People in Perspective

Cara E. Richards

Transylvania University

second edition

People in Perspective

An Introduction to Cultural Anthropology

Originally published as Man in Perspective

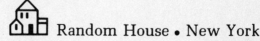 Random House • New York

Second Edition

987654321

Copyright © 1972, 1977 by Random House, Inc.

All rights reserved under International and Pan-American Copyright Conventions. No part of this book may be reproduced in any form or by any means, electronic or mechanical, including photocopying, without permission in writing from the publisher. All inquiries should be addressed to Random House, Inc., 201 East 50th Street, New York, N.Y. 10022. Published in the United States by Random House, Inc., and simultaneously in Canada by Random House of Canada Limited, Toronto.

The first edition was published under the title Man in Perspective.

Library of Congress Cataloging in Publication Data

Richards, Cara Elizabeth, 1927–
  People in perspective.

  First ed. published in 1972 under title: Man in perspective.
  Bibliography: p.
  Includes index.
  1. Ethnology. I. Title.
GN316.R52 1977   301.2   76–21283
ISBN 0–394–31202–3

Manufactured in the United States of America. Composed by Datagraphics. Printed & Bound by R. R. Donnelley & Sons Co.

*To Elmer Lawson,
who is responsible for
my writing this book,
and to Anne Sullivan,
a good friend*

Foreword

This second edition of *Man in Perspective* retains from the first edition the useful format of a general introductory textbook interspersed with selected readings from a variety of authors writing about a variety of cultures. These selections deal largely with the experience of concrete individuals in other societies, or in other periods or special segments of our own society, and provide a series of vivid images that are used to illustrate Professor Cara Richards' discussion of the theory and concepts of cultural anthropology. All of this material is presented within a volume that is of a size suitable for a semester's or quarter's course.

The discussion of the selected readings from a unified point of view, already a strong point of the first edition, has been strengthened and expanded in this edition. Cultural anthropology as treated by Professor Richards is an open discipline. The study of humanity is a complex subject and may be usefully pursued by many methods. A major goal of anthropology is to synthesize a comprehensive picture of the development of human culture and of the range and central tendencies of its variation. The reader may note that nearly all of the readings discussed by Professor Richards were written by authors whose identity is something other than professional anthropologist. Nevertheless, these selections are relevant for the anthropologist.

In her discussion, likewise, Professor Richards has taken a broad view of the scope of anthropology, and has freely touched on the work of authors whose primary training is in other disciplines, as long as their findings or speculations help clarify anthropological problems and develop the student's interest in them. The discussion now includes major new findings and interpretations that have appeared since the preparation of the first edition. Among these might be mentioned discoveries of new forms of fossil man in Africa, experiments teaching nonvocal forms of language to chimpanzees, and the research of Alexander Marshack on forms of notation in Paleolithic artifacts.

Anthropological works based on a year or two of fieldwork in nonliterate societies have sometimes been charged with incorrectly presenting a static and rigidly bound cross-section of cultures which more extended research and more historical data would demonstrate to be changing. Yet anthropologists who have studied cultures comparatively keenly realize that these cultures are subject to change; today in particular most cultures are changing rapidly. Professor Richards imparts a sense of change and history into her presentation of cultural theory that increases its applicability to problems of our own society. Her use of examples from American cultures at different periods helps students apply anthropology so that they might understand where we are today and where we may be going. But this is more than a book on American culture. Professor Richards leads the reader from our own culture to those more alien cultures that are the achievements of peoples who are as much members of the human species as we are, and with whom we need to develop a deeper mutual understanding in these days of growing international and intercultural communication.

J. L. Fischer

Pittsburgh
April 1976

Acknowledgments

Many teachers, colleagues, friends, relatives, and casual acquaintances have influenced the contents of this book both directly and indirectly. Since it is impossible to list them all, I can only acknowledge grateful awareness of their contributions.

Specifically, I want to thank Ray Ware, Professor of Economics at Transylvania University, who patiently read each chapter of the first edition and made invaluable suggestions. I also want to thank Susan Warren who chased down elusive references and did the initial preparation of the bibliography, glossary, and index for this edition. Nell Main typed the manuscript.

I also want to thank John Fischer whose thoughtful criticism forced me to rethink some passages and expand others. Of course, nothing could have been accomplished without the editors, Murray Curtin, Barry Fetterolf, and Fred Burns, of Random House, who have been very patient with me. Charles Whitaker, York Dobyns, and Rosa Salas all helped at key points, and I never could have finished without their assistance.

Finally, I want to express my gratitude to Richard Honey of Transylvania University, Robert J. Smith of Cornell University, and the students who read portions of the manuscript and gave support, encouragement, and suggestions.

C.E.R.

Lexington, Kentucky
April 1976

Contents

Introduction

In speaking of "culture" we have reference to the conventional understandings, manifest in act and artifact, that characterize societies. ... Still more concretely we speak of culture, as did Tylor, as knowledge, belief, art, law, and custom. ... the quality of organization among the conveniently separable elements of the whole of a culture is probably a universal feature of culture and may be added to the definition: culture is an organization of conventional understandings manifest in act and artifact [Redfield 1941: 132–133].

This quotation from Redfield sets forth the main characteristics of the primary and basic concept of the field of cultural anthropology—the concept of culture. Culture consists of ideas, organized into a pattern, learned primarily from other people, and shared with other people. Culture cannot be studied directly, since it is ideational, but has to be inferred from the observable data. The description of a culture, therefore, is a construct of the analyzer, based on his or her observations of behavior (both physical and verbal) and of the material results of behavior—the artifacts of a society.

As we look at human groups the world over we see that ... all the activities in which they engage can be shown to function in the final analysis (1) to maintain the biologic functioning of the group members; (2) to reproduce new members of the group; (3) to socialize new members into functioning adults; (4) to produce and distribute goods and services necessary to life; (5) to maintain order within the group, and between itself and outsiders; and (6) to define the "meaning of life" and maintain the motivation to survive and engage in the activities necessary for survival. ...

   With regard to the activities so described, we can offer a hypothesis ... that these six classes of activities represent not only what various groups the world over actually do but, additionally, what these groups have to do if they are to survive and continue as human groups [Bennett and Tumin 1964:9].

These functional prerequisites of continuous social life form the basis for the structure of this book. In each of the first nine chapters there is at least one first-hand account that illustrates how a particular society provided for one of the functional prerequisites. The excerpt is then analyzed and the topic discussed in more detail. The last chapter of the book deals with some trends in anthropology and some of the conceptual tools of anthropologists.

People in Perspective

1 Survival: Hunters and Gatherers

In many species, including Homo Sapiens, *living in groups improves an individual animal's chances for survival. And, of course, individual survival is essential for the continuation of a group, since without members, there is no group. Individual survival in all animals requires the fulfillment of biological needs of nourishment and protection. In the human being (possibly the only self-aware creature who broods, questions, worries, and commits suicide) there are psychological needs that must also be satisfied. Culture, the chief instrument by which the human race has solved these basic survival problems, has provided a number of different solutions. The first chapter is concerned with some of the means by which members of different societies have provided themselves with food, clothing, shelter, and health care.*

Hunting and gathering wild food products from the environment was one of the earliest ways members of human societies ensured themselves adequate nutrition. Products of the environment were also used to make clothing and shelter in climates where these were necessary. Until recently, members of societies have not concerned themselves with the question of clean air, and the only people who considered adequate water to be a survival problem were those in environments where it was scarce.

Caring for sick or wounded individuals and restoring them to health have also been major concerns during much of human history. Methods of treatment have relied heavily on supernatural assistance (discussed in Chapter 9) for most illnesses, but in this chapter the more materialistic aspect of treatment is mentioned.

Human beings have also spent a considerable amount of time and effort decorating or modifying their bodies to conform to local standards of beauty. This attention to cosmetic detail has contributed more to morale than to biological health, but the search for beauty has affected diet and style of dress. Consequently, it too is briefly discussed here.

Since air and water are still minor problems (except to industrial nations), and clothing and shelter are not equally essential in all environments, we will concentrate in this chapter on the search for food, which must be available in quantity every day for long-term survival. Even though it is possible for individuals to exist without food for a day or so now and then, if deprivation is a regular thing, the individual will be weakened and will probably succumb to disease more readily than someone who is adequately fed every day.

In the following excerpt, pay particular attention to the way members of the society make use of the environment to meet individual needs. Note especially the kinds of food consumed, the sources of clothing and shelter, how these things were obtained, and how they were prepared for eventual use.

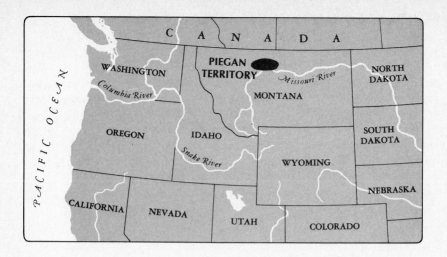

Survival and the Piegan Hunter

Winter came that year in the early part of November.* The lakes and streams froze over, there were several falls of snow, which the northwest winds gathered up and piled in coulées° and on the lee side of the hills. It was not long before the buffalo began to keep away from the river, where the big camps were. A few, of course, were always straggling in, but the great herds stayed out on the plains to the north and south of us. Since the buffalo did not approach the stream the Indians were obliged to go out on a two or three days' camping trip in order to get what meat and skins they needed, and several times during the season I went with them, accompanying my friends, Weasel Tail and Talks-with-the-buffalo. On these short hunts few lodges° were taken, fifteen or twenty people arranging to camp together, so we were somewhat crowded for room. Only enough women to do the cooking accompanied the outfit.

As a rule, the hunters started out together every morning, and sighting a large herd of buffalo, approached as cautiously as possible, until finally the animals became alarmed and started to run, and then a grand chase took place, and if everything was favorable many fat cows were killed. Nearly all the Piegans had guns of one kind or another; either flintlock° or percussion-cap,° smooth-bore° or rifle; but in the chase many of them, especially if riding swift, trained horses, preferred to use the bow and arrow, as two or three arrows could be discharged at as many different animals while one was reloading a gun. Some of the hunters killed twenty and more buffalo on a single run, but I think the average number to the man was not more than three.

*Abridged from *My Life as an Indian* by James Willard Schultz, pp. 39–40, 42–46, 108–110, 174, 177–179. Copyright MCMVII, Forest and Stream Publishing Co. Copyright © 1935 James Willard Schultz. By permission of the author's estate and Fawcett Publications, Inc. Schultz was a "squaw man" with the Piegan Blackfoot Indians during the latter part of the nineteenth century. He experienced their life both while they were an autonomous people and after they were settled on a reservation in a dependent relationship to the United States government. The book consists of his recollections.

°This gloss mark indicates a word to be found in the Glossary at the end of the book.

When on these short hunts a medicine man always accompanied a party, and the evenings were passed in praying to the Sun for success in the hunt, and in singing songs, especially the song of the wolf, the most successful of hunters. Everyone retired early, for there was little cheer in a fire of buffalo chips.

By the latter end of November the trade for robes was in full swing, thousands of buffalo had been killed, and the women were busily engaged in tanning the hides, a task of no little labor. I have often heard and read that Indian women received no consideration from their husbands, and led a life of exceedingly hard and thankless work. That is very wide of the truth so far as the natives of the northern plains were concerned. It is true that the women gathered fuel for the lodge—bundles of dry willow, or limbs from a fallen cottonwood. They also did the cooking, and besides tanning robes, converted the skins of deer, elk, antelope, and mountain sheep into soft buckskin° for family use. But when they felt like it they rested; they realized that there were other days coming, and they took their time about anything they had to do. Their husbands never interfered with them, any more than they did with him in his task of providing the hides and skins and meat, the staff of life. The majority—nearly all of them—were naturally industrious and took pride in their work, in putting away parfleche° after parfleche of choice dried meats and

A Piegan Indian camp as depicted by Maximilian Bodmer. *(Courtesy of the American Museum of Natural History)*

pemmican,° in tanning soft robes and buckskins for home use or sale, in embroidering wonderful patterns of beads or colored porcupine quills upon moccasin tops, dresses, leggings, and saddle trappings. When robes were to be traded they got their share of the proceeds; if the husband chose to buy liquor, well and good—they bought blankets and red and blue trade cloth, vermilion,° beads, bright prints, and various other articles of use and adornment.

. . .

One evening in the latter part of January there was much excitement in the three great camps. Some Piegan hunters, just returned from a few days' buffalo chase out on the plain to the north of the river, had seen a white buffalo. The news quickly spread, and from all quarters Indians came in to the post for powder and balls, flints, percussion caps, tobacco, and various other articles. There was to be an exodus of hunting parties from the three villages in the morning and men were betting with each other as to which of the tribes would secure the skin of the white animal; each one, of course, betting on his own tribe. By nearly all of the tribes of the plains an albino buffalo was considered a sacred thing, the especial property of the Sun. When one was killed the hide was always beautifully tanned, and at the next medicine lodge was given to the Sun with great ceremony, hung above all the other offerings on the center post of the structure, and there left to shrivel gradually and fall to pieces. War parties of other tribes, passing the deserted place, would not touch it for fear of calling down upon themselves the wrath of the Sun. The man who killed such an animal was thought to have received the special favor of the Sun, and not only he, but his whole tribe.

. . .

I joined one of the hunting parties the next morning, going, as usual, with my friends, Talks-with-the-buffalo and Weasel Tail. . . .

. . .

We started early . . . and never stopped until we arrived at a willow-bordered stream running out from the west butte of the Sweetgrass Hills and eventually disappearing in the dry plain. It was an ideal camping place—plenty of shelter, plenty of wood and water. The big herd with the albino buffalo had been last seen some fifteen miles southeast of our camp, and had run westward when pursued. Our party thought that we had selected the best location possible in order to scour the country in search of it. Those who had seen it reported that it was a fair-sized animal, and so swift that it had run up to the head of the herd at once and remained there—so far from their horses' best speed, that they never could determine whether it was bull or cow.

Other parties, Piegans, Blackfeet, and Bloods, were encamped east of us along the hills, and southeast of us out on the plain. We had agreed to do no running, to frighten the buffalo as little as possible until the albino had been found, or it became time to return to the river. Then, of course, a big run or two would be made in order to load the pack animals with meat and hides.

The weather was unfavorable, to say nothing of the intense cold; a thick haze of glittering frost flakes filled the air, through which the sun shone dimly. We were almost at the foot of the west butte, but it and its pine forest had vanished in the shining frost fog. Nevertheless, we rode out daily on our quest, toward the Little River. . . .

I cannot remember how many days that cold time lasted, during which we vainly hunted for the albino buffalo. The change came about ten o'clock one morning as we were riding slowly around the west side of the butte. We felt suddenly an intermittent tremor of warm air in our faces; the frost haze vanished instantly and we could see the Rockies, partially enveloped in dense, dark clouds. "Hah!" exclaimed a medicine-pipe man. "Did I not pray for a black wind last night? And see, here it is; my Sun power is strong."

Even as he spoke the chinook° came on in strong, warm gusts and settled into a roaring, snapping blast. The thin coat of snow on the grass disappeared. One felt as if summer had come.

We were several hundred feet above the plain, on the lower slope of the butte, and in every direction, as far as we could see, there were buffalo, buffalo, and still more buffalo. They were a grand sight. . . .

It seemed about as useless as looking for the proverbial needle to attempt to locate a single white animal among all those dark ones. We all dismounted, and, adjusting my long telescope, I searched herd after herd until my vision became blinded, and then I passed the instrument to someone beside me. Nearly all of the party tried it, but the result was the same; no white buffalo. We smoked and talked about the animal we were after; each one had his opinion as to where it was at that moment, and they varied in locality from the Missouri River to the Saskatchewan, from the Rockies to the Bear's Paw Mountains. While we were talking there appeared a commotion among the buffalo southeast of us. I got the telescope to bear upon the place and saw that a number of Indians were chasing a herd of a hundred or more due westward. They were far behind them, more than a mile, and the buffalo were widening that distance rapidly, but still the riders kept on in a long, straggling line. I passed the glass to Weasel Tail and told what I had seen. Everyone sprang to his feet.

"It must be," said my friend, "that they have found the white one, or they would give up the chase. They are far behind and their horses are tired. Yes, it is the white one they follow. I see it! I see it!"

We were mounted in a moment and riding out to intercept the herd; riding at a trot, occasionally broken by a short lope, for the horses must be kept fresh for the final run. In less than half an hour we arrived at a low, long, mound-like elevation, near which the herd should pass. We could see them coming straight toward it. So we got behind it and waited, my companions, as usual, removing their saddles and piling them in a heap. We realized, of course, that the buffalo might get wind of us and turn long before they were near enough for us to make a dash at them, but we had to take that chance. After a long time, our leader, peering over the top of the mound, told us to be ready; we all mounted. Then he called out for us to come on, and we dashed over the rise; the herd was yet over 500 yards distant, had winded us, and turned south. Whips were plied; short-handled quirts° of rawhide which stung and maddened the horses. At first we gained rapidly on the herd, then for a time kept at about their speed, and finally began to lose distance. Still we kept on, for we could all see the coveted

A travois. Babies as well as household goods were often transported this way. *(Courtesy of the American Museum of Natural History)*

prize, the albino, running at the head of the herd. I felt sure that none of us could overtake it, but because the others did, I kept my horse going, too, shamefully quirting him when he was doing his best.

Then out from a coulée right in front of the flying herd dashed a lone horseman, right in among them, scattering the animals in all directions. In much less time than it takes to tell it, he rode up beside the albino. We could see him lean over and sink arrow after arrow into its ribs, and presently it stopped, wobbled, and fell over on its side. When we rode up to the place the hunter was standing over it, hands raised, fervently praying, promising the Sun the robe and the tongue of the animal. It was a three-year-old cow, yellowish-white in color, but with normal-colored eyes. The successful hunter was a Piegan, Medicine Weasel by name. He was so excited, he trembled so, that he could not use his knife, and some of our party took off the hide for him, and cut out the tongue, he standing over them all the time and begging them to be careful, to make no gashes, for they were doing the work for the Sun. None of the meat was taken. It was considered a sacrilege to eat it; the tongue was to be dried and given to the Sun with the robe. While the animal was being skinned, the party we had seen chasing the herd came up; they were Blackfeet of the north, and did not seem to be very well pleased that the Piegans had captured the prize; they soon rode away to their camp, and we went to ours, accompanied by Medicine Weasel.

. . .

One evening a vast herd of buffalo had been discovered two or three miles back from the river—a herd so large that it was said the valley of Cow Creek and the hills on each side of it were black with them as far as one could see. Soon after sunrise many hunters, with their women following on travois° horses, had gone out to run this herd and get meat. An hour or so later they charged in among them on their trained runners, splitting the herd in such a way that about a thousand or more broke straight down the valley toward the camp, for the nearer to camp the killing was done, the easier it was to pack in the meat. Down the valley the frightened animals fled, followed by their pursuers. We in camp heard the thunder of hoofs and saw the cloud of dust before the animals came in sight. Our lodges were pitched on the lower side of the bottom, between the creek and a steep, bare, rocky ridge. Every man, woman, and child of us had hurried outside to witness the chase.

It was really far more exciting to see such a run near at hand than to take part in it. First of all, the huge, shaggy, oddly shaped beasts charged madly by with a thunderous pounding of hoof and rattle of horns, causing the ground to tremble as if from an earthquake; and then the hunters, their long hair streaming in the wind, guiding their trained mounts here and there in the thick of it all, singling out this fat cow or that choice young bull, firing their guns or leaning over and driving an arrow deep into the vital part of the great beast. The plain over which they passed became dotted with the dead, with great animals standing head down, swaying, staggering, as the life blood flowed from mouth and nostrils, finally crashing over on the ground, limp and lifeless heaps.

That is what we, standing by our lodges, saw that morning. No one cheered the hunters, nor spoke, nor laughed. It was too solemn a moment. We saw death abroad; huge, powerful beasts, full of tireless energy, suddenly stricken into so many heaps of meat and hide. Paradoxical as it may seem, the Blackfeet reverenced, regarded as "medicine," or sacred, these animals which they killed for food, whose hides furnished them with shelter and clothing.

A band of horses drinking at the river became frightened at the noise of the approaching [buffalo] herd. They bounded up the bank and raced out over the bottom, heads and tails up, running directly toward the [buffalo] herd, which swerved to the eastward, crossed the creek, and came tearing down our side of it. The rocky ridge hemming in the bottom was too steep for them to climb, so they kept on in the flat directly toward the lodges. ... Women screamed, children bawled, men shouted words of advice and command.

. . .

Now, the leaders of the herd reached the outer edge of the village. They could not draw back, for those behind forced them forward, and they loped on, threading their way between the lodges, nimbly jumping from side to side to avoid them, kicking out wickedly at them as they passed. For all his great size and uncouth shape, the buffalo was quick and active on his feet.

... We held our breath anxiously, for we well knew that almost anything —the firing of a gun or sight of some suspicious object ahead—might throw the herd into confusion. If it turned or bunched up in a compact mass, people would surely be trampled to death, lodges overturned, the greater part of the camp reduced to ruin. Finally the last of the herd passed beyond the outer lodges into the river and across it to the opposite side.

No one had been hurt, not a lodge had been overturned. But long scaffolds of drying meat, many hides and pelts of various animals pegged out on the ground to dry, had either disappeared or been cut into small fragments. That, indeed, was an experience to be remembered; we were thankful to have escaped with our lives. ...

The next day the trees and high bushes bordering the river were bright with the people's offerings to their Sun god. They gave always their best, their choicest and most prized ornaments and finery.

. . .

Nät-ah'-ki and I went once after buffalo, camping with Red Bird's Tail, a genial man of thirty-five or forty. There were few lodges, but many people, and we traveled as light as possible. We ... camped on the head of Armells Creek. . . .

. . .

... The sun shone bright and warm, there was a big herd of buffalo nearby, everyone rode out from camp in the best of spirits. I had changed horses with Nät-ah'-ki; while mine liked to run as well as hers, it had a tender mouth, and she could easily control it. Once into the herd, I paid no attention to anyone else, but did my best to single out the fat cows, overtake and kill them. I did not need the meat nor robes, but there were those with us who had poor mounts, and what I killed I intended to give them. So I urged the little mare on, and managed to kill seven head.

When I stopped at last, no one was near me; looking back I saw the people gathered in two groups, and from the largest and nearest one arose the distressing wailing of the women for the dead. I soon learned the cause of it all; Young Arrow Maker had been killed, his horse disembowelled; Two Bows had been thrown and his leg was broken. A huge old bull, wounded and mad with pain, had lunged into Arrow Maker's horse, tearing out its flank and knocking the rider off on to the backs of its close-pursuing mates, and he had been trampled to death by the frantic-running herd.

Two Bows' horse had stepped into a badger hole and he had been hurled to the ground, his right leg broken above the knee. Some of the women's horses were dragging travois, and we laid the dead and the injured on them and they were taken to camp by their relatives. We hurried to skin the dead buffalo, some of the hunters taking no more of the meat than the tongue and boss ribs, and then we also went back to the lodges, silently and quietly. There was no feasting and singing that night.

They buried Arrow Maker in the morning, placing the body in the fork of a big cottonwood, and then we prepared to move camp, which took all the rest of the day, as meat was cut and dried to reduce weight, and the many hides had to be trimmed, the frozen ones thawed and folded for packing. There was not a man in camp who knew anything about mending a broken leg, but we splinted and bound Two Bows' fracture as best we could. On the succeeding morning we broke camp early and started homeward, every one frantic to get away from the unlucky place before more misfortune should happen. The injured man was made as comfortable as possible on a couch lashed to a travois.

In the afternoon a blizzard set in, a bitterly cold one, which drifted and whirled the fine snow in clouds around us. A few decided to make camp in the first patch of timber we should come to, but the rest declared that they would keep on through the night until they arrived home. They were afraid to stop; more afraid of some dread misfortune overtaking them than they were of Cold Maker's° [personification of winter] blinding snow and intense cold. . . . Red Bird's Tail was one of those who elected to keep on.

The low flying snow-spitting clouds hid the moon as we hung on to our saddles and gave our horses the reins, trusting them to keep in the trail which Red Bird's Tail broke for us. We could not have guided them had we wished to, for our hands became so numb we were obliged to fold them in the robes and blankets which enveloped us. . . .

Red Bird's Tail and many of the other men frequently sprang from their horses and walked, even ran, in vain effort to keep warm, but the women remained in the saddle and shivered, and some froze hands and faces. While still some six or eight miles from home, Red Bird's Tail, walking ahead of his horse, dropped into a spring, over which the snow had drifted. The water was waist-deep and froze on his leggings the instant he climbed out of the hole; but he made no complaint, walking sturdily on through the deepening drifts until we finally arrived home. It was all I could do to dismount, I was so stiff and cramped and cold; and I had to lift Nät-ah'-ki from her saddle and carry her inside. We had been on the trail something like seventeen hours! I roused one of the men to care for our horses, and we crawled into bed, under half a dozen robes and blankets, shivering so hard that our teeth chattered.

When we awoke it was nearly noon; and we learned that a woman of our party had dropped from her horse and Cold Maker had claimed her for his own. Her body was never found.

Subsistence hunting is not all pleasure. A sportsman can postpone his trip if the weather is bad, or when he does not feel well. A hunter, needing to provide for family members as well as for himself, does not always have the same option. Hunters must go out with some regularity because their societies usually have little surplus food. If an epidemic (such as smallpox or influenza) hits a hunting band, a major cause of death may be starvation, not disease. Starvation also threatens if the weather is so bad that everyone is confined to camp for several days in a row.

On the other hand, daily hunting is rarely necessary. Modern hunters and gatherers have been pushed by stronger agricultural peoples into relatively poor environments, yet studies have found that even under these conditions, most of them have to work only a few hours a day a few days a week to provide an adequate diet (Holmberg 1969:75–76, 248; Lee 1968:37).

The Indians, or, more accurately, native Americans, described in the excerpt were an affluent group of hunters and gatherers. They had techniques for storing and preserving food; they had horses, guns, bows and arrows, all of which made their hunting quite efficient. Yet even for them, the hunt—exciting, challenging, even inspiring—could also be difficult, frustrating, and sometimes deadly. Hunters on foot usually have a more difficult time. The anthropologist George P. Murdock thought horse transport made such a difference in life pattern that he refused to include mounted hunters in his compilation of hunters and gatherers. He also excluded groups that obtain their food from intensive fishing and those that engage in any agriculture at all, even though they obtain most of their food from hunting and gathering (Murdock 1968:15).

Not all anthropologists agree with this classification. Some feel there is a significant difference between people who harvest what resources the environment naturally provides and those who modify the environment in such a way that it produces what they choose where they choose. Using this distinction, one can study the range of variation possible in societies based on harvesting natural resources as compared with those based on the domestication of plants and animals. Groups that use both methods may either be kept in a separate category or assigned to one or the other on the basis of an arbitrary distinction: all those who obtain more than half their subsistence from harvesting natural resources assigned to the hunters and gatherers; the rest to the food producers, for example.

Comparative study of different hunting and gathering societies can help isolate factors significant in the formation of social classes, complex political structures, and so on, and thus lead to a better understanding of how civilization began and what its dynamics are. This is important because human beings have been urban, industrialized creatures for only a short time. For two million years, perhaps more, they harvested their natural environment, as had their primate ancestors before them. What effect has this way of life had upon them? What demands did it make? What opportunities did it offer? What kind of individual was most likely to be successful at this type of life? And, finally, why was hunting and gathering abandoned for agriculture? Answers to these questions may help humans cope more effectively with modern complex conditions.

EARLIEST SURVIVAL TECHNIQUES: QUESTIONS AND CONTROVERSIES

The earliest phase of development of the human race is obscured by time. The role played by hunting is not clear, and reputable scientists sometimes find themselves embroiled in bitter controversy about it. Chimpanzees—the primates most closely related to *Homo sapiens*—are foragers who seldom, if ever, scavenge (eat meat they do not kill). They hunt only rarely, while most other primates do not hunt at all (Hulse 1971:208; van Lawick-Goodall 1971:81–82). When did humans first begin to hunt? How important was the contribution of hunting to their diet and development? Was all the meat in their diet from hunting, or were they also (or entirely) scavengers? Were the things they made used primarily as weapons, or were they simply tools for peaceful foraging?

When and why did humans lose the projecting canine teeth so characteristic of their primate relatives? This loss is among the first of the physical changes that slowly differentiated human beings from their closest relatives, but we are not sure why the change occurred. Perhaps human ancestors began to use weapons or tools that removed the need for the projecting canines. It has also been suggested that the loss was due to hormone changes as humans grew less aggressive (Holloway 1967:63–67). Projecting canines are useful for more than fighting, however; they enable animals to break through the hard outer covering of various nuts, fruits, and plants. Because of the multiple use for projecting canines, it would seem probable that the substitution of tools and weapons is the more likely explanation for their loss.

In non-tool-using animals differences in teeth reflect differences in diet. Since we do not know how early in the development of the human line tools were used, or just what they were used for, we cannot be certain of the diet of early humans. Yet the questions of the amount of meat in the ancestral human diet and how this meat was obtained are believed significant because many basic, innate human characteristics are thought to have originated in the way our ancestors lived during the several million years they were changing from generalized primates to human beings.

In spite of the controversy over hunting and diet, scientists have reached consensus on some things. Most researchers agree that at some point in time, descendents of a generalized primate (one not specialized in the direction of either apes or humans) began to deviate from the general pattern of primate behavior by walking erect and using tools. Why this happened is not entirely clear. Some scientists suggest that climate variation forced the creature to change (Ardrey 1961:264–265); others suggest the change was the result of random mutations that persisted and spread because they enabled the group to exploit an environmental niche untapped by other primates (Campbell 1966:29–30); still another writer has suggested that conflict with its own kind started the generalized primate on the path toward humanity and forced it along at top speed (Bigelow 1969:7, 11). The split between gorillas, chimpanzees, and man apparently began during the geological epoch called the Miocene,° which occurred from 28 to 12 million years ago. Sometime in this epoch, one variety of a widespread and varied type of generalized primate, collectively called Dryopithecines, began to change in the direction of humans while other varieties developed toward chimpanzees and gorillas. Currently, *Ramapithecus* is the favorite candidate for the type that started the human line (Buettner-Janusch 1966:126–127) but as new finds continue to be made ideas about this are likely to change (Edey 1972:51–53).

The most obviously distinctive physical characteristics of human beings, those that separate them most clearly from other primates, are found in their feet, pelvises, skulls, and perhaps most important, their brains. Consequently, it is logical to assume that the most significant behavioral changes involved these parts.

Physical changes must give a reproductive advantage (by increasing the survival potential or the sexual attractiveness of the individual who has them) or they will not be passed along to a sufficient number of the next generation to be spread through the group. Erect posture obviously accounts for the foot and pelvic changes, but how did erect posture give an advantage to human ancestors? What did it do that the posture of the ancestors of gorillas and chimpanzees did not? For one thing, erect posture raises the eyes higher off the ground. This would be of no particular advantage to tree-living animals, since the view from a tree is greater than from a height of a few feet (chimpanzees climb when they want to look around [van Lawick-Goodall 1971:102–103]), but erect posture is very useful on the ground away from trees, enabling the individual to see over low shrubs and moderately tall grass. This suggests that generalized primate human ancestors spent more time in the open away from trees than the ones who were ancestral to chimpanzees and gorillas. Another consequence of erect posture is that since the hands are not being used for walking, things can be carried in them, and sticks or rocks can be aimed and thrown, even on the run—an improvement in both defense and offense that might have given a survival advantage to a small primate caught in the open away from trees.

What about increased brain size? Changes in the brain that allowed for improved hand-eye coordination and greater manual dexterity would have given additional survival potential to an erect primate. The modern brain is a social as well as a technological instrument. One author suggests that a major factor in our evolution may have been conflict between human groups. He bases his theory on the concept that success in such conflict depended on increased coordination and cooperation *within* the group (Bigelow 1969:7, 11). In addition, he says that the small ancestral humans could not have hunted, scavenged, or even protected themselves successfully without efficient cooperation (Bigelow 1974: personal communication). The advantages of complex coordination and cooperation for getting food and for protection against human or nonhuman enemies placed a premium on increased mental ability.

To sum up, several behavior changes must have been involved in the physical alteration of the basic ancestral human form. Among those suggested as most likely are (a) living on open grasslands instead of in forests, (b) making tools instead of relying on biological equipment, (c) carrying and throwing things, (d) running erect, and (e) cooperative and coordinated hunting and defensive group maneuvers.

It is often stated today that hunting was strictly a male activity, with women waiting at a base camp for the men to bring back the game. This concept is based on Western historic hunting practices, however. The excerpt in Chapter 5 describes a hunting technique still common today that depends heavily on the cooperation of women and children, who spread out in a line or semicircle and make as much noise as they can to drive the game into some sort of trap where the men are waiting. The same technique is even used by male lions who frighten game into the clutches of the hidden females. Driving game into traps or over cliffs has been practiced all over the world, and archeologists have found evidence of its having been used 400,000 years ago (White and Brown 1973:77). Consequently, there is no justification for assuming that it is a late invention. Given the customary foraging pattern of primates that includes all the able-bodied juveniles and adults of both sexes, the personnel would have been available to mount such drives; only the ability and motivation to organize were lacking. Cooperative male hunting is occasionally practiced by chimpanzees (with the rest of the band in the area, however [van Lawick-Goodall 1971:81–82, 190–195]). It is *as* possible that the hominid° females and young were organized to help in the cooperative hunt as that they were left at a base camp. The larger number of individuals involved with the whole group participating would increase the effectiveness of the method. Isolated individual male hunting could have been a late development that depended on more sophisticated

Buffalo (American bison) being driven over a cliff. This hunting method dates back some 400,000 years. *(Courtesy of the American Museum of Natural History)*

hunting skills and more effective weapons. It is not likely to have been the first step toward a primary reliance on hunting.

Although the factors that influenced the direction of the major physical changes that occurred in human evolution are still being debated, at least the majority of researchers agree on the general pattern and order. Following the first hominid ancestor of the Miocene and descended from it were several (authorities differ on the exact number) varieties of more-or-less humanlike creatures living in Africa perhaps as early as 5 million years ago (Edey 1972:73). Though specialists argue over what to call each form, there is fairly substantial agreement on the general picture. Certain forms are large and heavy, often with a bony crest running from back to front across the top of the skull (called a sagittal crest°). Recent finds indicate at least one variety of this type had sexual dimorphism°—that is, males and females were quite different in size (Leakey 1973:57,61). This type Leakey calls *Australopithecus,*° while others call it *A. boisei, A. robustus,* or *Paranthropus* (Howell 1965:62–63; Le Gros Clark 1967:31; Edey 1972:138–141). There is general agreement that this kind was *not* ancestral to humans.

The other type is much lighter, does not have any sagittal crest, has a larger cranial capacity, and in all respects seems more human. Recent finds indicate this type was probably changing rapidly while the other had reached a plateau of development that lasted over a million years (Leakey 1973:53, 67). There is general agreement that the lighter type *is* ancestral to modern humans, although there is considerable argument over what to call the various examples that have been found. Leakey and many others prefer *Homo* as a generic° label, but some authorities still hold to the term first applied by Raymond Dart in 1924, *Australopithecus africanus.* All of the lightly-built, large-brained forms they regard as either geographical or evolved variants of it (Edey 1972:50, 138–139; Pilbeam 1972:13). Recent research around the shores of Lake Rudolph in Kenya and in the Omo Valley of Ethiopia has added enormously to our information, and as work continues there will be clarification of terms along with an increased understanding of the complex story of human evolution.

Whatever the ultimate outcome, we are still left with the main question: Why did the hominid line change the particular way it did? It has been suggested that tool-using, erect posture, and meat-eating gave the necessary impetus to the development of the human brain (Chard 1969:70, 71). The heavy form of *Australopithecus* was probably not bipedal to the same extent as modern man, another reason for disqualifying it as in the line of human ancestry (Leakey 1973:57). Because of the way the thigh bone joined the pelvis, the heavy form probably could not straighten its legs to stand comfortably erect with its head directly over its feet, or stride with the easy mile-devouring gait of modern humans. These creatures could run or shuffle along erect, but that is about all. Chimpanzees can do almost as well, according to recent studies, and they too use tools, hunt, and eat meat occasionally (van Lawick-Goodall 1971:80–82, 190–195; Pfeiffer 1972:312, 338). If hunting, tool-using, and occasional erect posture were enough to make the human being, why are chimpanzees not more human? Bigelow has suggested that since the brain is above all a social instrument, "the selective force that produced this rapid and complex change must have had something to do with social life" (1969:11). Since all primates have a relatively complex social life, he goes on to say that some factor not found in the typical primate behavior, and one that gave a major survival advantage to its possessor, must be sought. He suggests that improved group cooperation for effective conflict with other groups meets the necessary conditions. Groups with the largest, most efficient brains were able to organize and cooperate most effectively. Less competent cooperators were killed outright or driven into less desirable areas (where the more intelligent of them might survive while the less intelligent died). This situation would give a powerful survival advantage to more intelligent cooperators, perhaps powerful enough to account for the speed and extent of human evolution (Bigelow 1969: Chapter 1). Other experts, ignoring Bigelow's emphasis on cooperation, find this approach—with its incorporated violence—unacceptable. They argue that there is no good evidence for intergroup violence in the early years of human development and prefer to rely on less speculative factors, such as more meat in the diet. Leakey's work at Lake Rudolph provides good evidence of meat-eating, although it does not settle the question of whether the meat was obtained through hunting or scavenging (Leakey 1973:69).

Whatever the factors involved in the changes, and there were probably many, including others not yet suggested, the evolutionary selection process enabled individuals with the necessary abilities to have more offspring and pass on their genetic differences to an ever increasing number of individuals. Thus the human evolved and spread (Chard 1969:70–71).

Because the subject is *humanness,* even scientists have difficulty remaining objective in the debate over how much conflict human ancestors engaged in, how much meat there was in their diet, and whether it was obtained by hunting or by scavenging. Some who think the development of humankind began as a result of deliberate hunting for food also seem to believe that any carnivore must accept killing, violence, and bloodshed as natural. They therefore suggest that several million years of selection for the best hunter and the most successful carnivore in the group has made a taste for violence part of human biological endowment. Other scientists, deploring the violence humans display, reject this explanation as an attempt to excuse and condone aggression. These scientists insist that the human's immediate ancestors were peaceful foragers and got their meat by scavenging, not hunting. Therefore, they say, humans are innately peaceful; it is society that turns them into killers. Thus, political, religious, and humanitarian views enter the arena of the study of the development of the human race, causing individuals to promote certain hypotheses, not so much because the evidence supports them, but because they as individuals *prefer* one interpretation over another.

The entire question is complex, with little concrete evidence to support either side. There is no doubt that humans have been hunters for at least the last half-million years of their existence. But half a million years is a short time in terms of evolutionary change and could not be expected to have the same effect as several million years of selection. In addition, many of the assumptions on which the arguments are based have not been tested. For example, is a carnivore unique in accepting violence and bloodshed? Some generally tranquil grazers show a considerable capacity for violence at certain times of the year (usually the mating season) or in defense of their young. If the acceptance of violence cannot be limited to carnivores, then either carnivorous *or* vegetarian ancestors could account for man's pugnacious behavior.

Can one assume that the violence involved in hunting—normally directed toward other species of animals—encourages in-group violence of the sort that plagues man? Not all hunting animals engage in violence against their own kind; even the killer whale is good to its mother. Perhaps some of the difficulty with human beings lies in the way they define their in-group. Most modern scientists identify all humans as members of one species, yet even in the modern industrialized nations not everyone would agree with this classification, as any racist knows. Outside the industrial world, quite a few humans call or have called their own group "The People," "Human Beings," or "Real Men" while designating other groups as "Enemies," "Savages," "Almost People" (Dobyns and Euler 1970:2–4), safely removing them from consideration as fellow humans. Perhaps the violence that occurs between two such human groups—with neither regarding the other as quite human—is more comparable to the predatory out-group attacks of other animals than to in-group violence. So far as we know, humans have no instinctive mechanism for recognizing strangers as also being human. Like ants and rats, people are apt to attack strangers of their own species. Unlike many other animals, however, humans do not have instinctive mechanisms for turning off violent aggressive impulses (or if they do, those mechanisms are fairly easy to overcome). Lorenz states that in other animals inhibitory instincts evolved along with effective weapons, but that in human history, the cultural evolution of things to kill with happened so fast that inhibiting mechanisms had no time to develop (1966:232–234). Primates in general seem to lack the strong inhibitions against violence under certain circumstances that some other species have. The usual primate reaction to threats from others is a submissive gesture or flight. The submissive gesture does not always work, and in circumstances where flight is impossible, results can be fatal (Ardrey 1963:86–89; van Lawick-Goodall 1971:132, 152, 196). Actually, humanity does better than detractors seem to think. In most of the world today, we rarely attack strangers on sight as some other primates still do, and human history, full of violence though it is, also chronicles the development of increasingly effective techniques for incorporating more and more people into the in-group—the ones with whom we can live in peace. The process is far from complete, but people can travel unarmed in relative safety today over stretches of territory that barely 150 years ago were full of dozens of hostile groups ready to kill an enemy (that is, a stranger) without waiting to ask questions. Violence within the group—murder, assault, and so on—is still with us, but the whole question of violence in human societies needs more dispassionate study than it has so far received.

Can one assume that violence is the *only* characteristic selected for in hunters or warriors? Many of the hunting techniques used by humans (and even by some other carnivores) require close coordination and cooperation among a number of individuals. Under these circumstances, evolution would select for cooperative individuals as well as for violent ones. Bigelow points out that only a high degree of cooperation makes modern large-scale conflict possible (1969:3). Cooperative warriors, even today, are not so likely to be killed as isolated ones, who, without support from their comrades, can more easily be destroyed. So even incessant war would select for cooperative persons, rather than merely vicious ones. In addition, there is no evidence that violence and cooperation are mutually exclusive. Many human groups that have been ferocious to outsiders have been models of cooperation among themselves, and in fact *must* be.

Even if all the assumptions about the relationship between violence and hunting should prove to be correct, can it be assumed that these characteristics have become part of the *biological* heritage of humans? Humans are noted for lack of instincts and for the importance of learning in determining their behavior. Is there any evidence that violence is an exception? Some people feel that there is. If violence does not have some instinctive basis, why does it seem to be so easy to teach to each generation? And why is it so difficult to develop a peaceful society? If humans are basically peaceful gatherers, history shows precious little evidence of it. Regardless of the type of economic or political system in operation at any particular time, humans seem to have behaved violently toward one another. Indeed, descriptions of small peaceful groups living in total harmony with each other seem to be myths based partly on wishful thinking, and partly on the occasional discovery of isolated groups like the Tasadays in the Philippines, who do not fight other groups, and who show little aggression within their own group (if one overlooks the possibility that they practice female infanticide). The question of how practical war would be for a group of twenty-three people, half of them children, is rarely raised by promoters of utopian visions. Internal peace is, after all, not very difficult with so few people, even in our conflict-ridden modern society. How it would be possible to divide the world's total present population into Tasaday-sized groups, living on crayfish and wild plants, even if this would ensure peace—and there is no guarantee that it would—is another question seldom considered by admirers of the simple life. Such tiny societies have few answers *directly* applicable to the industrialized populations of today.

If the basis for human violence should prove to be instinctive, does this mean that nothing can be done about it? Sex is instinctive, but to admit that does not automatically condone promiscuity. Humans have apparently always regulated sexual behavior; societies have fallen into difficulties only when their members have tried to ignore the drive or to eliminate it entirely. Scientists who accept the position that humans are instinctively aggressive do not necessarily condone indiscriminate violence. Instead, they suggest that aggression can neither be ignored nor eliminated; like sex, it must be channeled into socially beneficial rather than disruptive patterns (Lorenz 1963:49–56).

Like many controversies, this one thrives on the lack of data. We do not yet know *how* early humans got most of their meat—by hunting or by scavenging. We do not know how much meat they ate. We do not know precisely how they used the tools they made; nor can we tell what other tools—of more perishable material and so unpreserved—they had. We do not know how—or even whether—they fought their own kind in the earliest stages of their development. It is difficult to imagine how the lighter varieties of humanlike primates could have fought, hunted, or scavenged without some sort of weapon. They were too small to kill any large animals unaided, and would have had difficulty competing with other scavengers for dead animals. Even acting in groups, they would have needed some kind of offensive or defensive weapon, since physically they had none—no claws, projecting canines, horns, or hoofs. Possibly the human's ancestors threw rocks to chase predators or scavengers away, to kill small animals and stun larger game. (Humans can naturally throw more accurately than other primates, although the chimpanzee can be trained to do quite well [Hulse 1971:176].) The tools that have been discovered in association with these humanlike primates may have been used for butchering, skinning, or opening hard-shelled nuts or fruits, rather than as weapons. Future archeological research may provide more answers.

TECHNICAL ADVANCES

Whatever the behavior of their immediate ancestors, early humans themselves were definitely hunters. The record becomes more complete as we approach the present, of course, so there are more data to use for speculation. Half a million years ago, humans were hunting very large animals, like elephants, cooperatively. They had some use of fire, and probably knew how to make it. Their weapons were improved over those of earlier periods, and they may have had some form of language (Howell 1965:83).

The discovery and control of fire was one of the more significant early technological advances, since shelter is a basic need for human survival. Control of fire made it possible for humans to live in areas where they could not survive without some protection. They could occupy roomy caves that would have been too damp and cold otherwise. They could drive (and keep) out formidable predators. With fire for cooking, humans could eat otherwise inedible foods, and could make edible foods more digestible. The presence of charred animal bones at Chou-kou-tien suggests that cooking food was one of the early uses for fire (Weidenreich 1939:53, 56; Roper 1969:436). In historic times, fire was used as a hunting weapon, and it has apparently been so used for at least 400,000 years (Pfeiffer 1972:167; White and Brown 1973:77). In addition, fire in a shelter at night served to lengthen the day—perhaps to encourage the development of language, but at least to give humans an advantage over other animals by providing more functional time. Fire by night and smoke by day could also signal the location of the main group and thus enable wide-ranging hunters and gatherers to find their way back to camp more easily. Fire could be used to protect children, the elderly, and the disabled, thus making it possible for the hunters and the gatherers to leave them for longer periods without endangering their survival.

The development of language was another highly significant step in human evolution. Its origin (like the origin of humans) is still subject to controversy. Since language left no direct traces until writing was invented, its existence must be inferred from indirect evidence. Some individuals have suggested that proof of cooperation in hunting demonstrates the presence of language, but this is a weak argument, since other predators hunt cooperatively without language. Such cooperation requires communication, true, but many animals other than humans communicate, some with highly elaborate call systems. Language, however, is something more than a call system. Most elements in a call system are instinctive and consequently difficult to modify. Language is learned and therefore relatively simple to change. Although the capacity for language is inborn, no specific language is instinctive. All children "reinvent" language for themselves, as shown by the fact that many of their earliest word combinations, such as "that doed," "more up," "all gone shoe," are things they have never heard from adults (Pfeiffer 1972:448). Any normal individual can learn any language, if he or she begins early enough.

The sounds of a call system cannot be broken down and recombined to give new meanings. Therefore, the more complex the life, the more calls have to be programmed into the individual. At some point the increase in the number of calls could have gotten so large that a brain that was capable of coping with them would have been equally capable of handling a more flexible system—language. This reasoning suggests that the first steps toward language may have been taken as long ago as 15 million years (Pfeiffer 1972:463–464). If so, language may have played a part in the changes that split the hominids off from the chimpanzee and gorilla lines.

Research today is probing the secrets of the mind to learn more about the mechanisms involved in language and its origin. One direction lies in exploring the ability of other primates to understand and use language. The most successful such effort has been with the chimpanzee Washoe, who was taught a modified form of the language of the deaf. Washoe learned to understand some 350 hand signals and was able to use about 175 of them correctly in a creative way that showed a previously unexpected level of mental ability. With language, researchers were for the first time able to verify directly something they had suspected but could not prove—that chimpanzees are self-aware enough to recognize their own reflections. While Washoe was looking in a mirror, they signaled to her "Who is that?" and she promptly signaled back, "Me, Washoe." This example indicates how crucial language is to certain kinds of communication (van Lawick-Goodall 1971:235–236).

In another experiment, chimpanzees were taught to use various plastic or pictured shapes to represent ideas—a kind of ideographic writing—and they, too, proved able to communicate in a creative way, indicating comprehension of the concepts behind the shapes in a manner that goes beyond a call system and approximates at least a lower limit of true language. The physical inability of chimpanzees to speak had impeded previous studies of their capacities to use symbolic communication (Pfeiffer 1972:450–458; Premack and Premack 1972:92–99).

Another approach uses electronic measurements within the human brain itself. The data, analyzed by a computer that permits the correlation of enormous masses of information that would defeat any other form of study, hold the promise of being able to decipher the "neuronal code" that underlies the development of language. According to Dr. Bechtereva, director of the Institute for Experimental Medicine in Leningrad, researchers at the institute have found that the pattern of electrical activity in specific areas of the brain "was markedly different for a known word and for a similar-sounding syllable that had no meaning." She feels that this difference identifies the part of the linguistic process that involves the ability of the brain to discriminate between meaningless and meaningful sounds (Jonas 1974:56). From there it may be only a short step to identifying the specific pattern that is associated with specific words.

Still another approach is the attempt to discover the linguistic capabilities of species such as dolphins that are a long way removed from humans. Dolphins have a highly developed audible communication system. The size and complexity of their brains lends support to the hypothesis that a high level of communication would be associated with a corresponding development of the mental equipment.

All these various approaches are helping us to understand more of what language is and why, in spite of all the intricate call and communication systems that exist, man is apparently the only animal that has developed true language. One of the most important ways in which language differs from a call system is that in the latter the sounds are made only in the presence of the specific stimulus associated with the call. An animal using a call system is therefore bound to the present, and tied to immediate places or events. Language makes humans time- and space-free. A person does not have to be in the presence of a particular stimulus to communicate about it. One can talk about events and objects from the past or future, and can even speculate about imaginary or intangible things such as pride, X-rays, and unicorns. A human is free to deal conceptually with the past and the future, as well as the present.

About 100,000 years ago, some early humans buried their dead in an elaborate manner, occasionally surrounding the bodies with animal skulls or grave goods° (Chard 1969:123). It is difficult to imagine a reason for this unless there was some sort of belief system surrounding the dead. The existence of such a system virtually demands language, for how could shared complex beliefs develop without some means of communicating abstract concepts?

The use of language gave humans a tremendous survival edge. For the first time individuals could pass their knowledge along to others by some means besides action and imitation. Members of a group could pool their knowledge more effectively, could discuss and ponder the significance of some unique event, could relive exciting or alarming events, and could verbally explore alternative ways of dealing with dangerous situations. When language was finally developed, humans could accumulate traditions, and their offspring could build on what had previously been learned, unlike other animals, who were forced to repeat the same learning generation after generation. The advantages for survival are obvious. A deer that has never experienced a forest fire must escape through its own native intelligence and good fortune, unless some other deer that has escaped one is around to provide a model. Without an actual fire, the experienced deer has no way of passing the knowledge along to the others of its kind, so its valuable information dies with it. Human beings, on the other hand, can prepare their offspring to cope with events that might not be repeated for years. Theoretically, a person might indirectly save the lives of great-grandchildren through information transmitted down two generations.

In addition to the development of fire and language, humans also steadily increased the complexity of their tools. The hand-held stone point was improved by the addition of a handle, making a knife, spear, or javelin. The *atlatl*° (spear thrower) was invented. This artifically extended the length of a man's arm and thus gave more force to the thrown missile. Ultimately, the bow and arrow were developed (apparently in northern Africa about 30,000 years ago [Chard 1969:135]) and spread throughout the world. The bow added greatly to the range and force of weapons.

By the time the bow and arrow were invented, the human creature was physically *Homo sapiens,* the modern species. The establishment of modern man all over the world occurred with surprising rapidity and has led to disagreement over what happened to earlier, not quite modern forms such as Neanderthal° man. It has been suggested that they evolved into modern man, were absorbed by modern man, died out naturally, or were killed off by modern man. The weight of expert opinion seems to be gradually shifting to support the position that earlier forms called *Homo erectus,*° such as Peking man° and Java man,° evolved into *Homo sapiens sapiens*°—modern man—by way of the Neanderthaloids° (*Homo sapiens neanderthalensis*°) (Brace 1964:19), but there is still resistance to this hypothesis, even though the concept of the descent of the human being from the australopithecines through the pithecanthropines (*Homo erectus*) seems entirely acceptable. The objection to a Neanderthal stage may be based on biased early studies and tradition more than on firm scientific grounds (Brace 1964:3–19). Or it may be that the so-called Classic Neanderthal was an isolated group that contributed very little genetically to human evolution, whereas their Neanderthaloid ancestors in other parts of the world had significant roles.

ANALYZING EVIDENCE: THE PIEGAN PATTERN

The history of human development includes the development of culture. The human being cannot be studied as a biological organism alone; culture has coexisted with humans from their beginnings. Culture and humankind have changed together, and one author has even made culture part of the definition of humanness by suggesting that the threshold of humanity was crossed when the human animal could no longer survive without culture (Chard 1969:75). It has also been suggested that the biological development of the human line was caused at least in part by culture and that without it, people would not have become the physical beings they are (Chard 1969:74, 75).

Archeological evidence is therefore not the only data that have been used in the attempt to reconstruct the human's early life patterns. Researchers have looked to the cultures of historic or modern hunters and gatherers for analogies to help them understand the way the human race lived for most of its history. This approach must be used with caution, because modern hunters and gatherers have as long a history as anyone else, and there is no way of being certain what changes may have taken place during that time. Nonetheless, it would be foolish to overlook any opportunity to learn more about the dynamics of hunting and gathering patterns. What do hunters and gatherers of various societies have in common? In what ways do they differ? What is the range of variation that seems possible within the pattern? What are the attitudes of hunters and gatherers toward violence? death? cooperation? Since cooperative hunting techniques require organization in a way that individual hunting does not, what forms of organization appear in hunting and gathering societies?

The excerpt at the beginning of this chapter answers some of the questions for one group of hunters and gatherers—the Piegan Indians—at one period of time (the end of the nineteenth century) and in one general location (the northern plains of the United States). No claim is being made that these native Americans were typical of all hunters and gatherers, and in any case, one brief excerpt on one society cannot possibly provide definitive answers to any of the questions. In analyzing the excerpt, however, one can practice gathering bits of information on significant questions from the observations or descriptions of societies. Answers suggested by the analysis can be checked against other observations or descriptions of the Piegan, then compared with similar data from other societies. Science proceeds through the patient compiling of data until the pattern finally becomes clear, or the hypotheses being tested are supported or rejected. In the process, new questions are raised while old ones are being answered.

Division of Labor

To analyze the excerpt, one can first ask: How did the Piegan get the necessities of life? Answering this question immediately reveals the existence of a division of labor. The excerpt indicates that both men and women were involved in providing the basic necessities of food, clothing, and shelter among the Piegan, but they did not duplicate each other's efforts. The labor of one sex complemented that of the other.

Men provided meat and skins. Other parts of the book from which the excerpt is taken indicate that men also provided horses (mainly by stealing them from other tribes), engaged in both offensive and defensive conflicts with other tribes, and traded, both with other tribes and with non-Indians. Women sometimes joined them in the trading, but did not normally take part in the rest of the men's activities. Women sometimes accompanied the men on long hunting expeditions, but, according to the excerpt, only to do the cooking.

Women gathered fuel for cooking and heating. They cooked daily meals, and they preserved food for future use by drying and storing it in rawhide containers they made themselves. Women also tanned the hides men provided and then made clothing and other articles from the tanned skins. Using trade beads and dyed porcupine quills, women decorated the articles they made. They also made the shelters, which were of tanned skins stretched over poles. (The male usually had the job of finding the poles, although the excerpt does not mention that.) Women put up and took down the lodges, and normally loaded and unloaded the horses. Men occasionally helped with some of these activities, but generally, according to the excerpt, women took pride in doing their own work, and the book indicates they were embarrassed to accept male assistance unless absolutely necessary. Neither the excerpt nor the book mentions the women's contribution to the food supply by gathering berries and other vegetable products, yet these formed an important part of the diet and a significant supplement to the meat provided by the men. Some chores, such as gathering wood, carrying water, and providing occasional meat by snaring small game, were often performed by the children, but neither the excerpt nor the book mentions these.

This division of labor is typical among hunting and gathering peoples. There is no hunting and gathering society that makes hunting large game a

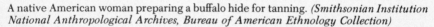

A native American woman preparing a buffalo hide for tanning. *(Smithsonian Institution National Anthropological Archives, Bureau of American Ethnology Collection)*

regular part of the woman's role, for example, nor one that confines men to activities around the home base. This is probably related to another normal part of the female role, bearing and rearing children. It is difficult to imagine a woman eight months pregnant stalking a deer with any ease, and a woman burdened with a toddler and an infant would have trouble dodging the charge of an enraged buffalo. Such activities would not promote the survival of the children, either.

These differences in activity patterns have often fooled observers who did not participate fully in the lives of the people they described. Such outsiders rarely accompanied the men hunting, where they were more likely to be a hindrance than a help if they did not know the customary procedures. Because the outsider usually observed hard-working women (whose activities were often performed around the camp) and resting, relaxed men, much of the literature paints the women of "savage" societies as overworked slaves to their lazy mates. The excerpt calls this view erroneous; the writer points out that the women worked at their own pace, and did it from choice (although the alternative—not working and being called lazy or being otherwise subject to strong disapproval—was so unattractive that any normal woman really had no option). It also makes clear that the "lazy" male was often away, engaged in exhausting and dangerous pursuits from which he might not return at all. In camp, he felt entitled to relax, and his wife, who often remained snug at home while he was risking his life, seldom begrudged him his leisure.

On the other hand, the Piegan excerpt does lend some support to the stereotyped image of the hunting band with stay-at-home women and far-ranging men, but that is at least partly because of the horse. In hunting and gathering societies that lack the horse, young able-bodied women are usually away from the base camp almost as much as the men are. Food-gathering is not a sedentary occupation. Since food close to camp is usually quickly exhausted, female gatherers range as far afield as men—or farther, depending on the specific hunting technique the men use. Men who wait for game at a blind, for example, may actually travel less than the women. Nor is meat provided only by the men. Both women and children may bring in small game or fish (Pfeiffer 1972:388–389; Gould 1969:9–11; Thomas 1959:102–113).

In hunting and gathering societies, female activities are almost always important to group survival. In many, the female contribution means the difference between survival and starvation, or between scarcity and plenty. Even when her contribution to the food supply is minimal (among Eskimos, for example), the woman's work is still essential. Life in the Arctic is so precarious, hunting so demanding and time-consuming, that the male food provider could not survive for long without the activities of the women, who spend all their time making, repairing, and maintaining clothing, processing food, and keeping a warm home base, in addition to caring for the children (Freuchen 1961:55).

Although Eskimos may be extreme in the amount of interdependence of the sexes, hardly any hunting and gathering society could afford to have half its adult members unproductive. A few societies can barely afford any unproductive members at all, and are occasionally forced to abandon the ill and aged.

(Some anthropologists who have worked with such peoples have suggested that they do not really *have* to abandon the sick and aged; they simply do not want to be bothered caring for them. It is difficult for some people steeped in Western traditions to accept this explanation, but it seems to be correct [Holmberg 1969:225–226; Lee and DeVore 1968:91].)

Since survival of the human species depends on *both* individual and group survival, and since the two sets of requirements may occasionally conflict, social institutions usually reflect the delicate balance required. In crisis situations, this complex balance may be disturbed. Obviously, if all individuals die, there is no longer any group, but also obviously, not all members of any group contribute equally to its long-term survival potential. That is, the short-term surival of certain people at the expense of other specific people may jeopardize the

An eskimo family in the Thule region of northern Greenland. One of the major activities of Eskimo women is repairing and maintaining clothing. *(De Wys, Inc.)*

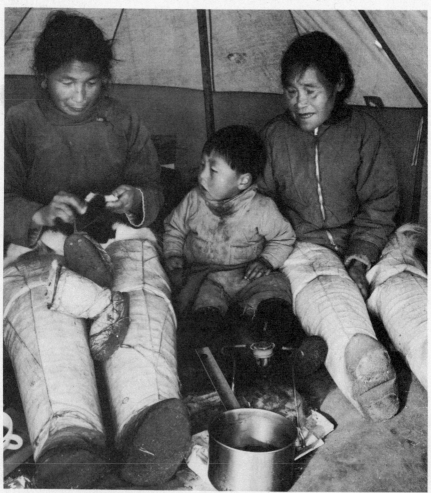

long-term survival of the group itself. So in crises, the demands of specific people may take second place to the demands of group survival. When that happens, instead of contributing to the survival of *all* members, the group contributes only to the survival of certain ones while other members are sacrificed.

Members of a society in which the male obtains all or most of the food will necessarily be concerned with preserving his life first, because without the food producer, everyone in the group will die. In a crisis situation, therefore, only the adult male is indispensable. In societies in which both men and women contribute significantly to the food supply, able-bodied adults of both sexes may receive approximately equal priority, but the aged, the sick, and the children are still expendable. Their deaths will not result in the extinction of the group so long as adult males and females survive to get more food and to reproduce. Lost members can be replaced by new ones.

In modern industrial societies, most people are able to avoid confronting such upsetting choices, but in the so-called underdeveloped nations, or Third World, some individuals still must make them. With the growing pressure of population on limited world resources, more of us may be forced to make this type of difficult decision and choice in the near future (Paddock and Paddock 1967:205–206). At the moment, we are not prepared, emotionally or intellectually, to do so, but under famine conditions, attitudes toward life and death are far different from those in modern industrialized societies. Only the affluent can be permitted the luxury of "women and children first."

The Piegan excerpt suggests another characteristic that may be common to many hunting and gathering societies—a difference in the steadiness of the activity of men and women. Women work day after day with little variation in the *total* amount of activity, although the *type* of work frequently varies. Men, on the other hand, tend to work very hard for one period of time and then relax for another. In a study that measured time spent in various activities, it was found that hunters averaged about as much time resting as they did in hunting, but that the daily routine varied sharply. Hunters sometimes went out several days in a row—particularly when they were unsuccessful—but after a fortunate kill, a man might remain in camp eating and sleeping for several days (Holmberg 1969:75–76).

It would be interesting to know if this difference in male-female activity patterns is typical of all hunting and gathering societies and if so, what effect (if any) it had on human development. What adjustments (if any) were required by the change to an agriculturally based system with quite a different activity pattern?

Environmental Constraints

Certain environments limit the number of possible solutions to the problems of survival. Without sophisticated technological control over heat, Eskimos can never be an agricultural people in the Arctic. Most of the year they do not even have a chance to *gather* plants. Hunting and trade remain the only sources for food. Desert environments similarly limit survival possibilities without sophisticated control over water. The environment also limits the possible solutions to the problem of shelter. Obviously, grass huts are no more possible or practical in the Arctic than snow houses and fur clothing would be in tropical rain forests.

Nevertheless, although it limits, the environment does not *determine* the solutions to the problems of survival. Given a moderately rich environment instead of the Arctic or the desert, a number of different solutions are possible. For example, in the southwestern United States the environment has been successfully exploited by hunters and gatherers, subsistence farmers, commercial farmers, stock raisers, merchants, and manufacturers. The northeastern coastal region has included the same range of possibilities, plus that for fishermen. The limitations of environment are modified by culture, especially technology. One can say either that the environment limits the size of the population a given technology can support or that the technology limits the size of a population a given environment can support. The two are in a dynamic interrelationship (referred to as technoenvironmental) that is difficult to disentangle even for the purposes of analysis (Harris 1968:655).

In areas where numbers have had to be strictly limited in order for the group to survive, infanticide has often been used as a means of population control when other techniques were lacking (Lee and DeVore 1968:11). People do not normally prefer infanticide and will stop the practice if their technology changes. Where infanticide is an accepted practice, general attitudes toward the preservation of life often differ from those in Western civilization. Another factor is also operative, however. In some societies, a baby is not regarded as a member of the group, or even human, until some time (occasionally several weeks) has passed. If the infant dies before that time, it is not publicly mourned and no funeral rites are held; the body is simply discarded (Hart and Pilling 1964:91). Such an attitude is difficult for people in advanced, high-technology Western societies to understand. Even in the United States, however, there is a sharp difference of opinion between those who believe human life begins at the moment of conception (and therefore regard abortion as murder) and those who believe human life begins only after birth, or when the fetus can survive outside the womb, or when brain-wave activity can be detected. Members of different societies can be placed along a continuum according to the point at which they believe human life begins. Since they hold that life begins at conception, Roman Catholics might be placed at the earliest extreme (although there are some groups that believe pregnancy begins when a spirit enters the womb [Hart and Pilling 1964:14]).

What is the "right" answer to this question of when human life begins? Each group can and will defend its position, but members of the other groups usually will not accept the justifications, the "evidence" offered, or the assumptions on which justification and evidence are based when these contradict their own. It appears, then, that the "right" answer depends on which premises, evidence, and definition of "human" one accepts. (The same cannot be said of *all* differences between cultures, however; some are susceptible to objective evaluation. This will be discussed at greater length in Chapter 10.)

Sources of Survival

What do hunters hunt? How does this affect the way they hunt? The Piegan excerpt describes a society heavily dependent on a single animal—the buffalo, more accurately called the American bison. The buffalo was not only the main source of meat, but also provided clothing, shelter, storage containers, and various tools through the use of skin, bone, muscles, and internal organs that were not eaten. In addition to buffalo, Piegan hunters killed deer, elk, antelope, and mountain sheep, although these did not play a major role in the economy. Since porcupine quills were used in decoration, that animal must have been hunted too. The book indicates that various predators, such as mountain lion, wolf, wolverine, and bear, were also killed, but only for their skins. Since the bear was thought to be supernaturally powerful, he was rarely hunted and was more often killed in self-defense.

Several societies have been heavily dependent on a single source of food —the Chipewyan Indians on caribou (Oswalt 1966:19), prehistoric Magdalenian peoples on reindeer (Chard 1969:25), the California Indians on acorns, the northwest coast Indians on salmon, and the Eskimo on seal (Spencer and Jennings 1965:124, 169, 233)—but such dependence is neither inevitable nor universal. Many societies exploited their environment so fully that few animals or plants remained unused, and the most important food source at any particular time depended on its relative abundance then. A band that exploits its environment extensively is usually better protected against famine than one that relies chiefly on one source. A recent symposium on hunters and gatherers revealed that the only societies that ran a real risk of starvation were those depending almost exclusively on meat obtained from relatively few kinds of animals. Those that relied on both meat and plant food, although they might suffer meatless days and times of scarcity, were never in any real danger of starvation (Holmberg 1969:83; Lee 1968:40–42).

With the buffalo gone, Piegan culture collapsed. Their life pattern was so dependent on the buffalo that they could not maintain it without them. Although the situation would not have been such a disaster had it not been complicated by hostile pressure from non-Indians, the disappearance of the buffalo alone would certainly have forced a major adjustment. The disappearance of the mammoth in the distant past, the permanent migration of the reindeer from southern France in the even more distant past, changes in caribou migration routes in historic times—all these have had repercussions on the culture and survival patterns of the people dependent on those animals. Just what changes were made, or how disruptive the consequences were, we do not know, except in the case of certain native American groups where the process was observed and documented. The changes must have been profound, however, since the artifacts characteristic of the mammoth hunters or the reindeer hunters cease to appear archeologically, and are replaced by others.

Food Customs

The excerpt mentions briefly another characteristic typical of many hunting and gathering peoples—generosity. The author killed seven buffalo one day, not because he needed meat or hides, but because he wanted to give them to other people. Almost all hunting societies try to make the sharing of game animals desirable to their members, and some make it obligatory (Freuchen 1961:108–131). It is not always popular, and descriptions of life in other societies frequently contain anecdotes of attempts to avoid mandatory sharing of food by various devious means, such as eating late at night, eating away from the main camp, sneaking into camp, or hiding food (Holmberg 1969:87–88). Yet sharing game is a form of insurance. No hunter is so skilled that he can always be sure of success; any hunter may have periods of sickness or be incapacitated as the result of an accident and not be able to hunt effectively. One who has shared game can demand a return when he is empty-handed. The gift of game almost always creates an obligation on the part of the recipient either to return the gift in kind when possible or else to return it in some other form—performing a service for the giver or doing a favor for a member of his family. A society in which each individual hunted only for himself and his family, and in which each family had to depend only on its own members, would not have the survival potential of one in which game was regularly shared. In addition, unshared food would often be wasted when a hunter from a small family killed a large animal. Unless the society had efficient food preservation techniques (and few do), his small household would not be able to eat all the meat before it spoiled. Sharing meat with the whole group is thus a more efficient utilization of the resources and consequently promotes group survival. This may be the reason why there are so few "selfish" hunting and gathering societies; they simply did not survive.

Food is, of course, basic to individual survival. In all but modern affluent societies, most individuals are directly involved in the food quest. In such societies, hospitality is usually obligatory. Even in the urban United States, some sort of food or drink is normally offered to visitors, but the significance of the offer has declined to such an extent that in most cases it can be rejected by a simple "No, thank you." If the visit is prolonged, however, the refusal often causes some anxiety and the host or hostess usually asks again, "Are you sure you won't have something?"

In less affluent societies, an offer of food is equivalent to an offer of friendship, and refusal is a rejection of friendship. It is therefore potentially dangerous to refuse food or drink. One of the hazards (and sometimes pleasures) of cross-cultural research is the variety of food items presented to the honored guest (the researcher). Almost all anthropologists have anecdotes about items they have been expected to consume (sheep's eyes, honey ants, and grubs are among the more disconcerting to American anthropologists). But although people in many societies eat things regarded as inedible in the United States, almost all societies reject some edible items in the environment. The reasons for specific prohibitions are varied, and not always clear; frequently, a member of the society can say only that the item is "no good" or that it is just "not eaten." Occasionally, something edible is believed to be poisonous. Tomatoes were not eaten in the United States for many years in this mistaken belief. Their red color was thought to confirm their poisonous nature, since "everyone knows" that red is one of nature's danger signals. The Siriono in eastern Bolivia refused to eat snake meat on the same erroneous grounds (Holmberg 1969:78).

Sometimes esthetic reasons are given for not eating an item. Asians are generally squeamish about drinking the mammary secretions of a cow, although people in the United States enjoy the taste of milk. Americans are squeamish about eating buzzards or other scavengers because of their food habits, yet will usually consume pork products from an animal whose food habits are equally questionable and whose meat in addition often carries a dangerous parasite (trichina) that can infect humans. The esthetics of eating parasite-infested meat apparently does not bother most Americans, although stories of Eskimos eating maggoty meat are apt to nauseate them.

An item may be rejected because it is not regarded as fit food for humans. Dog and cat meat is generally rejected in the United States, and meat from some other animals such as snakes, horses, squirrels and even rabbits is rejected in certain regions, or by certain segments of the population; yet all these animals are quite edible, and most are eaten in some parts of the world. (If such a rejected item is eaten unwittingly and the individual subsequently learns what he has done, he may become ill, even if he enjoyed the food before he knew what it was.) Another food regarded as unsuitable for humans is pet food. Perhaps some, or even all, brands do contain things that are harmful to people, although it is just as likely that they contain things that are edible but that do not meet government standards for human food. In any case, pet food has often been used by economically deprived minority-group members as a cheap source of protein, and with current inflated food prices, even people who are economically better off are wondering whether some pet food might be included in their diet.

Religious prohibitions against certain items frequently occur. The Judaeo-Arabic proscription of pork is well known, and the Christian Bible lists additional items still prohibited to orthodox Jews. The majority of the items on the list are not regarded as fit for human consumption in most Christian countries today, even though the prohibition is no longer consciously religious. (Examples of these items are camel, mouse, lizard, mole, bat, eagle, vulture, owl, pelican, and stork.) Most of these items were or are eaten in some parts of the world. A few of the items on the proscribed list are eaten today in Christian countries, although they are not usually part of the general diet; they tend to be regarded either as gourmet food or as food for the poor (examples are rabbit, tortoise, and snail). At least one group of items permitted in the Christian Bible is entirely rejected in the United States—the group of insects including beetles, locusts, and grasshoppers (Deuteronomy 14:4–20; Leviticus 11:3–30). (Some items regarded as "sophisticated" delicacies in the United States today—chocolate-covered ants, for example—are simply affectations. *Nobody* in hunting and gathering societies, or even in simple agricultural societies, eats such things. Australian aborigines still eat honey ants, but *not* chocolate-covered ones.)

Attempts to uncover a practical reason underlying each taboo have been made, with some success. Pork carries trichinosis, and therefore the prohibition seems to make some medical sense, although it is questionable whether the connection was at all understood by people who prohibited the eating of pig meat. And this medical explanation does not make clear why in this case only the pig is prohibited when other animal meat that is not prohibited may have different parasites or carry diseases harmful to humans. And what about the attitude toward dog or cat meat? In the United States, most people, even people who do not have pets, are reluctant to eat it, although there is nothing wrong with the meat and dog meat at least has been eaten as a delicacy in various parts of the world. After all, people eat lamb and rabbit, and these animals have often been made pets, even by the very individuals who eat both meats (though they may spare the specific animal that is their pet). The anthropologist Marvin Harris claims that materialistic reasons always underlie food prohibitions. It would be impractical for people in Arab countries to raise pigs, for example. Because of the habits and needs of pigs, the energy put into raising them would not be adequately rewarded. They compete with man for food and scarce water and need shade and cool, damp weather. They do not provide wool, milk, eggs, or transportation, are notoriously difficult to herd in large numbers over long distances, and so can only be expensive luxuries, tempting for their tasty meat but economically unjustified. A religious prohibition reduces the temptation considerably (Harris 1972*b*:32–36). Harris has made the most thorough attempt yet to explain apparently irrational beliefs and behavior concerning food. Although there has been disagreement over some details, no one has effectively challenged his major premise that there is a rational explanation based on technoenvironmental factors (Harris 1974:v,4–7).

No general food prohibitions are mentioned in the Piegan excerpt, but an incident in the book from which the excerpt was taken reveals at least one. At a treaty ceremony with Crow Indians, the Piegans were both revolted and fascinated by the Crow dog feast. According to the author, the Piegans regarded the dog as partly sacred, never to be killed and certainly not to be eaten. The Piegans left hurriedly before the actual feast, and the author reported that some were nauseated at the very idea of the dinner. Other tribes in addition to the Crow regarded the dog as edible and even as a luxury food (Jameson 1909:175).

Many food tabus among the North American Indians were specific to certain individuals as part of their relationship with the supernatural. Individuals often sought personal help from supernatural beings. To establish and maintain the relationship, the individual usually had to follow certain procedures, among which food tabus were frequent. The excerpt, for example, mentions a special tabu on buffalo meat. When the *white* buffalo was killed, the tongue (one of the best parts and regarded as a delicacy) was offered to the Sun, but the rest was left on the prairie. No one was permitted to eat it.

Women drawing water from the village well as Bisalpur, India. This task often provides women with their only chance to exchange news and gossip with people outside their own households. *(United Nations)*

Clothing and Shelter

As has been mentioned, in addition to being a prime food source, the buffalo also provided tools, satchels, robes, bedding, and shelter. The Piegan used the tanned skins, prepared by the women, to cover their lodge poles or to make satchels (parfleches°) for carrying food and various belongings. They made needles, spoons, and other tools from various bones, thread from sinew, and robes and bedding from the furred hides. Piegan clothing was traditionally made of animal skins, usually deer, prepared and sewn together by the women. Native North Americans in general wore clothing that was part of the "tailored" tradition found across the world in the northern half of the globe. In tailored clothing, the material is cut to fit the body closely, especially around the arms and legs. The modern American business suit and the Eskimo parka with trousers are also part of the tailored tradition.

Untailored clothing, common in warmer climates and more or less limited to the southern half of the world, consists of straight lengths of material wrapped around the body in various styles. The Asiatic Indian sari and the South Pacific sarong are examples. Bark cloth, made by beating together fibers from the inner bark of certain trees, was used for the South Pacific clothing. This same process, applied to animal fibers, produces felt, a stiff, almost waterproof material that was widely used for tents in Asia by nomadic herdsmen. Plant and animal fibers, twisted into string or cord, have been woven into nets, bags, belts, armbands, and headbands in many parts of the world, but true woven cloth did not become widespread until after the development of agriculture (see Chapter 2).

Such skirts as these are often worn on Pacific islands. *(Woodfin Camp & Associates)*

Although animal furs, leather, and spun fibers have provided clothing in most parts of the world, some peoples have taken advantage of other materials or have used the furs and fibers in unusual ways. Thin strips of fur from small animals such as rabbits were woven into warm blankets by prehistoric western and southwestern native Americans. Bunches of grass are tied together to a belt at one end and flared out at the other to make a skirt in various parts of the world. Fibers bound together in a series of coils, then looped around the body and bound together on the sides to rest on the hip bones, make another kind of skirt in New Guinea. In various parts of North America, and in parts of the South Pacific including Hawaii at the time of first contact with Europeans, bird feathers were made into spectacular cloaks for special occasions. Men in New Guinea wear specially shaped gourds to cover their penis. Men in parts of the South American jungle simply tie the foreskin closed over the end of the glans and consider themselves dressed.

Total nudity is rare in the world, partly because Western standards of modesty have been energetically spread by colonists and missionaries, and partly because clothing not only provides useful protection against cold, heat, sun, insects, and thorns or sharp grasses, but also can be used to carry any number of things. Women in New Guinea, for example, stow babies (along with pigs, melons, or tools) in net bags (worn in a series to keep the babies from being crushed by the pigs or melons) (Matthiessen 1969:20); Eskimo women stow their babies in their parkas and carry tools in their boottops (Freuchen 1961:27). Even Australian aborigines, who are otherwise naked, may wear string belts to thrust digging sticks or other tools through.

Basketry and net weaving are probably very old skills, but because the materials used are so perishable, it is only rarely that any archeological evidence of them is found. Woven sandals, about 9,000 years old, have been discovered in the Southwest, and three-thousand-year-old cloth has been found in Peru, but it is unreasonable to expect to find anything that is much older (Bushnell 1968:17, 31). From modern or historic peoples we know that basket and net making is world-wide in distribution. Fibers of different sizes and flexibility are twisted, braided, wound, or woven together in a number of ways to make a variety of objects, from watertight baskets or fingernail-sized miniatures to baskets that can hold a grown man, and from delicate gauze to nets strong enough to hold a frantic antelope.

Humans no sooner began making clothing than they decorated it. Leather shirts were brightened by paint or by naturally colorful things like shells, seeds, feathers, or stones sewn on in fanciful patterns. Designs were pressed on bark cloth with dye-covered wooden blocks in a process not far removed from early methods of printing. Among those people in the world who do not wear much clothing, many decorate their bodies instead, painting, tattooing, and scarring being the most common methods of such adornment. People who wear clothing also often paint, tattoo, and scar their skin, but they almost always confine this form of decoration to the face or arms where it is most likely to be visible.

In simple societies, both tattooing and scarring are painful processes. The skin is cut or pierced by thorns, sharp stones, shells, or other implements, and

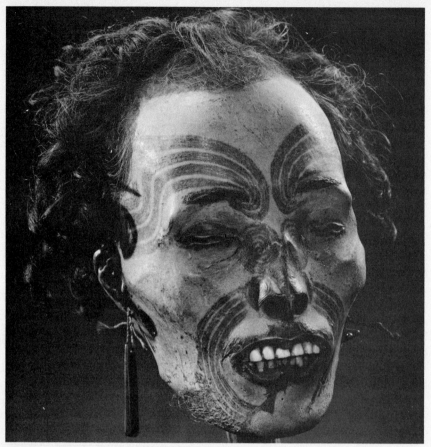

Facial tattooing on a (New Zealand) Maori smoked head. *(Courtesy of the American Museum of Natural History)*

ash, charcoal, or dye is rubbed into the wound. This either raises the surface of the wound and ensures a prominent scar or introduces the coloring into a level of skin where it will remain permanently. Anesthetics and disinfectants are not used, so the whole process is apt to be recognized as an endurance test by which members of the society may evaluate a person's courage. The more extensive the tattoo or scarring pattern, the more courage and stamina an individual has demonstrated.

As if these processes were not painful enough, other practices even more demanding have been popular in various parts of the world. Some of these— marking the passage from child to adult—are described in Chapter 7. Others, however, are employed more for the sake of beauty than to test the individual's readiness to assume the role of adult. These are often performed so early in life that the individual has no choice in the matter. For example, several peoples flattened the heads of their babies (in front, back, or on the sides) to give them a "beautiful" appearance.

Some native American groups fastened an object close to the middle of the baby's face, at eye level, to encourage crossed eyes—a sign of beauty. Other peoples in various parts of the world pierce lips, nose, or ears to provide a handy place to hang trinkets. Beads, feathers, jewels, animal teeth, wooden disks, rings of gold, silver, shell or any attractive, costly material have been hung from or inserted in various parts of the anatomy. Teeth have been filed to points, inlaid, covered with precious metals, or knocked out entirely—all for beauty. Canines and incisors are especially likely to be removed. Sometimes, teeth are removed to make room for fancy lip plugs, or for reasons presumed to be connected with health. The Dodoth in Africa remove all the baby tooth buds still in the gums to avoid the first teething experience, which is said to be hard on the baby's health. Later they remove the adult incisors to provide room for the lip plug. Dodoth women make interesting use of this body modification: when a female is annoyed, she removes the plug and sticks her tongue out through the hole at the person who angered her (Thomas 1965:5).

Housing

Piegan housing was made of skins, which were stretched over a framework of poles. The whole lodge was cared for, put up, and taken down by the women. The lodge was portable; in fact, the poles of the frame could be used to make the travois (see page 9). Well staked down with furs on the floor and around the sides, the skin lodge made a warm, comfortable shelter in winter. In summer the sides could be rolled up and flaps at the top opened for better ventilation.

Mobile hunters and gatherers almost always have easily built shelters, unless they stay in caves. They generally use materials that can be found on the spot, because it is not worth hauling heavy objects any distance. The most common type of dwelling is a framework of poles covered with a variety of materials—skins, as in the Piegan lodges, or other material such as branches, woven mats, thatch (bunches of leaves or grass tied together and placed in overlapping rows), large leaves, or long grass according to climate and available material. Eskimos, who live in a climate where substantial shelter is needed at least part of the year and where building materials are scarce, solve the problem in several ways. In fall, before the ground freezes hard, they dig pits two feet or so into the ground, and build walls and roof up with stones and turf. This type of house has a wide distribution in areas where the climate is severe. When families travel, with deep snow on the ground, central Eskimos build their famous igloos. Very few Eskimos live all winter long in igloos, however, and of course no igloo lasts all year, since the snow melts in summer. In warm weather, most Eskimos use skin or canvas tents.

The log cabin, familiar as the pioneer shelter in the United States, was a European import brought over by immigrants from the Scandinavian countries, particularly Sweden, who settled in Delaware in the 1600s. Its practicality made it immediately popular and its use spread so quickly that few Americans today realize that it did not originate with the first settlers.

Until quite recently in human history, houses with several rooms were limited to the most powerful and wealthy members of complex societies.

Houses with six rooms or more did not exist at all until after urbanization took place (see Chapter 2). Although most of the world's population today still lives in one or two rooms per family, homes in some heavily populated parts of the world such as India, the Middle East, and traditional China appear larger because several families live in a compound structure built around a central courtyard and consisting of a number of separate "apartments" (of one or two rooms each) where related families live. The case is much the same with the Pueblo peoples in the southwestern United States. Each family has only one or two rooms, but since these are built attached to one another, the impression given is of a single large building.

In many simple societies, the entire band may shelter under one roof. The Yanomamo and the Siriono are examples in South America. In such cases, each family has its own particular section. In more complex societies, there may be several such houses, with each one containing a number of related families. Multifamily "longhouses" are found in many parts of the world (C. Richards 1955:1200). Among the Dodoth, a large fence encloses the living area for several related families, each with a separate, private, enclosed segment (Thomas 1965:13, 16). This solution is frequent in societies that allow a man to have several wives, each wife having her own section for herself and her children. In other societies where polygyny is allowed, the women live all together in one section of the main dwelling—the famous harem, for example.

There are wide variations between solutions to the problem of shelter, yet all of them can be classified within a relatively small number of types. One main basis for classification is whether the housing is permanent or temporary. ("Per-

An igloo, built by Central Eskimos during winter travel. *(C. Bonington/Woodfin Camp & Associates)*

manent" in this context means only that the house will last more than one season.) Within these two major categories, houses can be classified by shape (round, square, rectangular, irregular); by number of rooms; by degree of isolation (that is, by whether the houses are separate units at some distance from all others, are clustered in patterned groups, or are attached to others); and by whether each house is for a single family, or is a multiple-family dwelling. When a correlation is made between these classifications and other characteristics of a society, it is apparent that the type of houses people live in are not randomly distributed. Certain kinds of subsistence methods, certain levels of complexity, and certain kinds of social organization are associated with certain classifications of houses. Throughout the book, we will continue to explore some of these associations.

Hunting Tools and Techniques

What tools and techniques do hunters use? Horses were an essential part of Piegan technology. They enabled hunters to get close to game, to keep close after the buffalo began to run, and to carry large amounts of meat back to camp. Not surprisingly, horses were highly valued, and individuals constantly tried to increase their herds. The excerpt indicates that they spared the horses when they could. On the hunt for the white buffalo, the men walked the horses as much as possible to save them for the run they knew was coming. When they stopped to wait for the buffalo to come closer, the native Americans "as usual"

Typical housing of so-called Pueblo Indians (a number of different peoples including Hopi and Zuñi) in the North American Southwest. This particular example is in New Mexico. *(Courtesy of the American Museum of Natural History)*

removed their saddles (these were obviously not the bareback-riding television Indians). On the other hand, the excerpt also indicates that they used quirts freely to force their horses on after they began to tire. Many peoples of the world—not just hunters and gatherers—are known for their casual (by American standards cruel) treatment of animals. The Piegan were no exception.

The culture of the Piegan was almost as dependent on the horse as it was on the buffalo. Only a few hunters and gatherers have had animal transport, and all the examples date from relatively late in human history. Animals large enough and fast enough to serve a hunter's purpose were not domesticated early anywhere, and did not exist in the New World until the Spanish brought in horses. Other forms of transportation—boats, canoes, kayaks, dog sleds, travois, cars, planes—also developed relatively late. So far as we know, all early hunters traveled only by foot.

The new means of transportation affected man's range, his affluence, and some of his behavior, yet hunters with these more advanced transportation techniques still share many characteristics with hunters on foot. One reason may be that in most cases the new methods served more to increase the mobility of the group, bringing the hunter into richer hunting grounds, than to increase his effectiveness in killing game. That is, the hunter used the transportation only to get to the hunting area and to bring the meat from his kill home. He did not hunt from his bull boat, raft, or dog travois. The horse and the kayak or dugout used in deep-water fishing are obviously exceptions. The excerpt makes it clear that the horse was an essential part of the Piegan hunting method. In fact, the horse made buffalo hunting rewarding enough to induce some native American farmers to leave their fields and take it up. (This was one of the few instances in human history where farming was abandoned for hunting as a subsistence method.) Hunting from horseback is by no means the only way to hunt large herd animals like buffalo, however. Early hunters, in both the Old World and the New World, were rather efficient at driving herds over cliffs or into bogs. The drive technique could be wasteful, since a small group might easily get more meat than members could eat, preserve, or transport. It might have reduced the game animals too drastically in certain areas. However, it could also provide a reason for small groups to cooperate and establish ties and relationships that might later form a basis for larger societies. Later hunters did not use this method so often, since more effective techniques were apparently developed, such as individual hunting with bow and arrow.

Hunting with bow and arrow gave a number of advantages, and increased use of this method may have been a factor in the decline of the fire drive or surround. For one thing, if the elephant or buffalo drives of early hunters were organized in the same way as they are by modern hunters and gatherers, it probably required the cooperation of the whole band, and possibly even several bands acting together. The drive uses women, older children, and the spryest elders in addition to the able-bodied hunters, because the chances of most of the animals veering away from a trap are too great if only a few hunters try to herd them. But getting full or joint group cooperation must always have been somewhat difficult. How much simpler it must have been, then, for a hunter to go out alone, or with one or two friends, and still be able to bring home meat, as he could do with the bow and arrow. In certain environments, the bow and arrow probably had other advantages, since hunters using this method caused less waste. An individual hunter, confronted with a herd, could kill only what he needed and let the rest live. An individual, particularly if he went after deer or similar animals more vulnerable to an arrow than the tough-skinned buffalo or elephant, could usually provide meat for one or two wives, their children, and even their (and his) parents. Spread of the bow and arrow, therefore, might well have significantly altered hunting technology and consequently the organization for the hunt. It is the bow and arrow that makes the stereotyped division of labor more feasible—the hunter stalking game to bring back to the waiting woman (or leave for her to collect). Women are active participants in the game drive and the surround, so in the earliest period of human hunting they were hardly likely to be waiting unproductively at a home base. And if they were not participating in the game drive, they were most likely out after plant food. The image of early hominid females waiting patiently in the cave for the males to bring back meat is one of the less likely modern myths.

According to the excerpt, the Piegans had guns as well as bows and arrows. Interestingly enough, many preferred to use bows and arrows for hunting buffalo because they could shoot more arrows than bullets in a given period of time. Guns had the advantage of being effective over longer distances, but they were both noisier and slower. In general, even after the repeating rifle eliminated the difference in speed of firing, native Americans continued to use bows and arrows in situations where noise was a factor and distance was not. They shifted to guns when firepower and long range were more important. A steady supply of ammunition was also an important variable in the adoption of the gun. A man could always make his own arrows, but after the development of the cartridge containing both powder and bullet, the average individual (native American or not) could no longer make his own and had to obtain supplies by purchase or theft.

The rifle is the last dramatic technological development in hunting. The first advance over hand-thrown missiles was the spear thrower, just as the composite spear (stone or bone points on a wooden shaft) had been a technological advance over wooden spears or unshafted stone points. The spear supplemented or replaced the bolas,° stone balls tied together on long strings and thrown to entangle the legs of game animals. The bolas is still used in South America (Martin, Quimby, and Collier 1947:247). Early hunters may also have used the sling, but there is no certain archeological evidence of this. They probably had many tools and weapons made of perishable materials such as plants, leather, and wood that have not survived. Some form of throwing stick is certainly possible. In historic times, such a weapon has been reported from places as far apart as Australia and the southwestern United States (Simmons 1966:11). So much time has passed since the period of early hunters that it would be more surprising to find evidence of these perishable materials than

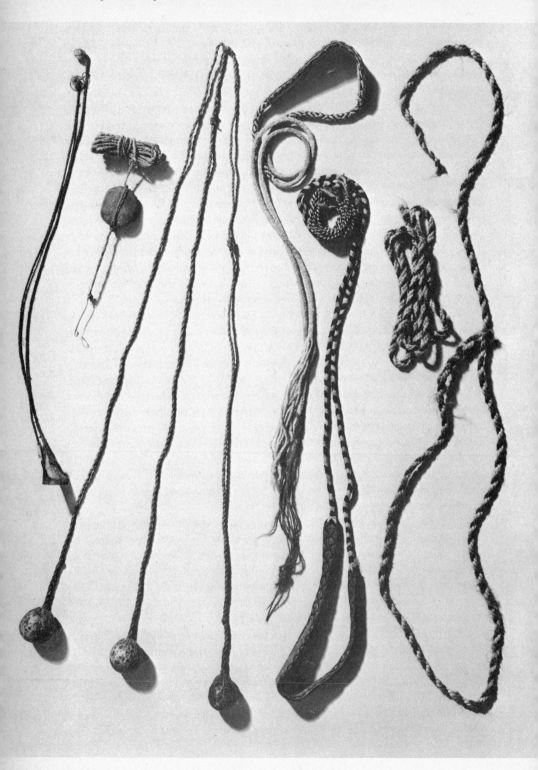

it is not to. Traps, nets, snares, and poisons are all hunting devices that leave little or no archeological traces. Some remnants of fish weirs° have been found, but they are only a few thousand years old (Martin, Quimby, and Collier 1947:93). Other than these, there is little direct evidence of the full variety of techniques early hunters may have employed.

In this regard, the sling and the bolas present special problems. The sling itself, like the thongs tying the bolas stones together, is perishable, but the sling missile and the bolas stones are not. Sling missiles that have been identified as such in early historic sites are ovoid, biconical, or egg-shaped, rather than round (Korfmann 1973:39, 40). Sometimes they are modified stones, sometimes molded clay; but often they are simply stream-smoothed pebbles. As such, they would be difficult for an archeologist to identify as parts of tools. Bolas stones, which are usually round, present a particular problem because they may be the same shape as hammerstones (stone hammers). At present it is difficult to distinguish the two unless the context in which they are found gives some sort of clue (Pfeiffer 1972:412). Evidence of use might be the only distinguishing characteristic that would separate hammerstones from either bolas stones or sling missiles, which, of course, should not show any intensive use (Korfmann 1973:38).

The whole question of tool use is more complex than one would guess. The purpose of manufactured objects is not always obvious, especially if parts are missing. Indeed, we cannot always recognize the intended use of objects made by our own ancestors as recently as colonial times. Problems are especially great when an object is of a shape quite different from that of its contemporary counterpart (i.e., hammerstones and modern hammers), or when the use for which the object was designed is no longer part of the culture (warming pans, for instance, are not part of the culture of people living in centrally heated houses). It is a joke among archeologists that any time they cannot identify the use of some object, they call it a "ceremonial object."

Land animals, fish, water mammals, and birds are snared, netted, trapped, speared, poisoned, or shot by modern hunters. The blowgun and sling are usually limited to use on land animals or birds, whereas the hook and line or harpoon tend to be limited to use on fish or water mammals. With these exceptions, virtually all techniques used on land have been adapted to water use, and vice versa.

Some animals are more efficiently hunted cooperatively; others, individually. Animals that move in herds and animals that are either very large or very small are usually more effectively hunted by groups that can surround the game, or drive it into a trap or bog or over a cliff. Rabbits and other small game are still hunted by surrounding an area with a circle of people who gradually close in. Dangerous solitary animals (bears or tigers), besides being surrounded and frightened by noise makers, may also be hunted by small groups of men

Examples of early tools and weapons. From left to right: a lasso; a fishing line with sinker and bait holder; a bolas; two slings; two bridles. *(Courtesy of the American Museum of Natural History)*

who protect one another and jointly bring down the game (Steward 1968:326–327). Medium-sized animals (deer, elk, antelope) are probably more often hunted by individuals.

Most societies employ a variety of techniques and consequently organize their hunters in various ways for different situations. The excerpt provides an example of this. The author usually went hunting with a group rather than alone. When he was part of the group, he cooperated with the others and accepted certain rules. In hunting the white buffalo, for example, everyone agreed not to start the buffalo running until either the white one was found or they were ready to give up the search. In general among Plains Indians, no one was allowed to hunt individually before a tribal hunt, because if the buffalo were frightened, the whole tribe might go hungry for a time. The Cheyenne Indians even gave one of their military associations the responsibility of policing the camp just before the hunt to see that no one sneaked out early (Hoebel 1960:53). Cooperative hunting is practiced by many peoples (see the excerpt on Pygmies in Chapter 5), and always places some restrictions on the behavior of the individuals involved.

On the other hand, the excerpt indicates that along with the cooperative hunting went a great deal of individuality. Once the buffalo run started, each

Indians hunting the bison. *(Courtesy of the American Museum of Natural History)*

hunter was on his own, and the game he killed (through his endurance, skill, and the ability of his horse) belonged entirely to him. This made his generosity all the more admirable. He did not *have* to share his kill, so if he did, he was highly respected for it. In this attitude, the Piegan resembled many other hunters and gatherers. The excerpt indicates that among the Piegan a man was free to hunt by himself whenever he cared to. He was also free to hunt with only one or two friends instead of a larger group. Hunters and gatherers tend to be pragmatic; if the usual procedure fails for any reason, almost all such societies have several alternate techniques.

Attitudes and Beliefs

What were the views of the Piegan concerning violence? What data does the Piegan excerpt provide on the general question of human aggression? Reread the excerpt to see what information it yields on the attitudes and beliefs related to this matter. As you do this, one of the major problems of anthropological research should become obvious. Clothing can be seen, weighed, measured, photographed. The processes for making it can be observed and recorded. The materials used to make it can be analyzed. But who has seen an attitude or photographed a belief? Like all things of the mind, these can be studied only indirectly, through observable manifestations—that is, through what people do, and what they say. From these manifestations we must try to construct attitudes, beliefs, and indeed, all of culture (which, as Redfield points out in the definition on page xv, is a thing of the mind). An additional difficulty is that, according to psychological data, even the most insightful of us do not always understand our true motives and desires. A researcher is therefore confronted with problems on several different fronts simultaneously. First, attitudes are on a different level of abstraction from physical artifacts (what some people call material culture). Second, there are different levels of reliability in the data the researcher has to work with. People may lie about their attitudes and motives, they may tell the truth as they perceive it but be unaware of their true motives, or they may describe their attitudes and motives accurately. On still another level of reliability, people's behavior, based on their attitudes and motives is, at least, observable, but the bias of the researcher may cause trouble here. (The problem of researcher bias—a serious one, into which a great deal of effort has gone trying to overcome, reduce, or at least allow for it—is discussed in the last chapter.) These research problems will be mentioned again at various times. For the present, it is sufficient to become aware of them and to begin to evaluate data in terms of levels of abstraction, reliability, and bias.

Turning to the excerpt again, we confront another problem in trying to answer the broad questions of the relationship between hunting and intrahuman violence and whether aggressive behavior is inborn in man. (Of course, any attitude revealed by this excerpt could be unusual and atypical. It *is* one example, however, and the controversy can be settled only by the examination of actual cases, not by armchair discussions of what human behavior "logically" should be, or what people are "really" like.) The excerpt makes only a few specific statements about attitudes toward killing game. Once, when the buffalo were headed toward camp and people could see the killing, "No one cheered the hunters, nor spoke, nor laughed. It was too solemn a moment. We saw death abroad; huge, powerful beasts, full of tireless energy, suddenly stricken into so many heaps of meat and hide." Note that the observer is reporting on more than one level at once. When he states that no one cheered, spoke, or laughed he is reporting observable behavior, so unless he is lying (and there seems to be no reason to suspect he is), the description is probably accurate. When he is explaining inner reactions, however, there is no way of telling whether he is reporting feelings that only he had or ones shared by the Piegan. He *thought* they shared them, but did they? If they did, it hardly seems as if the Piegan took killing lightly. Certainly the excerpt does not support the position that because hunters kill often they grow casual about bloodshed or death and consequently can more easily kill one another. Again, when Medicine Weasel killed the white buffalo, "He was so excited, he trembled so, that he could not use his knife, and some of our party took off the hide for him . . ." Of course, killing a white buffalo was something quite special. (The same passage, incidentally, disposes of the myth of the stoical Indian.) The book makes it clear that animal killing was frequently a highly emotional experience for the Piegan—at least as the author saw it. Nonetheless, the Piegan engaged in considerable violence against other people. They gloried in raids against other tribes; they responded to conflicts within their own group by assault, corporal punishment, suicide, and murder. Killing a Piegan exposed one to retaliation from the victim's relatives, but aside from concern over this danger, killing a human does not seem to have been taken as seriously as killing a white buffalo.

The Piegan example does not contradict the hypothesis that hunters are apt to be violent against humans as well as against animals, but neither does it fully support the suggestion that intrahuman violence results because hunting leads people to take violence and killing casually. The excerpt indicates that the whole relationship is more complex than it first appears. The Piegan attitude toward violence is not a simple one of "accept" or "reject." Instead, members of the society seem to classify cases of violence according to the perceived necessity for it. In the book, attitudes toward any specific act of violence between humans vary from complete acceptance through reluctant acceptance to complete rejection, according to the circumstances. People in most societies seem to make a similar distinction between acts of violence that are regarded as fully justified and those that are in every way repulsive. Is it possible to channel an instinct in so many diverse ways? Human sexuality, certainly based on a biological drive, shows much the same kind of variation. So the argument continues. The Piegan excerpt does not solve the problem; it only adds some depth.

The anecdote about the stampede mentioned in the excerpt suggests that the Piegan shared what seems to be an almost universal human tendency. The buffalo had been driven near the camp by the hunters so they would not have to pack the meat far once they had finished their killing. The desire to save time and energy is a characteristic that has affected the direction of culture since the beginning of human history (Titiev 1963:378–379). Given a choice of alternatives, human beings have almost invariably chosen that which would take less time and less human muscle—except in the areas of art, recreation, and religion, in which the choices are usually made on some other basis (see Chapter 9 for further discussion).

The excerpt also suggests that the Piegan were not expert conservationists, at least not by conviction. The white buffalo was madly pursued, although if left alone, white buffalos might have appeared more frequently in the future. Fat cows were singled out for killing as often as possible, since the meat was tenderer and had more flavor. Studies show that most subsistence hunters have this approach to game. It is mainly herdsmen and sportsmen who are concerned about keeping productive cows and their offspring alive to ensure future plenty. Hunters and gatherers tend to resort to fertility magic instead. Reported instances of subsistence hunters concerned with conservation are rare, and usually refer to protests against outsiders killing off game the hunters regard as rightfully theirs. On the other hand, subsistence hunters rarely kill for sport and seldom waste any of their kill.

The description of the hunt for the white buffalo and that of the ride through the blizzard reveal why so many hunters and gatherers place a premium on strength and endurance, especially for males. Hunting and gathering societies often incorporate endurance training into their child-raising techniques—making young boys roll naked in the snow every morning, for example, or go all day on a minimum of food or water. Sometimes the ceremony marking the change from child to adult also incorporates a test of courage, strength, or endurance (see Chapter 7). When adults frequently have to call on resources of courage and physical endurance to survive, this is likely to be reflected at some point in child-training.

Beliefs about the supernatural are closely interwoven with pragmatic hunting knowledge among the Piegan. The white buffalo hunt provides one example; the incident in which Arrow Maker was killed and Two Bows wounded another. Trouble indicated to the hunting party that the supernatural environment was hostile. They did not know why and did not try to find out; they simply wanted to get away quickly. Most were willing to risk the dangers of the blizzard to put as much distance as possible between themselves and the dangerous location. When the buffalo stampede passed through camp without doing any major damage, people attributed their safety to supernatural intervention and responded with sacrifices to indicate their gratitude. Interestingly enough, no one seems to have blamed either the supernatural or the hunters for directing the buffalo into the camp in the first place. If people had been harmed, the supernatural (though in response to human action or inaction) rather than the hunters would probably have been held responsible.

In most hunting and gathering societies, both hunting skill and favorable relations with the supernatural are thought to be essential to success. A successful hunter is confident of supernatural favor; an unsuccessful one usually consults specialists to find out what his problem is. Specialists are expected to perform ceremonies to ensure success, to increase or attract game, and so on.

The excerpt mentions that a "medicine man" accompanied the group on all the long hunts, and members of the party passed the evening in prayer or in singing special songs associated with hunting success.

Most writers now assume that much of the Paleolithic° cave art in southwestern Europe was part of hunting magic, performed either to celebrate success or to ensure it. Some art may also have been associated with fertility magic, to ensure plenty of game. (A substantial amount of the Paleolithic art may have been related to storytelling, writing, and astronomical observations. This is discussed in Chapters 2 and 9.) All hunting peoples have had enough experience to realize that the most skillful hunter may return empty-handed at times. Resort to the supernatural can restore a man's confidence, maintain it, or explain his misfortune and thereby reduce anxiety.

Unusual animals such as the white buffalo are often thought to have supernatural qualities themselves, or at least to enjoy a special relationship with the supernatural. An animal that is peculiarly hard to kill or one that behaves in an uncharacteristic way is also often thought to have special powers, and the individual who kills such a beast may prove and even strengthen his own power by doing so. Of course, he may also run the risk of antagonizing the supernatural by killing a favored animal. Greek mythology contains several stories illustrating this danger (Leach 1949:76), and most schoolchildren are familiar with the tale of the Ancient Mariner. In societies where the dangers are emphasized, killing a special animal may be an omen of disaster.

Some hunting societies believe in a generalized spirit for each animal: a giant beaver, symbolizing all beavers; a special elk, representing all elk. The body of a slain animal must be treated with proper respect, or all animals of that type will avoid the hunter in the future. Quite a few hunting societies believe that animals allow themselves to be caught or that their representative spirit sends his "people" to the hunter for the community's benefit. Consequently, Eskimos give seals a "drink" of fresh water to encourage other seals to let themselves be caught (Jenness 1959:50, 204), and in the 1600s Huron Indians would not allow the bones of deer, moose, or fish to be thrown to dogs for fear others of their kind would learn of it and refuse to allow themselves to be taken (Thwaites 1897, 10:167). Some societies also extend feelings to plants and perform rituals before gathering them.

The excerpt reveals that the Piegan thought the supernatural controlled the weather (a widespread belief in the modern United States too—witness prayers for rain during drought). When the chinook began to blow and cleared the air of the frost haze that had been hampering the search for the white buffalo, one of the men exclaimed that since he had prayed for the "black wind," its appearance proved his power. (Of course, if it had not come, it would simply have shown that his power was weak. Either way, the belief in the supernatural was supported.)

Although the excerpt does not mention it, the Piegans believed there was a supernatural component to illness, as well as to accidents. Sickness and wounds from accidents or violence have threatened humans, as they have all animals, throughout their existence. Human beings are perhaps the only animals to seek to prevent or cure disease and heal wounds through cooperative action—possibly because they are the only animals that can. Most adult or juvenile animals, even those living in groups, must fend for themselves if they are sick or hurt. The amount of assistance the group offers its disabled members varies among species, from none at all to, at most, protection from predators or supplying food. Protection tends to be limited in time to a few hours or a few days for all but infants. Carnivores seem to be the only animals that supply disabled members with food. Occasionally individual animals may lick the wounds of others, but this response is not typical of all species, or even of all members of one species (van Lawick-Goodall 1971:132). No other treatment has been observed. Among primates other than man, ill or injured animals are on their own generally, and if they fail to keep up with the group, they are almost invariably killed by predators. If they cannot get food for themselves, they starve. Infants are exceptions, of course. Since they get food by nursing, and since among primates they are carried around by their mothers, several of these statements do not apply to them. Even nonhuman primate mothers do not give medicines or bandage wounds, however.

As soon as humans began to have a base camp where the sick, disabled, and feeble (either young or old) could remain while the able-bodied went after food which they brought back and shared, members of that group had a survival edge over other animals. The base camp would afford some protection from predators even before the control of fire, and the simple fact that the sick individual could rest and still be fed would probably increase chances of survival. With fire, even if it did no more than keep the sufferer warm, thereby reducing danger of shock or chill, the probability of survival increased again. Active group cooperation in helping the sick or disabled undoubtedly led to a further improvement in the survival potential of individuals and consequently of the group as a whole. The Piegan excerpt indicates what may have been one of the earliest practices of group cooperation to assist a member—transport of the injured to a place of safety. This and immobilization of broken limbs were probably the first things humans added to the animal repertoire of care for the sick and disabled.

Use of raw plant remedies and, after the invention of cooking, the discovery of useful medicines that could be extracted from plants by boiling or heating, undoubtedly increased the survival rate still more. We have no information on how soon people began to make use of plant remedies, but since some knowledge of this sort is virtually universal, it is probably quite old in human history. (Attempts to obtain supernatural assistance to cure the sick and disabled are also virtually universal, and are probably associated with the origins of religion which apparently began at least a million years ago with *Homo erectus,* if not before. This aspect of curing will be discussed more fully in Chapter 9.)

THE CHANGE TO AGRICULTURE: WHY?

One interesting discovery in recent studies is that most hunters and gatherers live well on a minimum of effort. Only those in rigorous environments where plant food is unavailable most of the year live a precarious existence (Lee 1968:42). The old idea that hunters and gatherers lack the necessary leisure to be able to build a complex society is apparently incorrect. Something else must be missing.

Along with leisure, a large population and a surplus food supply are regarded as necessary for the development of civilization. If by working a bit longer, hunters and gatherers could obtain more food, couldn't they have a surplus, increase the population, and thus meet the requirements for developing a civilization? It certainly sounds possible, but there are difficulties because of the interrelatedness of the various factors. First, if the hunters and gatherers work harder, they lose their leisure. Second, if they increase the population, food that would have been surplus with their smaller population will instead be needed to keep the additional members alive. With more food and more people, the question of how much additional hunting and gathering the environment can support becomes highly significant. It has been estimated that hunting and gathering bands today—all in poor, marginal environments—have a population that is only 20 to 30 percent of the average carrying capacity of the land (Lee and DeVore 1968:11). One suggestion as to why they remain so few is that population is determined by the *minimum* carrying capacity of the land, not by the average (Lee and DeVore 1968:84–85). Thus, even if the population increased during normal years, it would be brought down sharply again through starvation in the first bad year. It seems, then, that the potential of hunters to increase their population, provide a food surplus, and still have sufficient leisure to develop a civilization may be more imaginary than real.

Discovery of the amount of leisure available to hunters raises a second puzzling question, almost the reverse of the first. That is, if we have partially answered why hunters do not develop civilizations, we still have to answer the question of why some of them did. Why, after at least a million and half years as highly successful hunters, living a good life, with plenty of food and leisure, and with no knowledge of any alternatives, did humans turn to agriculture at all? Why work longer, and harder, and build up food surpluses? The answer *seemed* fairly obvious when the image of the life of hunters and gatherers was that of desperately poor savages, barely clinging to survival, a hair's breadth from disaster all their lives, struggling each day simply to exist. Under such conditions the life of a farmer would seem ideal. Now that we have learned that this image is false—that even today when hunters and gatherers have been forced into the least fertile, least productive areas, the image only partially applies to a very few groups—the question of why humans turned to agriculture has been reopened.

Increasing population may be the answer. As new behaviors and discoveries added to the chances of survival of this primate-becoming-human, his numbers must have grown. (There is evidence of a population explosion in the upper Paleolithic [Pfeiffer 1972:242, 246].) For a long time, the solution to the problem of too much pressure on the environment was for groups to split and for some to move on. Mute evidence for this solution lies in the spread of humanity throughout most of the Old World during the time of *Homo erectus,* into the

New World, Australia, and all of its present range after the appearance of *Homo sapiens* (Chard 1969:94, 117, 140, 167). The change to agriculture came after humans had occupied every continent but Antarctica. It occurred in central areas, surrounded on all sides by territory already occupied by hunters and gatherers. The change did not occur overnight; it took several generations. Archeological evidence gathered in the last decade indicates that populations were growing and people were staying in one place for longer and longer times even before the domestication of plants, at least in the Middle East. Perhaps to cope with the problems of more people, less game, and no open hunting territories to move to, individuals in particularly favorable environments began to "help nature along" a little by planting seeds where the grains had once grown (but had disappeared because of overgathering), or by pulling up undesirable plants competing with the preferred ones. From that it would have been a small step to planting seeds in areas that looked favorable, and from that another small step to improving less favorable areas by lengthening a natural backwater into a rudimentary irrigation canal or by extending a small natural rise in the ground to hold floodwater on a larger area, and so on. Some hunters and gatherers today do things of that sort, planting their seeds and leaving them to grow with no further help while the group follows its normal hunting and gathering round. If they are lucky, when they return at harvest time they have some additional food. If they are not, they simply depend more on their other foods, and try again the following year. This pattern is called incipient agriculture, and may have been one of the life styles from which full agriculture developed (Chard 1969:167, 180–182; Braidwood 1975:93–120). To the relatively sedentary gatherers of the Middle East, who were able to watch and tend their plants more consistently during the growing season, the reward was probably correspondingly greater. Recent archeological work in the Middle East indicates that the sedentary village came *before* plant domestication (Pfeiffer 1972:274; Leonard 1973:22–24), thus supporting the suggestion that domestication was a solution to a pressing survival problem and not just something somebody thought might be a clever thing to do. In the New World, domestication of a few plants occurred long before settled village life, but the people who grew those plants did not depend on them for even half their diet (Leonard 1967:15). Increasing dependence on domesticated plants came very slowly, and only the improvement in yield after the hybridization of maize allowed the type of food production Middle Easterners were able to get even from wild wheat. (See Chapter 2 for more detail on this matter.)

Most kinds of hunting require considerable mobility, which is not compatible with large accumulation of goods of any type, particularly when no animal transport is available. Hunters and gatherers in a stable relationship with an environment that ensures them an adequate and steady food supply also do not need to plan for the future, or stock food (Steward 1968:328). Sedentary hunters who exploit a seasonal abundance, preserving and storing enough food to last them through the season of scarcity, are an exception. They almost alone among hunters are apt to have highly complex societies, with a considerable difference in power and wealth between various segments of a large population. Tribes such as the Haida and the Tlingit (southwest Canada and Alaska) lived in just such a favored environment and developed a complex, elaborate social system based on the seasonal abundance of salmon (Drucker 1963). Without techniques for preserving and storing fish, these peoples would have fed heartily for part of the year, but then would have had to travel in search of food. On the other hand, location on a bay near the mouth of a river with easy access to a forested hinterland may have permitted sedentary living even without any efficient food-preservation technology. Fish, sea mammals, shellfish, and game would then have been available with a minimum amount of travel. Sedentary hunters and gatherers can also accumulate a considerable store of material goods, and engage in long-range planning. It is possible that it was a society of this sort that first turned to agriculture to maintain a way of life under pressure from increasing population and with nowhere to go without conflict.

Another type of hunting and gathering society that may have been the first to turn to agriculture is one that depended heavily on plant products instead of game. These people, more gatherers than hunters, may have practiced incipient agriculture. Both patterns—sedentary hunting and gathering, and nomadic collecting of plants and small game with incipient agriculture—may have led to domestication in different parts of the world. This could account for the archeological evidence indicating that village life preceded domestication in the Middle East but came considerably after domestication in the New World (Armillas 1964:292–300).

SUMMARY

The survival of the individual is basic to the survival of groups. With humans, life in a group is also basic to individual survival. The dynamics of human behavior, therefore, have both individual and group components. The term *culture* is one anthropologists use to refer to the organized ideas, beliefs, knowledge, and concepts that individuals learn from and share with other members of the group in which they live. Culture, rather than physical genetic adaptation, is the mechanism through which humans cope with their world. In this chapter, we have discussed some group solutions to the problem of individual survival. With regard to specific survival needs—food, water, air, shelter, and health care—we have dealt mainly with the topic of food, since it has posed the most immediate and persistent problem. Until recently, air and water (except in desert and arctic environments) have, for the most part, been taken for granted. Actually, pure water has been a problem ever since people began to congregate in cities, but only a few of the ancient cities of the world (and not all the modern ones) have shown any awareness of the difficulty. Cities in technologically complex societies at one time had virtually solved the problem of water pollution, but recently increasing population and additional sources of pollution have once again made difficult the task of obtaining pure water.

Shelter as protection against the elements and predators has posed more of a problem to humans in the past than it does at present. Once the problem was solved, however, it tended to stay solved for some time. That is, once an individual found a particularly good cave, or built a durable house, the problem was solved for generations. Some caves show occupational sequences covering thousands of years. Even human-made shelters have sometimes been occupied for hundreds of years. Temporary shelters, although they do not last long, have the advantage of being easily built by almost anyone from the materials at hand. The shelter problem has therefore only occasionally been serious.

Illness and injury from violence or accidents have always posed serious threats to individual survival. Like the shelter problem, however, the problem of disease or injuries as a life threat tends to be sporadic rather than constant, except under unusual circumstances.

Food, however, is a daily requirement if the individual is to continue to function at full efficiency. Although the problem of food supply may be solved for months through the use of preservation techniques such as drying, freezing, pickling, dehydrating, smoking, salting, and canning, most societies in human history have relied on short-term solutions.

Humans have had a long history as hunters and gatherers. They started (and continue) as animals living off the environment, but with a gradually increasing development of and dependence upon culture. This adds a variable that through the centuries has become increasingly important. Because of culture, the power of the environment to determine the human physical form began to diminish. More and more, the environment simply provided a framework within which a number of different solutions to survival were worked out. Culture became a screen interposed between the individual and the direct effects of the physical environment. Humans began, in fact, to change the physical environment itself. They did not grow fur to survive in a cold climate; they built fires to heat their environments, shelters to protect themselves from cold and storms, and they used the furry skins of other animals to keep warm. They did not grow internal water-storage areas so that they could live in deserts; they made watertight containers and aqueducts to carry water into arid environments. They made weapons with which to kill animals otherwise too strong, too large, too fast, or too fierce for them.

The problems of survival remain the same for human beings as for all other animals, but with culture, they no longer have to depend on their own physical equipment to solve them. In the most technologically complex societies of the present day, this screen of culture has cut people off so effectively from the direct influence of the environment that some have forgotten how intimately and ultimately they are involved with it. Fortunately, other individuals have never lost that awareness and have succeeded in calling attention to the damage being done to the environment. In the United States today, probably more individuals are conscious of their relationship to the environment than at any time since humans were exclusively hunters and gatherers. Certainly there is more widespread concern now about the quality of the environment than there has ever been in the past. Humans have been polluters for hundreds of thousands of years, but because their numbers were relatively few, they did little damage and were able to remain unconcerned about what damage they did do. Only recently have they begun to accept some responsibility for their actions in this area. One hopes they have accepted it in time.

2 Survival: Food Producers

Hunting and gathering is not the only way of obtaining food. Producing food in quantity is another means of providing for basic nutritional needs. The domestication of plants and animals, which was a relatively late discovery in human history, has had profound consequences, providing new opportunities for settlement, clothing, and housing, and making different demands.

In the following excerpt, take particular note of what foods are consumed, what material goods are available, how they are obtained, and what is done to prepare raw materials for consumption. Also pay attention to who does what in this type of subsistence system. Be alert to the various ways in which food production differs from hunting and gathering, but also look for ways in which the systems are similar, particularly in the demands they place on the people who follow them.

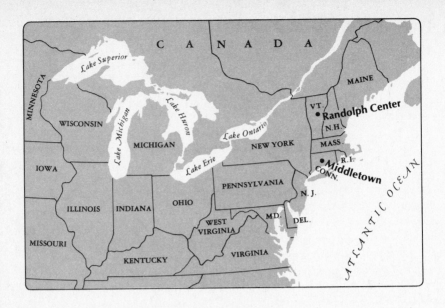

A Rural Childhood in Vermont

All five of us went to normal school—my three sisters, Rebecca, Adelaide and Martha, as well as Closson and I.* But we boys always had to hustle home, get into overalls, and do chores, no matter what the weather was like. . . .

. . . I loved the farm animals, and Martha and I spent much of our spare time during the winter training calves to drag us around on our sleds. We had one black and white heifer we could drive anywhere. Years later Father took that grown-up heifer out with some of the herd, to lead them down a road to a distant pasture. He had a terrible time with the one we had trained. At last he gave up and rushed into the house dripping with perspiration and wildly excited. While he was being calmed down, I sneaked to the barn. Imagine Father's chagrin when he saw me driving the recalcitrant cow down the road with a horse's bridle on her head and the reins through a saddle on her back!

. . .

Father was a small man with a majestic beard and an excitable manner. He met large issues calmly but was in a continual ferment over trifles. His native Vermont reserve was shot all through with a strong dash of peppery temperament . . .

To understand Father one would need to know something of his own bitter childhood. At the age of three he walked to school, a considerable distance, experiencing the rigors of a New England winter almost before he was free from his cradle. One day his father picked him up when he got home from

*Abridged from *Forty Years a Country Preacher* by George B. Gilbert (New York: Harper & Bros., 1939), pp. 10–11, 15–23, 35–38, 41, 134–137, 141, 145–147, 192, 242–244. Reprinted by permission of Virginia Gilbert, copyright holder.

school, kissed him and told him that his mother was dead. After that he had a stepmother who was so cruel to him that it shaped his attitude to women for the rest of his life. In his teens he ran away from home and by the time we got to know him, there was little softness left in Father. But life under his roof was never dull, for he had the knack of dramatizing every simple event around the farm. . . .

He had all the ingrained pessimism of the farmer and the beauties of nature left him cold. If he looked at the sky at all, it was merely to see whether it was going to rain, and usually he was sure that it was. The flowers and birds might have been so much cardboard, except that the birds would undoubtedly damage the corn and the flowers were traps for weeds. If a stretch of fine days came along, it was a "weather breeder" sure. We would have to get the corn in before it rained, or rescue the buckwheat from the deluge. A sunny stretch was bound to presage drought. Early in the fall he began to worry about frost. . . .

. . . One night he got us up at three o'clock to go down back of the barn and cut corn as, sure enough this time, the frost had come. We had no mittens, since it was too early for our woolens, so I remember Father holding the lantern while we boys, half asleep and shaking with cold, gripped the icy stalks with one hand and tried to wield the cutter with the numb fingers of the other.

. . .

The old north bedroom where Closson and I slept was terribly cold. Our covers were usually like ice. We slept on corn husk mattresses with socks on our feet and long woolen toques° with tassels on our heads. . . .

The winter cold of these days lives more strongly in my memory than the blossoming springs and fine autumns we had in Vermont. Father was more solicitous of his horses than his sons, so when Closson and I wanted to go somewhere, we generally had to walk, no matter what the weather was like. It was bad enough doing the mile and a quarter trek to school in the snow, trying to keep in the narrow ruts made by sled tracks, but getting back late at night in the dark from a church function was worse. Often there would be an icy crust on which I kept slipping, and the wind would cut right through me. I remember once getting so discouraged that I sat right down in the snow, despairing, and after a while crawled along on my hands and knees. It really seemed as though I never could get home that night. But I didn't get any sympathy from Father. "Nonsense," he would say, dismissing the subject, when I dared to complain of the cold.

. . .

Our sufferings were greatly aggravated by chilblains° [painful swellings or sores caused by exposure to cold]. Can I ever forget them? We wore hard, cold, cowhide boots made by our Grandfather Blodgett, and sometimes rolled on the floor with pain, in spite of the woodchuck grease rubbed into the leather to soften it. There was one pair in particular from which we all suffered in turn, boys and girls. No one could tell on whose feet those awful shoes would land. They must have been a child's size twelve, and were made of heavy, unsplit cowhide just as stiff as a board. There were cut holes for the strings and no shaping in the back to fit the heel. Just low and painfully straight. How we hated them! They were summered in an old chest over the shed. Four of my generation had worn them and finally they fell to poor Martha. One thing I know, they never wore out. The one redeeming feature was that after going barefooted all summer, our feet would spread and the abominable shoes would not go on, no matter how much woodchuck grease, well-colored with lamp black, Father might apply from his three-legged iron kettle with its rattail handle, all of which gave off a worse smell than the fried salt pork we had every morning. But when I was about twelve years old along came a new kind of shoe—a felt moccasin covered with rubber. I shall never forget the difference this made to me. My feet were warm at last. I was no longer driven half crazy with chilblains and blisters.

. . .

. . . We had two fine maples and some big elms on the farm. There was a maple right in front of the house and a swing hung from one of its limbs. If a rope broke when the beds were being corded, we got the worn pieces to make swings for ourselves. . . . in my boyhood no one would think of buying a new rope for a swing. That would be mad extravagance. We made up all of our own games, of course. We hunted through the barn for odds and ends to help in making sleds and for pieces of straps to hold on old skates. . .

I can never forget the rattrap Father made. He got a big box, at least a yard square, made a sliding door for it, and put a hook over the door. This he put up in the cellar. A string ran up from the sliding door, through a knothole in the floor, and was tied to the bedstead right by Father's pillow. Some corn meal was put in the box as bait for the rats, and any old time that Father happened to wake up in the night, he pulled the string, just on general principles.

The morning after the box was first set up, there was a grand rush for the cellar. We hit the box and listened. Yes, it was occupied all right. We heaved it step by step up the cellar stairs and into the living room. Closson had been dispatched to the hay mow to hunt for the cats. . . . They were to help conduct the massacre when the box was opened.

The women came downstairs from their bedrooms, and the men of the house armed themselves with clubs. The cats were all present or accounted for, and we opened the door of the box. Man alive, what a time we had for a few minutes! Men, boys, cats, rats, chairs, weeping and wailing and gnashing of teeth! We went through that performance a dozen times, whether there was one rat in the box or eleven, which was our score on one occasion. The women soon learned to absent themselves from those rat-killings, and to show up only after the carnage was over. . . .

Another time, Father and I went down to the cellar to open a barrel of cider. Cider, of course, begins to "work" [ferment] about three or four days after it is made. Father had rolled a barrel of it to the foot of the cellar stairs and I noticed that there were decided signs of pressure and agitation within. But he said nothing until after supper that night. Then he exclaimed, "By thunder, George, I forgot about that barrel of cider. We've got to knock the bung° out of it. Get a hammer and a lantern."

He took the light and I followed him down the cellar stairs with the hammer. We rolled the barrel over on its side and worked it around until the bung was on top. Father reached for the hammer. Now, you don't hit the bung itself in a cider-barrel. You strike the stave near it, with a downward blow. Father was never a man to do things by halves. When he hit a barrel, it stayed hit. And he hit this one. Bang! The thing blew out like the rear tire of a Model T. A two-inch stream of overworked cider hit the ceiling. Father, acting on impulse, pushed his hand down over the hole, to stop it. He might just as well have tried to stop the Mississippi, for he merely spread the shooting stream sideways. I ducked to the floor and Father got the full benefit of the flood. He was literally soaked with cider. His whiskers dripped streams of it. . . . He was a sight to behold. The deluge put out the lanterns and we groped our way upstairs, in the dark.

Well, I never found that bung. Out of sheer curiosity I used to look for it, but it never did turn up. The force with which it hit the ceiling may have broken it to bits—who knows? Neither did I ever refer to this incident in Father's hearing. Whenever I thought of it, I had to get out of his sight, back of the kitchen stove, until I could quiet down. No one ever laughed at Father and survived.

. . .

A barrel churn, used to make butter. *(The Bettmann Archive)*

Mother and Kate Robinson, who worked for us, were great cheese makers. This was always an elaborate ceremony. First, when a calf was killed, its stomach was stretched on a board, as one might stretch a woodchuck skin. There it dried and the pieces were then used to make cheese. One piece of rennet,° an inch square, was put in four-and-a-half quarts of milk to curdle it for the making of a pound of cheese. When the milk was properly curdled, it was poured through a basket to remove the whey. Then the curd was seasoned with salt and sage, both well mixed together with the fingers. (The sage was raised in the garden, dried in the attic, and crumpled up, ready to sift into the curd when needed.) The cheese was then put in a round wooden cylinder and thoroughly pressed down until hard, remaining in this state at least overnight. Finally, the cheese was removed and covered with a cloth, ready for use. It was cut with an army sword, a flourish favored by Father.

The churning was a great headache to Closson and me. We had the usual barrel churn that flopped over and over. If you didn't get the cover on just so, with all the "fingers" under the "hooks," then off it would come, as you turned the churn over, and the whole mess would go all over the floor. Besides the loss of the cream, there was the task of cleaning up, with the prospect of Father's fury hovering over us like a thunderbolt. "Has it come to butter yet?" was the cry that pursued us all over the farm for years, it seemed to me. Sometimes the wretched mixture would take a whole day and would even run over to the next —stubbornly frothing and foaming, everything but coming to butter, and in the end going to the pigs. Closson would get so bored that he would try to read and churn at the same time.

. . .

. . . I prefer to remember the good times we had sugaring. During my normal school days, I used to work at it all night, leaving home in the morning just in time to get to class. I love sugaring, as I suppose all boys do who have tried it. There would be a fine crust of snow at that time of year, and we would slide over it through the bare maples. Afterwards would come the big roaring fire, the steam, and plenty of syrup around for us to spread on our slices of bread.

On Saturdays Mother sent us our dinners from the house. There would be a six-quart pan with mashed potatoes and now and then a fried egg, depending on how Father's hens were doing. . .

. . .

In those days there was no such thing as an evaporator with a regulated flow of sap. If the sap got scorched, that meant a lot of trouble. . . . But the great thrill came at "sugaring off," when the sheet-iron pan was pulled off the fireplace and the syrup dipped out. Father would stand by the pan with a long-handled dipper, stirring the boiling mess to and fro, holding it up every minute or two to watch the syrup drip off the edge. If two or three drops ran together and made a big flat drop, it was called an "apron." This meant that the sap was boiled down enough for syrup, but if the drip came off the dipper and made a long "hair," it was done well enough for granulated sugar. Father would get excited when it aproned. "She's down," he would yell, and we would run around to the other side of the fireplace to lift up each end of the pan, so that

An early one-room school in Sturbridge Village, Massachusetts, similar to the one in which Gilbert first taught. *(Marc and Evelyne Bernheim/Woodfin Camp & Associates)*

he could push a board through. Down would come bricks, ashes and all sorts of debris, right into the tops of our boots. A delay of half a minute meant that the mixture would be scorched and spoiled so we had to work fast, no matter what the consequences to ourselves. The last run of sap, when the leaves had started, made a ropey syrup that turned into vinegar. We were sorry when sugaring time was ended. It was hard work but great fun.

· · ·

Father preached education to us all the time. Both he and Mother had high respect for academic attainment, so it was not strange that Closson and I should turn our attention to teaching ... My first school was at Brookfield. ... I was sixteen. ...

... It was a winter term. I had twenty-four scholars representing eight or nine grades. ...

· · ·

... In summer I worked on farms for a dollar a day. One season I loaded and pitched off 119 big loads [of hay], earning enough to pay for a two-horse spring-tooth harrow° for Father's farm. It was a grand affair that ran on four wheels and had a seat. After studying it carefully, Father put the seat down cellar and stowed it well out of sight over a beam. Nothing as lazy as this could get a footing on his farm. ... Father was ever a critic of the soft and effete.

· · ·

[After the author married, he bought himself a farm.] ... As I approached the place on foot, I kept my eyes open. Father had told us many a time: "If ever you buy a house, boys, look well to the cellar and the underpinning. And if you ever buy a farm, look well to the water supply—a farm with stock takes an awful lot of water."

. . .

Before I bought the farm I asked the owner's son how wide the farm was, for I knew its depth. "Why," said he, "if you start hoeing a row of potatoes on a blazing hot day, you'll think it long enough." And he was right. It was forty rods across [660 ft.]. . . .

. . .

. . . how we slaved on that farm during the next few years! It didn't have a single fence, and the land was run down. At the start we sold butter and buttermilk, cream, eggs and lambs. . . . The blankets we have on our beds were made from the wool of our own sheep. One year we had cloth made from our sheep's wool and we all had suits of it.

. . .

As we had a brook and a good deal of water, we went in for geese. . . .

. . .

At one time or another we have had all sorts of animals on the farm, even a Shetland pony and an Angora goat, but now we confine ourselves to sustenance farming. We have a horse and enough hens to supply the table with eggs and chickens. We generally raise two pigs every summer, and smoke our own ham and bacon. We have our own beef and we sometimes can thirty or forty jars of it. When we kept sheep we had sheep bakes every year, but we gave them up because with sheep the ground soon becomes infected and they need to be moved around. Our land is not extensive enough for that.

. . .

. . . I've always liked to fish and as far back as I can remember I've been crazy about a pond, so when I got to wondering one day what I could do with that old hen yard, suddenly I thought of pond lilies and how I had always longed for them. Father never would bother with flowers in Vermont. A garden to him was a place to grow good filling vegetables, and not rows of flowers. Anyway, the pond lily is a fine bloom to raise if you have water. You don't have to hoe or water it.

. . . You need soft mud for the lily roots and rather stagnant water, so it doesn't do to clean out the pond too thoroughly—they thrive on decaying matter. . . .

The big pond [the second pond] is about 200 feet long and 60 feet wide. We had to dam up our brook, just as we used to do in Vermont, and with pretty much the same results at first—the rains would come, the floods would flow, the dam would be washed away. Remembering how many times this happened in my boyhood, after one washout on my own farm, I decided that we must dig the hole aside from the main channel of the brook; otherwise it would soon fill up with mud. We started digging on the flat near the brook and we worked on it off and on for ten years. The pond from the first took its place as one of the most important activities of the farm. Its enlargement, care and use were discussed as much as the crops. Just as the boys helped me with corn, potatoes and hay, so I helped them with the pond. Sometimes we used wheelbarrows, but most of it was done with horse and scraper. Help came from an unexpected source when the neighbors found that it was a fine place to cut their ice. Instead of going farther afield, they came to our place, often with two horses and a big scraper, and between one thing and another the hole steadily grew bigger and deeper until it reached its present proportions.

It has provided good swimming and skating for the whole neighborhood. . . .

. . . We always have a row boat on the pond, and visitors think there ought to be fish in it, but fishing and a good swimming pond do not go together. Even with the brook running in, it will fill up with mud at the bottom, and for good swimming, of course, it has to be cleared out. Fish require weed growth. . . .

. . .

On the old farm in Vermont we had a pump that brought up soft rain water from the cistern in the cellar to the kitchen [for washing] but we had to go down cellar for all our drinking and cooking water, and lug it up the stairs in kettles and pails. It was a great nuisance. When I began earning money, one of the first things I did for Mother was to put in another pump at the other end of the kitchen sink with a pipe running down cellar to the drinking water. This was a great help to her. It is terrible to reflect on the tons and tons of water that have been lugged up just such stairways by generations of women and children, lifting the pail up one stair at a time. An investigation made in Litchfield County showed that in one year a woman carried thirty-six tons of water from the outside well into the house—something like ten pails a day.

. . .

[The author's father, who was a Democrat in Republican Vermont, was appointed postmaster by President Cleveland.] Father lost the post office when Cleveland went out, and the building [that he had constructed on rented land] had to be moved off the rented ground and down the road a mile and a quarter to our farm. It was a job we never would have tackled had we known what was coming, but we had a lot of fun out of it too—thanks to Charlie Blodgett, comical, dirty, fat and disreputable, but a soul I hope to meet in heaven. I learned one of the most valuable lessons of my life from Charlie, and that was to maintain perfect cheerfulness under the most trying circumstances. . . .

. . . even Charlie was stumped by that plagued post office. Day after day we struggled with it, Charlie cursing like mad—hot, red and filthy, but always cheerful . . .

We worked with planks and rollers, moving the post office on a capstan,° with a horse going round and round. When we got it down to the edge of the hill we decided to have a bee and get people to bring their oxen and horses to help in our mighty task. I was dispatched to ask the people to come, and the bait was the dinner we would give them. The people grumbled. They didn't see why they should use Republican horses to pull a Democratic post office. Well, we finally hitched on seven pairs of horses and seven of cattle and did we have a time! We had to feed this army of men and animals. . . . Charlie . . . did turn a heartbreaking job into a holiday. Father in the same circumstances would have had a thousand fits, but Father was steering clear of this undertaking. . . . Well, in the end Charlie's horses triumphed and the building found a resting place after a week's labor.

The moving bee took place less than eighty-five years ago, and Gilbert was running his own farm less than sixty years ago, during the childhood of individuals still alive today, yet for most of us, it sounds like a different world. The percentage of people working on farms in the United States has steadily decreased during the last half-century to less than 6 percent today (Toffler 1970:13–14). Some figure near this percentage is common among the highly industrialized nations, but it is unique to them and has been true only during the last few decades. Most people in the world today are still directly involved in the food quest, but—unlike their early ancestors—as farmers instead of as hunters and gatherers.

Humans domesticated plants and animals after about 2 million years of hunting and gathering, and the world has not been the same since. The pace of change has steadily increased; children now live in a world dramatically different from the one their parents knew, and their children will inherit one still different. The excerpt illustrates the extent of change during just the last two generations. To people over forty, some elements in the excerpt may be familiar, but the younger and more urban the reader, the stranger the life described seems. For example, in this day of the school bus and the automobile, how many children have had to walk miles through ice and snow to get to school, or have had to make their way home on foot on a bitter winter night? How many people under fifty have churned butter by hand? Or made cheese at home? Or worn home-made shoes? Or used woodchuck grease as a lubricant? No doubt some have, but not many, at least in the United States.

THE SHIFT TO FARMING: CONTINUITIES AND CHANGES

The shift from hunting and gathering to full-time farming took generations in some areas, and although it carried the potential for drastic change, this was not apparent at first. A comparison of the excerpts in Chapters 1 and 2 will reveal some of the differences and similarities between farmers and hunter-gatherers. A few of the differences are obvious—the increase in the number and kind of human-made things in the environment, the change in the way food is obtained, the relative lack of mobility. Some consequences of these differences are explored later in the chapter. Other differences are less obvious, partly because the two excerpts are not parallel in the aspects of life they mention. The similarities also may not be apparent at first reading. But note, for example, the need in both cases for endurance, courage, and perseverance. The farm boy as well as the hunter had to cope with extremes of weather, and had to complete certain tasks, regardless of climate or inclination. (In some ways, the farmer's life in the excerpt is more demanding than that of the hunter. Hunters rarely have to get up in the middle of a cold night to save their food supply, as the farm boys did. When crops are ripe, they must be harvested or they will be lost —unlike game. In many parts of the world, planting cannot be postponed for long either.) The farm boy, like the hunter, must be able to face pain with courage. For example, the children in the excerpt suffered terribly from the cold during the winter, but endured it, paralleling the endurance of the Piegan coming home through the blizzard. In environments where winters were severe, members of both societies responded with stubborn endurance. Red Bird's Tail simply continued walking after he fell into some water during the trip home in the blizzard. Gilbert, in Vermont, crawled home from a church function when the ice crust made it difficult to stand up. Similarities should not be overemphasized, however, for the differences between the two life styles are considerable, and have important consequences on all areas of life.

Compare the two excerpts again for differences in what people ate and how they obtained it. The Piegan excerpt mentions only meat. The book from which the excerpt is taken and ethnographic studies of the Piegan show, however, that they ate plant products, too. Nonetheless, the interest, the concern—at least of the men—was with hunting and meat-eating. The diet of the Piegan differed from that of the Vermont farmers because, except for food obtained in trade, none of the Piegan's food was produced. In Vermont, on the other hand, all but the maple products were obtained from domesticated plants and animals. The interest, concern, and focus of male attention in Vermont was on plants, not game animals.

Recent nutritional studies have shown that domesticated plants often differ significantly from their wild relatives in terms of protein or other nutrients. Wild wheat, for example, is higher in protein than domesticated varieties (Pfeiffer 1972:417). We also know that, historically, whenever groups of hunter-gatherers (such as the native Americans) have been "civilized," settled in one place, and urged to take up farming, their diet has suffered, mainly because they stopped gathering the balanced variety of wild plants they were accustomed to and had neither knowledge nor money to take advantage of the full variety of foods available to farmers. Although the situation today is due to social and economic problems rather than to the potentials of the two methods, it may parallel what occurred in early farming communities when gathering had declined sharply (because nearby supplies were exhausted, and because people were working too much to take the time necessary to gather) and domesticated supplies were limited to one or two items. Nutritional effects of domestication in its earliest form are naturally hard to study because it is not possible to work with living subjects, and modern situations are not precisely comparable. Skeletal material is the only thing available to work with, and not only is it limited in quantity but it may not be at all representative of the whole population. As a result of these and other factors, nutritional studies of this crucial period are virtually nonexistent.

The situation in Vermont was quite different from that of the first people to use domesticated plants and animals for most of their diet. Gilbert and his family were taking advantage of a long history of development. Their diet was probably comparable in variety and nutritional value to their remote hunting and gathering ancestors, rather than to their more immediate farming progenitors, with the additional advantage of being somewhat more under their control. For example, they had a steady supply of eggs. Hunter-gatherers also eat eggs; however, they can get them only when the wild birds are nesting, whereas the Vermont farmers had a supply all year long. The Vermont farmers also had some items (such as milk) that are hardly ever available to hunter-gatherers, and a few things (such as cheese and hard cider) that are entirely outside the diet of nonfood producers. The meat the Gilberts ate in New England was probably more tender and differently flavored than the game consumed by the Piegan. The muscles of a domesticated calf, or even of an old milk cow, cannot compare in toughness with a buffalo or elk that has spent its life running from predators, or trotting miles over the landscape. Anyone who has ever eaten game is also aware of its often strong flavor under ordinary cooking methods.

Food-Producing Techniques

The skills and techniques required to get food differ sharply. Gilbert did not need to know how to track game, stalk a buffalo, aim a bow and arrow, or outwit a bear. His sisters did not need to be able to identify the root of a food plant by its dried stem. On the other hand, a Piegan did not need to know when

Sowing by hand (broadcasting seed) in Iran. *(United Nations)*

to plant, how to distinguish weeds from food plants by their first early sprouts, or how to geld a calf.

At present, we do not know much about the techniques used by the early domesticators of plants. Modern Middle Eastern villagers usually scatter seed broadcast on plowed ground (Pierce 1964:27). Archeological finds in early civilizations indicate that in Mesopotamia a seed funnel was attached to the plow so that the grain was deposited in the furrow (Frankfort 1964:353; Barnouw 1971:224). Both techniques are relatively late, since they obviously developed after the domestication of animals and the invention of the plow. The only archeological evidence from earlier periods consists of harvesting tools, rather than planting implements. In other parts of the world, people domesticated different kinds of crops, and therefore developed different techniques of cultivation. Root crops, for example, are typically grown by placing a piece of an old root in the ground; seeds are seldom used. The root pieces are usually placed either in individual mounds or in rows; they are never just scattered over a field. Maize—the staple crop in the New World, known to most people in the United States as corn—was traditionally planted by seed in individual mounds, never scattered. Today it is usually planted in rows. In the Valley of Mexico, farmers developed a unique type of agriculture called *chinampa*. Working in the shallow lakes, they dredged rich bottom silt and aquatic plants into artificial islands, often called floating gardens, although they did not float. These permitted intensive agriculture with high yields (Armillas 1964:321).

In many parts of the world the most fertile fields did not have enough water. Irrigation works of varying complexity are among the earliest evidence of agriculture. Some are not more than small earth dams to channel or hold flood water in specific places, or a natural backwater deepened and lengthened into a canal. Others are long, complex systems that must have required a considerable amount of planning, engineering skill, knowledge, and man hours of labor to complete. The relationship of elaborate systems to a society's social organization is explored in later chapters. Here, it is necessary only to point out that elaborate systems would not have been needed, and could not have been built or maintained, by a hunting and gathering band of twenty-five to fifty people—or even by the Piegan.

In areas where irrigation was not used, where fertility of the land was not maintained by periodic floods (as in the Nile valley) or by regularly dredging silt up from the lake bottom (as for the *chinampas* in the Valley of Mexico), fields lost fertility after a few years. How long it took depended on the kinds of crops grown, the amount of nutrients in the soil to start with, rainfall, and a number of other factors. Early farmers coped with the problem of decreasing fertility in their fields by abandoning the old fields and clearing new ones. The old fields might be permanently abandoned as the people moved on, never to return, or they might be abandoned for a regular period of time, ranging from one to twenty growing seasons, while the people moved in a slow, regular pattern that eventually brought them back to their previous fields. The techniques for clearing new fields usually involved cutting down the trees and brush, letting the debris dry, and then burning it on the spot, allowing the ashes to mix with the soil. This method of shifting cultivation, called slash and burn, or swidden, is still practiced in many parts of the world. People who use it may have to move their village every few years, if all the nearby fields become used up, but as mentioned above, many of these communities move in a slow, roughly circular or oval path that, possibly after decades have passed, returns them to their starting point. So long as population pressure is not too great, and there is a steady supply of new land to clear, swidden cultivation may be the best possible for the environment. In cases of high land fertility, or where there is a stable balance between population and available land, swidden cultivation may even support permanent villages (Carneiro 1968:133). In recent years, however, the method has caused problems as increasing world population and changing land-use patterns have cut down on the available new land. Path circles are getting smaller and fields have to be put into use again sooner, sometimes too soon. The path swidden agriculturalists usually follow may be evidence of population increase in the past; that is, such a pattern possibly results from one farming community's encountering others in the direction it has been moving, and being forced to turn. If a circular path, rather than a steady movement in one direction, were the natural pattern for communities of this type to follow, plant domestication might not have spread as far or as fast as archeological evidence indicates.

Planting rice seedlings in Indonesia. *(United Nations)*

In some parts of the world, fields are devoted to a single crop. This is typical with the cereal grains, such as wheat and barley, and with rice. In other parts of the world, fields contain several crops. This is particularly true with root crops such as potatoes, yams, and manioc, which are often grown with other vegetables. A traditional combination in the New World was maize, beans, and squash, the bean climbing the corn stalk, and the squash sheltering in its shade. The system of small fields containing multiple crops planted and tended entirely by hand is usually called horticulture,° or gardening, to distinguish it from what is called plow agriculture, or simply agriculture: the system of large fields containing a single crop and requiring animal or mechanical power at various stages of the production process.

The two systems frequently have a different division of labor. The excerpt describes a division fairly typical of plow agriculture. Women worked in and around the house (although as children the girls sometimes participated in rounding up or herding the few cows the family had). Men were responsible for work in the fields. In plow-agriculture societies in which women do help in the fields, their work is generally secondary, and the men are normally responsible for the work using animals or machinery. Although some variation is permitted to allow for the exigencies of life, when the pattern is broken—even in an emergency—it may be a subject for scorn or amusement. For example, in the comic strip "Barney Google and Snuffy Smith," when Snuffy's wife Loweezy does the plowing, it is both a source of amusement and additional evidence of the bad character of her husband (Laswell n.d.). Similarly, in the 1860s, Mary Livermore expressed her shock and disgust at women working in the fields, until she realized that the Civil War had made it necessary by taking so many men from the fields (Livermore 1890:146–147). In horticultural systems, on the other hand, women normally work in the fields, either with the men or alone. Both sexes often perform the same tasks, although in some societies men do the heavier work of clearing the fields. In a few places, the women are entirely responsible for the plant produce, while the men concentrate on cattle herding or some other prestigious activities (Gatheru 1965:17; LeVine and LeVine 1966:12).

If we compare the division of labor between hunters on the one hand and agricultural peoples on the other, some similarities are apparent. In both, the activities of women seem to be concentrated near the home. Horticultural peoples may differ somewhat in this regard, yet the gardens are not too far away to take children to, and women can still keep an eye on them as they work. In this sense horticulturists are similar to gatherers whose women range rather widely, with their children, collecting plant foods, and who often travel farther from the home base during the day than do Piegan women or women in societies that depend primarily on plow agriculture.

MOBILITY AND STABILITY: CAUSES AND CONSEQUENCES

This fact of mobility—both of individuals within a society, and of whole societies—is a significant one that deserves further attention because of its consequences for social organization, child-raising, values, and attitudes.

Tents made of felt used by Iranian nomadic herders. *(United Nations)*

Most hunters and gatherers have to move every few days. The Piegans and other mounted hunters could stay in one place longer than people on foot because the horse allowed them to travel greater distances in search of game. Even so, Plains Indians normally moved many times a year, often every four or five days in winter, spring, and fall, and stayed in one place only during the most severe winter weather, or during productive late summer months when hunting and gathering were best. Horticulturists, at least those practicing swidden cultivation, also must move often, but usually not more than once every four or five years, and sometimes not more than once a decade. Intensive fishing-hunting-gathering peoples may be as sedentary as swidden farmers. Plow agriculturalists usually have the greatest stability, along with those horticulturists who plant in land naturally fertilized by floods, or who use fertilizer of some sort. Communities of this type may not have to move for centuries. A few specially favored locations show an archeological record from hunting and gathering up to historic civilizations (Hamblin 1973:15, 33).

As mentioned in Chapter 1, this residential stability coupled with population increase may actually have provided the stimulus for the development of domesticated plants and animals in some parts of the world. In other parts, residential stability extending over generations does not exist even *with* domesticated crops and herds. In fact, one type of life style based on domesticated animals (nomadic herding; see below) has a degree of mobility comparable to that of hunters and gatherers on foot.

The question of whether people choose residential stability or have it forced on them by their method of subsistence is a complex one. Archeological evidence would seem to indicate that in some places the prior existence of residential stability dictated a change in methods for obtaining food, leading to the shift to agriculture. The method of food production, however, also dictates the amount of residential stability. Normally, a hunter either follows game wherever it goes or, if he has moved on his own initiative, hunts whatever game is available in the new area. In addition, some hunters and gatherers may plant a few seeds, wander off after other foods, and, if they are lucky, harvest something on their return. Full-time farmers, on the other hand, dependent on their crops for most of their food supply, are tied to a particular locality once the crops are planted. If they leave their fields, they may lose their food supply.

Growing crops also led to a change in attitudes toward land itself, which reinforced the tendency toward residential stability. Hunters and gatherers are much less interested in the land per se than in the animals on it. They have no desire to control a geographic place empty of game. The situation is different for farmers; although they too are interested in what is growing on the land, the nature and control of the land itself is important. It is probably a general human characteristic to value something according to the amount of time and effort invested in it, and farmers have often invested a considerable amount of both into making a particular piece of land productive. Certainly, individual farmers who have spent time and effort producing a crop do not willingly give it up even when each one knows she or he could survive by hunting or gathering if necessary. Similarly, the more effort individual farmers have put into making a particular spot of ground productive, the more likely they are to be reluctant to abandon it. They cannot take improvements with them if they leave. If farmers are forced off the land, they lose all the rewards of their labor.

Thus, with the development of farming, people not only *had* to stay with their crops, they *wanted* to stay. Just as many hunting peoples develop a positive attitude toward the ability and opportunity to move freely, farming peoples often develop a positive attitude toward stability. They "grow attached" to their land. The peasant's craving for land is notorious. Land characteristically serves as a major basis for prestige and power in farming societies, or in those societies recently emerged from an agricultural orientation. (Land loses much of its importance as an indicator of status in highly industrialized societies, however. Factories, businesses, and money, among other specific status symbols, become more significant.) Thus, agriculture fostered a fundamental difference in attitudes toward land and stability. The excerpt reflects some of the basis for this attitudinal change in descriptions of how hard the author worked on the farm he purchased, and how proud he was of the improvements he made.

Residential stability led to other unanticipated consequences. In Chapter 1, it was pointed out how generosity is highly valued among hunting peoples. The generous person attains prestige and receives esteem. Among some farming peoples, however, the accumulation of goods began to take the place of generosity as a source of prestige. Perhaps the change was a logical one. Mobile hunters cannot accumulate much in the way of tangible goods because they are constantly faced with the problem of transporting them. Since farmers may remain in the same place for years, however, they can accumulate material things. (Students are often amazed at how many things they manage to accumulate in their dorm rooms during one school year.) Furthermore, a farmer who continually gave away his produce not only would have nothing to show after a year of effort, but in addition might even lack the seed to plant the next crop. A successful farmer not only *needs* a surplus (to provide seed and to ensure against a bad year or two in which there might be no harvest), he also *wants* one, since it relieves his anxiety. Thus the emphasis easily shifts from giving away to accumulating.

In stressing this change of means for attaining prestige and power within the group, one must not overlook the continuing trends stressing cooperation. It is too simple to classify certain societies as altruistic and others as selfish or acquisitive. Human societies are invariably more complex than such labeling would suggest, and individual motivation is even more so. There is also a tendency when classifying a society as "altruistic" or "selfish" to imply that its members usually feel selfish or altruistic. But people in a society may share their goods without feeling the least bit generous, just as a person in our society may pay taxes without feeling any desire to help the government. In both cases, people act to stay out of trouble. The society in the excerpt is one in which the accumulation of goods is important, private property is highly respected, and prestige is largely obtained from possessions. Yet cooperation is evident not only as an ideal, but in practice. Cooperation within the family was, of course, taken for granted. The family was an economic production unit, and all its members had tasks that contributed to the well-being of the family as a whole. Although the family was self-reliant, and valued being so, it still maintained cooperative relationships with other families. The excerpt mentions that neighbors found it convenient to cut their ice in winter from the Gilberts' pond, and the Gilberts were pleased to let them. The neighbors usually responded to this generous gesture by going to the trouble of enlarging the pond hole as they were getting ice—thus saving the Gilberts a considerable amount of labor. In another example, community members, although political opponents of the Gilberts, helped them move their post office building in exchange for a dinner. The Gilberts reciprocated by feeding all the workers—not from generosity necessarily, but because it was the only way to keep them working.

The pattern of labor exchange—a favor for a favor—is widespread among agricultural and horticultural peoples. In return for the help of neighbors during harvest and planting, a man or woman works in their fields when called. Anyone who fails to contribute a fair share of labor is left out of this exchange system and may lose much of the crop in consequence. Like the system of shared game among hunting peoples, labor exchange provides social insurance. Individuals who are incapacitated can expect the same help from neighbors as they would get if healthy, with the understanding that they—or their family— will reciprocate at the first opportunity. Exchange also makes possible a more efficient use of labor during peak agricultural periods, and therefore gives those societies practicing it a survival edge that may account for its wide distribution. Societies that did not practice it may not have survived.

Residential stability also fostered changes in relationships between people. With the increasing differential possible in possession of material goods, an everwidening gap developed between rich and poor in farming societies. Hunters also have their poor, but the difference between rich and poor is not great in regard to material possessions or in the amount of food each consumes. The richest family has the same transportation problem as the poorest (particularly in societies without animal transport), and even the best of hunters would go hungry occasionally if he did not receive food from others. The same factors do not apply in farming societies. Control over the most productive land and over labor becomes a crucial variable; consequently, social stratification increases sharply in farming communities.

Another change in human relationships that probably depended on residential stability was the development of slavery. Male slaves are not much use to mobile hunting bands. They have to be fed; one dares not send them out hunting because they probably would not come back; one dares not leave them behind in camp, since they might not only escape but take the women and children with them as captives. Female slaves usually rapidly improve their position by becoming mothers of hunters.

With the development of farming, however, the utility of male slaves increased enormously. There was plenty of hard labor for them to do; free men were not away hunting and so could supervise and guard them; and even better, slaves produced not only the food they ate, but a surplus as well. Female slaves usually produced more slaves, and did not improve their position so easily as they could in the hunting band. Consequently, slavery became an important human institution whose legitimacy was never really questioned until the morality of the concept itself was challenged by English and American Protestant humanitarians (Quakers and others) in the late 1600s and early 1700s (*Encyclopaedia Britannica* 1966, 20:780–781). The opposition to slavery gained strength with increasing industrialization. Slavery—the absolute ownership of the person of the slave by another—is almost as inefficient for industrialists as it is for hunters and gatherers since reluctant workers can all too easily commit sabotage or learn new techniques of organization and evasion. Uneducated slaves are usually inefficient and educated ones are apt to be difficult to control (Lacy 1972:58–59). Transportation improvements that increased mobility undoubtedly added to the problems of controlling slave labor.

Farming and residential stability apparently encouraged a sharp increase in technological development. The excerpt indicates an emphasis on developing more efficient techniques for doing things (the "better mousetrap" is an example). This emphasis seems to have been characteristic of many agricultural communities, particularly during the early phases of development. In the Old World, the domestication of plants was followed fairly rapidly by new discoveries and inventions in metallurgy, pottery, fermentation and brewing of alcoholic beverages, textiles, architecture, and many other areas. Pottery itself was actually developed before plants were domesticated, and probably in a different locality entirely, but it was so thoroughly accepted and innovative improvements were so routinely made by agricultural peoples that for years archeologists and other researchers assumed pottery was an inevitable part of the complex of domestication, developed in response to the needs of these peoples. It has been only in the last decade that archeological evidence of the development of pottery independent from agriculture has reached the textbooks, and consequently the classroom (Chard 1969:204).

Residential stability also apparently encouraged, or perhaps demanded, another change. Among mobile hunters, if people within the group quarrel and cannot be reconciled, it is fairly easy for the group to split. The enforced stability of the farmer may prevent this—except as a last resort. When everyone must stay with the crops, people cannot escape frequent confrontation with others whose interests conflict with their own. Such confrontations may lead to violence that is highly disruptive to the group. Studies of humans and other primates show that a clear-cut determination of who can give orders to whom and who must submit to whom saves a great deal of trouble by eliminating a large share of open conflict (Homans 1950:418–419). For ants the problem of precedence and rank is solved by instincts. Ants are programmed to know and keep their place. They cannot do anything else. Humans, however, learn. They do not know these things by instinct. For a system with highly structured ranks to succeed, children have to be well indoctrinated to "know their place." Encouraging independence of thought and action is not the best way to instill obedience and submission. The emphasis that a plow-agriculture society may place on these characteristics is shown at several points in the excerpt. In spite of the pain caused by the ill-fitting shoes, none of the children refused to wear them. Neither the author of the excerpt nor his brother tried to remain in bed when Father called them to cut corn at three o'clock on a cold morning to save the crop from frost. No one rebelled at churning butter, although everyone hated it. Many farming societies, residentially stable, expect children to obey parents as long as the parents live, and children rebel at their peril (as the author put it, "No one ever laughed at Father and survived"). Hunters and gatherers do not usually regard submission as so desirable. Societies that encourage originality or independence of thought and behavior are seldom agricultural (more than 50 percent of the productive adult population directly involved in farming). Conversely, societies that demand long-term submission of sons and daughters to parental authority are rarely based on hunting and gathering. Unquestioning obedience may not be a useful attribute among hunters, who often have to exercise rapid and decisive independent judgment when pursuing game.

With the development of agriculture and residential stability, new techniques for resolving quarrels and conflicts had to be invented. Demanding submission and obedience to parents and, by extension, to other authority figures may have been two of these "new" techniques (although submitting to dominant figures in the group is very old). Others, less speculative, were the new institutions that led ultimately to the development of the formal legal and governmental structures we know today.

POPULATION GROWTH AND CONCENTRATION

Stability was not the only impetus to the development of formal legal and government structures; the size of the society was another factor. So long as a group remains small, informal means of social control are usually effective; but once the group exceeds a certain size, other methods must be developed or the society will split into smaller, more manageable units again. (This subject is discussed in more detail in Chapter 4.) With the spread of agriculture, the overall human population increased enormously, but the distribution was as significant as the overall increase. For the first time in human history it became feasible for several hundred people to live in permanently close contact with each other. Once the new techniques for keeping the peace in larger groups had been developed, so that they no longer fissioned when they grew over fifty, villages could grow to enormous (by the standards of the time) size. Conditions were right for cities to develop. A growing population poses a series of problems even to farmers, however.

One effect of the concentration of population in sedentary villages and large cities was the increasing importance of epidemic disease. That this probably had genetic consequences is indicated by the history of depopulation in the New World after the introduction of Old World diseases. Illnesses that were relatively mild among the Europeans were deadly to New World natives who had never developed any kind of immunity—genetic or otherwise—to them.

So long as humanity lived in small groups, in scattered hunting bands that had little contact with one another, epidemic diseases were relatively limited in the amount of damage they could do. Once populations began to concentrate in settled communities, however, sanitation problems increased the speed with which epidemics could spread, and people crowded together increased the number of potential victims. Villages and cities provided a more suitable envi-

Epidemics in the past often caused so many deaths that normal burial practices had to be abandoned. Here a cartload of bodies is dumped into a common grave during one of the epidemics of the Black Plague. *(Culver Pictures, Inc.)*

ronment for rats, mice, and the vermin they carry than did the mobile hunting camps. This increased the potential for certain diseases, such as plague and typhus, that may not have been serious problems before. The greater amount of long-distance trade, along with the habit of fleeing a city or village when an epidemic struck, also increased the distance over which an epidemic could spread. Disease has played a major role in human history, but only a few individuals have ever commented on its significance (Zinsser 1935:150–165; Dobyns 1966:441–442).

Invention of techniques for controlling larger numbers of people was probably a major factor in the appearance of urbanization, one of the characteristics of the life pattern we call civilization.° The word *civilization* as used here refers to a society with certain typical attributes. Those accepted by most scholars are monumental architecture and public works; formal governmental structure; formal legal structure; a significant increase in technical specializations other than farming; scientific advances, particularly in the fields of metallurgy, astronomy, mathematics; invention of writing; large complex social units, including cities, national states, and empires; and social stratification (Chard 1969:222). Not all civilizations exhibit every attribute, and no single element is diagnostic, but all civilizations have most of the characteristics mentioned or they are not defined as civilizations. Obviously, it is quite possible to have a civilization in this technical sense without members of it being "civilized" in a humanistic sense. The two meanings should not be confused.

Urbanization and civilization are not inevitable consequences of the domestication of plants, since many societies based on agriculture have remained on a small-village level of organization for centuries and have never become urbanized. The small village is apparently a stable adaptation, evolving to urbanization only under the stimulus of other factors, which are not at present identified with any certainty. Agriculture of some sort does appear to be necessary for the development of a civilization, however, because apparently none based on hunting and gathering has ever appeared. Therefore, we say that agriculture is a *necessary* but not a *sufficient* condition for the development of civilization. There were several centers of civilization in both the Old World and the New World. Mesopotamia, Egypt, the Indus valley in Pakistan and India, and the Yellow River valley in China were among the earliest centers in the Old World; Mexico, Guatemala, and Peru had the earliest centers in the New World.

Comparison of the different centers indicates that urbanization and civilization should be considered separately. Although they are correlated, they may not be causally related, at least in the early stages of the development of each; that is, cities have developed in some areas before a civilization appeared, and in other areas the civilization was present first. In the New World the first so-called cities were actually enormous ceremonial centers, where few people lived (Leonard 1967:32–33). In the Old World, Jericho was apparently a rich trading center and a city, having developed urban characteristics along with or even before agriculture (Hamblin 1973:29). But although agriculture might be necessary for the full development of both cities and civilizations, it was not

A model of Tenochtitlán, the Aztec capital, as it appeared when Cortés saw it. *(Mexican National Tourist Council)*

sufficient for either. Just as farm villages did not automatically grow into cities, so not all farming societies built civilizations. What were some of the factors that led to the development of a city? Location seems to have been a significant factor for Jericho. It was at a major water source in an area where water was scarce, and it was at an intersection of major trade routes. These factors may have been responsible for the growth of other centers too. They may never have been farm villages (Hamblin 1973:15, 19). But what about farm villages?

FACTORS IN URBANIZATION

Since human population increased rapidly after the domestication of plants and animals, why did all the early farm villages not develop specialists and grow into cities? Some did, but for a city to develop out of a farm village, most of the farmers would have to leave, or else give up farming, since one of the characteristics of a city is that it is a concentration of nonfood-producing specialists who exchange their specialties for food produced outside its boundaries. All cities are symbiotic with their hinterlands. No city population produces enough food to feed itself. Instead of a farm village growing gradually into a city, it is more likely that a concentration of specialists served as a nucleus.

Another problem about urbanization was suggested earlier. Even with a concentration of specialists, as a community grew in size, its people had to develop new methods of social control to settle the inevitable disputes and conflicts of interest. If the villagers were not able to make successful innovations in this area, the community could never grow into a city, since after a certain point it would lose population as individuals and families were forced out, voluntarily went in search of a more satisfactory location, or were killed in quarrels and feuds. Only villages successful at social control were able to grow.

Why would specialists gather and settle in a single location? What groups were likely to develop new forms of social control, so that a city could grow? What kinds of specialists were likely to congregate? Was there only one category or were there several? We do not yet know the answers with any certainty, but archeological evidence increasingly indicates that certain religious systems, as well as trade, played an important part in the urbanization process. The earliest city-states in Mesopotamia were centered around a temple, which was the focus of economic, scientific, and governmental, as well as religious, activity. Religious specialists organized and managed agriculture, trade, and manufacturing, as well as religion. The temple building was a workshop, a storehouse, a market center, an employment agency, an inn, and a dining hall, as well as a place of worship (Frankfort 1964:350–356).

Obviously, not all religious systems, even among agricultural peoples, acted as catalysts for urbanization. What did religions that encouraged urbanization have in common? We do not yet know. The mounting evidence of the significance of religion in the development of urbanization is so recent that this question has not been investigated and so remains unanswered for the moment.

The development of civilization apparently depended on many of the same factors that led to urbanization, with the addition of at least one other: size of the population and area involved. In other words, most civilizations are far larger than any single city. List again the characteristics of a civilization (page 78). All except "large, complex social units" (plural) are also characteristic of cities. The cities included in a civilization need not be under a unified political control. The Sumerian and Greek civilizations consisted of several autonomous city-states. Conversely, as mentioned earlier, civilizations may not have true cities. Olmec and Mayan civilizations in the New World had ceremonial centers rather than true cities. Perhaps where trade was a significant factor in the development of civilizations, true cities were characteristic, whereas when religion alone was the significant catalytic factor, ceremonial centers were more characteristic. A third factor in the formation of civilizations appears to have been pressure from "barbarians" (who were often nomadic herdsmen in the Old World; see below). Villages or cities, banding together for protection, could have provided the larger social structure necessary for the development of civilization. Cooperation against barbarians, whether mounted or on foot, would therefore have given the same sort of stimulus for new techniques of coordination and control over large groups of people that Wittfogel suggests large-scale irrigation provided (see Chapter 5). He believes some sort of stimulus of this nature was essential to the development of civilization. Pressure from barbarians, trade, religion, and the need for large irrigation systems may each have played a significant role in the development of civilizations in different areas. It is not necessary to assume only one cause operating everywhere.

DOMESTICATION OF ANIMALS: NEW LIFE STYLES

It has not yet been determined precisely where or why animals were first domesticated. The domestication of grazing animals may have followed the domestication of plants, and it has been generally assumed that the first animal of any kind to be domesticated was the dog. The latter assumption has recently been challenged, however. Archeological evidence in the Near East indicates that sheep and goats were domesticated there before dogs (Chard 1969:200–201). Nevertheless, the case for dogs is still good in other parts of the world. Since dogs are carnivores and scavengers, they can easily survive on the scraps around a hunting camp. If the ancestors of dogs did begin to hang around hunting camps, there are a number of reasons why their presence might have been tolerated. First, the domestic dog tends to bark at the approach of strangers. We do not know whether his wild predecessor did so, but if he did, notification of the approach of an outsider could have given a survival advantage where relationships between hunting groups were hostile. Second, if, like their descendants, the immediate ancestors of domesticated dogs were scavengers, they could help to keep a camp clean. Hunters might not be esthetically concerned with cleanliness, but since dogs eat human excrement as well as garbage that draws flies, the health of groups with dogs might well have been better than that of groups without them. If true, this was another survival advantage for the hunters. Third, dogs are a handy food source in times of emergency. Their presence around a camp would have added still another survival advantage. Later, the advantages of dogs for hunting, transport, sheep-herding, providing hair for textiles, and so on, made them even more popular. Another reason for considering them the earliest of the domesticates is the fact that there are few human groups that lack dogs. Dogs accompanied man into the New World and probably into Australia, both populated long before any grazing animals were domesticated, so the case for the primacy of dogs still seems strong.

Grazing animals, since they do not eat bones, hide, meat, refuse, or similar items available in hunting camps, were probably not domesticated until humans had supplies of forage to maintain them. It has been suggested that the first animals were kept by farmers for the purpose of having sacrifices for the gods available at short notice (Chard 1969:201). Since wild grazing animals do not have the surplus milk, woolly coats, or other useful characteristics that evolved under domestication, it is difficult to suggest a motive for their domestication other than that of having meat easily available. Since the human *can* survive without meat, certainly long enough to hunt for it or trade for it if hunting is impractical, there are not many conditions that would require the immediate availability of meat other than the demands of gods or rulers, both of which are notoriously impatient. It is also possible, of course, that the human tendency to save effort led the farmer to keep animals around so that he would not have to hunt for them when he or his family wanted meat. The only difficulty with this suggestion is that farmers frequently seem to regard hunting as an enjoyable activity. It is also questionable whether raising animals is really easier than hunting them, and farmers seem rather reluctant to kill their domestic animals (particularly when they do not have many) except on special occasions.

Large herds of animals are not common among farming peoples. Instead, a farmer is likely to have only a few animals of several different types. The excerpt illustrates this pattern: chickens, kept for both eggs and meat; a horse or two; some pigs; a few cows (for milk and meat); some sheep, which were given up because the farm was not large enough to move them around as much as the author felt was necessary; a pony; a goat; and fish. Middle Eastern farmers often have chickens, sheep, and goats, with perhaps a donkey or a mule in addition; Southeast Asian peoples often have chickens, water buffalo, and pigs. When there are enough of the larger animals, such as cows or water buffalo, in a community, they may be placed in a single herd in the charge of the children of the village, or the community may hire a herder (Beals 1964:5, 15; Kipling 1936:102).

In areas where environmental conditions demand that animals be moved seasonally to better pasture, there are several possible alternatives open to the community. The village may hire specialists to herd; families may take turns sending members away to herd for periods of a few weeks at a time; or the whole community may move with the animals—a pattern called transhumance.° Farming cannot be practiced with transhumance unless the seasons and the environment are unusually cooperative, so that the herds can be brought to the agricultural area at about the same time the planting needs to be done and removed only after the harvest. When the environment is not suitable for this, the people must make a choice between splitting up the community for long periods of time or giving up either farming or large-scale herding. Nomadic herders do little or no farming and depend almost entirely on the animals they herd. These people are not truly the "wanderers" their name suggests—few groups are. Instead, they travel within a specific range over fairly specific routes, on a more or less regular schedule. Their movements are quite predictable to anyone who knows them well.

Although this pattern is similar to many hunting patterns in amount of mobility, it may be a secondary development following the domestication of plants and animals, and not a direct evolution from hunting. The values of hunters and herders tend to be quite different in regard to the animals they depend on. As mentioned in Chapter 1, hunters seem to prefer to kill young animals and cows when they can because the meat is tenderer. Herders prefer to kill old, barren, unproductive animals. They also care for their animals physically, carrying and protecting the young and weak, feeding the motherless animals (the frequent biblical references to the concern and care of the shepherd for his flock illustrate this attitude). This behavior is alien to hunters, who do not know the proper techniques and usually lack both the skill and the inclination to perform necessary tasks (such as aiding in difficult births and castrating the male animals). Attempts to convert hunting peoples into herders have generally been unsuccessful, so the possibility of the shift being a "natural"

Reindeer herding in Lappland. *(Werner Bischof/Magnum)*

evolutionary development seems unlikely. Hunters have been known to convert to herding under outside stimulus, but even with this encouragement the transition seems difficult (Lantis 1952:127ff.). Archeological evidence is not clear, however. In some areas, herding seems to precede farming. The two developed so close together in time that precedence of one over the other cannot be decided at the moment. The sequence described above seems logical, but until more evidence is gathered, the question must remain open.

Nomadic herders tend to concentrate on only one or two types of animal, the particular one chosen varying from one environment to another. Northern peoples such as Lapps or Tungus base their economy on the reindeer (Service 1971:91–111). People on the Asian steppes raise horses (Forde 1968:299–309). People in the Himalayas depend heavily on the yak (Ekvall 1968:11). Occasionally, nomadic herders do depend on a variety of animals instead of just one. Some desert peoples, for example, rely mainly on sheep and goats for meat, milk, and wool or hair to make into textiles, but also raise camels and horses to ride and to transport goods (Richardson and Batal 1949:496). The nomadic-herder pattern apparently never developed in the New World, where the only domesticated animals were the llama, the alpaca, the guinea pig, and (possibly) the turkey—none of which are suitable for riding, hauling, or transporting heavy loads. Although the llama was and still is used as a pack animal, most cannot carry more than sixty pounds. Consequently, they are not as useful for hauling or transport as are Old World animals that can carry far heavier loads. No animals suitable for these purposes existed in the New World centers of plant domestication (the bison lived north of the main centers).

The nomadic herder's life style never has been one of the most popular, and today it is limited to a relatively few peoples in isolated parts of the world. It has rarely, if ever, been a completely independent way of life, since its members are normally in a symbiotic relationship with some farmers. But the herders, who are as mobile as hunters and gatherers, have had an influence on Old World history quite out of proportion to their numbers. With the horse and the camel giving them a great advantage over peoples on foot, nomads were in a position to raid villages and cities, and did so with some regularity. They were frequently the "barbarians" so familiar in history books. Villagers sometimes bought them off with "gifts" of grain or local artifacts, a practice that often developed into mutually beneficial trade relationships, the herders contributing meat and animal products in return for the villagers' grain.

Some of the herders collecting tribute from cities yielded to temptation and lived a luxurious life on the riches they milked from their conquests. In a generation or two, these conquerers were apt to become a ruling class, virtually indistinguishable from their former enemies as they lost their distinctive cultural characteristics. For many years, it was assumed that this was the process by which all nation-states and empires were established (conquest from the outside), and it may be true for some of them (Hoebel 1964:154). Not all villages

A view of the Pataling section of China's Great Wall. *(United Nations/T. Chen)*

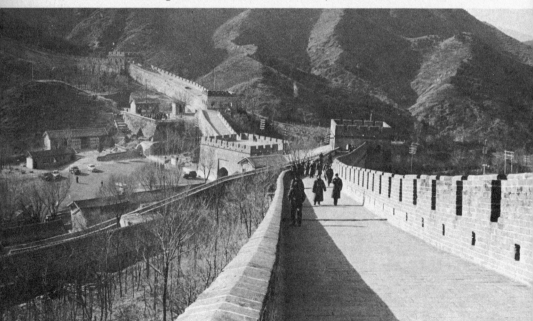

and cities were conquered, however. Some apparently fought back. The Great Wall of China was constructed to keep out mounted barbarians. Some nation-states apparently had their beginnings in organizations formed to combat the incursions of these invaders (Cohen 1968:237). (Other factors involved in the formation of nation-states and empires are discussed in Chapter 5.)

In the Old World, the discovery of the technique of castrating male animals to make them docile enabled even people who were not specialist herders to use some of the larger animals—geldings and oxen, for example—to haul loads and to plow. The development of the wheel (and subsequently the cart and the chariot) revolutionized both transportation and warfare, just as the invention of the plow radically altered agriculture. Again, the lack of suitable large domes-ticated animals in the New World prevented these innovations from developing there. Even though archeological evidence shows that the concept of the wheel was present in the New World (Ekholm 1964:493–495), it was never applied. For the wheel to be accepted during its early development, apparently a combi-nation of factors was necessary, only one of which was the concept of the wheel itself. Others were the need to move heavy loads over land; large expanses of firm, flat land to support the clumsy early wheels; easy access to wood from which to make wheels; and large, strong domestic animals to pull the heavy carts (Chard 1969:222). This combination of factors simply never occurred in the New World.

Evolution of animals under domestication led to increased milk supplies and changes in the nature of the coat of certain of them (wool appeared on domesticated sheep, for example). In the western part of the Old World, these changes were utilized: techniques for making butter and cheese were invented, and textiles using wool were developed. If you had been given no information about the source of the excerpt at the beginning of the chapter, you would still be able to tell that the farming system described had its origins in the western part of the Old World by the mention of wool bedding and cloth and cheese making, because none of these were used to any significant extent in Asia (except by nomadic herders). Animal power and meat have been and remain the primary uses for animals in most of the Orient. In India, cows are sacred, and meat is not eaten by pious Hindus. Clarified butter is extensively used, however, both for cooking and for religious purposes. Pigs, which were a late domesticate and are notoriously hard to herd, were not acceptable animals for all peoples; they were rejected in several places in the Middle East. However, they form a mainstay in parts of Asia and in the Pacific Islands (Oliver 1971:62; Hogbin 1971:27).

ATTITUDES AND VALUES

In hunting, herding, and plow-agriculture societies, major decisions are usually made by adult males, and the influence of women is often slight and indirect. Women tend to be somewhat more influential in horticultural soci-eties, but, overall, the weight given to the opinion of women varies sharply from one society to another regardless of subsistence base, and even within the same society there are considerable variations depending on the individual personalities involved. No society known (except for mythical or legendary ones) relegates men to a secondary position in regard to decision making. The occasional presence of a female ruler does not invalidate this statement, since all of those known to history have been surrounded and guided by male advisors who made or influenced most of the decisions. In any case, the pattern of decision making in the society at large was not appreciably altered to any great extent by the existence of a female ruler. (This subject is discussed further in Chapters 4 and 5.)

One difference in value orientation can be discerned at the very outset of plant domestication. Members of some societies—for what reasons we do not know at present—came to look on nature as an enemy, the environment as a foe to be conquered, subdued, and forced into cooperation with them. Members of other societies seem to have conceived of nature as a friendly or beneficent force that would provide them with abundance if treated properly. The concept of nature as a hostile—or at best, indifferent—force seems almost to be limited to societies with plow agriculture; it is rare among horticulturists.

As a result of the difference in attitudes and needs, technology in various parts of the world has taken divergent paths. The need to protect stores of grain, for example, which is universal among agricultural peoples, led in some areas to the development and improvement of means for trapping or killing animal thieves. In other areas, people concentrated on building better and stronger storage facilities.

The problem of the priority of technology or values—like the chicken-or-the-egg debate—is currently a matter for controversy. Are the values responsible for the technology, or is the technology the cause of the values? As in many anthropological controversies, a strong case can be made for both points of view, and the truth may well be that both are correct in different situations. For example, the logistic demands of agriculture dictate that certain techniques will be more effective than others. Farmers, in this case, often make virtues of necessities. As mentioned earlier, they not only must stay in one place, they want to. They not only must store a surplus, they like to. But the excerpt indicates that the reverse may also be true, and that values may affect the technology. When the author bought his father a spring-tooth harrow with a seat, his father removed the seat and stored it before using the harrow, because it was "lazy" to sit while harrowing. The father was also apparently unwilling to install a pump in the kitchen for the drinking water (which would have saved the labor of the women and children who had to haul it upstairs in buckets), although he had installed a pump for washing water—presumably in the interests of efficiency. (The author indicates his different attitude by reporting that with the first money he earned, he installed a pump for his mother.) The apparently universal human tendency to save time and effort has led to the development of labor-saving devices in almost all areas of the world, although strongly held values have sometimes kept this trend from developing very far. Values rejecting labor-saving devices are often imbedded in a religious system.

The Amish, for example, reject mechanical devices in general for religious reasons (Clark 1937:235). Various inventions have been denounced as "the work of the devil" (Taylor 1962:75).

In the section on the rat massacres, the excerpt indicates an orientation toward the destruction of rodent pests. The father's pessimism regarding the weather, his lack of interest in nonproductive plants such as flowers (which were "traps for weeds"), and his refusal to sympathize with his son's sufferings from cold confirm the existence of the concept that nature is an enemy one must be strong and vigilant to overcome. The son, however, seems to show a more positive attitude, several times in his book revealing a love and respect for nature. In the excerpt he demonstrates his awareness of natural forces and his willingness to work with rather than against them by his approach to the swimming pond. Instead of replacing each washed-out barrier with a newer and stronger one, trying unsuccessfully over and over to dominate the stream as his father had done, the author dug the swimming pond off to one side of the main stream after the first washout.

A change in values apparently led Gilbert to develop an alternative (and more successful) method of stream control than that used by his father. The two concepts illustrated by this example—conquer or cooperate—are both present in the United States, but only recently has the cooperative concept begun to influence the thinking of significant segments of the population, primarily as a result of the excesses to which the "conquer" notion has led. A value change on the part of many researchers in this country has already led to exploration and use of new directions in dealing with insect pests. Instead of insecticides, the instinctive mating behavior or various natural enemies (including diseases) of the unwanted insects have been used against them. The success of these methods may change attitudes and values of people who use them, but it was often a difference in values that encouraged some people to look in new directions, to ask the questions they did, and so discover new techniques. Just as a mental shift makes the reversible figure of the Necker cube appear to change orientation, so a change in attitude may suddenly allow an investigator to see something that was obvious before, but hidden from him by the blinders of covert culture (discussed in more detail in Chapter 7).

On the other side of the argument, religion is an aspect of man's life that changed as a result of the domestication of plants and animals. Like all peoples, hunters and gatherers are concerned with the supernatural (see Chapter 9) but

A Necker cube. A shift in mental perspective makes the Necker cube appear to change orientation.

Survivors file through a flooded field in East Pakistan (now Bangladesh), past a victim of the disastrous cyclone-tidal wave. *(UPI)*

the focus of their concern differs from that of farmers. For example, the hunter is not so preoccupied with weather. His food supply is not likely to be destroyed by an early frost, a violent storm, or even a flood. Since different foods are available at different times, hunters and gatherers usually do not depend on the abundance of a single brief season for most of the year's food supply. When they do (as is the case with the sedentary fishers of the northwest coast of the United States) their life pattern tends to resemble that of village farmers.

Weather is a central concern of farmers and horticulturists, however. After all their labor, an unforeseen weather disaster can wipe out the harvest and leave the people in danger of starvation, if indeed it does not kill them immediately. The sea flood in East Pakistan in 1970 (which inundated° vast areas of land and killed over 200,000 people) indicates that farmers are not exempt from these problems even in this time of advanced technology. Farmers in all parts of the world have tried to predict and control the weather, often turning to the supernatural to do so. Again, the examples illustrate the dynamic interplay of technology and values.

Attitudes toward time may also be influenced by the manner of subsistence. To hunters and gatherers, one day is much like another, seasonal differences come gradually, and time is often measured in relatively large units, such as "moons" or "winters." Farmers and horticulturists in many parts of the world, though, must plant at just the right time or crops will not ripen before bad weather arrives. Wanting to know the best time to plant is widespread and may be responsible for the development of sophisticated calendars by such widely separated agriculturalists as the Sumerians of Mesopotamia and the Maya of Guatemala.

Some sophistication in keeping track of time need not have been a totally new invention of the farmers, however. Research by Alexander Marshack suggests that by 20,000 years ago, people were already knowledgeable about moon phases, seasonal variation, and other astronomical matters, had developed a symbol system for keeping track of astronomical events, and had invented stories to account for them. The legends and myths that appear in the oldest known forms of writing, the sophisticated astronomical observations responsible for Stonehenge and other megalithic constructions, as well as the pyramids and the Middle Eastern calendar, all appear to come out of an ancient and widespread tradition that could well have had its start during the time of *Homo erectus* or even earlier (Marshack 1972:112–120, 125–127). The Mayan calendar in the New World does not appear to have any direct relationship to the Middle Eastern one. Despite a number of popular books to the contrary, the evidence seems to support independent invention in the two locales. Since all calendars are necessarily based on the same astronomical phenomena, some similarity is inevitable. Additional resemblances could be explained by a parallel descent from a common ancient tradition, such as that suggested by Marshack, rather than by a direct transfer from the Middle East. Since the New World was

Stonehenge—one of the best-known prehistoric monolithic constructions, now thought to have been built to mark astronomical events. *(Charles Gatewood)*

apparently first entered by modern man, and not by the earlier *Homo erectus* forms, any already established traditions would have entered with them. This theory can account for a number of Old World and New World similarities without resorting to the unlikely voyages so beloved by popular writers.

Other attitudes that might have responded to the methods for obtaining subsistence are those toward delayed gratification and planning for the future. Farmers are more accustomed to wait for deferred rewards than are hunters. Even though a hunter is sometimes unsuccessful, he usually returns home with game that is consumed immediately. Hunting people are famous (or notorious) for the tremendous quantities of food they are able to eat when it is available. Observers in the 1800s reported that in one sitting a Plains Indian could consume as much as ten pounds of buffalo meat (Ambrose 1975:11)! Frequently, no matter how large the kill, people in a camp ate continuously (with brief periods for sleep or other essential activities) until it was all gone. More than one observer has wondered why hunters do not preserve some of the kill to provide for the inevitable (to the observer) days of shortage to come (and of course some do, as the excerpt in Chapter 1 shows). Hunters do not seem to have the same sense of the inevitability of hunger as do the observers, although they have usually experienced meatless days. Hunting people are also famous for their lack of anxiety about the future. They generally express the feeling that tomorrow is likely to bring better fortune, and game, to the camp. Farmers, on the other hand, *must* plan ahead. They cannot have immediate rewards for their labor, since it takes time for crops to grow and ripen. They cannot gorge on the harvest until it is all gone or they will have neither seed nor food for the future. Farmers in areas where crops cannot be grown on a year-round basis (i.e., in most of the world) must engage in heavy work for several months to a year before they have any edible reward—and then they may lose it at the last minute because of some human or natural disaster. In the light of this difference in the demands of the subsistence methods, one could predict that in values, as reflected in child-training, religion, and other areas of life, hunters and gatherers would probably most often stress immediate rewards and have only a shadowy concern for the future (or an afterlife). Farmers, in contrast, would be more likely to stress future rewards. It would be surprising to find a hunting and gathering people whose values were focused on future rewards, or an agricultural people whose main concern was with the immediate present.

The excerpt indicates an emphasis on deferred rewards in child-training. A great deal of effort was invested in a variety of tasks whose reward was expected in the future. The emphasis on education is an illustration. Education is rarely immediately useful, yet the parents of the author stressed it to such an extent that he felt "it was not strange that Closson and I should turn our attention to teaching." (He was fortunate that his education began to "pay off" in terms of a job when he was only sixteen, and barely one jump ahead of his students. Today, because of the requirements of certification, teachers have to invest much more time and effort before they are able to reap even meager rewards from their education.) The elder Gilbert's emphasis on education is surprising compared with his attitude toward such things as flowers, birds, and other "useless" items. Obviously, he did not consider education useless, in spite of its lack of immediate visible benefits and the fact that it deprived him of farm labor for a major part of the day and the year. From this, one may conclude that he was looking toward future rewards.

Another consequence of domestication is said to be increasing specialization. Yet in spite of the development of technology that accompanies domestication, the excerpt indicates that specialization is associated more with urbanization than with domestication itself. The children in the excerpt used scraps to build play equipment; the women in the family made cheese; the father built a rattrap; the boys churned butter; a grandfather made shoes; the family made mattresses of corn husks and "bedsprings" of rope; woodchuck grease was rendered out of animals family members had probably killed. When the author had his own farm, he raised pigs, slaughtered them, and prepared hams and bacon; the women canned beef from the family's own cattle; and for a while the family used wool from their own sheep for bedding and clothing —but notice, they did send the wool out to be made into cloth. In many societies, the women (or men) would have spun the wool into yarn or thread and either woven it into cloth or knit it into a variety of items.

In a modern, industrial, urbanized society, almost all these goods and services are purchased from specialists. This is a recent development, however, as the excerpt indicates. The early farm village was nearly as self-sufficient as a hunting and gathering band. Most individuals in the farm village were full-time farmers. Specialists, if there were any, worked at their specialties only part of the time. The great upsurge of full-time specialization appears along with urbanization.

The domestication of plants provided humanity with an alternative life style for the first time in its history. Now people could live either as hunter-gatherers or in rural villages as food producers. The domestication of animals added still another life style—that of the nomadic herder. The development of the city provided a fourth alternative—that of the urbanite. For the first time, we have a large group of people whose life style was not directly involved in the food quest. This group did not become a majority in any society until the past few decades in some of the modern industrial states. The four alternatives were the only ones for thousands of years, but recently, under pressure of increasing industrialization, the differences in life styles have continued to increase. At some point, a quantitative change becomes a qualitative one. Surely the contemporary "urbanite"who does not live in the city—the commuter whose social and business lives are almost completely separated; the executive who directs a vast economic empire without having any physical contact with it, yet who can communicate directly with almost any member of it at a moment's notice; the internationalist, who maintains homes in several countries and commutes between them regularly, traveling thousands of miles a year—deserves to be categorized separately from the "urbanite" of a few centuries ago. The tremendous increase in speed and distance of communication combined with an almost unimaginable increase in technological complexity have created new opportunities for life styles as different from the first urbanite's as his was from the hunter-gatherer's (Toffler 1970:12).

The development of industrialization and what Toffler has called the super-industrial world (1970:14, 421) has placed another set of demands on humans, who were just beginning to adjust to the consequences of agriculture and city life. In the modern, so-called developed nations, less than 15 percent of the population is engaged in agriculture. The rest are "working," spending their time and energy at nonfood-producing tasks for which they receive payment (see Chapter 3) that they cannot eat but must spend for food, clothes, and all of the other survival needs that hunters and gatherers or village farmers provide directly for themselves. Many of the jobs people have are hard to relate to any particular perspective. A file clerk may do a vital job without ever knowing how or why it is vital, or even whether he or she is doing it well or poorly, unless told by a supervisor. (Innumerable writers have concerned themselves with the alienation and boredom this situation may cause, although possibly boredom with a factory job or alienation because of it does not occur as often as a liberal arts professor might think. For people who are particularly interested in this problem, books on industrial psychology, sociology, or labor relations may be helpful.) Modern businesses also tend to move personnel around the country with dizzying speed. The conditions many people presently have to cope with, therefore, include a return to high mobility, but without the closeness of the hunting and gathering band or the nomadic herder. The human's emotionally intensive world has shrunk to the nuclear family, which breaks apart when the offspring are grown. Parent-offspring ties, therefore, are not lifelong, and the duration of the new ties formed is also uncertain. Individuals have many "acquaintances" (a relationship totally unknown in small societies) but few deep and lengthy involvements. No wonder a common assumption is that one person can never really know another. That is a task that takes a lifetime and almost none of our relationships last that long. No one in the United States is likely to know even a close relative the way members of a small hunting band know each other.

The amount and variety of information individuals need to know today to have even a minimal control over their own destinies have increased drastically. The Piegan and the people in the Vermont farm family began to learn many of their occupational skills as soon as they could notice anything, and spent their lives learning and practicing them. By observing and copying the people around them, they learned most of what they needed to know. No one can do that in modern society. Some means of cramming stores of information into people's heads had to be developed. A great deal of time today is spent on mental rather than physical activity—with what consequences we do not know.

We are still trying to learn what the demands of an industrial society are on the individual, how much and what kinds of strain such systems place on people, and by what methods people may effectively cope with the requirements of modern life. There is a high degree of controversy about all the suggested answers, indicating that we are still a long way from defining the problems properly, or gathering the right information needed to answer the important questions. Currently, answers are formulated and defended more on emotional grounds than logical ones.

SUMMARY

The survival of individual members is an essential condition any group must meet if the group itself is to survive. One basic need for individual survival is food, along with air, water, clothing, and shelter. Chapter 1 dealt with one means of satisfying the basic need for food—hunting and gathering. This chapter deals with other alternatives that developed after the domestication of plants and animals.

Another way of looking at the means for satisfying the survival need for food is in terms of the demands the various subsistence methods make on individuals. The two major alternatives (farming and hunting-gathering) have subtypes that make similar demands on people; for example, the demands on the sedentary hunter (whose subsistence is usually based on intensive fishing) are not so different from those on the small village farmer. The life of the nomadic herder and the nomadic hunter are similar in many ways. On the other hand, the demands made on the village farmer are far different from those made on the commercial farmer in a modern industrial state. The urbanite, past or present, has still a different set of demands to cope with.

The city is a recent development in human history. It has posed problems to human survival that were only beginning to be solved at the start of the twentieth century. Now, even as we are still trying to solve the problems of the city, it may be that modern technological developments have made the city obsolete (Hoebel 1966:530). One question that is often asked today is whether cities as we know them are really essential to contemporary society. With modern transportation and communication, do people have to be physically concentrated in one place? Perhaps cultural centers, trade centers, manufacturing centers, industrial parks, and living centers—all separated from each other but linked by efficient mass transportation and sophisticated communications of all sorts—are the trend of the future (Toffler 1970:401–403). We live in an exciting time, a transitional time, and a difficult time, possibly equivalent to the early days of agriculture and civilization (Toffler 1970:12). It is not easy to predict the trends of the future, but it is profitable (and fun) to try.

3 Distribution of Needed Goods and Services: The Small Societies

In addition to solving the problems of how *to obtain the basic necessities for biological survival, a society must also ensure that individual members have sufficient access to them. The distribution of goods and services is essential in all human societies because all have some division of labor. No one individual obtains all the basic necessities of life for himself. Even in the simplest societies, where the division of labor is based only on sex and age, some individuals do or have something that other individuals need. The division of labor makes people interdependent, and thus holds the group together, but it also creates problems of distribution that the group collectively must solve to persist as a group.*

Goods and services are produced; they are distributed; they are used. Throughout this process choices of various kinds are made. This chapter focuses on what some of the choices are. Since not all choices are equally feasible, the chapter also deals with the factors that limit the number of alternatives as well as those that make certain choices more likely for a particular society. In reading the excerpt in this chapter, concentrate on what appears to be valuable in the society, who gives what to whom, and under what circumstances.

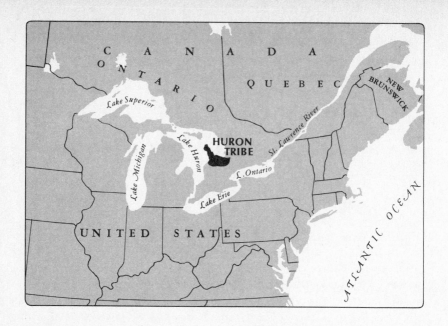

Huron Indian Life: Dreams, Cures, and Reparations

In addition to the desires that we generally have that are free—or, at least, voluntary in us, . . . the Hurons believe that our souls have other desires, which are, as it were, inborn and concealed. . . .*

Now they believe that our soul makes these natural desires known by means of dreams, which are its language. Accordingly, when these desires are accomplished, it is satisfied; but, on the contrary, if it be not granted what it desires, it becomes angry, and not only does not give its body the good and the happiness that it wished to procure for it, but often it also revolts against the body, causing various diseases, and even death.

. . .

In consequence of these . . . ideas, most of the Hurons are very careful to note their dreams, and to provide the soul with what it has pictured to them during their sleep. If, for instance, they have seen a javelin in a dream, they try to get it; if they have dreamed that they gave a feast, they will give one on awakening, if they have the wherewithal; and so on with other things. And they call this *Ondinnonk*,—a secret desire of the soul manifested by a dream.

Nevertheless,—just as, although we did not always declare our thoughts and our inclinations by means of speech, those who by means of supernatural vision could see into the depths of our hearts would not fail to have a knowledge

*Abridged from "Relation of What Occurred in the Country of the Hurons . . . in the Years 1647 & 1648" by Father Paul Ragueneau, in Ruben G. Thwaites (ed.), *The Jesuit Relations & Allied Documents* (Cleveland: Burrows Bros., 1898), Vol. 33, pp. 189–195, 199, 203–209, 229–235, 239–249. Odd-numbered pages are in English; even-numbered, in French. The writer was a French Jesuit who lived for several years with the Huron Indians in Canada.

of them,—in the same manner, the Hurons believe that there are certain persons, more enlightened than the common, whose sight penetrates, as it were, into the depths of the soul. These see the natural and hidden desires that it has, though the soul has declared nothing by dreams, or though he who may have had the dreams has completely forgotten them. It is thus that their Medicine-men ... whom they call *Saokata,* acquire credit, and make the most of their art by saying that a child in the cradle, who has neither discernment nor knowledge, will have ... a natural and hidden desire for such or such a thing; and that a sick person will have similar desires for various things of which he has never had any knowledge, or anything approaching it. For ... the Hurons believe that one of the most efficacious remedies for rapidly restoring health is to grant the soul of the sick person these natural desires.

. . .

Now the ways in which those Medicine-men ... claim to see the hidden desires in the soul of the sick person are different. Some look into a basin full of water, and say that they see various things pass over it, as over the surface of a mirror—a fine collar of Porcelain;° a robe of black squirrel skins, which are here considered the most valuable; the skin of a wild ass, richly painted in the fashion of the country; and similar objects, which they say are the desires of the sick person's soul. Some seem to fall into a frenzy, ... and, after exciting themselves by singing in an astounding voice, they say that they see those things as if they were before their eyes. The others keep themselves concealed in a kind of tabernacle, and in the midst of the darkness pretend that they see around them the images of the objects for which they say that the sick person's soul has desires, which are frequently unknown to him.

But to return to ordinary dreams, not only do most of the Hurons try to gratify their souls' pretended desires for the things that are pictured to them in their dreams; but they also have a habit of giving a feast when they have had a propitious dream. For instance, if any one has dreamed that he captured an enemy in combat, and split his head with a war-hatchet, he will give a feast, at which he will tell his guests of his dream, and will ask that he be given a present of a war-hatchet. And it never fails that some one among the guests will offer him one; for on such occasions they make it a point of honor to appear liberal and munificent.

They say that these feasts are given to compel the soul to keep its word, because they believe that it is pleased at seeing this expression of satisfaction for the propitious dream, and that, consequently, it will set to work sooner to accomplish it. And, if they failed to do so, they think that that might be sufficient to prevent such a result, as if the indignant soul withdrew its word.

. . .

The Hurons recognize three kinds of diseases. Some are natural, and they cure these with natural remedies. Others, they believe, are caused by the soul of the sick person, which desires something; these they cure by obtaining for the soul what it desires. Finally, the others are diseases caused by a spell that some sorcerer has cast upon the sick person; these diseases are cured by withdrawing from the patient's body the spell that causes his sickness.

. . .

. . . When a person falls ill, his relatives call in the Medicine-man . . . who is to decide as to the nature of the disease. If he says that the sickness is natural, they make use of potions, of emetics, of certain waters which they apply to the diseased part, and sometimes of scarifications or of poultices. . . .

But, as a rule, these Medicine-men go further, and assert that it is a disease caused by desires . . . And sometimes, without much ceremony, they will mention to the patient four or five things which they tell him his soul desires—that is to say that he must try to find them, if he would recover his health. . . .

. . . when they see that the patient is a person of note, they usually . . . give a medical prescription that will arouse the entire public to activity. They will say that the sick person's soul has fifteen or sixteen desires,—some of which will be for very expensive and valuable objects; others for the most diverting dances in the country, for feasts . . . and for all sorts of pastimes.

When the prescription is given, the Captains of the village hold a council, as in a matter of public importance, and deliberate whether they will exert themselves for the patient. And, if there be a number of sick who are persons of note, it is impossible to conceive the ambition and intrigue displayed by their relatives and friends to obtain the preference for them, because the public cannot pay those honors to all.

When the Captains have decided in favor of one of these, they send a deputation to the sick man to learn from his lips what his desires are. The patient knows very well how to play his part on those occasions, for, though very often the illnesses are very slight, . . . he will reply in a dying voice that he is exhausted; that his involuntary desires are causing his death, and that they are for such and such a thing.

This is repeated to the Captains, and they set about procuring for the sick man the fulfillment of his desires; to that end they hold a public meeting, at which they exhort all to contribute. And private individuals take a pride in showing themselves munificent on such occasions, for all this is done by sound of trumpet, each one striving to outvie his companion; so that, frequently, in less than an hour the patient will be provided with more than twenty valuable things which he has desired; and they remain to him when he recovers his health, or go to his relatives if he happen to die. Thus a man becomes wealthy in a day, and is provided with all that he needs; for, besides the things that are prescribed by the Medicine-man, the patient never fails to add many others, which, he says, have been shown to him in dreams,—and whereon, consequently, the preservation of his life depends.

Afterward, the dances are announced that are to be performed in the cabin, and under the eyes of the patient, during three or four consecutive days, and on which, it is also said, his health depends. . . .

It is the duty of the Captains to see that all is done in an orderly manner, and with much display. They go into the cabins to exhort thereto the men and women, but especially the élite of the young people; each one tries to make his appearance there dressed in his best, to keep up his importance, and to see and be seen.

Afterward, the relatives of the sick person give very splendid feasts, to which large crowds are invited; the choicest morsels fall to the lot of the most notable persons, and of those who have made the best show during those days of public magnificence.

After that, the patient never fails to say that he is cured, although he sometimes dies a day after the solemnity. But, as these illnesses are usually . . . slight passing ailments, the sick man is often really cured; and that is what gives those remedies so great a reputation.

Such is the occupation of our Savages throughout the Winter; and most of the products of their hunting, their fishing, and their trading, and their wealth, are expended in these public recreations, and moreover, in dancing the sick are cured.

. . .

Since we have given the finishing touches to our Relation, Our Lord has caused such various accidents to happen to us . . . that we had enough material for a new Relation. But I shall leave for another season what cannot be said in a few words, and I shall speak only of a murder committed on the person of one of our servants, named Jacques Douart. That young man, who was twenty-two years of age, wandered a short distance from the house on the evening of the twenty-eighth of April, and was killed by a blow from a hatchet . . .

We could not doubt that the murder had been committed by some Hurons, and we have since obtained positive information of it. . . .

. . .

The whole country was in commotion, and the most notable persons among the nations who dwell in it were summoned to attend a general meeting on the matter. . . .

. . .

. . . it was publicly decided that reparation should be made to us in the name of the whole country for the murder. . . .

. . .

. . . Here, therefore, is what occurred.

When the Captains had come to their decision, we were summoned to their general meeting. An elder spoke on behalf of all, and, addressing himself to me as the chief of the French, he delivered a harangue to us . . .

"My brother," the Captain said to me, "here are all the nations assembled. . . . A bolt from the Heavens has fallen in the midst of our land, and has rent it open; . . . Have pity on us. We come here to weep for our loss, as much as for thine, . . .

. . .

". . . Speak now, and ask whatever satisfaction thou wishest, for our lives and our property belong to thee. And, when we strip our children to bring thee the satisfaction that thou desirest, we shall tell them that it is not thee whom they must blame, but him who has made us criminals by striking so evil a blow. Against him shall our indignation be turned . . ."

After replying to that harangue, we placed in their hands a bundle of small sticks, a little larger and thicker than matches, tied together; these indicated the number of presents that we desired as satisfaction for the murder. Our Christians had informed us of all their customs, and had strongly urged us to be firm if we did not wish completely to spoil matters . . .

The Captains at once divided the sticks among themselves, so that, as each Nation provided a portion of the presents demanded, reparation was made to us according to the custom of the country. But it was necessary for each one to return to his own village, to gather all his people together, and to exhort them to provide that number of presents. No one is compelled to do so; but those who are willing bring publicly what they wish to contribute, and they seem to vie with one another in proportion as their wealth, and the desire for glory or for appearing solicitous for the public weal, animate them on such occasions.

When the day designated for the ceremony had arrived, crowds flocked to it from all parts. The meeting was held outside our house.

In the evening, four Captains were deputed by the general council to come and speak to me . . . They presented themselves at the door. Here not a word is said, nor a thing done, except by presents; these are formalities that must be strictly observed, and without which no business can be considered as properly transacted.

The first present of those Captains was given in order that the door might be opened to them; a second present that they might be permitted to enter. We could have exacted as many presents as there were doors to be passed before reaching the place where I awaited them.

When they had entered, they commenced to speak to me by means of a present which they call "the wiping away of tears." . . . Then came the present that they call "a beverage." . . . "to restore thy voice which thou has lost, so that it may speak kindly." A third present was to calm the agitated mind; a fourth, to soothe the feelings of a justly irritated heart. Most of these gifts consist of porcelain beads, of shells, and of other things that here constitute the riches of the country, but which in France would be considered very poor.

Then followed nine other presents, to erect a sepulchre for the deceased, —for each gift has its name; four presents, for the four columns that are to support the sepulchre; four others, for the cross-pieces on which the bed of the deceased is to rest; and a ninth present, to serve him as a bolster.

After that, eight Captains, from the eight nations that constitute the Huron country, brought each a present for the eight principal bones in the frame of the human body,—the feet, the thighs, the arms.

Here their custom compelled me to speak, and to give a present of about three thousand porcelain beads,—telling them that this was to make their land level, so that it might receive them more gently when they should be overthrown by the violence of the reproaches that I was to address to them for having committed so foul a murder.

On the following day, they erected a kind of stage in a public place; on this they suspended fifty presents, which are the principal part of the reparation and which bear that name. What precedes and what follows are only accessories.

For a Huron killed by a Huron, they are generally content with thirty presents; for a woman, forty are demanded,—because, they say, women cannot so easily defend themselves; and, moreover, as it is they who people the country, their lives should be more valuable to the public, and their weakness should find a powerful protection in justice. For a stranger, still more are exacted; because they say that otherwise murders would be too frequent, trade would be prevented, and wars would too easily arise between different nations.

Those to whom reparation is made carefully examine all those presents and reject such as do not please them; these have to be replaced by others which satisfy them.

That is not all. The body for which a sepulchre is erected must not lie naked therein; it must be clothed from head to foot,—that is to say, as many presents must be given as there are articles of clothing required to dress it, according to its condition. To that end they gave three presents that bear only the names of the things that they represent, a shirt, a doublet, trunk-hose, shoes, and a hat; and an arquebus, powder, and lead.

After that, it was necessary to draw out from the wound the hatchet with which the blow had been struck,—that is, they gave a present bearing that name. As many presents are needed as there have been blows received by the deceased, to close all the wounds.

Then came three other presents,—the first, to close the earth, which had gaped in horror at the crime; a second, to trample it down; and, thereupon, it is customary for all the young men, and even for the oldest, to commence dancing, to manifest their joy that the earth no longer yawns to swallow them in its womb. The third present is for the purpose of throwing a stone upon it, so that the abyss may be more inviolably closed, and may not reopen.

After that, they gave seven other presents,—the first, to restore the voice of all our Missionaries; the second, to exhort our servants not to turn their arms against the murderer, but rather against the Hiroquois, the enemies of the country; the third, to appease Monsieur the Governor when he should hear of the murder; the fourth, to rekindle the fire that we always kept up to warm passers-by; the fifth to reopen the door of our hospice° to our Christians; the sixth, to replace in the water the boat in which they cross the river when they come to visit us; the seventh, to replace the paddle in the hands of a young boy, who has charge of that ferry. We could have exacted two other similar presents to rebuild our house, to erect again our Church, and to set up again four large Crosses, which stand at the four corners of our enclosure, but we contented ourselves with those.

Finally, they concluded the whole with three presents given by the three principal Captains of the country, to calm our minds, and to beg us to love those people always. All the presents that they gave us amounted to about one hundred.

We also gave some, in return, to all the eight nations individually, to strengthen our alliance with them; to the whole country in common, to exhort them to remain united together, that they might, with the French, better resist their enemies. . . . We also gave them some presents to console them for the loss they had recently suffered through the killing of some persons by the enemy.

Finally we ended with a present which assured them that Monsieur the Governor and all the French of Quebec, of Montreal, and of Three Rivers, would have nothing but love for them, and would forget the murder, since they had made reparation for it.

. . .

. . . The whole matter was concluded on the eleventh of May.

Murder was an expensive business among the Hurons! The French Jesuits did not agree with Huron concepts of justice, but their leader, Ragueneau, was wise enough to recognize that it would be futile and foolish to try to impose French concepts of justice in this situation.

Gift-giving to settle conflicts within a group and between groups is widespread. Its manifest function° (the one explicitly intended by members of the society) is to compose the differences between individuals or groups, and thus restore social tranquillity. But a latent function° (real, but unintended and sometimes unrecognized by members of the society) is to distribute wealth.

CONCEPTS: WEALTH, PROPERTY, OWNERSHIP

What constituted wealth in the Huron culture? In any society, according to economic theory, things are valuable if they are scarce in relation to the demand for them. In most of the Western world, the last part of this sentence is taken for granted because there is a great deal of similarity in the things regarded as desirable among various Western cultures. Westerners therefore usually assume an item is valuable simply because it is scarce. The clause "in relation to demand" must always be kept in mind when dealing with non-Western societies, however, since items that may not be at all desirable in Western eyes may be in great demand in other societies, and vice versa. Many of the native Americans of the northeastern United States were so uninterested in gold and silver, for example, that when Europeans asked to be shown deposits of gold or silver, they were unwittingly guided to deposits of lead, copper, or (in one case) even salt (Clinton 1817:7; Quinn 1955:820–821). The only metals these native Americans used before contact with Europeans were copper and occasionally meteoric iron. After contact they were avid for objects of iron and steel, but still relatively uninterested in gold or silver. They also desired glass beads, another item that was novel to their American culture.

Because the Europeans were ethnocentric° and culture-bound° (that is, they thought solely in terms of their own society's values), they assumed the native Americans were stupid, since they would give valuable furs for cheap knives, kettles, and beads. But from the native-American point of view, the stupid Europeans gave precious knives, kettles, and beads (which the native

Americans could not produce themselves) for cheap furs anyone could get with a little effort—at least during the early years of contact. This point of view was, of course, as ethnocentric as the European one, but the Western world has no monopoly on ethnocentrism. Who was exploiting whom? In this case, it was probably even. Both felt they were getting a good bargain. Later, of course, when unscrupulous traders resorted to trickery (getting Indians drunk and cheating them out of goods they had paid for, or just outright robbing them of their furs), the exploitation was obvious, and led to a great deal of bitterness and violence.

All known societies have some items that are regarded as more desirable than others. When these are scarce in relation to the demand for them, they constitute the wealth of the society. Ragueneau mentioned some things Hurons regarded as valuable—fine porcelain collars, robes of black squirrel skin, and shells. The cultures of all societies contain rules concerning proper and improper ways to obtain these good things. (Rules and rule making are discussed further in Chapters 5 and 6.) The excerpt describes two ways that were considered proper among the Huron: through compensation for a wrong and in fulfillment of an expressed soul desire. The excerpt also mentions several other proper methods by which goods were obtained either directly or indirectly: through ceremonial feasts, inheritance, trade, or by hunting or fishing. Other reports indicate that the Huron were accomplished agriculturalists and that maize was a major item of their trade, particularly when they traded with other native Americans. Some of the intangible things that Hurons coveted are also mentioned in the excerpt: the glory that comes from war, the pleasure from taking part in, witnessing, or sponsoring dances, the prestige from giving gifts and feasts, or from being singled out for special treatment at a feast. The excerpt itself does not mention any ways to obtain wealth that were considered improper by the Huron, but other Jesuit reports make it clear that a Huron who took something from another Huron without permission was going about it the wrong way and was subject to punishment (they also make it clear that taking something from the French without permission was not viewed in the same light). This indicates that Hurons had a concept of private property and personal ownership.

All societies seem to have some concept of property.° Property consists of both the valuable thing itself (whether tangible or intangible) and the network of rights and obligations people have toward one another in regard to the thing. Note the words "toward one another." There are no legal relations between people and *things,* only between people (Hoebel 1964:47, 58). This becomes significant when discussing theft as a violation of norms (see Chapter 5) rather than as a means for transferring wealth. The significance of theft as a method of distribution may be appraised from the crime statistics in the United States that show some 1.66 billion dollars' worth of goods were stolen (and thus transferred from one owner to another) in 1973 alone (FBI 1973:120). In spite of its effectiveness as a method of distribution in large complex societies, stealing from a fellow group member is not usually regarded as proper in any society. Cultures differ, however, not only in who is defined as a group member, but also

Sign to discourage shoplifters in a large store. Theft is a disapproved method of wealth distribution in most societies, although in complex ones some segments may approve of theft from other segments. *(Charles Gatewood)*

in what is defined as theft. Taking property that belongs to others without their permission is not always regarded as theft by members of every society. Among Eskimos, for example, anyone in need may use meat found in a cache, regardless of who put it there (Freuchen 1961:126–127). Cheyenne Indians allowed fellow tribesmen to "borrow" guns, horses, and other equipment without asking, but whatever was taken was supposed to be returned within a reasonable time. If it was not, action might be instituted to get the item back, or to punish the individual who took it (Llewellyn and Hoebel 1941:128). What is defined as stealing may not be equally condemned by all members of one society. In societies with sharp social divisions, for example, members of one class or caste may regularly steal from members of another. In this situation, although technically part of one political entity, people do not regard those of another class,° caste,° or subdivision of the society as fellow group members and consequently (as was the case with Hurons in regard to the French) consider them legitimate prey.

Property rights° usually include rights to control, exploit, use, enjoy, or dispose of the valuable thing (Hoebel 1964:58). All societies recognize the individual's rights over some things, but no society leaves such rights absolutely unrestricted. That is, all societies recognize private property, but all societies also limit it. Even in the United States, where great emphasis is placed on private property, there are numerous restrictions on individual property rights. Real estate can be taken away from its private owner if the public need for it is great (the right of eminent domain°) or if the owner fails to pay the public regularly (taxes) for the privilege of exercising ownership rights, and the owner is often restricted in the use that may be made of the property (zoning laws). An author or composer with a copyright° (rights over a certain organization of sounds or words) can benefit from it only for a certain period of time; then that particular organization becomes part of the public domain and can be freely copied by anyone.

Societies differ considerably in the things members regard as legitimately subject to individual control and those they deem more appropriately controlled by the group. Members of most small societies—hunting and gathering bands, nomadic herders, or small horticultural villages of twenty-five to fifty people, for example—regard most natural resources as not subject to anyone's control, or as legitimately controlled only by the group as a whole. In the former case, any human being can hunt, gather, drink water, live on or pass through their territory (but remember, people in many small societies often classify only band members as human beings). Strangers—even those classed as human—usually must ask permission, although normally it would be granted on a temporary basis. Newcomers (except for individuals who join the band) are expected to move on soon, and if they do not, relations between the two groups are likely to become strained.

Few groups are so casual with *all* natural resources in their area. Scarce resources—bee trees, water holes in arid areas, rare groves of favorite fruits or nuts, and so on—are usually much more carefully guarded, and may even belong to individual families rather than to the band or village as a whole.

Most societies, even simple ones, recognize the principle of individual effort. That is, if a person invests time and effort in something, most societies grant that person certain rights over it. (In industrial societies the employer extinguishes workers' rights over the items they work on by giving them money in exchange for their labor.) Even in societies whose members regard natural resources as group-owned, people tend to think of game, once it is killed, as belonging to the hunter (or hunters). Often, however, there is an elaborate set of rules surrounding the division of game, and the hunter may be required to give away all or most of the meat. This forced sharing does not mean that the game is group-owned, although to superficial observation it may appear so. Formal ownership is often most important, and sharing therefore creates a network of obligations, debts, and privileges among the band members that strengthens group ties (Thomas 1959:50). Even though sharing is compulsory, it is rewarded by other members of the society. A hunter who gives game on one occasion is entitled to receive game when he returns home empty-handed on another. A man who is able to give game more often than he receives it has many people obligated to him. Consequently he wields more influence in the band than a less successful hunter. Like a dominant alpha male in a baboon troop, he becomes attractive to women, young men, and other people, so the number of individuals associating with him increases. Up to a certain point, the increase in numbers will add to the group's potential for survival.

In addition to making it appear that game is group-owned, forced sharing may also give the appearance of altruism. Sharing behavior, however, as mentioned earlier, need not be motivated by generous impulses. Since an individual can get needed food, become more influential, gain supporters, receive esteem or respect, and in addition avoid punishment or conflict by sharing, it is clear that only a madman or a fool would try to hoard. Feelings of generosity need not be a factor at all.

The principle of individual effort is also recognized in small horticultural villages where natural resources such as land are group-owned. In these societies, usually based on slash-and-burn gardening, land ownership tends to depend on use rather than on some abstract right to a particular piece of land. Thus, land may be allotted by the group, or simply taken over by whoever clears and plants it. It then belongs to the users so long as they cultivate it, but becomes available to anyone else who cares to work it if the original users neglect it. This form of land ownership (usufruct,° i.e., based on use) may result from a pattern of shifting agriculture. When a village regularly moves to a new, distant, location, ownership of fields where the village once was is no more useful than ownership of land is to the hunter once the game is gone. If villages

Livestock often are a measure of a person's wealth, yet are frequently cared for by children. These goats are herded by a young Sudanese. *(United Nations)*

did not return to their original site within a few years during the early period of cultivation when the pattern of shifting villages was being formed, permanent ownership would have been so meaningless that it probably never developed as a concept.

This same factor may be involved among nomadic herders. They, too, recognize the principle of individual effort and have the concept of private property, since animals are all owned by individuals. Grazing land, however, is open to all. Once again, individual ownership of grazing lands for the highly mobile herds would be useless. Even today in the United States, cattle raisers tend to find ownership of grazing land prohibitively expensive and unnecessary. Cattle ranchers often simply pay the government or a native-American group for the privilege of allowing a specific number of cattle to graze at will on its land.

Stable residency patterns seem to be associated with a different form of land ownership. In an account of the Dodoth, a cattle-herding people who have been forced into a more settled residential pattern fairly recently, Thomas indicated that fenced-in pasture for individually owned herds may be developing, although there is a strong emotional resistance to it (Thomas 1965:192–194). Most societies based on plow agriculture—with the highest level of residential stability—regard land itself as subject to individual control, and land ownership as permanent. Original ownership may have been based on the principle of individual effort, so the person (or persons) who cleared and worked the land owned it, just as in the case of the horticultural village. Then, since the village did not shift location, and the same land could be worked for generation after generation by the same family, the idea of a permanent right to a piece of land could easily have developed. A claim to land could become fixed, regardless of use. The concept of permanent ownership may have been assisted in its development by the appearance of writing and record-keeping, but these are not essential. Permanent land ownership occurs in areas where no one is literate. In such cases, boundaries between land parcels are memorized and passed along from generation to generation. (Sometimes in a special ceremony to teach the boundaries, the young people of the community may be whipped, thrown into boundary streams, or otherwise forcefully encouraged to fix key points in their memories [Leach 1949, 1:129].)

Land is by no means the only item that is variable in regard to whether members of the society think it appropriately group-owned or held by individuals. In some societies salt, matches, or other useful and desirable items are a monopoly of the government; private individuals are not permitted to make or sell them. Conversely, it has occasionally happened that members of a society will permit individual ownership of things that people in the United States now feel should be controlled by the group. Private currency or coinage and private ownership of highways, bridges, and even rivers are not so far in our own past, and in some societies are still allowed (*Encyclopaedia Britannica* 1970, 3:101; 1966, 22:400).

In regard to patterns of ownership, the behavior of a hunting and gathering band or that of the small horticultural village is analogous in many respects to

the behavior of a large extended family in more complex societies, even to one in the United States. Although the analogy should not be pushed too far, since there are also significant differences, in many respects it is more appropriate to compare the small, simple society to an extended family of roughly the same size in a complex society than to insist on a comparison between whole societies regardless of the size differential. (The size of a society is extremely important in determining the kinds of relationships that can exist between its members, the technology its members can support or must practice, and in fact, all aspects of life [Wilson and Wilson 1945:24–30; Pfeiffer 1972:375–379]. Comparing the life style of the Tasadays, for example, with the life style of the population of the United States as whole is like comparing paramecia to horses. Both may have certain things in common, but knowledge gleaned from studying one will increase understanding of the other only if applied with great care, and in an appropriate way.)

It is clear that the Huron recognized private ownership and also that they placed some restrictions on it. People who owned things were expected to give them away under certain circumstances—for the public good, or for the assistance of other individuals. In one situation (described elsewhere in *Jesuit Relations*) a Huron family was forced to share its grain during a famine on the threat of having its storehouse and living quarters burned down. It is also clear from the excerpt that gift-giving in case of sickness was rewarding to people who gave. Thus Hurons, at least, did not depend solely on generous feeling to promote the behavior they wanted. They also rewarded people who behaved properly. (This is discussed at greater length below.)

REDISTRIBUTION°

The problem of who gets what in a society began early in human history —began, in fact, as soon as there were fewer indivisible items available than there were people who wanted them. Human societies, like all other groups, have a dominance structure°—that is, certain individuals have preferential access to the "good things" of life, usually food, space, and mates. Dominance plays a major part in determining who gets what in the society. The methods by which the dominant individual is decided upon are considered in more detail in Chapter 5. Here, our concern is with the problem of distribution itself.

If five hunters cooperate to kill a mammoth, who gets the tusks? If three help kill a bear, who gets the hide? If they kill a deer and share the hoofs (to make rattles), who gets the extra one? How do they divide the meat? Some way of deciding such questions also had to be developed in response to the division of labor. If men kill the animal, how do women get any meat? If women cook the food, how do men get any? There must be some method of distribution, and

Where animal power is used, as here in Nigeria, men usually do the plowing. *(Courtesy, British Information Services)*

human societies have developed a variety of ways to accomplish it. Distribution is the general term used when goods change hands. Redistribution is the term used when goods are collected (by an individual or specific individuals) from some members of a society and given to others. Taxes are an example of redistribution in complex societies; the reparation payment to the French in the excerpt is an example of redistribution in a simpler society. The excerpt deals with reparations° between societies, but Ragueneau reported that murders within Huron society were settled the same way. He even mentioned the specific value the Huron placed on human lives. In spite of the relatively precise economic evaluation of different victims, however, the function of reparations as a means of distributing wealth apparently went unnoticed, even by Ragueneau. Therefore, this function was latent rather than manifest among the Huron.

It is difficult to determine just how large a proportion of wealth was distributed by reparations in Huron society. Other parts of *Jesuit Relations* indicate the amount was larger than one might expect from the excerpt alone, since reparations were not limited to cases of murder. A variety of crimes and social offenses were settled in the same manner. In the case of theft, for example, the victim had the right to confiscate the possessions not only of the robber but also of his extended family.° (The extended family among the Hurons included parents, brothers, sisters, all the sisters' offspring, plus maternal aunts, uncles, and distant cousins.) For most offenses, the entire family of the culprit was considered responsible, just as all Hurons were considered responsible for the intersocietal conflict described by Ragueneau. If it proved impossible to determine precisely who the culprit was, residents of the village nearest the scene of the crime were collectively held responsible and had to pay reparations (Thwaites 1898, 19:85). If a crime took place within a village and the culprit could not be determined, presumably all the people not related to the victim would be held responsible. No such case was reported in *Jesuit Relations.* When a crime took place within a single village, there was apparently never any doubt about the identity of the guilty party.

Note that when collective responsibility was accepted, the cost was theoretically borne by everyone except people related to the victim, but actually, since the contributions were voluntary, those who were wealthy or who were trying to increase their status in the society contributed most. Contributions were made publicly, and, according to Ragueneau, the people seemed "to vie with one another in proportion as their wealth, and the desire for glory or for appearing solicitous for the public weal, animate them on such occasions." The same motivation can be seen at work in the United States when moderators of telethons for charitable causes publicly announce the names of contributors along with the amount each has given or when donors challenge others to match their contribution. War bonds were sold at public auction during World War II to encourage people to compete publicly for prestige. The method presumably resulted in people contributing more than they would have had their contribution been private, for there are apparently many societies in which people do not want to appear stingy or selfish in front of their fellow citizens.

However frequent and significant reparations may have been, they certainly did not account for so large a proportion of wealth transfer as did the distributions that occurred as a result of illness. Ragueneau stated that this was the major occupation of the Huron during the winters and that "most of the products of their hunting, their fishing, and their trading, and their wealth, are expended in these public recreations." There is little real evidence that the Huron recognized the distributive function of the activity, although Ragueneau assumed they did. In several places in the excerpt, he implied that the invalids were faking, that they took advantage of the occasion to ask for more than even the medicine man had suggested, or that they exaggerated the seriousness of their condition in order to get more goods. It is difficult to know whether Ragueneau was making an accurate inference, or whether he was misled by knowledge of the motivation that could have been correctly attributed to a Frenchman in the same situation. This is another example of problems that researchers using documents have, parallel to the problem mentioned in Chapter 1. Ragueneau presumably reported behavior accurately, but can we be equally sure of his interpretation of the Huron state of mind?

Since Ragueneau did not believe that desires of the soul could cause illness (not having had the benefit of modern psychological literature), he apparently assumed that the Huron did not really believe it either and used it to their own advantage. (Although if *no one* believed it, the trick could not have worked.) Studies of other societies, however, show that most people really do believe concepts of their culture regarding the cause and cure of diseases. It is only after alternative explanations are persuasively presented to them that a few doubters appear. Even then, the experience of doctors and missionaries has demonstrated that it is quite difficult to shake people's beliefs in this area, so it is probable that the Huron did not recognize the latent distributive function of the ceremony, but were aware only of the manifest function of healing the sick.

The same assumption of collective responsibility that appeared in cases of crime also held in cases of sickness. Illnesses resulting from desires of the soul were beyond the individual's conscious control, so people could not be blamed for wanting something that belonged to someone else. If people did not receive what the soul wanted, they might die, and the blame for the death would rest on the shoulders of those who refused to grant their wishes. This can easily be inferred from statements in the excerpt, and the inference is supported by other Jesuit reports. Most Jesuits agreed with Ragueneau and believed the sick were lying to get something for nothing, or, if they did believe an individual was telling the truth, assumed the dream was inspired by the devil. In either case, Jesuits usually refused to contribute anything in response to dreams or soul desires. The Huron, naturally, interpreted the refusal as malicious and accused the Jesuits of trying to kill them off. Since epidemics were brought into Huron country either directly or indirectly by Europeans (even though Europeans were usually unaware of it), the charge was not totally irrational. This belief was a factor in the martyrdom of several Jesuits (Talbot 1956:207). Possibly the large amount of ceremonial distribution reported by Ragueneau was due to the increased incidence of illness. Such distribution patterns may have been less significant in the precontact period.

Other redistributive methods are used in various cultures. Taxation has already been mentioned. Another method is giving gifts to a leader, king, or priest, who then redistributes them to other members of the society. In a redistributive pattern, the donor normally does not expect an immediate direct material return for his gift. A major difference between this and distribution through a market system therefore seems obvious: redistribution does not involve profit. If the word *reward* is substituted for the word *profit,* however, the difference largely disappears, since most ceremonial or redistributive gift-giving does involve some kind of reward. The giver in Huron society anticipated and received increased respect from other members of the society. With one act he might increase his prestige, gain more power, and also improve his

An ancient Egyptian rendering of a ceremonial offering. *(Brown Brothers)*

relationship with the supernatural. The excerpt states that "private individuals take a pride in showing themselves munificent." At the return feasts given by the sick person's relatives, "... the choicest morsels fall to the lot ... of those who have made the best show." The generous person therefore was ranked among the "notables" of the country. This was clearly reward enough to inspire the Huron to considerable effort. The excerpt says that each one tried to outdo his companion, and within less than an hour, the patient received more than twenty of the valuable items he had asked for. Monetary profit, therefore, is not the only motivation that inspires competition; competition can and does occur in redistributive systems.

Systems that require individuals to give heavily to their leaders or to supernatural specialists (taxes, tithes) may create a different motivation. Even though expensive gifts to priests may inspire esteem or improve relations with the supernatural, a primary motivation (especially in paying taxes) is often to escape punishment. (Nonetheless, the taxpayer has his reward in escaping penalties.) This motivation existed in the Huron situation too, but it was secondary.

Redistributive systems exist alongside market systems in complex societies. The United States has both redistribution and ceremonial distribution. Gifts are given to individuals on Christmas, Easter, birthdays, and other significant anniversaries; contributions are made to charitable, research, and religious organizations that redistribute them to others; and, of course, taxes are paid. Some financial profit may be involved in the charitable contributions because of tax savings, yet many individuals would contribute to such organizations even if the contributions were not deductible. The cost of personal gift-giving is not usually deductible in any case.

Even when financial profit is not involved, Americans and people in other societies make precise (if unconscious) calculations of the value of gifts. There is a good reason for this. The culture prescribes what is an appropriate gift for a particular situation. Almost anyone can recall a time when he or she was embarrassed by either giving or receiving a gift that was too expensive (or too cheap) for the occasion. A certain delicate precision of calculation is required to determine just how much should be spent on a gift to impress or please the recipient without causing embarrassment. Occasionally, someone deliberately sets out to humiliate another person (usually a rival) by giving an overly expensive gift, or to insult that person by a gift that is obviously too cheap. If the rivalry is, say, between two boys over a girl, a gift may be given to her instead of to the rival. In that case, the calculation must be even more precise, since the gift should humiliate the rival but not embarrass the girl. The most significant factors involved in the calculation include the socioeconomic status of both donor and recipient, the nature of the relationship, the intensity of the relationship, and the occasion.

RECIPROCITY°

Technically, redistribution systems are not exchange systems because there is no immediate return. All societies have some sort of exchange system *if* there is both a demand for something and a differentiation in suppliers. That is, there will be *no* exchange if the person who wants something supplies it himself. In the New England farm excerpt in Chapter 2, the man wanted cider and made his own. In the Piegan excerpt in Chapter 1, the person who wanted buffalo went out and killed one. There was no exchange under those circumstances. Exchange can occur only when someone wants what someone *else* has. The Huron excerpt does not illustrate exchange, but exchange based on several different principles did occur in the Huron culture. One principle was reciprocity, where goods are given with the expectation of a return, but no profit; the exchange is mutual. The return corresponds in value to the initial transfer of goods but is in the opposite direction. Among the Huron this form of exchange took place first within the family, stemming from the division of labor. Men hunted and did some work in the fields. Women worked in the fields and in the home. The work organization was similar to that of the Piegan, with agriculture added. Family members automatically exchanged the results of their labor without keeping an elaborate account of who contributed how much. Some societies *do* keep an account of what one family member owes another in regard to food, shelter, and so on (Pospisil 1964:30). Other societies keep such an account only for things that are not normally part of the family exchange pattern—for example, large loans between adult siblings in the United States. In most societies, however, even though members indignantly deny paying attention to exchange within the family, if a husband or wife does not fulfill economic expectations (if the wife, say, is lazy, a poor housekeeper, does not cook or sew for her husband, or if the man does not hunt, work in the fields, or somehow provide food), members of the society condemn the negligent party, and marital beatings or divorce may result. When this happens, it seems inaccurate to say that *no* attention is paid to the exchange process within the family. This form of exchange (where no one will admit to keeping careful track of the value of the return) has been labeled generalized reciprocity (Service 1966:14–15). In some societies, usually small ones with social interactions strongly directed by kinship ties, generalized reciprocity is the only kind of exchange practiced.

When members of societies are more openly concerned with calculating the values involved in an exchange and being careful that one party does not maintain an advantage, anthropologists speak of balanced reciprocity (Service 1966:14–15). There are at least two types of balanced reciprocity: identical and equivalent. In identical reciprocity, the same goods or services are exchanged. For example, men may work in each other's fields by turns, or the families involved in a wedding may exchange the same items to validate the marriage. In identical reciprocity there is usually a time lag between the original act and its return. It would be rather silly for two individuals to hand each other identical sacks of potatoes, for example, unless the exchange were merely symbolic, as at a wedding. What usually happens is that the return is made hours, days, weeks, months, or even years after the original "gift." In equivalent reciprocal exchange, however, the whole transaction is more often completed at approximately the same time and involves exchange of different things members of the society regard as equivalent—fish for vegetables, food for labor. People do not interpret this exchange as producing a profit for anyone.

Nevertheless, the items involved in an equivalent reciprocal exchange are often "equivalent" only in the eyes of the members of the society. Are steel knives really equivalent to furs? Are two bushels of corn really equivalent to one bushel of fish? On the other hand, if both parties to a transaction interpret it as a reciprocal exchange of equivalents, not involving profit, does it make any sense to impose the evaluations of a totally different society and claim that one party is exploiting the other? Use of the word *reward* may be helpful again. In the case of equivalent reciprocal exchanges, both parties feel the exchange has been rewarding. Each one has received something he wanted, and to get it has had to give up only something he was willing to part with—something he wanted less than what he got in exchange.

An objective evaluation of comparative worth of the two things involved in reciprocal equivalent exchange might be based on the amount of energy required to produce each one. This can become a bit difficult in cross-cultural trading, however, when products of simple societies are compared with those of complex ones. It is possible to make highly refined calculations on caloric requirements for particular jobs and the energy flow (input and output, including contributions of the sun, various chemicals, and so on), but that topic is a bit too specialized to be included here in detail. (Interested readers might consult Kemp 1971:104–115; Rappaport 1971:116–133; and Cook 1971:134–

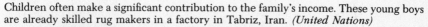

Children often make a significant contribution to the family's income. These young boys are already skilled rug makers in a factory in Tabriz, Iran. *(United Nations)*

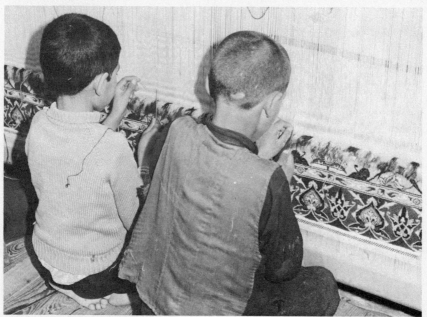

144, for a start.) For now, it may be enough to point out that human muscle power may be all that is used in a simple society to manufacture a rug. The amount of energy needed to produce the rug may, therefore, be expressed in terms of man-hours. If a mass-produced steel knife is given in return for the rug, man-hour calculations look very unequal. The rug maker had to gather the raw material for the rug and prepare it (which might involve spinning and dyeing the fibers). In a simple society, it is quite possible that the individual who sells a rug was the only individual involved in its production from raw material to finished product, so calculating the energy that went into it is relatively straightforward. But even ignoring the energy required to bring the steel knife to the place where it is traded, the calculations involved in the production of the knife are far more complicated. In the first place, the trader who gives the mass-produced knife did not make it, and that alone renders the calculation difficult. The knife was fashioned in large part by machines which were tended by workers, none of whom spent more than a few minutes—perhaps even only a few seconds—of time on that particular knife. In addition, it is necessary to take many more things into account because of the high degree of specialization that is involved in an industrialized society. The machines that did most of the actual work must be included into the calculations somehow. That means one must consider the labor involved in building the machines, in mining and smelting the ores that provided the metal that went into the machines, and the transportation of the raw materials to the machine factory and of the finished machine to the knife factory. In addition to all the labor that went into building the factory machines, it is necessary to consider the labor that went into the materials of the knife itself—again, mining, smelting, casting the metal of the knife blade, cutting trees, sawing and shaping wood that went into the handle (let's not even discuss what is involved in producing plastic handles!)—plus the work involved in producing the electricity that powers the factory machines, in stringing the wires that carry the electricity to the factory, in making the wires that were strung and the poles that hold those wires up, in building the machines that generated the electricity, and so on and on. All of these were part of the energy it took to make the knife that was exchanged for the rug. It is true that only a small fraction of the energy that went into all those separate items was directly involved in the production of one specific knife, but those fractions add up. Ignoring all those hidden energy costs and being unaware of the thousands of interconnected parts involved in the production of *anything* in an industrialized society are factors that have led to many of our modern economic and environmental mistakes. The superficial comparison of the work of the individual rug producer with that of a single worker in the knife factory or of the trader is highly misleading. Consequently, making objective evaluations of the relative value of items traded cross-culturally based on the energy needed for production is probably not worth the effort. In any case, when one party is forced to continue in an exchange perceived as unsatisfactory or when goods are stolen or forcibly seized, a legitimate charge of exploitation can be made, although the more emotionally neutral term of negative reciprocity may also be used for this kind of exchange (Service 1966:15).

The Huron engaged in identical reciprocal exchange of services between families within the tribe, and in balanced reciprocity (usually of equivalents) with outsiders. Hurons traded maize to other tribes for furs, meat, and fish; and traded both maize and furs to Europeans for European-manufactured goods. Except in cases where Europeans were involved, none of the exchange was through a market system. Even exchanges with Europeans were sometimes made on the basis of fixed trade arrangements with the tribe, rather than by individual sales based on market principles (Hamilton 1951:389–391).

In reciprocal "gift" exchanges (reciprocal gift-giving), the recipient has an obligation to return the gift. When a gift is given to someone specifically to create this social obligation, the process is called prestation° (Belshaw 1965:48). Prestation is the driving force behind some economic systems. As with ceremonial gift-giving, there may be no direct or immediate return for the gift, but the reward expected is usually explicit, although often deferred. In a prestation system, the donor frequently expects to be repaid by services of some sort (such as political support or preferential treatment) rather than by a return gift. Other members of the society also expect the recipient to repay the donor, and there is usually a consensus on both the proper amount and the nature of the repayment. In such societies, when recipients do not perform as expected, they lose respect in the eyes of their fellows and are not trusted in future dealings.

Prestation, like ceremonial distribution, can and does occur in societies with market systems. Its presence in the United States is indicated by the reaction people have when they learn that some influential political figure has accepted an automobile or other expensive gift. Watergate and the recent investigations of political contributions and payments to foreign officials by large United States businesses have focused strongly on various obligations people have created by gifts of money or tried to pay off by services. In such cases the public is not concerned about possible repayment in kind; it fears that a gift will be repaid by preferential treatment. (When money is given, it is called a bribe, rather than a gift.) There is a general reluctance in the United States to accept expensive gifts from people to whom one does not want to feel obligated. Parents, particularly mothers, are apt to act distressed on learning that their daughter has accepted an expensive gift (other than an engagement ring) from a man. They tend to worry about how the obligation might be repaid.

One of the difficulties in the economic study of simple societies has been considerable controversy over whether modern economic theories can be applied to those societies that are without a market system or a cash economy (Cook 1966:323ff.). Obviously some of the more elaborate conceptualizations concerning prices, market fluctuations, regressive taxation, and so on cannot be applied, but basic principles ought to be applicable. On the other hand, data should not be forced into an alien mode. It is unscientific to violate descriptions of a behavior pattern by ignoring salient characteristics simply in order to have tidy categories. Economic theories meant to apply to highly complex systems must not be mindlessly transferred to simple systems. The process of attempting to apply economic theories to simple systems, however, may be illuminating and helpful in increasing understanding of basic economic dynamics that are sometimes obscured in complex systems. Belshaw, for example, has improved our understanding of exchange through application of modern theory to simple systems (1965:1–46). Principles that can be applied to both simple and complex systems should be extremely useful, since *some* of the complexity of modern systems is due to the fact that they have a variety of ways of dealing with production, distribution, and consumption, whereas a simple society has only one (although it may be the same as *one* of the ways used in the complex society).

In the simplest of societies each individual is a producer who also consumes much of what he or she produces. Distribution is normally in the form of generalized or balanced reciprocal exchange along kinship lines, with blood relatives or in-laws. In such societies there is a constant exchange of food and services, continually creating and fulfilling obligations between husband and wife, spouses and in-laws, parents and children, siblings° (brothers and sisters), and other more distant relatives. In such societies, there is usually little redistribution, even through inheritance. There are few material possessions, and such things as there are most often are destroyed, buried, or abandoned when their owners die.

As more complex societies develop, additional techniques for distribution may occur. One of the earliest is probably redistribution of game and of some plant food that can be gathered in large quantities. The hunters or gatherers give most of what they have to others, who consequently receive food from several sources; everyone who receives anything distributes it to still others. Then after the food is cooked or otherwise prepared, it is distributed still again to different people. In the end, a hunter or gatherer may eat little of what he or she originally brought back but will make a meal from food obtained through the complex redistribution network (Thomas 1959:50, 215).

The hunters and gatherers in Chapter 5 practice ceremonial redistribution. That is, everyone contributes food to a common basket, for ceremonial purposes. All the people who participate in the ceremony eat the contributed food. This type of indirect sharing is common in many small, simple societies yet need have nothing to do with generous feelings, since it is socially required behavior, and not left to individual impulse.

In both redistribution and reciprocity, the social aspect may be as significant to the participants as what is distributed. When the emphasis in the society is on the social relationships between the participants rather than on the economic exchange itself, the system is called particularistic.° (The opposite system is called universalistic,° and is discussed in more detail in the next chapter.) Individuals in the society may claim that *what* is given or exchanged is not nearly so important as the fact that the distribution has occurred or that specific people were involved in it. This claim may have precisely the same value as the one familiar in the United States to the effect that it is not the gift but the thought behind it that counts. In some cases the claim accurately reflects the feelings of the person who makes it; in others it is a formal expression of an ideal, and the person who makes it would be the first to complain if the value of the gift or service were not appropriate to the occasion.

A society with both reciprocity and redistribution is obviously more complex than a society with only one of the two. Either or both may occur without a market, since the term *market* like the term *civilization* has a technical meaning. To have a market, there must be a number of buyers and sellers, and the price of the items sold must vary according to what is offered and asked by the different buyers and sellers (Fraser 1937:131). None of these conditions are met by the kinds of reciprocity and redistribution we are presently concerned with. (The concepts of sellers, buyers, and price will be discussed in more detail in the next chapter.) Besides reciprocity and redistribution, there are other forms of exchange and distribution in which the conditions necessary for a market do not occur. Extensive trade may take place between members of different societies, for example, without any market. The most common arrangement is for the members of the two societies to pair off and establish "trading partners." Each individual then exchanges goods only with the trading partner or partners (Belshaw 1965:13). Usually in this situation, traditional items are exchanged in traditionally fixed quantities between pairs of individuals who have a long-established relationship with each other. Change of partners, items, or amounts is not something that is easily done. It requires delicate and long-drawn-out negotiations (Belshaw 1965:17). If whole communities engage in this type of trade at one time in one place, the process may appear very much like a typical market to a superficial observer, but in reality all of the essential characteristics of a market are missing.

So-called dumb, or silent, barter° is another form of trade that lacks the essential characteristics of market exchange. In this form, one party places the items to be traded in a particular location—beside a well-known trail or at a waterhole, for example—and then withdraws from the area. The other party may remove desired items, leaving others in their place, or may lay out items being offered in exchange beside those of the first group. The first party returns, takes the items left in trade (or chooses from among them), and leaves. If necessary, the second group may return to complete the trade, but in no case is there direct contact between the groups. This form of trade may occur when groups are hostile, or fearful of each other for some reason. It is a method sometimes used to make initial contact between groups that are not known to each other.

It should be noted that the definition of a market does not require the use of money: conditions for a market may easily occur when two groups barter goods face-to-face. A society with a market form of distribution (even one based on barter) and reciprocal exchange is clearly more complex than societies that lack any form of market. Of all the various methods of exchange, a market system is usually the most complicated. Since one does not expect to find complex patterns where even simple ones do not occur, it would be surprising to find a market system occurring in a small society that has no evidence of redistribution or reciprocal exchange, and no other complex institutions.

EMIC AND ETIC INTERPRETATIONS

Notice that the terms used and the interpretations given by members of a society may not coincide with those of the analyst. The Huron interpreted gift-giving as a healing process; Ragueneau interpreted it as ignorant people succumbing to deception; and here we interpret it as a form of wealth distribution. Which interpretation is "correct"? The answer depends on the point of reference. For the Huron, a man who gave away a black squirrel robe was being morally responsible and helping heal a fellow citizen. For Ragueneau and other Jesuits, he was either deceived or in league with the devil. Classification of the characteristics of the society based on the members' viewpoint is called emic° (Price-Williams 1968:307). When the classification is made according to some external system of analysis, it is called etic.° Some anthropologists are currently arguing over which method is valid, or more valid.

Comparisons between societies involve etic classifications, and without cross-cultural comparisons, there is no way to discern general patterns (where they exist). Without generalizations there is no "science" of humanity, there is only the history of individual groups of human beings. The study of humankind then becomes limited to description and anecdote. Needless to say, anthropologists who are attempting to arrive at theories of human behavior reject the argument that each individual and each society is unique, without any common patterns, processes, or characteristics (Harris 1968:316–318). On the other hand, particularly in the areas of knowledge and thought processes, gross errors have been made by attempting to force the categorizations of one culture into the categories of another. Emic-oriented studies add a great deal to the body of information about man's thought processes and psychology. Ethnobotany, for example, deals with the way in which different societies classify their botanical knowledge; ethnomusicology is the study of the musical idiom of different societies. Emic-oriented studies can provide new insights and can be highly productive of increased understanding of the subject matter itself. We know more about music in general after learning non-Western ways of arranging and producing musical sounds. Such knowledge can enrich our own musical idioms. Both emic and etic approaches, therefore, can be useful, but for different purposes. The emic/etic controversy has been particularly vitriolic in connection with economic studies, yet together the two approaches may not only increase our understanding of the society under study but of economic processes in general.

SUMMARY

The division of labor, common to all human societies, has two obvious consequences. First, it makes humans dependent on one another and thus contributes to group solidarity. Second, it makes it necessary for some kind of distribution to occur to ensure individual and consequently group survival. Rules for distribution also become necessary when cooperative endeavor produces some indivisible but desirable product. Rules are necessary to settle the question, for example, of how the meat is divided if five hunters cooperated to kill the animal.

There are a number of ways in which distribution may occur. A simple society may have only one or two ways, whereas a complex society may have several. In small, simple societies where most contacts are direct and face-to-face, distribution is usually highly personal. Goods and services often travel exclusively along kinship (real, fictitious, or affinal°) lines. The guiding principle may be one of equivalent or identical reciprocity, wherein no individual is expected to gain at the expense of another and both must be satisfied. In this situation, goods and services are usually exchanged directly. Acceptance of a gift usually places the recipient under obligation to repay it either in kind or with some service. Distribution may occur without exchange, that is, through ceremonial distribution, where the donor expects to get his or her reward from someone or something other than the recipient (prestige from society, esteem from one's fellows, or good fortune from the supernatural), and through redistribution, reparation, and inheritance. Trade, in simple societies, is usually reciprocal, frequently between trading partners, with traditional prices and items. A true market does not usually occur in the simplest societies. In slightly more complex societies, if it does occur, it is usually based on some form of barter. Money does not usually come into prominence or general use until societies have reached a comparatively high level of complexity and sophistication. The next chapter deals with distribution, production, and consumption in one of these more complicated social systems.

4 Distribution of Needed Goods and Services: The Complex Societies

As societies grow larger, they necessarily also grow more complex. A system of distribution that is effective for fifty people will not work for a thousand. The same is true of the system of production, or subsistence. Hunting and gathering will not normally support a large number of people. The increase in size requires a variety of changes. Nonetheless, one of the factors that makes a society complex is that it usually continues to have many of the patterns common to small simple societies in addition to the new ones necessary to cope with its greater number of people.

In the following excerpt look for the same kinds of things that were mentioned in the Huron excerpt: what is considered valuable in the society, who gives what to whom, and under what circumstances. In addition, look for the new concepts and behavior patterns that are required by the larger society.

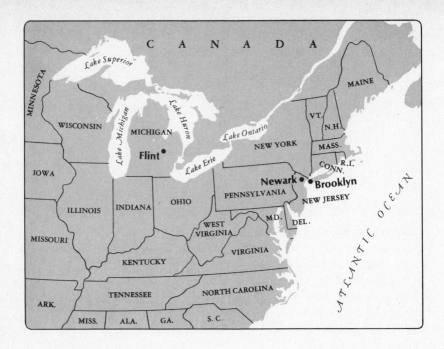

Captaining an Industry

. . . I was the eldest of five; four boys and a girl.* There was excitement for us all in the fact that I had a job in the mechanical field, so that my education would count. From the time I was eleven and began attending Brooklyn Polytechnic Institute I had been interested in mechanics, in engineering.

. . .

. . . Father certainly was not rich, but he had always managed to keep us in comfortable circumstances. As a rule, there was a cook in our kitchen, but if there were not, my mother well knew how to cook. She was the daughter of a Methodist Episcopal minister. Father was the son of a private-school master. Neither had any business forebears.

Well, I am bound to admit the first sight of my opportunity was disappointing. It was a gloomy, machinery-cluttered loft in a building in Market Street in Newark . . . I worked there as a draftsman for several months, pending removal of the business to near-by Harrison. But that was even more disappointing. . . .

*Abridged from *Adventures of a White-Collar Man* by Alfred P. Sloan, Jr., in collaboration with Boyden Sparkes (New York: Doubleday, Doran & Co., 1941), pp. 7–12, 18, 21–22, 24–27, 32–40, 43–44, 48–49, 57–59, 72–75, 77–78, 83–84, 86–87, 94, 98, 100, 102, 107, 133–135, 143–147. Reprinted by permission. The adventures begin in 1895.

Not far from a city dump on a weed-grown marshy plain was an old weather-worn building, like an overgrown barn. . . . Once the factory had been painted brown. Only one word describes it: "dirty." Smoke from the dump carried an acrid odor. Eventually across the wall nearest the railroad track there was lettered in black this legend: HYATT ROLLER BEARING COMPANY.

. . .

The antifriction bearing put at the disposal of engineers a workable instrumentality of priceless value. Hyatt was a gifted, practical, hard-working inventor in a period when inventors were able to work with reasonable hope of producing something as individuals rather than as cogs of great research organizations.

. . . Today John Wesley Hyatt—and many inventors of his time—with all his accomplishments would find himself regarded as scientifically illiterate. As a matter of fact, he would be. The modern research laboratories of industry demand men having years of training in some form of science, whose talents can be coordinated on a specific problem. . . .

. . .

I soon began to wonder how secure my job was. Literally, the business was being operated from week to week. Each payday was a crisis. . . . For months the gross business of the company had totaled only a few thousand dollars, but the pay roll and the other charges, for raw materials, freight and other things, had amounted to much more. The difference had always been supplied by Mr. Searles out of his own pocket. But Mr. Searles was becoming grumpier by the week, according to Pete [the paymaster]. Consequently all of us . . . were relieved each time Pete returned, bearing another check drawn against the Searles bank account.

. . .

The business was being operated badly. We seemed to capitalize only a fraction of our opportunities. Both Pete Steenstrup and I saw that plainly, but we could do little. . . .

. . .

Mr. Searles . . . decided that he would put no more money into Hyatt. . . . Unless some new backer could be found, it would be necessary to close down the works.

Because of the friendship of my father and Mr. Searles, they had discussed the situation . . . My father and a man named Donner, an associate of Mr. Searles in the American Sugar Refining Company, . . . bought into the company. I think Mr. Donner and my father each put up $2500. That was as far as Mr. Donner would go, but my father said he would advance more if the business showed any promise. Thereafter Pete, instead of going with the pay roll to Mr. Searles, went to my father. Pete and I had become partners.

. . . my salary was $175.00 a month. . . . We had six months to put the business on its feet, and we made good. With Pete selling and with me handling the production end, in our first six months we made a profit of $12,000. I'm not likely to forget that. Pete was given the title of sales manager. I was general manager.

. . .

But for a long time after we had shown we could make money the business faced a crisis each Saturday. Pay-roll worry has whitened a lot of hair in this country, mine included. . . . When a business is making money and expanding, it is to be expected that it will always be short of capital, simply because it is too successful in relation to its resources.

. . .

One day in our mail we found a letter from Kokomo, Indiana. A man named Elwood Haynes wanted to know about our bearings. He was making gasoline-powered road cars—automobiles. This inquiry came to us in 1899 and he had been making his gasoline-engine machines since 1894, never more than a few each year. . . .

. . . That was the beginning of our real adventures. It woke us up. If one automobile manufacturer wanted something better than ordinary greased wagon axles, why not sell all of them? . . .

. . .

On the first big order he got in Detroit, Pete recklessly called me on the long-distance telephone. . . . he had a trial order from the Olds Motor Works. They wanted 120 bearings, four for each rear axle on thirty automobiles. Pete was beside himself, and so was I.

. . .

A wildfire of experimenting in machine shops and barns was becoming a boom almost like a gold rush. In 1896, when Ransom E. Olds turned away from steam and made his first gasoline car, probably there were no more than thirty self-propelled carriages in America. But three years later, when we got our first order from Elwood Haynes, at least eighty separate business projects for making horseless carriages were under way. . . .

Speed! That was the most important word of all to Ransom E. Olds. He was a pioneer in the field of quantity production. . . . But to Henry M. Leland [general manager of Cadillac Motor Car Company] the most important word was not speed; it was precision. . . .

. . .

I remember how this was brought home to me. The white beard of Henry M. Leland seemed to wag at me, he spoke with such long-faced emphasis. . . .

"Mr. Sloan, Cadillacs are made to run, not just to sell."

. . .

"Your Mr. Steenstrup told me these bearings would be accurate, one like another, to within one thousandth of an inch. But look here!" I heard the click of his ridged fingernail as he tapped against a guilty bearing. "There is nothing like that uniformity.

. . . "Mr. Sloan, do you know why your firm received this order?"

. . . He pointed into the factory yard, where a lot of axles were piled like cordwood.

"The bearings in those axles out there did not stand up under the Cadillac load. . . . We canceled the order . . . Unless you can give me what I want, I'm going to put five-hundred Weston-Mott axles out there beside those other rejects."

That was a terrible threat. We'd lose the business of the Weston-Mott Axle Company. They'd have to change the design of their axle to use another bearing, which might end forever the relationship between Weston-Mott and Hyatt Roller Bearings. To Mr. Leland I spoke as softly as I could. . . .

. . .

But Mr. Leland interrupted, "You must grind your bearings. Even though you make thousands, the first and the last should be precisely alike." We discussed interchangeability of parts. A genuine conception of what mass production should mean really grew in me with that conversation.

I was an engineer and a manufacturer, and I considered myself conscientious. But after I had said good-by to Mr. Leland, I began to see things differently. I was determined to be as fanatical as he in obtaining precision in our work. An entirely different standard had been established for Hyatt Roller Bearings.

. . .

This may seem inconsequential, but truly it is of great importance, because the ability to produce large quantities of parts, each one just like the other or sufficiently alike, within a predetermined allowance of inaccuracy, is the foundation of mass production, as we understand that term today. . . .

. . .

In 1905 a considerable part of our bearings were shipped to Utica, New York, and one day I learned that one of our biggest customers was considering an important change. . . . The Weston-Mott Company, of Utica, was being tempted to move its axle plant out to Flint, a small town in Michigan. . . .

. . .

. . . The men trying to effect this change were William C. Durant and his partner, J. Dallas Dort. They were carriage manufacturers who had refinanced Buick.

That was a trivial incident of itself, but I believe it marks the first step in the integration of the automobile industry. Thereafter, bit by bit, we were to see a constant evolution bringing the manufacture of the motorcar itself and the manufacture of its component parts into a closer corporate relationship. . . .

. . .

Why had Durant and Dort been so anxious to get Weston-Mott's axle plant established next door to the new Buick factory in Flint? Every piece of the motorcar is essential in the sense that the automobile is not complete unless every part is available. Delay in delivery of any part stops the work. A dependable supply of parts might well make the difference between success and failure. Distance added uncertainty. It was natural, therefore, for the industry to correlate all its manufacturing within a rather narrow geographical area. . . .

. . .

The Hyatt Roller Bearing Company was dependable. We had to be in order to survive in the automobile-parts business. Literally, it was a capital offense to hold up a production line. . . .

Too much, too many jobs depended on keeping the schedule of deliveries. . . .

No excuse was any good if you failed to deliver. Often in the caboose of a freight train that carried a carload of Hyatt roller bearings you might find a Hyatt man who would cajole, bribe or fight, as the occasion demanded, to keep our bearings moving toward their destination. Eventually we kept two men in Buffalo, just to make absolutely sure no cars of Hyatt freight could go astray.

. . .

The confidence of the Ford organization in our roller bearings and in our ability to deliver was a most important factor in making Hyatt what it ultimately turned out to be.

. . .

Naturally, we had an indifferent product in our beginning at Hyatt. Our costs were necessarily high. But all that was true of . . . the automobile itself. To start out for a ride was an adventure; to return with no parts missing, and all parts functioning, was a miracle. . . .

Then the public seemed to be willing to pay a big price for an indifferent piece of apparatus—and like it. They forgot its shortcomings because it provided a new thrill. Fortunately before people's patience wore out, the cars improved.

Early automobiles were subject to frequent breakdowns. *(Automobile Manufacturers Association)*

As the parts of the motorcar became better, we continued to improve the standards of our Hyatt roller bearings. . . .

. . . Mr. Ford had determined that he had to have better steel in order to make stronger cars, at the same time avoiding the tendency to make them heavier and heavier. As a result of Mr. Wills' [C. Harold Wills] efforts, the answer was found in vanadium steel. When Mr. Ford prepared to introduce this new material into his Model T, I did the same at Hyatt.

. . .

. . . I had been so busy trying to make more and better Hyatt roller bearings that I had had little time to consider the economics of Hyatt's position. . . . my first realization of the importance of price as affecting volume was taught to me by Henry Ford. He had the vision to see that lower prices would increase volume up to the point that would justify such lower prices through reduced costs. . . .

. . .

. . . Ford was growing as no industrial enterprise had ever grown before. Hyatt Roller Bearing Company was obliged to grow with Ford, or else give way to some other supplier who would keep pace. The whole trick of that growth was to keep improving the technique of manufacture and to keep lowering the price of the car to reach an even bigger market. However, an even more amazing thing was the discovery that as the price of the car was reduced, wages could be raised. I well remember the consternation that spread through the industry when Mr. Ford made the dramatic announcement of a five-dollar-a-day minimum wage for his workmen. Many thought cars could not be sold on that basis. Who would pay the price?

At that time industry's practice was to set wages low, the lower the better. Reduce when you could, increase when you must. The power of an economic wage rate to stimulate consumption had not been realized. The five-dollar rate made good, but only because the Ford worker was enabled to produce more. From 1909–10 to 1916–17 the price of Ford's Model T was lowered year by year as follows: $950, $780, $690, $600, $550, $490, $360. The magical result of that was a volume which overwhelmingly justified the cost of the factory changes which preceded each cut in price. In those same years his production schedule grew as follows: 18,664; 34,528; 78,440; 168,220; 248,307; 308,213; 533,921; 785,432. . . .

. . .

. . . Closer integration was inevitable as the automobile industry passed out of the pioneering stage. But few had sufficient daring for the accomplishment of such vast trades as were even then in the making. William C. Durant was one. Ben Briscoe for a time was another.

. . .

Every deal made by William C. Durant for another automobile company after he organized the General Motors Company touched the interests of many parts manufacturers. Repeatedly I was to discover that Durant had taken over a Hyatt customer. . . .

. . .

. . . We were pouring profits into new buildings, new machines. It was a time of terrific growth in the industry. . . .

. . .

However, I was not altogether happy about the increase in our business. The process of integration was raising a problem for me. Actually, we had two gigantic customers. One was Ford, and one was General Motors. Suppose one or the other or both decided to make their own bearings? The Hyatt Roller Bearing Company might find itself with a plant far bigger than it could use and nowhere to go for new business. I had put my whole life's energy into Hyatt. Everything I had earned was there in bricks, machinery and materials. I was, I feared, out on a limb. But I was not alone. Other parts makers were out there, too.

. . .

. . . The same uncertainties that troubled makers of parts were valid worries of those who bought our parts. Suppose Buick or Willys-Overland or Ford suddenly got the idea it might be cut off from an important source of supply? Lack of one tiny part might hold up their assembly line. That fear was the nightmare of the business.

. . . In my heart I felt I would be acting soundly for our business if I made a deal with Durant.

. . .

. . . What they were forming was United Motors Corporation, destined to become an affiliate of General Motors.

. . .

They made me its president. . . . There were to be 1,000,000 shares of United Motors, and in 1916 there was a wild sound to that alone. I think we were about the first ever to issue so many shares. Today the practice of having sufficient shares to keep units of ownership small is generally approved. . . .

. . .

. . . in 1918 United Motors was consolidated with General Motors Corporation and later on was liquidated. I became a director of General Motors on November 7, 1918 and six weeks later, a vice-president. . . .

. . .

In bringing General Motors into existence, Mr. Durant had operated as a dictator. But such an institution could not grow into a successful organization under a dictatorship. Dictatorship is the most effective way of administration, provided the dictator knows the complete answers to all questions. But he never does and never will. . . . If General Motors were to capitalize its wonderful opportunity, it would have to be guided by an organization of intellects. A great industrial organization requires the best of many minds. . . .

. . .

Up to the time Mr. Durant left I had not had any direct responsibility for the manufacture of automobiles. My activities had been confined to the accessory group of operations. But I now began to have a broader scope as a sort of principal assistant to the president. Mr. du Pont ... gave us his time and the benefit of his great ability without limit until he resigned as president in May 1923, when I succeeded him.

The prime responsibility of General Motors now became mine. ...

... In the two years that Mr. du Pont had been president, much time had to be consumed in meeting the daily administrative problems. ... At the same time we had to give thought to a fundamental plan upon which we could build ... The prime consideration in that problem was a definite concept of management. The first step was to determine whether we would operate under a centralized or decentralized form of administration. ... We realized that in an institution as big as General Motors was even then ... any plan that involved too great a concentration of problems upon a limited number of executives would limit initiative, would involve delay, would increase expense, and would reduce efficiency and development. ... After forty years of experience in American industry, I would say that my concept of the management scheme of a great industrial organization, simply expressed, is to divide it into as many parts as consistently can be done, place in charge of each part the most capable executive that can be found, develop a system of co-ordination so that each part may strengthen and support each other part; thus not only welding all parts together in the common interests of a joint enterprise, but importantly developing ability and initiative through the instrumentalities of responsibility and ambition—developing men and giving them an opportunity to exercise their talents, both in their own interests as well as in that of the business.

. . .

My responsibilites had expanded enormously. At Hyatt, big as it was, I had been obliged to consider the interests of only a few stockholders, a few customers and three or four thousand workers. But as president of General Motors, I realized our thinking affected the lives of hundreds of thousands directly and influenced the economic welfare of many important communities, in some of which we were almost the sole provider. In some way, visible or invisible, as we expanded, the economic welfare of millions was becoming linked with the welfare of General Motors. ...

. . .

Bigness is essential in many branches of business and industry if the community is to be served on the best economic basis, and without bigness in some ways it cannot be served at all. ... On the other hand, some see danger in bigness. They fear the concentration of economic power that it brings with it. That is in a degree true. It simply means, however, that industrial management must expand its horizon of responsibility. ...

... An advancing standard of living means that more workers are becoming bigger and better consumers. Therefore industry's wage level is an important factor in this broader responsibility of industry because it involves the matter of purchasing power. ... Many believe the wage level is wholly at the discretion of management. That is not so ... Because, other things being equal, as we raise wages we increase costs and selling prices. ... Higher prices mean reduction in consumption, less employment. ... I wish most sincerely that there could be

One of the first assembly lines at a Ford plant—a production method that made automobiles cheap enough for most people to afford. *(Courtesy of the Ford Archives, Henry Ford Museum, Dearborn, Mich.)*

a broader recognition of the fundamental economic fact that the wage level depends on the amount of the productivity of the workers. Entirely so. Also the productivity of the worker depends upon the tools that the employer gives him to work with. The more efficient the tools, the more the worker produces and the higher wages he will inevitably receive.... the only true answer to the great question of more things for more people everywhere is more work efficiently performed....

THE HURON AND THE AUTOMOBILE INDUSTRY: COMPARISONS

How can Sloan's society be compared with the Hurons'? They seem like two entirely different worlds. The differences are great, of course, but there are also important similarities. Valuable things do exist in both societies, for example, and people make a considerable effort to get hold of them. Desire for esteem and respect motivate individuals in both societies, leading them to do things that at first glance would appear to defeat their attempts to accumulate the valuable goods in the society. Instead of hanging on to their valuables once they had obtained them, Hurons took pride in giving them away. Instead of saving his money, or spending it on personal luxuries, Sloan kept putting it back into his business, and was always worried that there was not enough (at least in the early expansion of the business). In both cases, however, although the short-range view would appear self-defeating, the long-range goal was an improved position in society, and in each case this aim was best accomplished in precisely the way the individuals went about it.

In both societies, relatives play a significant part. Hurons practiced intrigues to get public support for their sick relatives, gave reparations to compensate for wrongs relatives had committed, sponsored feasts to honor people who had fulfilled the dream desires of relatives, gave valuable things themselves to enable sick relatives to get better, and so on. Sloan owed his first opportunities to the active intervention of his father. Although the excerpt does not include it, the book specifically mentions that he got his first job through his father's friendship with Mr. Searles. Later, when Mr. Searles got tired of putting money into what appeared to be a losing cause, Sloan's father provided considerable financial support until the business was economically secure. (Notice also that while Hurons were involved with many relatives, Sloan was limited to very few. This is discussed at more length in Chapter 7.)

There is a general assumption that in industrialized societies, family ties are weak and, if strong, must be broken or they will impede economic advancement. The nuclear family° (parents and offspring) is said to be the only important family unit, and even *it* is on shaky ground in the modern world. This picture is not necessarily accurate. In a society changing from an agricultural to an industrial base, extensive family ties may prove a burden for individuals, true. For example, if one person in a large family discovers a way to make money in a society just beginning to shift to a cash economy, the financial demands of his relatives may make his economic progress impossible by preventing him from building up a store of capital, or doing what Sloan did— pouring his money back into the business. Unless the family is willing to postpone gratification, even to sacrifice immediate comforts, the only way an individual can save or invest is to break family ties. The same is true in many small societies when an individual tries to make money by opening a store or small business: relatives demand credit, refuse to pay, insist on special prices below cost, and in general make it impossible for the enterprise to succeed (Bauer and Yarney 1957; Higgins 1959). This is only one side of the story, however. Lack of business know-how rather than family ties may be the real culprit in many cases (Isaac 1971:294). Furthermore, there are instances of whole families or kindreds° dedicating themselves to increasing capital or building a business (Levy 1964:225–230; Wilkinson 1964:123–127). Under these circumstances, family ties may be essential for success rather than being a hindrance.

One of America's richest families in 1937. Left to right: John D. Rockefeller, Jr. (son of the founder of Standard Oil) and his sons David, Nelson, Winthrop, Laurence, and John D. III. By the time John, Jr., died the family had already given away more than $3 billion. *(U.P.I.)*

Once a society becomes more heavily industrialized, or the wealth of an individual reaches a point where it can provide for a large family, family ties may once again become useful rather than a burden. The Kennedys, Rockefellers, Rothchilds, du Ponts, and others are examples of families in which strong kinship ties actually helped increase the power and wealth of individual members, as well as of the family as a whole. In turn, the ties were strengthened by the improved economic position of the family.

Comparing the excerpts again, accumulation of wealth in both American and Huron societies was a goal, but not a final one; Hurons accumulated wealth to give it away, Sloan to reinvest it. But in both societies the accumulated wealth was used as a means to build prestige and influence. Although American culture, in comparison with that of the Huron, did not strongly pressure Sloan to be generous or to consider public welfare before his own, yet this pressure was not entirely absent. The book from which the excerpt was taken shows a clear awareness of responsibility to the public and consideration for the common good. Sloan's sincerity might be questioned. Did he really feel the sense of responsibility he expressed? After all, he was a Captain of Industry, and such people's sense of social responsibility has been debated. Sloan's sincerity, however, is irrelevant to the point being discussed, that is, an awareness of social pressure for responsibility and concern for the public welfare. As has been mentioned earlier, people do not have to feel generous to act that way in public. If Sloan had not believed the attitudes he expressed would draw public approval, he probably would not have mentioned them. Consequently, his statement, whether sincere or not, indicates that social pressure toward socially responsible behavior existed in American culture at this time. And the extent of the contributions made by rich persons to various organizations that benefit the general public also testifies to the existence of some such social pressure. If the *only* motivation for charitable contributions were to avoid taxes, they could be made anonymously. The fact that individuals usually want their name associated with large contributions indicates that they expect to receive some public approval for their act. Nonetheless, it is clear that Hurons were under much more direct pressure to be socially responsible.

At least part of the difference in the degree of direct pressure in the two societies is due to the great disparity in size between them. Direct social pressure is always much easier to apply in small groups than in large ones (see Chapters 5 and 6).

MONEY

Major differences between American and Huron practices result from the cash economy. Use of money as a medium of exchange has many consequences. The Hurons did not use money at the time of the excerpt, although in later years porcelain (glass) beads assumed many of the functions of money. Shell beads made into belts or collars had been in use prior to contact with Europeans, but apparently had not served as money in any sense. The belts and collars had many of the characteristics of money,° however. They could be broken down into individual beads—small change, as it were; the shells were relatively standardized, durable, portable, and remained stable in value for years. Having the characteristics of money, wampum (beads) could and quickly did assume the functions of money under the impetus of European contact. Wampum was legal tender in some parts of the frontier. The value of the beads was relatively stable in the colonies; it was even put into church poor boxes, and was occasionally stolen (Munsell 1850:8–10, 90–91; Orchard 1929:63). It was used as a standard of value, a store of wealth, a source of ready capital,° and a medium of exchange. Insofar as it fulfilled these functions, it was equivalent to money. Shells, cacao beans, and various other items have served the same purposes in other parts of the world.

Money is often symbolic of value rather than valuable in itself. That is, usually the thing serving as money cannot be eaten, used for tools or weapons, lived in, or otherwise directly utilized to improve one's chances for survival. Even things like cacao beans, tobacco, or whisky, that have been used as money and are consumable, are not absolutely necessary for survival, however enjoyable their use may seem. Until the industrial period arrived, precious metals and gems had little practical utility, although now some, such as diamonds, silver, and so on, are used in certain industries. The value of money decreases, sometimes seriously, in times of crisis. During a famine, for example, people may not be willing to sell food for any amount of money, or conversely, may be willing to part with all their possessions in exchange for food. The Judeo-Christian story of Joseph in Egypt claims to account for the pharaoh's right to ownership of all the land, relating how people gave their money, their animals, and finally their land for grain during a prolonged famine (Genesis 47:13–26). In India, agricultural workers sometimes demand a share of the harvest instead of money for their wages, since at least they can eat that (Srinivas 1955:14). Even gold or diamonds may be valueless when food is scarce, because neither can be eaten.

Money makes it possible to have a more complex and also a more impersonal exchange system. Under a barter° system, exchange can get cumbersome, since the things to be traded have to be brought to market and the items traded for brought home. Exchange usually takes place on a face-to-face basis. Exceptions such as dumb, or silent, barter are possible, but rare. Trade in a market situation where there are a number of buyers and sellers and the price asked and received by each depends on the decisions of the others is usually universalistic exchange, in which decisions are made on the basis of technical factors such as cost and quality, with emphasis on the exchange rather than on social factors (Belshaw 1965:79–80, 114). But even in a marketlike situation, barter remains personal because of the face-to-face contact of the participants.

In barter, the individual is simultaneously a buyer and a seller. In exchanging one's chickens for potatoes, one is simultaneously selling chickens and buying potatoes. Consequently, there is little specialization. The presence of cash makes greater specialization and greater impersonality easier. Increased specialization is the hallmark of the complex societies. It is one of the distinguishing characteristics of civilization. It is associated with what the anthropologist Titiev calls one of the "laws" of cultural development—the declining percentage of individual knowledge (Titiev 1963:376–378). That does not mean that people know less now than they used to; it means only that individuals know less of the total knowledge available, because the total is so much larger now. In a small, simple society, each adult individual may know almost everything there is to know in the culture: each person knows just about as much as everyone else. As societies grow larger, however, there is simply too much to know. No one can possibly know it all. The larger the society grows, and more complex it is, the less of the total any individual can know.

OCCUPATIONAL SPECIALIZATION

Comparison of the Ragueneau and Sloan excerpts illustrates the difference between the two in occupational specialization. A Huron was normally a producer, a distributor, and a consumer, sometimes almost at the same time. A few people engaged in trade with other native Americans and with Europeans. In

A meat market in Peking, where exchange is based on the personal relationship between buyer and seller. *(Marc Riboud/Magnum)*

most cases, however, the individual doing the trading had obtained or made the things he was trading with—he had killed the animals, worked in the fields, or made the artifacts, or his wife may have tanned the skins. Occupational specialization was minimal.

The Sloan excerpt provides a tremendous contrast. Here occupational specialization was extensive. Sloan's original company, Hyatt, did not make a car or even a major part of a car. It made only bearings, some of which were used in axles, most of which were put into cars. Sloan himself did not sell, design, or even make the bearings personally. What he did was to organize their production. Hyatt invented and designed bearings, unnamed workers made them, and Pete Steenstrup sold them. Other individuals packed them for shipping, transported them to the railroad, and loaded them on trucks. Just getting them to their destination was the work of hundreds of men Sloan did not even know. Although the company employed people to help get the shipments through on time, Sloan never had any personal or direct contact with the railroad workers who also had a part in the delivery.

This lack of direct contact with all the people involved in production, or in distribution, is characteristic of a complex society. Among the Huron, even if some individuals did not produce a particular thing themselves, they were usually acquainted with or had some direct access to the person who did. Even

The New York Stock Exchange, an impersonal exchange system where buyer never meets seller. *(Cornell Capa/Magnum)*

if they were not specialists in something, they were usually familiar enough with any given speciality to evaluate the specialist's performance accurately. The Sloan excerpt indicates how difficult, if not impossible, this sort of familiarity and access are in a large, complex society. Mr. Leland, for example, was not able to evaluate the ability of the Hyatt factory to perform to his specifications; he had to trust the salesman's promise. His dissatisfaction with the first results indicates that either Steenstrup (the salesman) lied, or that even he was not able to predict Hyatt's performance accurately. The presence of discarded axles, "stacked like cordwood" in the factory yard, indicated that the experience with Hyatt was not unique. When evaluation must wait for the results of performance, there may be a great deal of waste, as was the case with the axles. Even worse, the consequences may be fatal, when evaluation can be made only after the performance of such specialists as medical doctors, pharmacists, and airplane pilots. Some other social reactions to the problem of evaluation are suggested in Chapters 5 and 6.

Specialization has additional consequences. It results in increased interdependence of the people in the society. In the simplest societies, although individuals are not entirely self-sufficient, extended families may be. The Vermont farm family in Chapter 2 was not far from being self-sufficient. Farming villages in agricultural societies need little that community members cannot provide. Luxuries may come from outside, but survival does not depend on anyone beyond the community group. The larger and more complex a society grows, however, the more specialization increases, the less each individual does for himself, and the more people depend on each other. (This topic is explored further in the next two chapters.) In Sloan's day, American society had already grown quite complex and was in the process of growing even more so. Sloan was aware of the significance of this, as the excerpt reveals, for example, when he mentioned that the thinking of the General Motors board of directors "affected the lives of hundreds of thousands directly and influenced the economic welfare of many important communities" and added that "the economic welfare of millions was becoming linked with the welfare of General Motors."

The Huron system was simple: there were relatively few different things for people to do, and fairly direct contact between the producer, the distributor, and the consumer. Sloan's society supported a highly complex system with hundreds of different specializations and a tight interdependence between people who never knew or even saw one another. Such a society is heavily dependent on blind trust. Unless Durant could trust Sloan to deliver on time, for example, he could not be sure he could produce and sell cars, or (ultimately) pay his workers. Sloan was dependent on the reliable performance of the railroad workers. The factory workers at Ford, Weston-Mott, and Cadillac were equally dependent on Sloan and his workers. How could anyone be sure that all these unknown individuals would perform as required? Obviously, since most of the interdependent people did not even know each other, no one could rely on the informal social pressure and the direct influence on their fellow citizens that was available to the Huron. Hurons who did not do what they were supposed to could be beaten, could have their possessions confiscated, or their property burned by the people they injured. Sloan, Durant, Leland, and all the unnamed workers involved in the production of automobiles had no such recourse.

Sloan explains one of the levers available in a complex society. Leland threatened to cancel his order if Sloan did not make the axle bearings to precise specifications. If Weston-Mott lost Cadillac business, Hyatt would lose Weston-Mott's business, would not be able to meet its payroll, and would probably be forced out of business entirely. Sloan acted to preserve his business, but he did more. He accepted the reasoning of Leland about the need for standardization and incorporated it into his own thinking. He passed it along to his workers by insisting they follow the specifications exactly. If they did not, his lever was to fire them. How much of Leland's reasoning Sloan's employees accepted (or even knew about) is not certain. Studies of factories show that quite a few workers regard the demand for precision as an annoyance to be evaded when possible (Selekman 1947:120–121), which would seem to indicate that they either do not know or reject the rationale behind precision manufacture (or are hostile to their bosses and indifferent to the quality of the product).

The threat by Leland and the consolidation process initiated by Durant are characteristic of a universalistic system. Leland and Durant were making economic decisions on the basis of technical factors such as quality, convenience, and cost. They were not overtly influenced by personal, social factors. The Huron on the other hand operated on a particularistic basis. Economic decisions were made on the basis of social and personal factors—for example, what their relationship was with the individual or what the individual's relationship was with the community.

The excerpt reveals levers one company could use on another (cancel or increase orders) or on workers (hire or fire them). It also mentions another lever employers could use on workers—wages. Ford increased wages until they were the highest in the industry at that time, believing that that way he could get and keep better workers, and encourage more production from the workers he had.

New York's major newspapers were shut down by strikes several times during the 1960s. Here, strikers picket the *New York Times* building. *(U.P.I.)*

Workers are by no means helpless in obtaining better conditions from employers, although they must act together rather than individually to have the most effect. Americans are all familiar with the strike as an employee technique for influencing employers. Employers may respond to the strike by closing their doors entirely. When this tactic is used to force strikers back to work, it is called a lockout, but occasionally owners go out of business completely because of a strike. Several newspapers in New York City, for example, were forced to close down permanently as a result of prolonged strikes. Strikes, therefore, may have results workers do not intend, so cautious workers resort to it only in extreme cases.

The customer is in the most precarious position of all in the economic pattern, in one sense, although in another sense he has the most power. Like workers, customers must act in groups to have any effect, but because customers are scattered, and do not usually know one another, effective organization is difficult. When consumers do organize, however, boycotts (refusals to buy) have been powerful enough to force businesses to change practices or close. Special publications today—such as *Consumer Reports,* published by the Consumer Union—advise consumers about products and make organization somewhat easier. One form of unorganized customer power is public taste, which

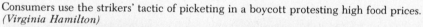

Consumers use the strikers' tactic of picketing in a boycott protesting high food prices. *(Virginia Hamilton)*

often changes unpredictably, forcing some businesses to close and allowing others to expand. The development of the auto industry is an example. As that industry increased, industries connected with horses and horse-drawn transportation declined.

Today business tries to predict public taste through market research and analysis, or control it through advertising, which strongly affects public buying habits by informing people of new products, creating new desires, or persuading people that one company's product is better than another's. The advertising industry, whose members are quite knowledgeable about how to influence opinion, is constantly under attack from one source or another for creating artificial needs, for lying or misleading the public in a variety of ways, and for contributing to a wasteful consumer attitude that puts unnecessary harmful pressure on the natural environment. Defenders of advertising insist that it informs the public and serves a vital function in the economy. As usual, there is some truth on both sides of the argument.

The consumer has still one more recourse in the United States when boycotts fail: government intervention. Laws can be passed and enforced against misleading advertising, against the adulteration of food products, against conspiracies to raise prices unnecessarily, and against various other business practices that could harm the consumer. Local and federal governments can and do set standards of safety, purity, ethics, and so on. In other words, consumers can get the government to act for them but, again, this requires cooperative action on the part of the consumers. (Questions of how groups organize and how public decisions are made are discussed in greater detail in the next two chapters.)

None of the levers mentioned in this section will work under all circumstances. In most cases, alternatives have to be available: a consumer cannot boycott a food producer unless another source of food is present. A monopoly in any desirable commodity puts the consumer at a great disadvantage, since alternatives do not exist, leaving government intervention as almost the only potentially effective avenue of protection. (If the government is also the producer—that is, where there is a governmental monopoly—the consumer is in an almost hopeless position; to get any relief the government must be influenced, and channels for doing this, other than rebellion, may not be available.) A monopoly similarly handicaps the worker. If there is no other employer in the area, a worker cannot safely threaten to quit. On the other hand, one problem that strikers have is the availability of alternatives to the employer, that is, the presence of other potential workers. A strike will be ineffective if the employer can simply hire other workers. That is why strikers usually establish a picket line—to keep other workers from taking over their jobs. In other words, competition between workers and between consumers weakens their position, while it strengthens that of business. On the other hand, competition among businesses provides worker, consumer, and other businesses with a lever to ensure quality performance and productivity, while it weakens the position of individual businesses. Competition is a two-edged sword.

Economic competition, rather than social pressure, served to ensure the necessary levels of performance in Sloan's society. In Huron society, where individuals had to provide required gifts or lose status, competition was social as well as economic. Emulative competition°—exerting oneself to do better than a competitor—can be used to great advantage by a society, since it harnesses individual energies that can then be channeled to produce social benefits. But competition can also be destructive.

It can take the form of attempting to pull down rather than to outdo a competitor; this predatory competition° is socially disruptive. The resulting battles can stall any attempts at change or improvement (Richards, C. 1975). In some societies, the individuals who move out ahead of the majority in any way are faced with strong social condemnation. Individuals and group members are ridiculed, scorned, and ostracized until they give up the new behavior. If new possessions are acquired or made, they may be damaged by those who do not have them (Madsen 1964:21–23). On one American Indian reservation, a woman was afraid to have plumbing put into her house because "people would say I stole the money" (Richards, C. 1957:24). In a Latin-American community, a European immigrant was forced to give up her varied diet of vegetables and subsist almost entirely on rice because her in-laws accused her of trying to copy the upper classes. Since alienating her in-laws might have resulted in losing her husband, she was forced to modify her diet. There was no question of the in-laws trying to outdo their new daughter-in-law by providing an even better diet; they just forced her to give up hers. In predatory competition the reaction of the majority of the group destroys any advantage obtained by individuals and thus restores the status quo.

The two forms of competition are different in their results for individuals and for societies. In the United States, the first type of competition is regarded by the middle-class majority as "healthy," and the second type as counterproductive and harmful. Several different minority groups, however, either do not distinguish between the two kinds of competition or are familiar only with the predatory type, and consequently condemn all competition as destructive. By not encouraging the first type, they are apt to practice the second; the result is resistance to change and the preservation of the status quo unless the whole group can change at once.

Competition is closely related to cooperation. Sloan touches on it only lightly in the excerpt, but describes various examples in the book. In cooperative, or team, competition,° individuals cooperate with others in their group but compete with other groups. Sports often provide examples of team competition. The rivalry of Ford and General Motors is an example Sloan describes; nationalism and warfare might be examples on a larger scale. Team competition can take both the emulative and the predatory forms described above, with the same results for groups as for individuals.

One of the reasons for confusion about cooperation and competition is that people have not carefully distinguished units or levels of analysis. In team competition in sports, for example, a game can be analyzed in hundreds of ways. It can be studied from an economic point of view, in terms of how much spectators pay for tickets; the wages of players, coaches, managers, and other participants; the cost of operating the stadium; what concessionaires make; and

so on. It can be studied from a psychological point of view, as leisure-time activity, as a profession, and in other ways. It can be studied as a single event or as hundreds of individual events. Participants can be divided into categories such as management, coaching staff, players, spectators. If the teams are considered together, and the game is the unit of analysis, the behavior is competitive, one team against the other. If each team is considered separately, however, the same behavior is cooperative—although if the sport in question is football, there is another possible level, since there are offensive and defensive units on each team that may compete with each other. Considered at an individual level, a single action—for example, blocking for a running back in football—may be simultaneously (1) competitive in regard to a member of the opposing team; (2) cooperative in regard to the running back; and (3) competitive toward other members of the same team who play the same position, or who are also expected to block for the runner.

A particularly significant aspect of this last complication, which may be called competitive cooperation,° is that often competition and cooperation cannot be separated by either level *or* unit of analysis because the individuals involved are both competing and cooperating *with the same people at the same time.* Another example would be an old-fashioned husking bee or barn raising in which people work together to get a task done (husking someone's corn, or building someone's barn) but also try to outdo each other at certain tasks. The one who husks the most corn, or hauls the most lumber, or splits the most shingles is rewarded.

Bigelow indicates his awareness of the close relationship between competition and cooperation in his book *Dawn Warriors.* The main thesis is what Bigelow calls "cooperation for conflict" (1969:8–11). Many of human beings' most savage acts against other humans have been cooperative endeavors. People who thoughtlessly condemn competition without distinguishing the kind of competition they reject do not realize that they are, as the expression goes, throwing the baby out with the bath water. By condemning *all* competition instead of just *predatory* competition, they are unknowingly rejecting not only a significant factor in social change but also an aspect of cooperation itself. Competition and cooperation are not mutually exclusive behaviors or values.

CONCEPTS EXCLUSIVE TO INDUSTRIALIZED SOCIETY

The Sloan excerpt reveals several concepts characteristic of highly industrialized societies but not of hunting and gathering or agriculturally oriented ones. Money, the high degree of specialization, and the interdependence of individuals and various segments of society have already been discussed. Impersonal economic levers for ensuring proper job performance have also been men-

Amish men and boys cooperate to raise a barn for one of the group. The barn owner will reciprocate with labor for his helpers. *(David S. Strickler/Monkmeyer)*

tioned. Although, as can be seen in the next chapter, economic levers are used in all societies, it is the impersonality with which they are applied—the universalistic aspect—that is unique to the complex society. The market is also characteristic of complex societies. In societies where money is widely used in exchange, the market can become different in character from a market based on barter. The increased impersonality of the cash market has already been mentioned, but it should be noted in addition that the introduction of money makes the introduction of other symbols such as checks or stock shares relatively easy.

Ownership of a particular item of property in simple societies is usually limited to an individual, or to a group bound together by kinship and marriage ties. Property may be tangible (land, meat, weapons), or intangible (a song, a magical spell, a formula for medicine), but it is usually a relatively unified thing, easily identifiable. In complex societies, on the other hand, ownership may be divided into many parts and spread among strangers who not only are not related to each other but do not even know each other's names. The property owned may be a business organization (with more people in administration alone than there are in an entire small society), located in several different parts of the world, and engaged in production, distribution, and consumption of a variety of things. Ownership is symbolically represented by stock shares that are themselves bought and sold symbolically by verbal or written promises of people who do not own them but merely represent the owners. This sort of paper transaction regularly goes on in the nearest approximation of the theoretically "perfect market" that current technology and human capabilities permit —the stock market, where stock brokers, representing owners, sell shares of stock, representing ownership, to other brokers. Even money (the symbol of wealth) or crops that have not yet been harvested (symbolic food, in other words) can be bought and sold at this level of abstraction. The market *principle,* however, is the same as in the barter market, that is, a number of buyers and sellers dealing in a variety of things whose prices vary according to what is asked and offered by each buyer and seller. The theoretically perfect market would be one in which the amount offered and taken in each transaction in a commodity would be simultaneously known to all the buyers and sellers. The barter market does not come very close to the theoretical ideal, but the stock market does. The stock market, therefore, is a unique characteristic of the most complex societies, related to but also different from the barter market and the other forms of exchange that occur in simpler societies.

Another of the concepts characteristic of complex societies is profit. As mentioned earlier, redistribution and reciprocal exchange—the only distributive mechanisms available in most simple societies—lack profit in the economic sense. As the term is generally used, *profit* means the excess of returns over the outlay of capital; more technically, it refers to the surplus product of industry after deducting wages, cost of raw material, rent, and charges (*Oxford Dictionary* 1955:1953). Capital refers to wealth in any form that is or could be used to produce more wealth. In a hunting and gathering society, where an individual distributes what he or she has killed or gathered, there is no money, no capital outlay, and no profit, in this technical sense. Reward, which may be a profit in a humanistic sense, is not the same thing as a profit in the narrower technical economic sense. In an individually owned business, any surplus (profits in a technical sense) belongs to the owner. It could be regarded as the owner's wage. When there are many owners, the profits may be divided among them, as their wages for having risked their wealth to help the business. Complaints about excess profits would indicate that members of the society do not feel the owner or owners deserve the amount of "wages" they are getting.

This is a simplistic way of looking at a complex subject, of course, but even at this elementary level it is apparent that the questions of who gets the profits (what happens to the surplus of industry's production) lies at the bottom of major ideological arguments in the world today. People in the so-called capitalist countries believe that the profits of most industries legitimately belong to individual owners. People in so-called socialist or communist countries believe surplus products of industry should belong to the state, which is identified with the people. The question of how much profit is "legitimate" is also hotly debated. Since both of these controversies are matters of "should" and "ought," opinions about them are not easily subject to objective support. Why "should" the state get the surplus products? Why "should" private owners get them? Why "should" company X make such high profits? How much surplus "should" there be? Arguments in this country over the level of profits of the oil companies during the recent shortage crisis show how emotional and confusing the controversy can become. As is the case with many such arguments, there may be no "right" answer. The answer people in any particular society decide to be the right one will depend on the interplay of survival demands and the several different sets of values that are applied by those people at that time in that society. (The ways members of various societies try to settle these vexing issues will be examined in the next two chapters.)

Still another concept, unique to complex societies, is that of high-turnover–low-unit profit leading to increased total profits. Ford was able to increase wages to his workers and at the same time lower prices. He did this through more efficient (less expensive) production and by increased sales, which brought in a greater total profit even though the profit on each individual car was smaller. (As an illustration: An item priced at $100 makes a $50 profit, but only 10 are sold each week. This provides $500 a week profit. The same profit can be made if 100 a week are sold at $55, and twice as much profit if 1,000 are sold at $51. Since there are usually more people who can pay $51 than $100, the potential market is greater and so is the potential profit at lower prices. If, in addition, the cost of production drops to $25 as a result of the larger number being produced, the advantages of the lower price are even more obvious.) Ford demonstrated clearly that in an industrialized society, under certain circumstances, *everyone*—workers, consumers, and managers—can get more.

The significance of this has not spread to all societies, particularly those still in or recently emerging from an agricultural economy, whose members tend to retain the traditional orientation (even in the United States it is occasionally forgotten). In an agricultural society, unless new land can be brought under cultivation or new technology increases crop yield, the only way one person can get more is at the expense of someone else. People in such societies tend to think of the good things in life as strictly limited in quantity, and therefore may regard all success in life as occurring at the expense of someone else. The anthropologist George Foster called this the image of limited good and said it was characteristic of peasant (agriculturally oriented) societies (1965:293–315).

It is possible to have other views of the world, such as the concept that the good things of life are unlimited and require only effort to be accessible to anyone; or that the "good things" in our worldly existence are quite irrelevant and that the afterlife will provide every conceivable good thing to anyone who has earned them by proper performance in this life. Individuals who hold either of these world views are not likely to regard themselves as gaining at the expense of someone else. Nomadic herders with ample pasture lands, and societies that are growing geographically or economically, are less likely to hold the image of limited good than societies that are agriculturally based with limited land.

The Sloan excerpt indicates another trend of American industry: consolidation combined with limited autonomy. First, the automobile industry physically and economically consolidated the manufacture of various parts in order to ensure the economic safety of the main manufacturer. Sloan felt Durant had shown insight and wisdom in consolidating the different companies into one area and under one control. He felt Durant was a dictator, however, and dictatorship an effective form of administration "only so long as the dictator knows all the answers." Such omniscience was impossible in an organization as complex as General Motors became. Sloan's philosophy of organization was quite different. He felt that the best individuals should be selected on the basis of technical factors (knowledge, skill, and competence) and then placed in charge of a department and given the freedom and authority to run it, so long as each maintained the necessary coordination with other departments. This particular philosophy has been widely followed in American industrial organization and has led to a success that has aroused envy and admiration all over the world (Servan-Schreiber 1968:203). More recently, the philosophy has led to the development of special "problem-oriented" production teams, planning boards, consultant firms, and other variously named groups created or employed for a specific task, given considerable autonomy for the duration, and then disbanded or dismissed when the task is finished. These temporary, high-powered groups form the basis of what Alvin Toffler calls "Ad-hocracy" and regards as the inevitable successor to bureaucracy in the superindustrialized state (Toffler 1970:109).

Another innovation that the Sloan excerpt illustrates is one that has had a profound effect on the American economy. In 1916 United Motors issued a million shares of stock, an amount almost unheard of at the time. There is no space to discuss this development in detail, but issuing large quantities of low-priced shares has made it possible for millions of relatively poor people to take part in the development of and profit from American industry. In 1916 this was a risky game, because the small stockholder was (and still is in many countries) ignorant, powerless, and unprotected. The development of the Securities Ex-change Commission (SEC), the passage of laws requiring disclosure of financial matters, the demands that companies trading large amounts of stock maintain certain standards of business procedure, and so on, have provided a measure of protection to the small stockholder that is unequaled in other parts of the world. It has made investment of small amounts of money both safer and more profitable, with the result that industry has been able effectively to tap this generally unavailable source of development capital. In other parts of the world, people put any surplus cash into land or hoard it, rather than invest it in industry. There are always more poor people than rich, so a small amount of money from many poor people often adds up to a larger total amount than any rich person can (or dares) risk. The American economic system has resulted in a much wider sharing of both risks and profits than occurs in other areas of the industrialized world. For example, statistics show that one out of every six adults in the United States owns stock. In 1968 almost 55 percent of the individ-ual shareholders had incomes under $10,000, and large corporate or institu-tional holdings amounted to only 22.4 percent of the total value of stocks (New York Stock Exchange 1969:43–45). A recent decline in the number of small stockholders caused such concern that the SEC immediately moved to encour-

Workers using a technique known as the sit-down strike at a Fisher automobile plant. *(U.P.I.)*

age small investors again by abolishing certain brokerage commissions on small orders and requiring agencies to deal in the smaller purchases instead of refusing all but large orders. Television commercials have also expressed the value of stocks to the small investor, indicating that some brokerage houses share the concern of the SEC. It is too early to tell how effective these moves will be, but the fact that they were made so quickly indicates recognition of the importance the private, relatively low-income investor has to the economy.

There are problems and drawbacks, of course. Ownership of large businesses has become so diffuse that the "owners" often exert little real control over the direction and procedures of the company they "own." Management of the business, far from being controlled by the founder or by a man vitally interested in it, often is controlled by paid employees who may have little real concern for the company or for the public. Even when they own large blocks of shares, people in management are apt to be more concerned with ensuring the profits of stockholders than in making risky innovations or costly but socially responsible changes. Management of large business is less susceptible to public pressure (except from a significant number of stockholders) than is the individual owner. The consequences of this are obvious in the areas of minority relations and environmental pollution. People such as Ralph Nader attempt to make large concerns more responsive to public opinion by trying to persuade the owners of large amounts of stock to make their position known on matters that affect the public welfare. In the book (although not in the excerpt) Sloan points out the need for this kind of responsibility on the part of big business, and implies that if large companies like General Motors do not develop some form of responsibility, the public will force it on them. His words have a prophetic ring.

The last sentence of the Sloan excerpt contains a major part of the credo of the modern industrialized world. Although it is basically true, there is some controversy over whether it is *desirable*. Modern methods of mass production are infinitely more efficient in producing *things* than the old handicraft techniques. If everything in industrial societies had to be made by hand, we would have a world in which the very few live in luxury while the majority lack almost all material comforts—a situation that in fact currently exists in many parts of the world, and that was characteristic of all nations and empires until less than a century ago.

In most highly industrialized nations today, although there may be wide gaps between rich and poor, the average citizen has comforts his ancestors could not have dreamed of. Some of these did not exist a hundred years ago, of course—electric lights, television, washing machines, refrigerators, indoor plumbing, central heating. But others—privately owned homes with several rooms; oranges, melons, and fresh vegetables in winter; fashionable, easily cleaned clothes; private transportation—are the results of a technological revolution that has brought incredible material prosperity to the majority of people in the United States and a few other high-technology societies. An ordinary worker in the United States lives in luxury hardly surpassed by members of the elite in some underdeveloped countries.

None of this material affluence could exist without techniques that make it possible to produce an enormous quantity and variety of goods quickly and cheaply. Such production strains the environment; the United States consumes a highly disproportionate share of the world's resources. Partly because of this, people in other countries (and in the United States itself) have become highly critical of America, which is called a selfish and ruthless exploiter of poorer nations. Unfortunately, however, the population of the rest of the world is not really interested in decreasing American consumption so much as it is in raising its own living standard to the level of that of the United States. No country seems about to dedicate its citizenry to remaining forever without the material luxuries commonplace in the United States. Instead, communist, socialist, and capitalist countries *all* seem to be making every effort to industrialize so that they too can produce more goods more cheaply for their citizens. The main argument dividing countries today is not so much what they are trying to do as how they are trying to do it. All of them at least give lip service to the goal of increasing production, but argue about the "best" (both most efficient and most ethical) way of attaining that goal.

SUMMARY

The excerpt from Alfred Sloan's autobiography provides a firsthand account of some of the events that took place during the expansionist phase of the automobile industry, certainly one of the prime examples of American industrial organization. Comparison of this excerpt with the one on the Huron reveals both similarities and differences. Social pressure for economically responsible behavior, economic levers, and desire for prestige and esteem exist in both societies, but a cash economy, increased specialization, increased interdependence, and greater impersonality in economic transactions differentiate the complex American system from the relatively simpler Huron one.

Simple societies distribute goods through reciprocal exchange and redistributive techniques. Distribution in highly complex societies may include these patterns as well as market distribution, a method that is rare but not entirely absent in simple societies (Pospisil 1964:18). This form of distribution or something similar to it may be almost inevitable in large societies with a great deal of specialization. Distribution and exchange in the market are frequently impersonal, and in large complex societies there usually is no direct face-to-face contact between producer and consumer. Economic decisions are made on the basis of price, quality, and other technical factors, rather than on the basis of personal relationships between people, although these continue to operate informally to a limited extent. There is usually some medium of exchange (money) in terms of which all goods and services are valued.

Studies of a society with a market system tend to be complicated by the fact that systems of reciprocal exchange and ceremonial or redistributive distribution coexist with it. In addition, personal and social factors are almost never entirely absent in economic decisions, which adds confusion to the study of a system that is theoretically supposed to be impersonal.

The values of a society interacting with the size of the society and the practical demands of the technoenvironmental situation determine the way in which its distribution system works. The goals toward which people strive and the manner in which they try to attain those goals are determined by what members of the society agree are "good" and "proper" goals and methods, as well as by what they can produce with their technology in the physical environment. In the following two chapters, social goals are discussed—how they are developed, how a society deals with people who do not use the approved means for attaining goals, and how such factors as population size are related to forms of organization and technology.

5 Maintaining Order and Organization: The Small Societies

One of the characteristics that distinguishes a group or a society from a simple collection of people is interdependence. When people are interdependent, individuals must behave predictably or the society cannot run smoothly. Humans are social animals, and to survive both individual needs and the prerequisites for group continuity must be met. The first two chapters focused on how individual needs are met through group living. Chapters 3 and 4 dealt with the ways individual and group needs of distribution were met. Chapter 5 again deals with problems of meeting both individual and group needs, this time for order and organization. The group protects the individual and thus enhances individual survival, but to keep conflicting interests from disrupting the group, the individual must be required to give up a certain amount of freedom of choice and action in some areas. By complying with this requirement, the individual gains freedom of choice and action in other areas, and more important, gains freedom from certain kinds of life threats. On balance, members of a group must gain more than they lose through group living or the group is not likely to survive, because its individual members die or leave. Societies differ widely in how much freedom of action they allow and how much conformity they demand, but in no group are individuals free to do exactly and only what they please. Such a society (in which all members did exactly as they pleased) could exist only if each individual were so indoctrinated or programmed as to want to do just what had to be done precisely when it was needed. This can happen only when social behavior is entirely controlled by instinct (as in insect societies), or by effective indoctrination, which is usually beyond man's technological capabilities or his dedication.

In the first four chapters we have dealt with various ways in which different societies satisfy the functional prerequisites of providing and distributing nourishment, shelter, the "good things" of life, and necessary services. In this chapter we focus on the range of permissible behavior and the ways members of small societies keep behavior within tolerable limits of variation. In the excerpt, pay particular attention to what is expected of whom and what happens if those expectations are not met.

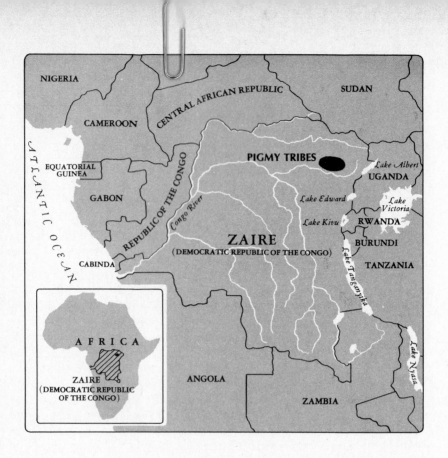

Pygmy Life: Cooperation and Castigation

I remember one morning in particular when we went to kindle the Fire of the Hunt outside the camp, because it was the day that old Cephu committed one of the greatest sins possible in the forest.*

I doubt if any of us had managed to snatch more than two hours' sleep, and we were all quiet while preparing for the hunt. In a Pygmy camp this is the surest danger signal of all, for usually everyone is talking and laughing and shouting rude remarks from one end of the camp to the other. It was not only that we were tired, but of late Cephu had refused to contribute to the molimo° [both a ceremony and the instrument used in it] basket, and that morning he had been heard to call out, in his loudest voice, that he was fed up with the molimo of "that camp over there." Even though he always made his camp a short distance off it was close enough to be thought of as the same camp, and whether or not we appreciated his presence we thought of his camp and ours as being the same. Even his unwillingness to take part in the molimo was

*Abridged from *The Forest People* by Colin M. Turnbull, pp. 95–107. Copyright © 1961 by Colin M. Turnbull. Reprinted by permission of Simon and Schuster. Colin Turnbull has lived and traveled more closely with the Pygmy people than any other non-Pygmy.

accepted, to maintain some semblance of unity; but this sudden statement made it impossible to ignore Cephu's feeling of rivalry any longer. Rather than cause an open breach, everyone in the main camp kept his thoughts to himself and was silent.

About an hour after dawn, four or five youths with their nets and spears went off to light the hunting fire. I went with them . . . Shortly afterward we were joined by half a dozen of the younger married men, the most active hunters, and we lit the fire at the top of the hill. Leaves and twigs were piled around the base of a young tree, and an ember brought from the camp set them ablaze. More leaves were thrown on so that dense clouds of smoke went billowing up to the invisible sky, until finally the flames burst through with a great roar of victory. There was no great ritual or ceremonial, but somehow this act put the hunters in harmony with the forest and secured its blessing and assistance for the day's hunt. The Pygmies regard fire as the most precious gift of the forest, and by offering it back to the forest they are acknowledging their debt and their dependence.

As we sat around waiting for the others, one or two couples passed by. They were going ahead so they would have extra time for gathering mushrooms on the way. They paused to chat and then walked on, lightly, swiftly, and gaily. Before long the main body of hunters arrived and asked where Cephu was. We had not seen him. It seemed that he had left the camp shortly after us but instead of passing by the hunting fire had followed a different path. Someone suggested that he was building a fire of his own. This brought cries of protest that not even Cephu would do such a thing. There was much shaking of heads, and when Ekianga arrived and was told what had happened he stood still for a moment, then turned around, looking in all directions to see if there was any sign of smoke from another fire. He said just one word, "Cephu," and spat on the ground.

By the time we got to the place where we were to make our first cast of the nets everyone was more silent and miserable than ever. It did not make matters any better to find Cephu there already, contentedly sitting over a fire eating roast plantains. He looked up and greeted us in a friendly way, and when asked why he had followed his own path he opened his eyes wide and softly said that he had misunderstood and taken the wrong trail. There were angry remarks, but Cephu ignored them all and went on munching at his plantain, smiling at everyone in his kind, gentle way.

Ekianga and a few others made a brief reconnaissance, and when they came back they gave instructions as to the best direction for setting up the nets. The womenfolk, who had been foraging around for mushrooms and nuts, picked up their baskets and went ahead with the small children. They trod lightly and made no noise beyond an occasional crunch of a rotten branch, buried deep beneath the carpet of leaves. We all spread out in a long semicircle, each man knowing exactly who should be to his right and who to his left. I went with Maipe, who had been sent by Njobo with his net. We soon lost sight and sound of the others, but Maipe knew just where he would be expected to set up his net, and he took a short cut. I lost all sense of direction and could not even tell on which side of us the women were waiting for the signal to beat in toward our nets. We followed a little stream and paused by an enormous out-crop of huge stone boulders, almost perfectly square in shape, some of them eight feet across each face. Maipe looked around, then sat down to wait. After a few minutes, Moke's nephew appeared to our left, stringing his net out through the undergrowth as he came.

The end of the net stopped a few feet short of the boulders, and Maipe deftly joined it to his net; then, slipping each coil off his shoulder in turn, he hung his own net, fastening it to low branches and saplings. It stretched for about three hundred feet, so that one end was completely out of sight from the other. It stood about four feet high, and Maipe walked the length of it, silently adjusting it so that it touched the ground all the way along and was securely fastened above. If he found the net drooping where there was no support, he cut a sapling, stuck it in the ground and hung the net on it, bending the top sharply back, twisting it around and through the mesh so that the net could not slip. When this was done he took up his spear and casually sharpened it with a stone picked off the ground.

It was about another five minutes before he suddenly stood up and beck-oned me to do the same. He stood absolutely motionless, his head slightly on one side, listening; his spear was raised just a few inches from the ground. I listened too, but could hear nothing. The forest had become silent; even the crickets had stopped their almost incessant chirping. Maipe raised his spear higher, and then at some signal that I did not even notice there was a burst of shouting, yelling, hooting and clapping, as the women and children started the beat. They must have been about half a mile away, and as they came closer the noise was deafening. We saw one antelope, a large red sondu,° ears back, leaping toward the boulders as though it were heading straight for our net, but at the last moment it saw us and veered away to the left. Maipe could probably have killed it with his spear, but he said, "That is not for us. It will probably fall into Ekianga's net." Just then there was a lot of yelling from Moke's nephew. Maipe vaulted over the net and ran swiftly, leaping and bounding like the sondu to avoid obstacles. I followed as best I could, but was passed by several young-sters from farther down the line before I reached the others. The sondu had gone into Ekianga's net, just as Maipe had said, but while all the attention was in that direction a water chevrotain, the *sindula,*° had tried to fight its way through Moke's net.

The sindula is one of the most prized animals; it is not much larger than a small dog but is dangerous and vicious. Moke's nephew had been left all by himself to deal with it, as the others in that area were helping Ekianga with the sondu. The youngster, probably not much more than thirteen years old, had speared it with his first thrust, pinning the animal to the ground through the fleshy part of the stomach. But the animal was still very much alive, fighting for freedom. It had already bitten its way through the net, and now it was doubled up, gashing the spear shaft with its sharp teeth. Maipe put another spear into its neck, but it still writhed and fought. Not until a third spear pierced its heart did it give up the struggle.

It was at times like this that I found myself furthest removed from the Pygmies. They stood around in an excited group, pointing at the dying animal and laughing. One boy, about nine years old, threw himself on the ground and curled up in a grotesque heap and imitated the sindula's last convulsions. The men pulled their spears out and joked with one another about being afraid of a little animal like that, and to emphasize his point one of them kicked the torn and bleeding body. Then Maipe's mother came and swept the blood-streaked animal up by its hind legs and threw it over her shoulder into the basket on her back.

At other times I have seen Pygmies singeing feathers off birds that were still alive, explaining that the meat is more tender if death comes slowly. And the hunting dogs, valuable as they are, get kicked around mercilessly from the day they are born to the day they die. I have never seen any attempt at the domestication of any animal or bird apart from the hunting dog. . . .

Ekianga was busy cutting up the sondu by the time I reached his net, for it was too large an animal to fit in his wife's basket. Usually game is brought back

A celebration dance in a Pygmy camp. The hooded figure in the center is the witch doctor. (*Pickett/Monkmeyer*)

to camp before it is divided, and in some groups the dead antelope would have been sent back to camp immediately, around the neck and shoulders of one of the youngsters. But here the womenfolk crowded around as Ekianga hacked away, each claiming her share for her family. "My husband lent you his spear. ..." "We gave your third wife some liver when she was hungry and you were away. ..." "My father and yours always hunted side by side. ..." These were all typical arguments, but for the most part they were not needed. Everyone knew who was entitled to a share, and by and large they stuck to the rules.

Above all the clamor, and in the process of re-coiling the nets and assembling for the next cast, a disgruntled Cephu appeared and complained that he had had no luck. He looked enviously at the sondu and the sindula, but nobody offered him a share. Maipe's mother hurriedly covered the chevrotain with leaves to avoid argument. She worked efficiently, not bothering to take the basket off but using her hands behind her back, and bouncing the basket on her buttocks until the dead animal was completely hidden by the leaves.

We went on for a mile or two and made another cast. Once more Cephu was unlucky, and this time he complained even more loudly, accusing the women of deliberately driving the animals away from his nets. They retorted that he had enough of his own womenfolk there, to which he replied rather ungallantly, "That makes no difference; they are a bunch of lazy empty-heads."

Pygmy nets strung for the hunt in a forest of Zaire. *(Courtesy of the American Museum of Natural History)*

They were still arguing when they set off for a third cast. I had caught sight of old Moke and stayed behind to talk to him. He had not left with the hunt but had gone off on his own, as he usually did, with his bow and arrows. I was surprised to see him. He said, "Don't follow them any longer; they will deafen you with their noise. Cephu will spoil the hunt completely—you'll see." He added that he had happened to be nearby, waiting for the animals either to break through the nets or to escape around the edges. He picked up a large civet cat, the skin slightly stained where it had been pierced by an arrow. "Not very good for eating," Moke commented, "but it will make a beautiful hat. Cephu won't get even that—he is too busy watching other people's nets to watch his own. His is a good net to stand behind with bow and arrow!" He chuckled to himself and swung the cat high in the air.

We ambled back slowly, Moke talking away, sometimes to himself and sometimes to me. On the way he stopped to examine some tracks that were fresh . . . He announced that they were made by a large male leopard, and that it was probably watching us . . .

Back in the camp I was surprised to find that some of the hunters were back already, including Maipe. They had taken a short cut, and traveled twice as fast as Moke and myself. Some of them said it was because rain had threatened, but others, more bluntly, said it was because they did not like the noise Cephu was making. There were a number of women in the camp, and they seemed anxious to change the subject, so Moke told them about the leopard tracks. They laughed and said what a shock the hunters might get if they came back along that trail. One of them started miming the leopard lying in wait, its eyes staring from that side to this. The others formed a line and pretended to be the hunters. Every few steps the "leopard" turned around and jumped up in the air, growling fiercely, sending its pursuers flying to the protection of the trees.

This dance was still in progress when the main body of the hunters returned. They strode into camp with glowering faces and threw their nets on the ground outside their huts. Then they sat down, with their chins in their hands, staring into space and saying nothing. The women followed, mostly with empty baskets, but they were by no means silent. They swore at each other, they swore at their husbands, and most of all they swore at Cephu. Moke looked across at me and smiled. He was skinning the civet.

I tried to find out what had happened but nobody would say. . . .

. . .

The rest of the hunters came in shortly afterward, with Cephu leading. He strode across the camp and into his own little clearing without a word. Ekianga and Manyalibo, who brought up the rear, sat down at the kumamolimo° and announced to the world at large that Cephu had disgraced them all and that they were going to tear down the kumamolimo and abandon the camp and end the molimo. Manyalibo shouted that he wanted everyone to come to the kumamolimo at once, even Cephu. This was a great matter and had to be settled immediately. . . .

Trying not to walk too quickly, yet afraid to dawdle too deliberately, he made an awkward entrance. For as good an actor as Cephu it was surprising.

By the time he got to the kumamolimo everyone was doing something to occupy himself—staring into the fire or up at the tree tops, roasting plantains, smoking, or whittling away at arrow shafts. Only Ekianga and Manyalibo looked impatient, but they said nothing. Cephu walked into the group, and still nobody spoke. He went up to where a youth was sitting in a chair. Usually he would have been offered a seat without his having to ask, and now he did not dare ask, and the youth continued to sit there in as nonchalant a manner as he could muster. Cephu went to another chair where Amabosu was sitting. He shook it violently when Amabosu ignored him, at which he was told, "Animals lie on the ground."

This was too much for Cephu, and he went into a long diatribe about how he was one of the oldest hunters in the group, and one of the best hunters, and that he thought it was very wrong for everyone to treat him like an animal. . . .

Manyalibo stood up and began a rather pompous statement of how everyone wanted this camp to be a good camp, and how everyone wanted the molimo to be a good molimo, with lots of singing, lots of eating, and lots of smoking. But Cephu never took part in the molimo, he pointed out, and Cephu's little group never contributed to the molimo basket. . . .

Cephu tried to interject that the molimo was really none of his business. At this Masisi, who had befriended him over the chair incident, and who had relatives in his camp, rounded on him sharply. He reminded Cephu that he had been glad enough to accept help and food and song when his daughter had died; now that his "mother" had died, why did he reject her? Cephu replied that Balekimito was not his mother. This was what everyone was waiting for. Not only did he name the dead woman, an unheard-of offense, but he denied that she was his mother. Even though there was only the most distant relationship, and that by marriage, it was equivalent to asserting that he did not belong to the same group as Ekianga and Manyalibo and the rest.

Ekianga leaped to his feet and brandished his hairy fist across the fire. He said that he hoped Cephu would fall on his spear and kill himself like the animal he was. Who but an animal would steal meat from others? There were cries of rage from everyone, and Cephu burst into tears. Apparently, during the last cast of the nets, Cephu, who had not trapped a single animal the whole day long, had slipped away from the others and set up his net in front of them. In this way he caught the first of the animals fleeing from the beaters, but he had not been able to retreat before he was discovered.

I had never heard of this happening before, and it was obviously a serious offense. . . .

Cephu tried very weakly to say that he had lost touch with the others and was still waiting when he heard the beating begin. It was only then that he had set up his net, where he was. Knowing that nobody believed him, he added that in any case he felt he deserved a better place in the line of nets. After all, was he not an important man, a chief, in fact, of his own band? Manyalibo tugged at Ekianga to sit down, and sitting down himself he said there was obviously no use prolonging the discussion. Cephu was a big chief, and a chief was a villager, for the BaMbuti never have chiefs. And Cephu had his own band, of which he was chief, so let him go with it and hunt elsewhere and be a chief elsewhere. Manyalibo ended a very eloquent speech with ... "Pass me the tobacco."

Cephu knew he was defeated and humiliated. Alone, his band of four or five families was too small to make an efficient hunting unit. He apologized profusely, reiterated that he really did not know he had set up his net in front of the others, and said that in any case he would hand over all the meat. This settled the matter, and accompanied by most of the group he returned to his little camp and brusquely ordered his wife to hand over the spoils. She had little chance to refuse, as hands were already reaching into her basket and under the leaves of the roof where she had hidden some liver in anticipation of just such a contingency. Even her cooking pot was emptied. Then each of the other huts was searched and all the meat taken. Cephu's family protested loudly and Cephu tried hard to cry, but this time it was forced and everyone laughed at him. He clutched his stomach and said he would die; die because he was hungry and his brothers had taken away all his food; die because he was not respected.

The kumamolimo was festive once again, and the camp seemed restored to good spirits. An hour later, when it was dark and fires were flickering outside every hut ... From Cephu's camp came the sound of the old man, still trying hard to cry ... From our camp came the jeers of the women, ridiculing him and imitating his moans.

When Masisi had finished his meal he took a pot full of meat with mushroom sauce, cooked by his wife, and quietly slipped away into the shadows in the direction of his unhappy kinsman. The moaning stopped, and when the evening molimo singing was at its height I saw Cephu in our midst. Like most of us he was sitting on the ground, in the manner of an animal. But he was singing, and that meant that he was just as much a BaMbuti as anyone else.

Even a simple hunting and gathering society makes demands on its members. Cephu did not do what was expected of him. Men of the society hunt cooperatively by setting up nets alongside one another, and Cephu set his in front of the rest. He had already violated a series of social norms° (group consensus as to what should or should not be done) before the net episode (Greer 1965:24). He refused to contribute to the molimo, or even to participate in it. He failed to pass by the hunting fire the morning of the hunt. Although the other members of the society were annoyed, no concerted action was taken against him until he set up his net ahead of the others. Why did this act cause a strong social reaction? Perhaps because it was the last in a series of actions that were progressively less acceptable? The author seems to feel the act would have called forth the same reaction even if it had occurred without any previous offenses. He called it "one of the greatest sins possible in the forest." (Actually, it is better called a crime°—an offense against people. The term *sin*° is usually restricted to offenses against the supernatural.)

KEEPING VARIATION WITHIN LIMITS: LAWS

The dependence of the group on cooperative hunting makes the offense a grave one. If any hunter could set up his nets where he pleased, the hunt would become a contest for the best location. Men who got their nets set out in front would have an advantage over those in the rear, and there would be gaps in the line through which animals could escape. Instead of an effective hunting technique, the process would turn into an exercise in futility: it would produce more rivalry and hostility than meat for the group. Cephu simply could not be allowed to get away with his behavior because it would imperil the method by which the whole group survived. By "doing his thing" he threatened everyone's survival. There was a confrontation, and Cephu and his group were threatened with exile. In the Pygmy environment, this was equivalent to a death sentence unless he and his group could associate with another band, because they were too few to survive alone. (This indicates, incidentally, the significance of population size for certain technologies. The average hunting band universally has six to eight adult males, and although its total population may be smaller or greater in any specific band at any specific time, the frequent occurrence cross-culturally of twenty-five as an average suggests that it is an optimum [Pfeiffer 1972:376]. The Pygmy hunting method seems to require almost that many as a minimum.) Cephu gave up in the face of the exile threat and offered an alternative—surrender of the meat he had illegally obtained. The alternative was accepted, and Cephu was restored to the good graces of the community.

Even the punishment of confiscating his food was alleviated by one of his relatives, who carried food to the camp so that no one really had to go hungry. Clearly, the BaMbuti were not bent on revenge. Once Cephu's behavior was again within tolerable limits, members of the society were satisfied. Cephu began participating in the molimo once more, so the system worked even though the BaMbuti had no specialized law-enforcement personnel or formal legal code. Complex devices are not necessary in a small society where everyone interacts on a face-to-face basis. In such societies, everyone knows what is expected, which variations will be tolerated and which ones will not be. Crime of the sort that occurs in larger societies tends to be rare in small groups, where there is seldom any doubt as to the identity of the guilty party and where the whole paraphernalia necessary for the protection of the individual in complex societies is superfluous.

Note that even though members of the society eased the punishment and welcomed Cephu back without any apparent recriminations, they did not allow him to profit from breaking the rule. The "stolen" food was taken from him, and although he got some food later from a relative, this normally would have happened anyway if he had been unsuccessful in the hunt. The message from the society was unmistakable: "Abide by the rules and you are one of us, so we will take care of you. Violate them and we will cast you out, for you are no longer a BaMbuti." When Cephu heeded the message, he was reintegrated into the group. Note also that several people called Cephu an animal. The implication throughout is that if one is not a BaMbuti, one may be an animal, or equivalent to one.

When violation of a norm is met by a severe punishment (or the threat of one) imposed with the approval of society, the norm may be called a law° (or a legal norm). There is disagreement among anthropologists over whether this definition is adequate. Some (E. A. Hoebel, for example) say that the use of force or threat of force by an authorized agent of society as part of the response to the infraction is essential for distinguishing legal from ordinary social norms (Hoebel 1964:28). By this definition, not all societies have law. Other anthropologists (Leopold Pospisil, for example) say that the definition need not mention the use of force at all. Pospisil states that law has certain attributes, such as authority (it must be accepted by all parties to the dispute), the intention of universal application, *obligatio*° (both rights *and* duties), and sanctions that can be either psychological or physical. Since his definition is broader, Pospisil claims that all societies have some form of law (Pospisil 1967:27ff.).

Whatever definition of law is chosen, some form of social control is universal, even if it is only intense indoctrination that makes punishment for norm violation the guilt inflicted by the individual on himself. The anthropological controversy over what characteristics the social controls should have in order to be labeled "legal" is mainly a semantic one. Insisting on certain characteristics—for example, that law must be written and supported by specialized agencies—limits the number of societies that can be said to have *law,* but it does not change the reality that members of every society attempt to regulate behavior in some way to ensure that all members perform predictably.

Whenever *any* norm is broken, members of a society usually have a negative reaction at first. If the reaction is mild (indicated by expressed irritation, angry remarks, gossip, and so on), the norm is called social, which roughly corresponds to the sociologist Sumner's term *folkways.*° If the reaction is severe, however, the norm is more likely to be called a law, corresponding—more or less—to Sumner's term *mores*° (the singular is *mos,* not *more*) (Sumner 1911:23, 30). Evaluation of a negative social reaction—punishment—as "severe" should be based on emic categories. That is, a punishment is "severe" or "light" only if the people of a society perceive it that way. The evaluation of outsiders is not relevant here, because the punishment is inflicted on and by people in a particular society in order to affect *their own* behavior. An outsider might laugh at a punishment a member of the society felt was worse than death; people in various societies have committed suicide rather than face exposure to ridicule or censure from their peers, for example. It is thus apparent that "You must not set your net in front of others" is a legal norm among the BaMbuti. The other norms Cephu broke, such as "a man should contribute to the molimo basket" or "a man should pass by the hunting fire before a hunt," were apparently only social norms, not legal ones.

Cephu was judged by the adult males acting together, and punishment was administered by most of the group, who went together to his camp to get the stolen meat. Small societies often handle trouble this way. Among the Huron, (larger and more complex than the BaMbuti but still small and simple compared to modern nations) judgment was passed by a council of elders, and leaders in the society took an active part in enforcing the decisions (part of this process is reported in the excerpt in Chapter 3).

Judgment and punishment may also be carried out by individuals or small groups especially assigned to the task. Simple societies rarely have full-time specialists. Some—the Pygmies, for example—lack specialists entirely, but may appoint people for specific occasions. The Cheyenne Indians appointed members of one of the military societies to act as police for the period of a communal buffalo hunt. Members of the appointed group had the right and duty to apprehend and punish anyone violating the legal norm: "There will be no individual hunting until the group hunt is over." After the hunt ended, the military society gave up its task (Hoebel 1960:53, 54). Note that all the functions of apprehension, judgment, and punishment were performed by the same group, not by separate individuals or groups. Complex societies show an increase of specialization in the area of social control, as they do in the economic area. In simple societies everyone may be involved in judgment and in punishment. When tasks are delegated to part of the group or to individuals, the delegation is only temporary. Simple societies are more personal in the applications of social controls, as they are in exchange and distribution. For example, the punishment described in the excerpt as an alternative to exile was spontaneous, appropriate to the situation and to the people involved. If someone else repeated Cephu's crime in the future, the punishment might be different, or it might be the same. There were no specific rules made for such an event. In small societies, punishment for rule violations is usually spontaneous and varied according to both the circumstances and the individuals involved; such punishment is technically called an informal sanction.° (Sanction° is a rather unusual word in English, since it can mean both *punishment* and *reward.* The double meaning can occasionally cause confusion. For example, the sentence, "The Z——society sanctions polygamy" does not really make clear whether the society punishes polygamy or encourages it.)

Societies of under 1,000 people usually have informal sanctions, whereas formal sanctions°—which are explicit, known in advance, and impersonally applied to all violators—are needed to cope with large numbers of people. The figure 1,000 appears to be the maximum with which informal controls work, and even this number may be too high for optimum efficiency. In a symposium on hunters and gatherers, the typical size of human groups was discussed. Although the participants could not agree on the reason for it, they noted that while 25 was the average size of the hunting band (although actual groups ranged in size from 18 to over 50), the tribe, a loose association of local bands with a similar language and culture and recognizing a common group identity, was normally limited to about 500 people. The range was from about 100 to slightly over 2,000, but the upper levels were exceptional. When the population neared 1,000, the tribe usually showed signs of beginning to split (Lee and DeVore 1968:155, 156, 245–248; Pfeiffer 1972:376–377). Like the average band size of 25, the figure of 500 seems to be an optimum number for certain types of social organization. Leadership is usually somewhat more explicit than in the smaller bands, and rules and sanctions a bit more formal, although they are still

A group of Tasadays recently contacted in the Philippines. One of the most isolated of peoples known in modern times, they numbered twenty-three at first contact. *(N. Dolf Herras)*

far from the written, codified, impersonal formality of the industrialized modern world. New techniques for enabling people to get along together, for settling conflicts of interest and disputes over power distribution, and for coordinating individual behavior with group needs had to be developed for the band of 25 persons to grow into the tribe of 500. The Tasadays, those peaceful people, numbered 23 at contact. If their population should begin to increase sharply, it is a safe bet to suggest that they will either change their life style and develop new methods of relating to each other or they will not stay peaceful and will split into groups, the number depending on the size of the population. Even with more formal social controls, some societies tend to fission when the population is under 300 people. The groups may split up violently, as in the case of the Yanamamo (a tribe on the border of Venezuela and Brazil), or peacefully, as in the case of the Hutterites (a religious sect whose communities are located in Canada and the northern United States) (Chagnon 1968:120; Hostetler and Huntington 1967:105–108). But in either case, a group nearing 300 is not a stable one in societies like the Yanomamo and the Hutterite and will separate into smaller divisions of people who can cooperate and stay together under the methods and values of their respective cultures.

In small societies, the injured party is usually granted the right to revenge himself on the offender, if he can. This is called private law.° If the wronged individual does nothing, the other members of the society also do nothing. If the wronged individual takes revenge, the other members passively approve, unless he or she exceeds the consensus of what is proper revenge. Cephu's offense was clearly against the group, and the group acted in response to it. If he had robbed a specific man, however, what would the group have done? Since the society is small, group members probably would have allowed the wronged individual to take his own revenge. In most societies with private law, women are not expected to get revenge themselves; instead a close male relative (a father, husband, brother, or son) is generally charged with the obligation. Among the Huron, when a man was robbed, he was entitled to loot the robber's cabin and confiscate all his goods (Thwaites 1898, 13:11, 13). In such a case, the individual is the authorized agent of the society for the moment. He is *enforcing* the law, not committing another offense. The weakness of private law as a means of social control is that it will not work unless all parties to the argument accept the right of the injured party to take revenge. If all do not, the society becomes torn with conflict. In the most common situation, group A gets revenge in retaliation for the murder of one of their own members by killing a member of group B. Instead of accepting the retaliation as legitimate, members of group B feel that the original killing was justified, or that the choice of the revenge victim was inappropriate (he may have been of a much higher status than the original victim, for example). Consequently, group B members feel that now *they* are the injured parties and entitled to revenge. They kill another member of group A. This is the beginning of a feud, which is likely to continue until one group is exterminated or both groups decide the scales are balanced and that neither group is entitled to any more revenge. Without some overriding authority to make such a judgment and enforce it, however, the latter solution is unlikely, and disruptive violence may continue for generations. The need of members of society to reduce or prevent such violence can lead to public law,° by which the society as a whole takes the part of the injured person and regards the wrong done to that individual as a wrong done the entire society. Then the society as a whole or some specialized members of it apprehend, judge, and punish the offending party (Hoebel 1964:27, 28). This happens occasionally in complex societies even if the so-called victim does not feel wronged and does not want revenge. Cases of prosecution of prostitution, drug abuse, gambling, and so on, are examples. Even though in most such cases there is seldom a complaining victim, members of the society have decided through legislation that these acts are offenses against society's members as a whole and should be punished. However, many people are trying to change the legislation pertaining to so-called victimless crimes, on the grounds that what goes on between consenting adults should not be any business of the law (Schur 1965:169 and *passim*). Other people, who regard the law more as a set of guidelines as to how people *should* behave, are reluctant to approve acts so many people dislike, even if the parties involved are all consenting. In complex societies, such differences of opinion create social tension. In small societies, where there is no group action without group consensus, behavior that challenges group norms meets a very different response. If the group members reject the behavior, the individual (or individuals) practicing it must change or leave. Other group members often react simultaneously.

Even in the simplest of societies, however, not everyone is expected to behave exactly alike. The differences between complex and simple societies lie in the variety of behavior patterns available and not in a total absence of variation in one. Not only are there always some different statuses and roles, but the way in which any one individual performs his or her role is different from the performance of others—within socially acceptable limits.

STATUS AND ROLES

A person's position in society is called a status.° Sociologists and anthropologists differ somewhat in the way they use the term. Sociologists tend to concentrate on the individual's overall position, which is usually referred to as socioeconomic status. People with high status are powerful and wealthy; low-status individuals are neither. This is an example of scalar status,° status depending on rank or access to wealth and power. Anthropologists are usually more interested in functional status,° status based on what one does in the society (Greer 1965:23; Linton 1936:113–114). It is apparent that any individual occupies several statuses, functional and scalar, in a society. According to the excerpt, Cephu is an elder, a husband, a hunter, and a family head. The excerpt names sixteen to eighteen BaMbuti statuses (depending on whether "children," "youngsters," "relatives," and "kinsmen" are counted as two, three, or four statuses), two non-BaMbuti statuses ("chief" and "villager"), and suggests several others. Some of the named ones ("nephew," "brother," "married men," for example) have reciprocal statuses, and naming one implies the existence of the other. Where there is a nephew, the existence somewhere of an aunt or an uncle may be assumed; a brother implies the existence of a sibling; married men require the existence of married women, and so on.

Some statuses are universal—that is, they appear in all societies. The principal ones are man, woman, child, adult, mother, son, daughter, brother, sister. The list does not include a father status because the English word, which refers both to the *pater,*° the sociological male parent, and the *genitor,*° the biological sire, does not have an equivalent with this double meaning in all languages. Among the Trobriand Islanders in the South Pacific, as well as among some of the Australian tribes, for example, the word applied to those we would call father actually means "mother's husband" and does not carry the connotation of biological sire, or *genitor,* at all. This is discussed more fully in Chapter 8 (Hart and Pilling 1964:22; Malinowski 1929:5–6, 195).

Note that the universal statuses are almost entirely ascribed° (assigned to an individual whether he likes it or not). Most of us do not choose to be men or women, children or adults; we just *are* by virtue of certain characteristics we possess. In the United States, if a child lives long enough, he becomes a teen-ager. Then, if he continues to live a few years longer, he becomes an adult. He has no choice. Ascribed status is contrasted with achieved status,° which the

individual attains through some effort of his own (Linton 1936: 115–117). Ascribed and achieved statuses are simply extreme points of a continuum; many
statuses fall in between. For example, it requires effort to raise a child to an
adult (although less in the United States than in societies without Western
medicine, where a parent who manages to raise all his offspring is regarded as
almost incredibly fortunate). Once the child is an adult in the United States,
however, the additional status of husband or wife is achieved rather than ascribed, since marriage is not inevitable. (Some parents regard it as a *major*
achievement.) Once the person is married, his or her parents have no choice
in whether they become grandparents. The status of grandfather or grandmother is therefore to some extent both achieved and ascribed.

Societies vary in the ratio of achieved to ascribed statuses. In the excerpt,
most of the BaMbuti statuses mentioned are ascribed—"old man," "child,"
"man," "woman," and so on. Only "husband," "wife," "hunter," and perhaps
"father" and "mother" could be regarded as achieved. Societies in which most
statuses are ascribed may be called closed, or rigid; one in which most are
achieved is open, or flexible. According to the American value system, societies
with a high proportion of ascribed statuses are undemocratic and limit personal
freedom. Members of such societies may not feel the same way, however.
People in closed societies may regard an open system with great anxiety, for
the ladder of success can be fallen down as well as climbed. The insecurities that
go with potential failure are minimized in complex societies where one's posi-

Women pounding corn in South Africa, performing one of their prescribed roles. *(Courtesy of the American Museum of Natural History)*

tion is predetermined by birth or some other factor over which one has no control. On the other hand, in such societies no one has the opportunity to actualize his or her potential unless lucky enough to be ascribed into the right status. Individuals must be indoctrinated to fit their statuses; they cannot be allowed to strive to attain the ones they want or are best suited for.

The excerpt reveals several additional difficulties that result from a careless application of American values to other cultures. Americans, for example, place a high value on the concept of the simple life, and often assume it to be an ideal pattern. Because the BaMbuti have no elaborate machinery for law enforcement, no school, no business "rat race," Americans may be inclined to see them as free and unpressured. But the BaMbuti "freedom," and the freedom of the idyllic simple life itself, are more illusory than real. Cephu found out what can happen if one does not conform, at least in certain ways. A man has but one occupational choice—hunting; a woman must be a wife, mother, and homemaker. If a man does not care to hunt, or a woman to marry, neither can live as a BaMbuti. There are no alternatives. When a man hunts, he has two choices: he may hunt alone or with the group. But if he hunts with the group, he must hunt the same way the rest do; he cannot put his net up where he wants to; he must stay in his assigned place or he will be punished, like Cephu. A society where most statuses are ascribed is indeed rigid. The rigidity may have advantages unsuspected by Americans, but even when it is combined with a simple, apparently unpressured life, it may also have unsuspected disadvantages.

The BaMbuti statuses are almost all universal (that is, present in all societies). The only exceptions are hunter and father (see above). Even father is almost universal, and hunter was a universal status during the first few million years of human history. There are no specialty statuses (limited to one or two people in the society) mentioned in the excerpt. The book from which the excerpt was taken does mention that some men are especially noted as molimo players, and molimo owner might be considered a specialty status, since there are rarely more than one or two in any group, but other than those and the status of medicine man, BaMbuti culture lacks any special ones. A specialty status need not be full-time; it simply needs to be a position that members of the society do not expect many individuals to occupy. In complex societies there are specialty statuses for both sexes, but in the simplest societies, if there are any special statuses at all, they usually are for males.

There are no statuses without roles. The term *role*° refers to the behavior pattern expected of someone in a particular position (status) in society. There should be a stress on the word *pattern*; that is, a specific act of behavior (opening a door for someone, for example) may be common to many roles. It is the overall pattern that distinguishes the role of doorman from the roles of other individuals who might in particular circumstances open a door for someone else. Pattern is therefore crucial in the concept of role.

Although there are universal statuses, there are *no* universal roles. We will stress this point again and again: roles must be described for each specific society. For example, both Piegan and BaMbuti have the status of hunter. The role of hunter, however, differs sharply. Among the BaMbuti a hunter is expected to string his net in an assigned position, alongside the net of another hunter. Then he is supposed to kill game frightened into the net by women and children. The Piegan (in the excerpt in Chapter 1) expect a hunter to kill buffalo by riding into a herd on his horse and shooting the animals with a gun or a bow and arrow. Full participation of the Pygmy women is essential to the success of the communal hunt, since they frighten the game into the nets and carry the meat back to camp. Women among the Piegan stay in camp during the hunt, and come out to bring back the meat only if the kill is close by. Otherwise, the men bring it in. The roles of both men and women in hunting differ from one society to the other; all that those mentioned have in common is killing game.

Sometimes the same behavior may be expected from more than one status. For example, in the Pygmy excerpt, both children and women make noise to frighten game; both men and women forage for mushrooms; both men and women cook. These similarities are, of course, only parts of the total role. As mentioned above, the pattern makes the role, and the pattern for men differs from that for women and for children, even though some specific behavior may be the same. In other instances particular items of behavior are restricted to particular statuses. Women apparently never use bows and arrows among the Pygmies, and grown men never take part in the beat to frighten game. Each of the excerpts in this book may be reexamined this way to determine statuses and roles in the society described.

The way in which an individual performs one role may affect the way in which he is accepted in others. For example, Cephu's performance as a hunter threatened his status as a band member and consequently all his other statuses and roles. There are also times when role expectations are incompatible. In the United States, for example, a man cannot always be both a good son and a good husband, because to perform one role well may require him to perform the other badly. If his wife and his mother make conflicting demands on him at the same time, he has to decide which to neglect. This is known as a role conflict° and causes problems in any society. (Normally, we escape role conflict because we are called upon to perform only *one* role at a time.) To start a heated discussion in a group of Americans, simply pose this problem: If a man capsizes in a boat with his mother and his wife, neither of whom can swim, which one should he save (assuming he can save only one)? It is a drastic example of a role conflict for which American norms provide no solution. There is no consensus as to which should take precedence. The poor male will be condemned whatever choice he makes.

Some societies *do* provide an answer to that particular role conflict. In a traditional Chinese family, for example, a man's first loyalty was to his family of orientation,° the one into which he was born. His wife could never surpass his mother. Until she bore a son, the wife was at the bottom of the priority list in the family. (She got her turn at power later, when her son married and brought home a daughter-in-law for *her* to bully, and she therefore had a great desire to bear sons.) A traditional Chinese would have to save his mother and let his wife fend for herself, or he would be severely criticized (Yang 1945:54). Among the traditional Eskimo, on the other hand, the old were usually sacrificed for the young; old people were abandoned or strangled (if they did not kill themselves) to give the young a better chance at survival during emergen-

The interior of an Eskimo home in Siberia. *(Courtesy of the American Museum of Natural History)*

cies. A traditional Eskimo would have to rescue his wife and not concern himself with his mother (Jenness 1959:207, 261).

Setting priorities is one way to minimize role conflict; another is to try to make it unlikely that situations which call for simultaneous performance of different roles will occur. Mutual avoidance between a man and his mother-in-law is demanded in many societies. When this is scrupulously practiced, a girl is normally never placed in a situation where the roles of wife and of daughter can be activated simultaneously.

Conflict between certain statuses may also be inherent in a situation. For example, a foreman is expected to give orders to the workmen subordinate to him, and it can be assumed that at least some of them will occasionally resent these orders. Conflict between foreman and workers is built into the situation. A few societies try to minimize such inherent conflicts by demanding joking behavior as part of the roles of the potentially conflicting statuses. That is, people in these statuses are supposed to play tricks on, joke with, or tease one another. The behavior can occasionally get rather rough, but it is not entirely left up to the initiative of the participants (Simmons 1966:39–40, 280–281). This joking behavior is thought to head off more serious and socially disruptive conflict.

Of course, rules are seldom followed exactly. There is a difference between ideal behavior (what people think *should* be done) and reality (what people actually *do*) in all societies. The gap is almost always greater in some areas than in others, but it is present in all. It can create social tension, but only if people know what the real behavior is, and they rarely do. (Do you *really* know from personal observation or information what the sexual behavior of the older generation is?) Instead, people *presume* they know what other people do, and act on that basis. Consequently, it is the gap between ideal and presumed behavior that is significant, rather than that between ideal and real. If the ideal-presumed gap is large, social tension will be high and members of the society will make a considerable effort to reduce it. But it may even be unrealistically large: during the witchcraft hysteria of the Middle Ages, people tried to wipe out sorcery and eliminate witches; actually, there was little actual sorcery going on, and there were even fewer actual witches. On the other hand, if the gap between the ideal and presumed is small, there is little social tension, even when the gap between the ideal and *real* behavior is large (Richards, C. 1969:1115–1116). Americans are much more concerned about civil rights now than they were two decades ago, in spite of the fact that there is probably a smaller gap between the ideal and the real now than there was then. But as more and more people have become aware of a gap between what they think ought to be done and what they presume *is* being done, the social tension has risen. For some people, the gap between ideal and presumed has widened because their concept of the ideal has changed; for others, it has widened because of a change in what they think is being done. Since either will result in an increase in social tension, a society may deal with the situation by attempting to change real behavior, by changing the ideal, or by changing the presumptions about behavior.

All societies expect different behavior from males than from females, although in a number of Western societies recently there has been a trend toward increasingly similar sex roles. The move in that direction is not complete, so sex remains one of the universal bases (along with age and kinship) for classifying people into different groups and for determining status. In the smallest, simplest societies, the *only* subgroups that exist are those based on sex, kinship, or age. Membership in these groups, like status, is ascribed, and everyone with the proper characteristics is included. All the ways one individual should relate to another in the society are predetermined, since all relationships are based on reciprocal statuses with known roles. There are no strangers in the society and no room for sharply innovative behavior. Members can perform their roles only well or poorly: no one has much scope to try out new behavior patterns. Many of these societies do not have "friendships" as these are understood in complex societies, because association with others and ways of relating to others are already spelled out in the norms, with little room for choice. People like some individuals better than others, of course, but although that may affect which relative or in-law one associates with most often, it does not affect the overall pattern of interaction either with the preferred individual or with less preferred individuals in the same relationship. A person who behaves in an innovative way toward others only arouses anxiety because there seems to be no reason behind his behavior, and "irrational" behavior is almost always worrisome in every society.

The specific behavior expected of men and women varies widely from one society to another. The earlier statement that there are no universal roles means, of course, that there are no universal male or female roles either. This is difficult to believe because to an even greater degree than most kinds of roles, those associated with sex belong to covert culture.° (This is discussed further in Chapter 7.) Because roles do vary, it is difficult to predict how a particular individual will behave in a given situation unless the investigator knows something about the culture of the subject's group. But the more the anthropologist knows about an individual's culture, the more accurate his or her predictions become. For example, if you were asked to predict what a Botocudo man would wear to a community meeting, you would probably not even be able to make a guess (unless you already know he is a coastal Brazilian Indian), but if you were asked to predict what an American male would wear to his office in New York City in the winter, your prediction would probably be fairly accurate.

A Piegan does not seek esteem the way a New England farmer does; Sloan's methods would not be appropriate for a Huron. All individuals may seek esteem from their fellows, but the way they go about it is determined by the values of their group. To strive for a goal that is not valued or to use despised methods to reach one is unrewarding behavior because, as Cephu learned, an individual loses esteem instead of gaining it. One definition of society is that it is a "group of individuals competing for conventional prizes by conventional means" (Ardrey 1970:104). Among human beings, conventional prizes and methods are manifestations of conventional understandings—that is, of culture.

DISTRIBUTING POWER

Social and legal norms do more than establish guidelines for behavior among members of the society and settle trouble cases; they also distribute power. When people live together and the inevitable conflicts occur, who gets his way and who has to give way? If the question of precedence had to be settled each time a conflict of interest occurred, a society would be in continual turmoil. The function of a dominance structure seems to be to cut down on the amount of physical violence within the group or species. In an established system, individual animals *know* which among them takes precedence in any given situation. A challenger is met by a threat from the dominant animal, which is usually sufficient to put the challenger "back in its place." If the challenger persists, the dominant animal physically punishes it or drives it out of the group (Ardrey 1970:156; van Lawick-Goodall 1971:171–173). A successful challenge, of course, raises the challenger's status, but serious challenges to the established structure tend to be rare. When adult animals who are strangers to each other are thrust together, however, there is a high level of violent conflict that results in fatalities unless the defeated one can escape from the area. (The human is by no means the only animal that kills its own kind!) The violence continues until a stable dominance structure is established. After that, the group becomes peaceful. The weakest animals are always the ones who suffer most in a society torn by conflict. One of the functions of dominant animals seems to be to stop quarrels; they do this by almost invariably siding with the weaker of the quarreling animals—unless the quarrel is with them, of course

(Ardrey 1970:157). A dominance structure thus improves the survival chances of the individual by cutting down conflict and providing some protection even if the individual is not at the top of the structure. Naturally, the dominance structure is not always such an advantage to the weakest individuals, especially in cases of food shortage. When food is plentiful, the dominance structure, by limiting quarrels and protecting the weak, may ensure a more equitable division of the available supply. When food is short, however, it is likely to be monopolized by the dominant animals to the detriment of the weak. This may decrease survival chances of specific individuals, but, unfortunately, is probably essential for group survival, since it ensures that at least part of the group will remain strong and live through the crisis.

No known society has complete equality. There are scalar status differences in the simplest societies as well as in the most complex. The excerpt reveals some of the scalar differences in BaMbuti society. Not only did Manyalibo and Ekianga have more power° (ability to make binding decisions) than Cephu, but adult hunters in general had more power than youths. An illustration of Cephu's loss of power occurred when a youth refused to give up a chair to him. The youth usually would have done so without Cephu's asking him to move, just as a subordinate male yields his place to a dominant one in a baboon or chimpanzee troop. In the excerpt, Cephu had lost so much power that he did not even dare ask the young man to move. He went to another chair where Amabosu, usually lower in status, was sitting, was ignored again, shook the chair, and was told he was an animal—lower in scalar status than *any* person.

In small societies, each individual has a power rank all his own and no two people are precisely equal. In large complex societies, the same may be true, but groups of individuals may be so close in rank, compared with other groups, that they may be considered roughly equal. This group is then called a class° or caste° (discussed in the next chapter).

As a society grows, it either develops effective mechanisms for settling disputes and distributing power or it splits apart. In the history of the human's development, the societies that survived and grew were those that devised techniques of social control enabling greater numbers of people to live together peacefully. Techniques that work in a small band where contact is on a face-to-face basis and informal social pressure is effective (among the Pygmies, for example) do not work unmodified in a large, complex society where different groups hold different values and are not so susceptible to face-to-face pressures from those who disagree. Formal controls, laws, and governments are techniques that have come about in response to the social need for order and organization (Hoebel 1964:154). The next chapter goes into more detail on these complex structures.

The BaMbuti had no formal legal or political organization; in fact, in the excerpt Manyalibo specifically denied that any such thing existed among them. As mentioned earlier, many people have the impression that because there is no formal structure, the society has no social control or organization and everyone does exactly as he pleases. That is never true in any society. The excerpt provides another example of people abiding by informal rules when it describes what happened as Ekianga was cutting up the sondu. Women crowded in, pressing their claims for a share by reminding him of a number of obligations. Conflict potential was reduced by the fact that Ekianga did not have to make a personal decision about the merits of each claim since "everyone knew who was entitled to a share, and by and large they stuck to the rules." (Distribution can reduce conflict as well as cause it.) The control is there, although it may be informal. People who try to set up communes, or students who decide to rent an apartment together to escape the restrictions of dormitory life, often run into problems when they assume that they will not need any rules. If everyone in the group holds the same norms, there may actually be no need for *written* rules: all the rules will be simply "understood," and usually followed; but if, as more often happens, people in the group have different values and opinions, problems almost always develop. Since members of these particular groups often share a distrust in rules and a belief that they are unnecessary, the conflicts that occur quickly become insoluble, and the group usually splits apart, sometimes quite bitterly; yet consensus concerning a few rules would have solved the problems in most cases.

No matter how small a group is, decisions affecting it must be made. The excerpt makes this obvious. Somehow the BaMbuti had to decide where to set the nets, when to leave camp to hunt, when to begin and end the molimo, where to put the kumamolimo, and so on. How did the BaMbuti make these decisions? Many were made by the adult males consulting together, with Manyalibo and Ekianga usually exerting the most influence. Some decisions, such as when to go hunting, required little consultation. Everyone knew the best time to go and it took only one person starting off about the right time to get everyone moving. Of course, if anyone left too early, the other men would comment on it, and perhaps make rude or joking remarks. Fear of this gossip or ridicule would be enough to keep most people from any marked deviation from the norm. Cephu's apparent indifference to gossip led to the situation that caused the group members to take stronger action. Cephu's behavior was rejected, not copied, by the others. They followed the pattern of disapproval set by Ekianga and Manyalibo who de facto became the opinion leaders. In this case, the leaders expressed the general attitude shared by other members of the group; they did not create it. In small groups, the leader is frequently an individual who does this. Perhaps the leader senses group sentiment and initiates a course of action that other members are fully prepared to undertake but unwilling to start; or perhaps consensus grows out of discussion and the leader is the one best able to express it. The other members may not even be aware that they are ready to act until the leader makes a move or expresses an opinion. This type of leadership is much more fragile than the type in which the leader actually, by oratory or other means, forms and creates group opinion, but it is probably more common, particularly in small groups. The hunting-band dictator, ruling his people with an iron fist, is as much a myth as the notion of the totally free, anarchic group.

Small groups may not consciously or officially have a leader, but they inevitably accept someone, or something, as a legitimate "authority" to settle vexing problems of power priority, conflict of interest, and so on. This authority may be a specific set of norms that everyone knows and adheres to most of the time. Obviously, all societies have individuals who break rules. (Every individual in every society probably breaks some rules at some time in life.) What happens then? Where are the authorities to whom one can appeal? Whose opinion is most influential? Norms also determine this. In small societies such as that of the Pygmies, some individuals are better hunters and regarded as wiser men; they are listened to. These are the leaders. Ekianga and Manyalibo were clearly such men among the BaMbuti. When Manyalibo said the BaMbuti did not have chiefs, he was referring to the specific villager status, because the whole incident clearly indicates that the BaMbuti had leaders.

Opinion leaders in small societies are almost never female. This is not to say that women have no influence; they do in almost all societies, large or small, and in some they have a great deal. But in making public decisions, in dealing with public power, women have not been conspicuous in the societies of the world. A few complex societies have had several female rulers—the two Elizabeths and Queen Victoria of England, for example (but they were always surrounded by male advisors). There have been other exceptions. The strongly patriarchal Hebrew society was once led by a woman (Deborah) (Judges 4:4–24) and was even ruled by a queen (Athaliah) for six years (II Kings 11:1–17). The current prime minister of India is a woman (Indira Gandhi), as was a former prime minister of Israel (Golda Meir). But these rare exceptions do not invalidate the generalization that public decision making and public power are almost always in the hands of men. The reason for this is still being hotly debated, but whatever it may be, the preponderance of males in this area of formal public social organization is clear.

The leader in a simple society is not "chosen" for the position. There is no formal mechanism involved. A man leads so long as his decisions are followed. When people no longer listen to him, he is no longer a leader. There is no special means for removing him any more than there was for choosing him in the first place. You cannot remove a man from a position he does not hold. Is such a leader supported by law? There is usually no norm that states that the leader must be obeyed. In fact, such leaders cannot normally command; they can only suggest. Yet their suggestions carry weight. The excerpt indicates when Ekianga and Manyalibo told everyone to assemble at the kumamolimo Cephu did not dare delay his arrival too long. After Manyalibo said that Cephu should go and live somewhere else, Cephu apparently did not think he could continue to live with the band unless he made some concessions, which he immediately did. One of the problems involved in studying law and power in simple societies is that obedience often seems to be "understood" and unquestioning. Because of this, many early anthropologists and theorists said that the members of simple societies were bound by customs they were unable to defy. Bronislaw Malinowski indicated that this image of the "primitive" is inaccurate. The laws, the violations, and the punishments are there; they are simply less formal and less overt (Malinowski 1966:9–16).

SUMMARY

Societies, because they are made up of interacting, interdependent people, need order and organization to exist. Since human behavior is not fully predetermined by genes, conflicts of interest and questions of priority continually arise. All societies have developed means of coping with these problems to ensure that (1) what must be done gets done, (2) people can rely on each other to perform necessary services and to behave in a predictable manner, and (3) behavior beyond the tolerable limits of variation is eliminated or decreased.

All societies permit some variation, and all societies permit more in certain areas than in others. The severity, complexity, and effectiveness of the means used to control deviation vary, but in all cases, if behavior goes beyond what is felt to be reasonable bounds, members of the society take some action to correct the situation. If they fail, the society fractures into groups within which the conditions of acceptable variation can be maintained.

Members of any group *must* accept some binding authority to settle disputes. Those who refuse to do so threaten the society as it is constituted and become the potential focus for a new society. However, in order for the new society to survive, it too must solve the problem of settling conflicts of interest. History is full of accounts of both successes and failures at this game, and it is obviously an immediate concern in the present world. In the next chapter, we look at more complex societies and the ways they try to solve the problems of maintaining order and organization.

People in all societies occupy a variety of statuses and play a variety of roles. One difference between complex and simple societies lies in the total number of roles and statuses available to each member in one as compared to the other. Statuses are interrelated, and may also be arranged in groups within the society. The simple society has few statuses, generally just the universal ones with only two or three others. There may be no specialty roles for women and only one or two—if any—for men. Group membership—if there are any groups smaller than the society as a whole—is normally ascribed on the basis of age, sex, or kinship. Most statuses are also ascribed.

Since statuses are few, roles tend to be well known to all adults. Variation beyond tolerable limits tends to be rare and highly susceptible to group pressure on an informal basis. Violators are easy to identify, and pressure to change behavior can be tailored to fit the individual. All societies have decisions affecting all the members, that is, public decisions, that must be made. All groups have power that must be distributed. No group has complete equality. In small societies, all these questions are decided informally, by the group as a whole. Leaders are people who are listened to, who are followed because they are respected and esteemed. Their power is usually that of suggestion, not coercion. Such leaders tend to express group opinion rather than form it.

6 Maintaining Order and Organization: The Complex Societies

Members of complex societies are even more interdependent than members of simple societies, and the problems of coordinating their behavior to ensure that both individual and group needs are met are accordingly greater. Obviously, there are more statuses and roles available in a complex society than there are in a simple one. There are also more subgroups in a complex society, and although membership in some is still based on age, sex, and kinship, other criteria may serve as well. In addition, more positions are likely to be achieved than ascribed, techniques for settling conflicts are more varied, and some are more impersonal. In this excerpt, as in the previous one, pay particular attention to what is expected of whom, and what happens if expectations are not met. Note the new methods for organization as well as those that persist from simple societies.

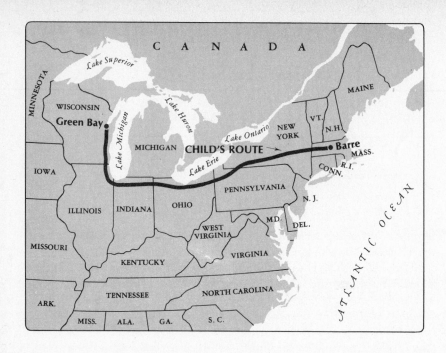

Authority and the Frontiersman

I was born in the town of Barre, Worcester County, Massachusetts, April 3rd, 1797.* At the age of ten, I was left an orphan, and never inherited a cent from any person. I was turned loose upon the wide world without anyone to advise or protect me, and had to struggle through poverty.

I remained in my native state until 1816. I was then nineteen years of age, and was hard at work at fifty cents per day, when the Town Collector called on me for a minister tax. The amount was one dollar and seventy-five cents, which appeared to me like a large sum to pay a minister, who performed no manual labor. I told the collector I had no money and inquired what would be the consequence if I failed to pay the tax? *"Pay or go to jail,"* was the reply; I didn't like the jail alternative, so I told the collector he must wait until I could get some money. He consented, and called again in a few days; but I was still moneyless. . . . It began to be close times with me—I must pay, go to jail, or run away. I determined on the latter course, settled with my employer on Saturday night, who paid me for my services, and made the necessary preparations for a quiet departure.

*Abridged from "Recollections of Wisconsin since 1820" by Colonel Ebenezer Childs, in Lyman C. Draper (ed.), *Collections of the State Historical Society of Wisconsin* (Madison: The State Historical Society of Wisconsin, 1906), Vol. 4, pp. 153–154, 165–167, 175–181. Reprinted by permission of the State Historical Society. Col. Childs was one of the early settlers in Wisconsin and a respected citizen at the time L. C. Draper recorded his recollections.

With a fine pony, and a few articles of clothing, which I packed into an old pair of saddle-bags, I started on Sunday morning after the people had gone to church. I went as much as I could across lots, and along unfrequented roads, in order to get past the church without being discovered. . . . I finally got safely beyond the limits of the town; but in passing through another town, I had necessarily to go close to the church, in passing which I was hailed from the front door. I cast a furtive glance in that direction, and saw a long-spliced Yankee coming towards me. I spurred up the pony, and kept out of Yankee's reach. Soon finding that his long legs could not overtake my nimble horse, he went back, and mounted a fine horse in the church shed, and gave me chase. . . . Had the tithing-man been a good rider, he would have overtaken me; as it was, after pursuing about two miles, he gave up the chase and returned. . . . I arrived at my sister's that night, and left early the next morning for the State of New York. My business took me off the main travelled road from Boston to Albany and when I regained it, I learned that a tithing-man and several assistants had passed in hot pursuit, but I was too smart for them, and evaded them all. It was at that time a violation of law for a traveller to journey on the Sabbath in Massachusetts, and if he could not be arrested on that day by the tithing-man, he could be followed and apprehended anywhere within the State. When I crossed the State line, and got into New York, I felt greatly relieved. I was then in the land of freedom, and out of reach of oppression. [He continued to travel and moved slowly west until, about 1821, he reached Green Bay, Wisconsin.]

. . .

Old Judge Charles Reaume lived about two years after I settled in the country. He was a man of great importance when I first came to the Bay, and for a long time previously. He had been appointed a sort of Justice, I think by General Harrison, when he was Governor of Indiana Territory. When Reaume held his courts, he would dress in his British uniform red coat, and cocked hat, and put on an air of pompous dignity. There was a noted case brought before him by a young lady for seduction and breach of marriage promise. After hearing the testimony, the honorable court rendered judgment in this wise— the seducer was sentenced to purchase a calico dress for the injured lady, and two dresses for the baby, and the constable to pay the costs by splitting a thousand rails for the Judge. This decision of the Court was complied with, though the constable was not well pleased with the part assigned him—not being able exactly to comprehend why he should be mulcted° in damages; but at length agreed to split the rails on condition that the Judge should board him while doing so. This was paying pretty roundly for the honors of office.

The first jury trial held at Green Bay before Robert Irwin, I was the plaintiff. . . . I gained my suit. The defendant in the case was a Frenchman. He and his friends were outrageous in their denunciations of the d——d Yankee court and jury. The next trial which was brought before Squire Irwin, was one in which a colored man claimed pay for labor done for L. Grignon. A jury was impanelled, when Grignon, the defendant, brought in his account as an offset against the negro's claim; and in the account, tobacco was charged at four dollars per pound, common clay pipes at fifty cents each, common calico for the Indian trade at one dollar and fifty cents per yard. The jury took the responsibility to reduce Grignon's account one half, and striking a balance, returned a verdict in the darkey's favor, at which he was greatly rejoiced, while his opponent was not a little restive ...

... In 1824, Hon. James D. Doty was appointed Judge for the North-Western district of Michigan Territory ... The first term of Judge Doty's court was held at Green Bay, when he charged the grand jury to inquire particularly in relation to persons living with women to whom they were not legally married. The grand jury found thirty-six bills of indictment against inhabitants of Green Bay for fornication, and two bills for adultery. I was a witness before the grand jury in eighteen cases, and I was also one of the jury. . . . The court was ... very lenient towards those who had been indicted; the Judge informing them that if they would get married within ten days, and produce a certificate of the fact, they would not be fined. They all complied with this requirement, except two, who stood their trial. Their plea was, that they were legally married, had lived a great many years with their wives, and had large families of children—that their marriages had been solemnized according to the customs of the Indians. The court took a different view of the legality of those marriages, and fined those two men fifty dollars each and costs. We all thought at the time that Judge Doty was rather hard in breaking in rough shod, as he did, upon our arrangements, but we had to submit, and make the best we could of the matter.

. . .

Fort Howard in Green Bay, Wisconsin, ca. 1850. *(The State Historical Society of Wisconsin)*

In the winter of 1827–28, Daniel Whitney obtained permission of the Winnebagoes to make shingles on the Upper Wisconsin. He employed twenty-two Stockbridge Indians, and one white man to superintend the party; and he engaged me to take the party up the Wisconsin, and supply them with provisions. ... When I reached Fort Winnebago on my return, Major Twiggs, the commanding officer of that garrison, informed me, that Whitney's men must be sent out of the country; that he expected the Indian Agent that day from Prairie du Chien, who would go up and conduct the whole party off from the Wisconsin; that Whitney had no right there, and if the Indian Agent needed any assistance in putting a speedy check to this trespass upon the Indian lands he should furnish the necessary quota of soldiers to effect it.

Major Twiggs then advised me not to attempt to go up where the men were making shingles; that if I did, I might get into trouble. I told him that I was employed by Whitney to supply his men with provisions; and that all the Indian Agents and soldiers combined could not prevent me from fulfilling my engagements. I told him furthermore, that this difficulty had all been brought about by false representations to the Agent; that I delivered provisions to the Winnebagoes for Whitney's men, and that they were all satisfied that Whitney should make as many shingles as he pleased. He flew into a violent passion, and told me that I would be sorry for my course, and for what I had said. I told him that I disregarded all his threats, and then left him.

I then went up to where the men were at work. They had made about two hundred thousand shingles. I delivered my provisions to the party, and was about leaving camp, when a Frenchman came on a clean jump. He told me that there was a great lot of soldiers and officers at Grignon's Trading Post a short distance below; that Mr. Grignon had sent him to inform me that the soldiers were after me, and that I had better go back into the woods, and keep out of the way. I told my men to take their teams a short distance down the river, and remain there until I should call for them; and with my own team I went down to Grignon's, where I found the Agent, one officer and twelve soldiers. The Agent informed me that he had come up to take all of Whitney's men out of the country. I asked him if he proposed to take me? He replied that he should take all he should find committing trespass on the camp. I went with them. When we arrived, the men were all out in the woods. I started to where they were at work, and I went to work shaving shingles. The Agent soon arrived with his party. I told the shingle-makers that they must quit work, which they did; but I kept on until all left, hoping they would attempt to arrest me, but they did not. After awhile I went to the shanty, where they were all assembled. The overseer asked me to go out of doors with him, that he wished to speak with me. When we got to the door, I asked him what he wanted of me; he replied that he wanted my advice as to what course he should pursue. I told him that if that was what he wanted, I would give him the best advice I had, in the house, before the whole party, Agent, soldiers and all; that if I were in his place, and had charge of the men, I would not surrender alive, but that he might do as he pleased. The overseer consulted with his men and they finally concluded to surrender.

At this juncture, I called on my eight stout Frenchmen who speedily came up with their teams. I told them that as the foreman and Indians were prisoners, that we would take charge of the shanty and property belonging to Whitney; upon which we all spread down our blankets, and turned in for the night. The next morning the overseer called to his men to get breakfast. I jumped up and told them, that as they were prisoners, they were out of Whitney's employ, and forbade them touching a single thing in or about the shanty. I called my men, and told them to get breakfast. That opened the eyes of the Agent and officer; and the latter remarked, that the commissary at the Fort had sent his compliments to me, requesting me to let him and his men and the prisoners have provisions enough to last them back to the Fort. I told him that he should not have a pound of anything—that they might starve first. Soon after the Agent came to me, and coaxed me until I concluded to let them have a supply; I sold them pork at fifty cents per pound, flour twenty-five cents, corn fifteen dollars per bushel, and let them have a horse and train° [a wooden sled with plank runners, drawn by a single horse] to return with for ten dollars. They took breakfast and left. I collected all of the tools, provisions, and other articles, and took them down to Grignon's, and stored them. The next day I started for the Portage, and encamped where Portage City is now located. That night a sergeant came to my camp to inform me that I had better not proceed by way of the Fort as Major Twiggs was in a high rage, swearing that if I should come nigh the Fort, he would have me arrested, put in irons, and set to Prairie du Chien; that I was as much a trespasser on the Indian lands as any of the party of the shingle-makers, as the officer and soldiers of the detachment . . . had seen me making shingles. The sergeant advised me to go across the country, and keep entirely clear of the Fort. I kindly thanked him for his good wishes, but told him that I had business with the sutler° at the Fort, and should go that way to see him; and that I was not in the habit of dodging any mortal man or set of men. The Agent sent me word, that I had better not go near the Fort; that he had heard what Twiggs had said, and it would be prudent to avoid coming in contact with him. Still I was determined to go by way of the Fort, while my teamsters were averse to it. I simply told them, if they were cowards they could go any way they pleased.

On the ensuing morning I got ready, and started for the Fort, my men all following. Nearing the garrison, I discovered all of the officers down at the river near the crossing place. The soldiers were getting out ice. When they saw me, Twiggs left, and went to the Fort. I crossed the river, and drove up to the sutler's store. I had not been there long, when a soldier came in and informed me that Capt. Gwin, the commissary, wanted to see me at the Fort. I told the soldier that I would endeavor to be more polite than the Captain had been— that he might give my compliments to him, and tell him if he wished to see me more than I did him, then he would find me at or near the store. The clerk was very uneasy, and requested me to leave the store, as he was fearful of trouble. I went out of doors. Soon after a number of officers came near where I stood —Capt. Gwin among them. The Captain asked me if I had really refused to let the officer and soldiers have provisions when they were up the Wisconsin? I frankly told them that I did; and if it had not been for the Agent, I certainly should not have let them have any, and that I was sorry that I had yielded to the Agent's urgent solicitations. Capt. Gwin was very indignant, and said that the officers had hitherto thought a great deal of me, but now I had forfeited all of their respect and confidence. I expressed my regret at losing their confidence; that I had my own views of duty, in doing which I could not consult their wishes. I got on my train and started; and in passing the Fort, I gave three cheers, and went on my way rejoicing. I did not see Twiggs again.

. . .

As early as June, 1825, Hon. John P. Arndt obtained a license to maintain a ferry across Fox River, a short distance above Fort Howard. Soon after, the commanding officer placed a guard on the west side of the river, to prevent the ferry-boat from landing—contending that no one had a right to cross without first obtaining leave of him. I was at this time boarding with Arndt, and took one of his boats, with one man with me, to try and see what the guard would do with me. As I approached near the opposite shore, the guard came down to seize the boat; I directed the man to turn the boat around, and throw the stern to the shore. He did so, and as I jumped out, the boat received an impetus which pushed it into the stream, when the man returned unmolested. I was arrested, went to the Fort, and laughed at the officers, and told them that I thought I was in a free country; and so believing, that I should go and come when and where I pleased, that they might all go to——.

Soon after, Judge Arndt thought that he would try the experiment of crossing and landing on the western bank of the river. But as soon as they landed, he and his companion were arrested, and taken to the Fort. Arndt was a little mulish, and refused to go, but was overcome by numbers, and dragged to the Fort by brute force. He was finally discharged with an admonition not to attempt to cross again without permission from the commanding officer. The court sat a short time after, and Arndt commenced a suit against the commanding officer for false imprisonment; the officer was fined fifty dollars and costs, and the court decided that Fox River was a public highway, and that any person had a right to obtain a license for a ferry at any point across the river, and the military had no right to interfere. The guard was withdrawn, and we had no further trouble about crossing and re-crossing Fox River.

SETTLING CONFLICTS

Laws are really effective only when the people in general support them. The failure of prohibition in the United States and the present difficulty in enforcing laws against marijuana use and segregation illustrate the problem.

Punishment is usually thought of as a deterrent to further misbehavior. Yet for it to be effective—if it is—it must be a probable consequence of norm violation. A $10 fine may be a more effective deterrent than twenty years in prison if there is a 99 percent chance that the lawbreaker will have to pay the $10 and a 99 percent chance that he will not have to serve twenty years. In addition, whatever happens must be regarded by the lawbreaker as a punishment. An Iroquois girl once complained to me that a judge had put her on probation instead of sending her to jail. Probation, she said, left her exposed to all the temptations that got her into trouble before, but with even more limitations on her behavior, making it now even easier for her to get into trouble. She said she would have been better off in jail where she could learn hair-dressing, a marketable skill. That is a sensible suggestion when being jailed itself is not regarded as a shameful, humiliating experience.

Furthermore, punishment must be imposed by individuals or groups that are in some way accepted as having the right to do so by the person being punished. Consider the resistance fighters in France during World War II. If one was caught, he was subjected to imprisonment, torture, and even death— all more severe punishments than we normally inflict on norm violators. Yet the threat of this treatment did not stop acts of sabotage and espionage. Resistance fighters regarded the danger as an occupational hazard, one of the risks they had to run to carry out a dangerous mission, not as a punishment for breaking a norm. Germans were not felt to have any "right" to make laws. They were the enemy, the outsiders, people to be defied and fought by any means available.

Much the same situation occurs with a counterculture° group in any society. Members of these groups, whose culture is opposed to that of the mainstream of the society, are not likely to be deterred by what *other* people (the enemy) regard as punishment. It is necessary to ask: "Does this person regard what we are doing as a punishment?" and "Does this person think the people punishing him have the right to do so?" If the answer to both questions is "No," then the proposed "punishment" will probably not be effective in bringing about any desired change in behavior. It will not even be satisfactory revenge.

Social pressure must be effective to some extent if a group is to survive at all. The individual who is completely insensitive to group pressure is more often a psychopath than a savior. Yet some frightening instances of inhumanity have also been the result of a too slavish adherence to group pressure. Atrocities such as those that occurred in Hitler's Germany or at My Lai in South Vietnam were carried out by people who claimed they were merely obeying orders. The sociologist Robin Williams pointed out that it was the "gentle people of prejudice who posed for us a basic problem" (Williams 1964:110). That is, the people who accepted discrimination and prejudice because everyone else did are more numerous and more troublesome than are the genuine bigots.

In a small society, where dissenters have no other people to turn to and where being cast out of the group may be equivalent to a death sentence, group pressure is naturally more effective than it is in a large society where almost any rebel can find at least some supporters. The problem of balance is crucial. All

American colonials protesting acts by what they regarded as illegitimate authority.
(Culver Pictures, Inc.)

extremes—individuals too resistant or too compliant and groups too tolerant of variation or too insistent on conformity—may be equally threatening to individual and group survival under particular circumstances. In complex societies, where individuals have difficulty in making their voices heard, the dissenter often plays a crucial role in calling attention to injustice, outmoded norms, or the abuse of power. Childs played such a role in regard to the army. In the excerpt, he was completely unmoved by the army threats. He *tried* to get arrested. In the shingle incident, when the foreman asked him for advice, Childs said he would die before surrendering. Note that Childs makes a distinction between an order he regarded as illegitimate and one he disliked but accepted because it emanated from legitimate authority (the judge). He obeyed the latter, but the former he gleefully defied and dared the bogus authority to do its worst. Childs was not exceptional; others on the frontier acted in a similar way. The parallel with the modern situation should be apparent. Militants are often acting in the good old American tradition of the Boston Tea Party. The justice—or lack of it—of a cause is not at issue. The point is that this behavior is apt to occur in any society when the norms and the legitimacy of its authorities are called into question.

Notice that two different things are involved—the norms themselves, and the authorities that make or enforce them. Variation in norms is one of the characteristics of a complex society (legitimacy of authorities is discussed later).

The economic rights and obligations people have toward one another in regard to valuable things (discussed in Chapter 3) are examples of norms that may vary or be called into question. The United States has a history of citizens violating norms of property under situations of stress. During the depression of the 1930s, for example, farmers used violence and extralegal methods (along with legal trickery) to try to keep their farms and to get more money for their crops. In the cities, people resorted to violence and rent strikes as well as to legal tactics to prevent evictions or seizure of property by creditors (Terkel 1970:239-265, 453-465). Today, some people may violate these norms for a variety of reasons: to attract attention, or obtain financial support, for their "cause," to harass other members of the society seen as "the enemy," or to correct perceived injustices of distribution. Naturally enough, members of the society who still regard the violated norms as legitimate want the violators stopped. However, the means adopted to do this may not work because they are usually designed for people who violate norms they themselves share (as was the case with Cephu), rather than for people who hold different norms.

Because the level of agreement about norms maintained in the simple societies does not occur in the complex ones, and indeed is probably impossible, new techniques for maintaining order and organization must be devised to allow larger numbers of people to coexist in relative peace—techniques such as formal laws, formal sanctions, and specialized personnel for both law and government, along with such concepts as delegation of authority, justice, public law, and impersonal enforcement. Injured individuals are no longer required to seek their own revenge or justice. Other members of the society cooperate to see that they are protected, revenged, or somehow compensated.

The functions of law (resolving conflicts, defining relationships among members of the society, and distributing power) are the same in either simple or complex societies, even though the mechanisms differ (Hoebel 1964:274). Increased complexity, however, is not only apparent in the development of specialized statuses and roles concerned with social control, and in the added informality and impersonality of procedures, but also in new sources of support for norms, problems of the identification of culprits, and determination of guilt or innocence of people accused of norm violation. Such things rarely troubled the BaMbuti; norms were supported by a general consensus of band members. The supernatural, for example, was rarely involved. But as societies grow larger, the supernatural realm often provides additional support for social norms. Violations may be interpreted as offensive to supernatural beings as well as to other members of the society. Individuals who break such supernaturally supported norms may expect misfortune, illness, madness, or death—all of which are regarded as supernatural punishments in various societies. So long as the supernatural is expected to punish sins, and so long as the punishment is limited to the guilty individual, members of society take no action. Sometimes, however, an offense by one individual is believed to expose the entire group to supernatural vengeance. Remember how in Chapter 3 all members of the Huron society were held responsible for the actions of one individual. This idea of shared guilt occurs in many societies around the world. In such cases, members of the community usually attempt to detect the guilty individual to punish him, and thus avert the wrath of the supernatural. A case of this type is reported in the Old Testament. The Israelites were badly defeated in battle. Their leader, Joshua, asked the supernatural for the reason and was informed that someone had disobeyed the strict command of God not to keep booty from Jericho. Joshua asked the supernatural to reveal the guilty party. First, Joshua cast lots to determine the tribe of the sinner, then the family, then the household, and finally the specific individual. When he was confronted with the results of the divination,° the man confessed, and the booty was found in his tent. Then members of the society killed him and his children, and destroyed his possessions. After they had thus removed the sinner from their midst, Joshua and his men again attacked the people who had defeated them, and this time the Israelites won. Of course, that convinced them that the divination and the punishment had been correct (Joshua 7:1–26; 8:1–27).

The story of Joshua not only illustrates group guilt and the danger of offending the supernatural, but also the problem of the identification of the norm violator. In small face-to-face societies, where everyone knows everyone else and where most aspects of life are highly public, it is hard to hide any kind of norm violation and there is seldom any doubt about the identity of the guilty person (as the BaMbuti excerpt illustrates). Larger societies such as the Huron

Notable persons in the French Cameroons wear ceremonial dress as they prepare to receive a UN mission. *(United Nations)*

made little effort to determine individual guilt because responsibility was collective—even if the culprit were known the whole family or community had
to pay reparations anyway. (The specific offender might be punished later by
the family or community, however, as was intimated in the Huron chief's
reparation speech.)

Complex societies have serious problems with identification. As a society
grows, the proportion of its members who know one another decreases. In
contemporary nations with a high degree of mobility and a population of several million or more, members of the society truly make up a "nation of strangers" (Packard 1972). Under these circumstances, identification of a norm
violator becomes difficult. Fear of misidentification, with the consequent suffering of a "good" citizen, is a concern in the United States (although it is not
necessarily so in all modern complex societies). This concern adds to the detec-
tion problem, since precise and accurate identification of the actual violator, not
just his or her community or family, is required. Group responsibility is not
acceptable in many modern societies, where because it is so easy for the individual to escape from social pressures applied by specific people, the group no
longer has much control over individual behavior. Consequently, members of
these societies feel it is unjust to punish everyone for the violation of one person
whose behavior is outside their control. Group responsibility still occurs on
occasion—in schoolrooms, prisons, and so on, where individual mobility is restricted and the group can effectively apply pressure—but it is not a general
mechanism.

Thus, population size and mobility are involved in both the need for social-
control techniques and the types that develop. Some societies have tried to
increase the effectiveness of the control through elaborate identification of
individuals and restriction on movement—such as requiring police permits
before individuals can move to another address; requiring citizens to carry
identification papers at all times; recording identification numbers whenever
bus, train, or airplane tickets are purchased; establishing checkpoints where all
travelers must identify themselves; and so on. This sort of close supervision of
the movements of individuals—regarded as a distasteful infringement on individual rights in the United States and seldom used—has been on the increase
throughout the world in the last few decades. This increase, which began
strongly after World War I and which has increased steadily ever since, is partly
due to the tremendous growth of population and increase in the speed of
transportation.

Before this trend took hold in industrial nations, supernatural means were
used (and still are used today in smaller, less complex societies) to indicate both
the identity and guilt of the accused. In addition to the casting of lots, there are
several ways the supernatural may be involved. One is the ordeal, where the
accused are given poison, forced to put a hand into boiling water, or to touch
their tongue to a hot iron, and so on. In these cases, the supernatural is expected
to protect the innocent and cause the guilty to suffer. During the witch trials
of the Middle Ages, there was a slightly different approach: suspects were tied
up and thrown into rivers or lakes. If they floated, it was assumed they had the
devil's help, so they were usually taken out and burned; if they drowned,

however, it was regarded as proof that God had accepted the innocent soul, so all was well—a case of "heads you win, tails I lose" for the accused. Trial by combat was another method for determining guilt or innocence. Either the accused or a champion willing to fight in the accused's defense battled the accuser (or the accused's champion). Women, children, and elderly or disabled men sought champions. An able-bodied man was supposed to fight in his own defense; if he sought a champion to fight for him he was likely to be suspected of cowardice or guilt and to have difficulty persuading anyone to "champion his cause" (the source of the saying). It was assumed that the supernatural would ensure the triumph of right (Leach 1949:829).

Trial by jury (jurors are supposedly ordinary citizens with no special legal training, selected from a random group without any connections to either defendant or plaintiff, and free from special biases) is a recent and unique institution confined to the English-speaking world (and to some former colonies). The presumption that the burden of proof is on the accuser is also unusual. In most legal systems, the accused is responsible for proving innocence. (It is much easier to disprove something than to prove it; a system in which one must prove innocence is biased against the accused, whereas one in which the plaintiff has to prove the accused's guilt is biased in the accused's favor.) Actually, in most such legal systems, the guilt of the accused is assumed and the purpose of a trial is simply to determine the degree of punishment that should be imposed. Even in systems in which there is some form of court and trial, the

A jury trial in Los Angeles in the 1920s. *(Brown Brothers)*

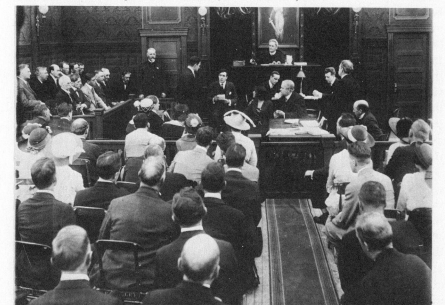

participants (other than the accused and witnesses) are usually members of the legal establishment rather than ordinary citizens. Such systems tend to be biased against the accused and *may* be more susceptible to corruption. On the other hand, if such a court and legal system is staffed with dedicated, altruistic, incorruptible individuals, it may render a more objective judgment than a jury. (Only the naive expect this to happen most of the time, however. Dedicated, altruistic, incorruptible people are seldom in the majority in any society. A system that depends on staffing all, or even most, key positions with such individuals is bound to function erratically.)

The adversary system, in which prosecutor and defense lawyers are competitors in a legal game, also causes some problems, since for most of the participants winning the contest may take precedence over establishing the facts or obtaining justice. (An example would be a case in New York State recently in which lawyers suppressed knowledge of several murder victims whose bodies their client had hidden. The lawyers' desire to win their case and protect their client took priority over a fair trial, the truth of the case, and justice.) The jury system is susceptible to some abuse under the adversary system also, because the selection process for jurors may be arranged in such a way that representatives of minorities or certain special groups are systematically excluded. Then, too, a lawyer who knows how to play on the emotions of the jurors may win his case even though the evidence is weak. Such things pervert the whole concept of a jury trial, in which the objectivity of the jurors is a major goal. Even though bias in favor of the accused is already built into the system through the expressed statement that the accused is presumed innocent until proven guilty, some people assume that jurors should favor the accused. But that would not necessarily result in justice any more than having jurors biased for the prosecution. A willingness to decide either way according to the strength of the evidence presented is the ideal behind the jury system.

The conflicting underlying assumptions of different legal systems have led to a great deal of misunderstanding between societies, since most people tend to believe other legal systems are like their own. Fidel Castro, for instance, was roundly criticized in the United States for condemning political prisoners without a jury trial—although Spanish justice and its New World descendants have never included such a thing. On the other hand, students in a Peruvian school insisted they would not have supported the cause of Carl Chessman (a robber sentenced to death by California courts whose case became a cause célèbre in the late 1950s) if they had known he had had a jury trial. In both cases, ignorance of the other system was partly the cause of the misunderstanding.

Complex methods for determining guilt and innocence—whether they involve the supernatural or secular institutions such as police and jury—are essential to large, complex societies. Detectives, police, judges, and juries are necessary when a society grows so large that victims are unacquainted with the criminal and cannot easily identify or find him.

The need for explicit rules and regulations in larger and more complex societies is indicated by some of the earliest writing we know. Business accounts, contracts, and disputes are among the first things to be recorded. In fact, it was the need for such records that apparently gave strong impetus to the development of writing. A law code of Ur-Nammu, a Sumerian king who ruled about 2100 B.C., is among the first examples of writing—about 300 years before Hammurabi, whose law code many history books still call the first (Hamblin 1973:106). In the Far East, too, matters of law and government are the subject of early writing although the Chinese oracle bones (the sources of the earliest records there) have a more directly religious orientation than the records of the Middle East (Chard 1975:297–300).

Once formal rules were made explicit and recorded in permanent form, specialists were usually given the task of explaining, administering, and enforcing them. A specialized army (at first as often used for internal enforcement as against external enemies) appears fairly early in written history, a specialized police force (distinct from an army), rather late. Both groups have been regarded with considerable suspicion by the general public. Until taxes were efficiently collected, and supply problems handled effectively, armies lived off local citizens, quartering in their houses and eating their food. In addition, soldiers in the ranks were usually from the poorest, least educated groups in the society. Consequently, populations were often menaced almost as much by their protectors as by the enemy. Police forces have suffered from similar problems. In many parts of the world they, too, are still recruited from the

A London bobby, ca. 1915. *(Culver Pictures, Inc.)*

poorest, least educated levels of the society and are given little or no special training. They often have a reputation as spies or tools of oppressive leaders. A different attitude appeared in some countries (England, for example) during the nineteenth century, when a majority of citizens began to regard police as sources of protection against "criminal" elements in the society. Today, in the United States, both attitudes toward the police can be found. Some segments of the society regard the police as agents of "the enemy," while others think of them as protectors. The difference in attitude depends on whether the police are perceived as supporting the values of one's own group or those of some other. In reality, values are not as significant as behavior. As the Wisconsin excerpt shows, in complex societies it is possible for a number of people and groups to hold quite different values—so long as *behavior* remains within certain specified limits. If behavior goes beyond those acceptable limits, however, the various law-enforcement specialists are called upon to use sanctions to bring the behavior back within the tolerable limits. Thus, despite the differences in the number of people involved, the specialization of some of them, and specific details of procedure, the underlying concept among the BaMbuti, the Wisconsin community, and the modern United States is the same: when someone has gone too far, has behaved "badly," that person must be punished, reformed, or both. Questions of concern in complex societies today are, Whose values are being protected and supported? How widespread is adherence to those values? Are majority values involved, or is a minority trying to impose its values on the rest of society? Only in complex societies can there be any doubt about these issues.

In Wisconsin, formal and explicit laws were passed by specialists called legislators, acting in council, and allowing the decision of the majority to be presented as the judgment of the group as a whole. Those specialists clearly did not share the same opinions as other people in Wisconsin regarding what was proper behavior—but then there was a much wider range of opinion in Wisconsin than there was among the BaMbuti. One reason for this is that there were so many more people in Wisconsin, but another reason is the result of another characteristic of social complexity—an increase in the number of statuses and roles.

STATUS VARIETY AND CONFORMITY

Comparison of the excerpts in this and the previous chapter makes the increase in societal complexity (due to the greater number of statuses and the variety of available options for interactions) obvious. There were only sixteen to eighteen named statuses in the BaMbuti excerpt. There are some fifty in this one. Almost all of the BaMbuti statuses are ascribed, whereas only twelve of the fifty named in the Childs' excerpt are ("orphan," "person," "Yankee," "sister," "man," "baby," "negro," "Indian," "woman," "child," "white man," "Frenchman"). As usual there are some ("wife," "lady," "guard," "coward," "witness," "inhabitant," "prisoner") that seem to be partly ascribed and partly achieved, but well over half of the statuses mentioned are definitely achieved ("minister," "General," "Town Collector," and so on). This variety of available options is one of the indications of societal complexity. It goes with occupational specialization. Among the BaMbuti no one individual collected the contribution to the molimo basket, a religious contribution. New Englanders had at least two specialists for collecting religious contributions, the town collector, who gathered the tax to support ministers (along with other town taxes, no doubt), and the tithing man, who was in charge of direct contributions by church members to their church funds. Similarly, the BaMbuti had no legal specialists, whereas Wisconsin had several.

Accompanying this increase in available options for behavior and variability in social expectations is an increased pressure to conform, at least outwardly, to these expectations. The relationship between societal complexity and pressure toward conformity is somewhat paradoxical. On the one hand, a large variety of acceptable roles are available in complex societies, but pressure for *outward* conformity to expected behavior not necessarily directly related to role performance is greater in complex societies than in simple ones, and directly correlated with the amount of specialization in the society. There may actually be a need for greater conformity in complex societies in order to reduce anxiety. For example, in the United States it is next to impossible for the average individual to determine directly the competence of the people on whom he or she depends. Our survival is constantly at the mercy of persons we do not know who must promptly and accurately perform tasks we know nothing about. For example, we usually do not know the farmers, meat packers, canners, water-works employees, and others who are significantly involved in our daily meals, nor do most of us have more than the barest understanding of their jobs. Yet the food we eat and the water we drink can kill us if they are not properly processed. With our lives at stake such uncertainty should produce unbearable anxiety. Why doesn't it? First, most of us don't think about the problem. Second, the presence of a large amount of diffuse anxiety is a common phenomenon of complex societies which suggests that there may be a concern about the problem on at least some level of our awareness. And third, outward conformity tends to reassure us.

When we do have some direct contact with people on whom our lives depend (such as doctors, police, pharmacists, or others), we tend to evaluate them by superficial visible characteristics. These may not be the best to use, but they are all we have. For example, suppose you are in a strange town and suddenly have a severe pain in your chest. Your left arm begins to go numb. You see a doctor's office and, terrified, you go inside. There you find a man in leopard-skin trunks and high leather boots, striding back and forth, cracking a whip and singing an operatic aria. A receptionist nods toward him and says, "The doctor will be with you in a moment." If you are a normal individual, you will probably go right back out the door in spite of your chest pain. On the other hand, if the same man comes out of an office door wearing a white smock over long pants, with a stethoscope around his neck, and if he speaks in a quiet, assured manner, you will probably relax, confident that this man can help you.

Actually, the first one might be the best heart specialist in a hundred-mile radius and the second one a fraud. But you have neither the time nor the qualifications to make any valid check of the man's actual competence, so you judge—in your urgent need—by outward conformity to the behavior expected of a physician in our society.

In a small society, on the other hand, individuals have plenty of time to get to know one another, and outward appearance need not be considered at all in evaluating competence, guilt, or reliability. The BaMbuti did not have to notice what Cephu was wearing, or how he combed his hair, to judge him; they knew him all too well. No matter what Cephu said, no one was fooled by his protestations of innocence or his false tears. Indeed, Moke had even been able to predict that Cephu would spoil the hunt long before he did. By the same token, however, because everyone knew him so well, no one doubted him when he gave in and repented. In large, complex, mobile societies, that sort of intimate knowledge of a person is possible, if at all, only with a few close friends and relatives. There is no way that most police officers can know most citizens in their area, or that most doctors can know most of their patients, the way Moke knew Cephu. Moke grew up with Cephu. He saw him, played with him, hunted with him, listened to him hour after hour, day after day, for thirty years or more. How could he help knowing him thoroughly?

Because of the high degree of pressure for outward conformity in modern industrialized societies, dress and manners are a major form of nonverbal communication. These things communicate in simple societies too, but there they seldom take on the significance for initial impressions that they do in a complex society. Many young people either do not realize the significance of this aspect of "appearance," or refuse to accept it, while members of the older generation often cannot explain just why they think long hair is disrespectful. Consequently, much of this kind of communication may be faulty. For instance, a young man to whom a beard and long hair may indicate only an awareness of modern styles may find that when he goes job-hunting, older people appear to be in doubt about his ability to perform properly as, say, a bank teller. Unfortunately, since prospective employers have not had the opportunity to watch him grow up and to follow his general behavior throughout his life, they have little choice but to react to his nonverbal communication—which in the case probably says to them that the applicant is an individualist who scorns the opinions and values of the older generation (i.e., his prospective employers). Naturally they question, if not his *ability,* at least his *willingness,* to perform the required tasks adequately and honestly. This kind of failure to understand or appreciate the communication function of appearance in complex societies has led to much unnecessary unhappiness and confused bitterness.

POWER

Some of the bitterness is related to frustration on the part of people who are trying to improve their power position in society or fear on the part of people who feel threatened with the loss of some of theirs. All people seem to want some control over their own lives, some voice in public decisions, some prestige and esteem from their fellows. Methods of gaining these valued goals differ widely from one society to another. In several, to gain public power it is necessary to avoid any appearance of seeking it. Anyone who obviously tries to gain power is apt to lose it. Thus Cephu actually lost his case when he claimed that he was an important man, a chief. The response was that if he was a chief he was not a BaMbuti, since they did not have chiefs. By openly claiming power, he lost all chance at it. In such societies, the man who actually has power tends to be one who claims there is no such thing as a chief and who always appears reluctant to push his opinions on anyone. That man is listened to, and his advice followed. He may claim not to want power, but he makes key decisions that affect the behavior of others in the society; whether he claims it or not, whether he wants it or not, he *has* power.

Complex societies have more power to distribute, public decisions affect more people, more material wealth is involved, and there is consequently a great deal more concern about power and its distribution in complex societies. The BaMbuti denied they had chiefs. They had no formally chosen leaders. They represent one end of the public power continuum. The other end, found in complex societies, is a network of statuses whose primary roles are political —that is, dealing with public power and decision making—one definition of *government*° (Swartz, Turner, *et al.* 1966:12). By this definition, the Pygmies do not have a government. Wisconsin did, although the only clearly political status mentioned in the excerpt is that of the Governor of Indiana Territory. Yet the Pygmies make group decisions and exercise public power even though they do not have specialized roles for doing so. All men are hunters and all occasionally make or help make public decisions.

The opinion leaders in the Pygmy group expressed the general consensus. The judges in the Wisconsin excerpt occasionally went against group consensus, but in both cases the members of the society supported their leaders and, one assumes, were ready to use force to do so if necessary. Force may be a factor in the support for authority, but it is important to realize that *no* system of social control could possibly rely entirely on force. If a political leader does use force to stay in power, he obviously has to rely on many others to apply it for him, and they, at least, must support him for some reason other than the force he commands, since they are that force. In addition, force is expensive and inefficient.

Childs expressed dissatisfaction with the judge's decisions several times, but he never suggested disregarding them. When he did have a conflict with the law in New England, he ran from the area rather than defy the officals. The excerpt makes it clear, however, that this behavior was not the result of sheep-like conformity or timidity; Childs had a strongly developed idea of what consti-tuted legitimate authority. He never questioned the right of the tithing man to arrest him. He simply escaped from his jurisdiction. He accepted Judge Doty's decisions and even served on the investigating jury, although he did not like the new rules and said so. However, he defied, ignored, and insulted Major

Twiggs. Childs did not grant Twiggs any right to control his behavior. Later, when the commanding officer of the fort tried to prevent people from crossing the Fox River without his permission, both Childs and Arndt openly challenged his right to do this. The army officer ultimately accepted the legitimacy of the court, since he withdrew the guard once the court decided the river was a public highway.

Notice how closely this topic is related to the question of acceptance of norms. The two things are not the same, but they are similar and related. It is possible to accept the right of an authority to make or enforce laws but to reject the laws themselves. In such a case individuals have several options, and among those most commonly chosen are the following: they can obey the laws and work to get legislation to change them; they can secretly disobey the law and try to avoid getting caught; they can openly disobey the laws and try to convince authorities not to enforce them (by persuasion, social pressure, or prestation); they can openly disobey the laws, challenging the law in court or proudly going to jail as a way of expressing their rejection of the law and acceptance of the authority's right to make and enforce it. Options are fewer if people accept the laws but reject the legitimacy of the authority since, in this last case, people would continue to abide by the law but would try to remove the authority—using either legal or illegal means to do so.

The acceptance of authority is an important part of any system of social control. If even one of the parties to a dispute does not accept the right of an overriding authority to make binding decisions, the system of social control is threatened. If the army had refused to accept the decision of the court, what could Childs have done? He could have surrendered, and no longer attempted to cross the river without permission. He could have tried to cross without getting caught, and run the risk of arrest and punishment. He could have fought. There were not many other alternatives available. The Civil War (correctly titled the War of the Rebellion) resulted from the refusal of certain states to accept the right of the federal government to make decisions that were binding on them. In simple societies, when the legitimacy of leadership is denied and its decisions defied, there is a change in leadership; in complex societies there is often civil disorder or violence either within one society or between two or more. The United Nations and the earlier League of Nations provide good examples of the ineffectiveness of organizations whose legitimacy of authority is not accepted by all the participants in a dispute.

LEADERSHIP IN COMPLEX SOCIETIES

In small societies, as mentioned and illustrated in Chapter 5, leaders are not formally chosen and the number of leaders is not very large (even though every adult male in the group may lead at one time or another) because of the size of the group. In large societies, the number of people in leadership positions increases, the formality of choosing leaders grows, there are more ways in which the choices are made, and (as in the case of economic or legal mechanisms) new forms are added to those that exist in simple societies. In addition, complex societies have several different levels of power in which only the lower ones correspond to leadership patterns in simpler societies. That is, the Pygmy band leader might correspond roughly in power to a family head in India, or to the minister of a fringe denomination or leader of a commune in the United States. Among the BaMbuti, band leaders are the top power level, but in India and the United States there are multiple levels above the family head, the minister, or the commune leader.

At the simplest level, leaders are determined pragmatically—as long as people follow them, they are leaders—but in complex societies, the highest leadership positions are determined in various ways:

1. The status is sometimes ascribed to an individual on the basis of his heritage.
2. Leadership can be revealed by the supernatural. The first king of Israel, Saul, was so revealed to Samuel. The Dalai Lama is chosen on the basis of supernatural signs.
3. Leaders may achieve their positions by conquest or competition.
4. A leader may be chosen by vote. Among complex societies, this method of choosing a leader is relatively recent.

Complex societies always have some intermediate levels of power between the highest and lowest positions. Councils, for example, are almost always involved at some point in the structure (Hoebel 1966:459). Even the most tyrannical dictator usually has a group of especially trained advisors. In fairly simple societies the council of elders may be the leadership. In the excerpt in Chapter 5 the "council" consisted of all the male adults and youths. Only the women officially took no part in making the decision about Cephu. From their behavior while returning from the hunt, however, it is clear that the women's disapproval of Cephu was at least as strong as the men's. None of the men involved in the actual decision could have been unaware of the attitude of the women, or of how the women would react if nothing were done. The women, therefore, influenced the decision although they took no active part in it. In a small society there is little need for elaborate mechanisms to learn the will of the people: everyone knows what it is, just as most of us know the opinions of our family and friends on matters of common interest. Remember, in a small society a person's entire life is spent with the same people, and usually they are fewer in total than the average American sees in a week. Under those circumstances, it is very difficult *not* to know what everyone is like and what they think about things. Councils in small societies often allow everyone likely to be affected by a decision to express an opinion, but this may be more to stir the group to action than to inform members, since often a consensus already exists.

Occasionally, however, members of the group may disagree sharply, and then the speeches at a council meeting do enable individuals to learn new information and to think more carefully about the problem. Usually members of small groups must reach unanimous agreement before taking any action. If they cannot agree and the problem is a serious one, the group may have to split up. The requirement of unanimity therefore places serious limits on the size of a group. The larger a group is, the longer it takes to reach unanimity, and the greater the possibility that the members will never agree entirely. Growth, therefore, must await the development of new techniques of organization.

One innovation for getting rapid decisions in a large group at a time of crisis was for members to delegate decision-making authority to a smaller council. Whereas all BaMbuti males were involved in decision making, in a larger society a council might be made up only of the heads of individual families; the unmarried men, young or old, would be left out of the process. For such a system to work, of course, these excluded individuals would have to agree to abide by the decisions of the family heads. If the society continued to grow, so that the council of family heads became too large to be able to act effectively, several related families might delegate authority to one person, who would represent them in council. As long as the council authority continued to be accepted, the innovation would permit a larger number of people to cooperate effectively in one society.

Still another step, again possibly prompted by the need for rapid decision making in a time of crisis, might be for a council to delegate power to a single individual and then revoke it when the crisis is past. If crisis situations arise often and last long enough, the position could become permanent. It has been suggested that this is how the status of king first came about in Mesopotamia (Frankfort 1964:356–358). Another innovation is to take a formal or informal poll of council members (or of all the adult males, or all the adults) and allow the majority opinion to decide the course of action for the group. This process is based on certain assumptions that most Americans take for granted but that are not so obvious to people experienced in other systems. For the innovations in decision making previously mentioned, only people who were not actively involved in the process had to accept the decisions made; but in majority rule, people *involved* in the decision making—the members of the minority—have to accept decisions contrary to their expressed wishes. The people excluded in the other systems have to accept the right of others to make decisions affecting them, and have to agree to abide by the decisions, at least for a time. For majority rule to work, minority members must *also* accept that the only legitimate way to change the course of the group is to change the decisions of members of the majority by education or persuasion and not by force. Failure to accept either of these conditions will disrupt the society and may cause it to fracture into smaller autonomous groups. Even if the society does not split apart completely, refusal of members of the minority to accept decisions of the majority, or the authority of the majority-chosen leaders, will certainly lead to conflict, possibly violent. Small societies avoid this difficulty by waiting for unanimous consensus. Because of the power of face-to-face influence in small groups, and also because of survival requirements such as those that forced Cephu to accept the group decisions (since his band could not survive alone), one or two individuals are usually not able to maintain strong opposition to a firm position taken by the rest of the members of the society. Even in our own society the influence of unanimous agreement is powerful. In a famous experiment, the psychologist Asch found that about one-third of the subjects, learning that they were the lone dissenters in their individual group, would deny the clear evidence of their own senses to bow to group opinion (Asch 1955:31–35). The importance of unanimity in bringing about conformity was shown in this experiment when only one of the individuals sided with the dissenter. When this happened, the power of the majority to influence the decision virtually disappeared.

In complex societies such as the United States, obtaining unanimity on any question is virtually impossible. The mechanism used in most democratic societies to allow continued functioning in the absence of unanimity is to select representatives for the citizens, and delegate to the representatives the responsibility for making decisions the rest of the population agrees to accept. Leaders, representatives, and law makers are chosen from among the people in the society by the process called voting. Ideally, voting permits all qualified individuals to express their opinion by their vote for a representative whose views coincide with theirs. Note that the qualifications for voting vary from country to country and from time to time in any given country. In the United States,

Exercising the right to vote, New York City, 1974. A voter signs the register in front of observers. A man stands by the voting machine, a device that has made illegal manipulation of votes more difficult. *(Jim Anderson/Woodfin Camp & Associates)*

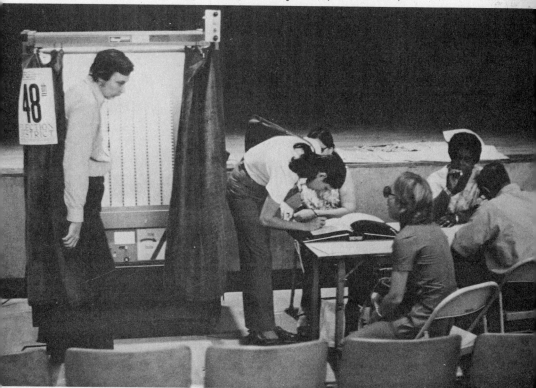

the belief is that the vote should be secret so that people cannot be influenced through terror or bribes to vote for someone they do not want. Actually, of course, this ideal is not always reached in practice. (In some countries, having the "secret ballot" means only that the ballot is *marked* in private. Since each party has a separate ballot, and voters have to choose the ballot they want in front of all observers before they take it into a booth to mark, *secrecy* is an empty word. The only thing a voter can secretly do in such a situation is token protest, by leaving the ballot blank. It is also impossible to vote a "split ticket," that is, vote for individuals in different parties. All votes are necessarily party votes.)

The area Childs described in the excerpt was still a territory, not a state, and consequently personnel in many offices were appointed rather than elected. This was accepted by people living on the frontier as a temporary, necessary expedient, but as soon as the population increased, agitation for statehood began. Americans were still too close to a time when they had been governed by appointees from distant England to be content for long with nonelected officials.

Another attitude prevalent in America is that voters should have a meaningful choice in an election. This belief is not universal among all societies that have elected government, however. In some countries where one party is especially dominant, only one candidate is presented, and again the only available protest is a blank ballot (or a refusal to vote—if voting is not compulsory). Subgroups within the United States vary in their adherence to this concept of choice. University faculties, church groups, and various organizations with nominating committees often present single slates (one candiate for each office) with the justification that since these are the best ones, there is no point offering others. There is enough resistance to this idea, however, so that almost all groups have some provision for "nominations from the floor," that is, for allowing names of other candidates to be presented at the last minute by people who were not members of the nominating committee.

GROUPINGS IN COMPLEX SOCIETIES

Distribution of power within groups in the United States tends to more or less follow the pattern for power distribution of the society in general. But what about the distribution of power among the different groups in the society? An increase in the number of groups is as characteristic of complex societies as is the increase in the number of statuses. In some of these societies, power priorities between groups are clearly specified. The military societies in native

A Sikh preacher addressing listeners in the Golden Temple (the major Sikh shrine) at Amritsar, India. In a number of societies authority figures are also religious leaders. *(United Nations)*

American societies and African age grades, for example, are discussed below. In the United States today, however, except for the political subdivisions whose relationships are spelled out in the Constitution, and the political parties, power relationships between groups are relatively unspecified. Laws have been primarily concerned with power relationships between individuals or between individuals and specified political units.

Although the law largely ignores the subject, there are group power differentials in the United States. Like other complex societies, we have classes and, according to some researchers, castes. Classes are made up of a number of people roughly equal in scalar status. One class differs from another in rank, but within each class there are only minor differences. (However, there are differences. Even within the same class, there is not complete equality; some people have more power or prestige than others.) A caste is almost the same as a class. The difference is that people can move—although sometimes only with great difficulty—from one class to another, but no mobility is permitted between castes. Caste membership is ascribed, and although the caste as a whole may improve its rank in relation to other castes, the individual cannot. Classes and castes are rare in small societies. Simple societies lack them by definition, since having a caste system automatically makes a society complex. As societies become more complex, the number of groups increases and criteria for membership change. Among the BaMbuti, the only groupings in the society smaller than the band itself were the individual families, and membership in families (except for the spouses) was ascribed. Larger, more complex societies have additional groups, such as elders, work crews, councillors, and so on, with membership in some ascribed by age or sex, but in others achieved. As societies grow more complex, new ways of classifying people into groups are added. Besides ascribed membership based on age, sex, or kinship, there are voluntary and semivoluntary criteria for membership. Subgroups within a complex society may be based on such things as residence, occupation, religion, special interest, and preference. Membership in preference groups (sororities, fraternities, and social clubs, for example) and special-interest groups (hobby clubs, some unions, political organizations) is usually voluntary, but groups based on residence, religion, occupation, and certain special interests—some unions, for example—are only semivoluntary; that is, a choice may be made at some point that determines a subsequent classification. A man who chooses to work for a particular company, for instance, may have his geographical area of residence decided for him.

Clubs, military societies, secret societies, age grades, and similiar organizations play significant roles in a number of societies. Among native Americans of the great plains, military societies were often responsible for keeping order or restraining eager hunters from stampeding the buffalo herd. In Africa, different age sets or grades (groups of males of roughly similar age, initiated at the same time) defend the society, legislate, or are assigned some other special task. Membership in the military societies is achieved; in the age grades it is primarily ascribed. Secret societies in a number of societies are in charge of religious ceremonies that are carried out for individuals or for the society as a whole.

However, at the level of complexity of simple horticultural villages or relatively affluent hunter-gatherers, only males belong to formal organizations other than the family. It has been suggested that a reason for this is that females do not have large blocks of leisure time, and that men object to their socializing outside the home anyway (Hoebel 1966:393). Whatever the reason, cross-cultural research indicates that special organizations for women are rare in simpler society but increase in number and significance as societies become more complex.

All complex societies contain subgroups whose members oppose some or most of the formal norms and resent representatives of the decision makers charged with enforcing those norms. Groups vary, however, as do individuals, in the extent to which their culture and the norms they share vary from those of the people in the mainstream culture. Some, perhaps regarded as the most dangerous by the majority, may actually have cultures more similar to the mainstream than groups perceived as "no problem." The Mafia, for example, has been notorious as a group pictured as posing a major threat to American society, yet Mafia members usually live side-by-side with other members of the society, sharing goals, participating fully in community or social activities appropriate to the people among whom they live, having identical aspirations for their children, and being fully accepted as "good neighbors" or friends, but always running the risk of rejection if they are ever identified as members of the Mafia. The norms they do not share are mainly those dealing with methods of acquiring wealth and power. On the other hand, a group such as the Amish may be regarded with tolerant interest, even approval, although their beliefs and values diverge sharply from the mainstream culture. The Amish are opposed to education beyond the eighth grade and reject almost everything modern, from machinery and conveniences to entertainment and morals. A key to the different attitudes held by members of the majority toward Amish and Mafia lies in the degree to which the actions of one group influence the lives of the other. The Amish can be ignored (or visited as a tourist attraction) by everyone except people living in their immediate neighborhood. Mafia activities, on the other hand, touch the lives of everyone, often in a detrimental way.

This discussion illustrates one of the problems facing a multinational society like the United States. How much and what sort of variation can people accept without destroying the continuity of the society as a whole? Are there basic values that *must* be accepted by almost everyone for a society to continue to exist? If so, what are they? Comparison of majority attitudes toward Mafia and Amish provides part of the answer, as does a look at the Wisconsin excerpt. So long as Childs and others in Green Bay were living in relative isolation, they could make their own "arrangements," as Childs put it, in regard to their family lives. Once their isolation decreased, and they began to be incorporated into the mainstream culture, however, sanctions were applied to bring their behavior into closer conformity with the norms of the larger society. The Mormons experienced the same thing during their attempts to have Utah declared a state. Polygyny° (having more than one wife) was no problem in Utah until Mormons wanted to unite with the larger society. In a complex society, therefore, the greater the isolation, the greater the cultural variation can be. Conformity is necessary or desirable only in the specific areas where the lives of the members of the two groups touch and interact.

SUMMARY

The specialization in law and government historically has accompanied specialization in other areas of life—economic, scientific, educational, religious, and artistic. Impersonality in law and bureaucracy in government, are linked with impersonality in distribution, production, and consumption of goods, mass-produced art, formal organized religion, and organized industrial team research. All these trends are related to (as a cause or an effect of) growth in the size of societies. There is a dynamic interrelationship—a feedback effect—between size and the other elements. Without new concepts in law, government, and social organization in general, people would not be able to maintain cohesion long enough to grow large enough to support the technology necessary to allow continued growth. Without a large population, new concepts and practices would be neither necessary nor possible. Not only is there no need for specialized law officers or rulers in a group the size of the BaMbuti; there would not be enough people to fill the positions anyway. Similarly, without a large population, new technological developments would neither have been necessary nor possible. More people are involved in discovering a single new antibiotic than make up the entire BaMbuti group described; there are fewer Tasadays (the previously mentioned group recently discovered in the Phillipines) than there are top management officers in a single automobile factory in the United States.

The degree of cooperation required for a modern nation is far more than is necessary for a hunting and gathering band, although it is a different type of cooperation on a different level of abstraction. Cooperation among the BaMbuti, Piegan, and similar groups is on a direct, face-to-face, personal basis, whereas much of the cooperation in modern societies is between strangers and is indirect and impersonal. Both kinds of cooperation exist in complex societies, just as reciprocity and prestation occur in a market economy. Indeed, one of the problems faced by people in complex societies is how to encourage both types, and also how to ascertain which type is required in a given situation. Some of the ways members of different societies have tried to solve these problems are discussed in the next chapter.

Norm violation in any society can be handled in only a limited number of ways:

1. Violators may be forced to conform to the norms or be removed in some way from the society.
2. The norm itself may be changed so that the behavior is no longer a violation (if enough people accept the violation, it becomes a new norm).
3. The limits of toleration may be increased so that the violation is permitted even if it is not fully accepted. It does not become the new norm, but it does become an acceptable alternative.

4. Violators may form a subgroup within the society and continue to struggle with supporters of the norm.
5. The society may split into two or more societies with different norms. In this alternative, there will no longer be any conflict over norms within each new group, but the groups may be in conflict with each other.

Government and law are two institutions° that complex societies have developed to deal with questions of public power, public decision making, and norm violations. Small societies may lack these institutions (it is a matter of definition), but no society lacks ways of carrying out the functions of government (making public decisions) or the functions of law (settling disputes, defining the relationships of members of society to one another, distributing power, establishing guidelines).

Wars occur when nations refuse to accept any overriding authority and yet cannot settle their conflicts of interest. One great barrier to settlement both between and within societies is a refusal of either side to compromise. A stand in support of "nonnegotiable demands" means that one of the parties to the dispute must surrender completely. If neither will do so, violence is usually inevitable unless one side can or will leave the vicinity of the other. Another barrier to settlement is a difference in the covert culture of the groups. Actions are misinterpreted, intentions are misunderstood. Increased understanding and tolerance on both sides of the quarreling groups is essential if problems arising from this source are to be reduced.

In social living, human or nonhuman, it is impossible for each individual to have his own way immediately all the time. There are no "inalienable rights" except those that members of the society choose to grant. This is an unpopular statement, but the physical world grants no rights. Ask the avalanche about the rights of villagers in its path; talk to the flood about the rights of the farmers. Even in the social world, unless individual members of a society agree, no one has any more "right" to "life, liberty, and the pursuit of happiness" than his or her own strength and ferocity can provide. The Declaration of Independence says: "*We hold* these truths to be self-evident." The first two words have been italicized to emphasize that the statements that followed were those the signers of the Declaration could agree on. The American Revolution itself, as well as the behavior of countless people in thousands of societies before and since, is clear proof that the "truths" are *not* self-evident. Even after they were pointed out, not everyone agreed with them. Biologically, they are not true. Socially they *may* be, if everyone in the society agrees they are. Laws and norms spell out the rights members of a society grant to one another as well as the responsibilities they owe each other. People trying to change their own rights and obligations are automatically also altering the rights of others. Anxiety, hostility, and disruption are an inevitable consequence, at least for a time.

A complex society has at some level all the mechanisms for maintaining order and organization that a simple society has, but it also has a much wider range of techniques for applying them. Without these additional techniques, the society would never have grown large enough to become complex.

At the basic level of status and role, a complex society has many more of both than does a simple society, and more of them are achieved than ascribed. A complex society also has more subgroups within it than a simple society does, and membership in these groups is based on a number of criteria in addition to those of sex, age, and kinship. Although offering more alternative statuses than simple societies do, complex societies often place a high priority on outward conformity, possibly because it helps alleviate the anxiety that specialization coupled with increased interdependence may lead to.

Norm violation in complex societies is usually punished by formal sanctions applied by specialists. The problem of determining the guilty party and protecting innocent people from unjust accusation requires elaborate mechanisms in the complex society that are unnecessary in simple ones.

In addition to the increased complexity of statuses, roles, and methods for settling conflicts and determining relations, complex societies also usually have more elaborate formal, and impersonal ways of distributing power. Although force often is involved at some point in maintaining power and social control, it is never the only support of a government. Most citizens have to want to do what has to be done if a society, simple or complex, is to function effectively all or most of the time. How does a society go about getting people to want to do what has to be done, and to accept rules as proper and authorities as legitimate? In the next chapter we deal with the most common way this is accomplished—the process of socialization.

7 Socialization

There must be order and organization for a society to survive, but societies vary widely in their norms and structures. In addition, the members cannot all be forced to follow the rules. A society functions smoothly only when its members want to do what has to be done. How does a new member learn what he needs to know to get along in the group? How does he come to want what the group wants, and shun what it disapproves?

Most new members are born into the group; while they are growing up they are taught openly, subtly, or unconsciously the things they must know. Since humans have so few instincts, they obviously have to be taught the most elementary survival skills. But the more elaborate, if not more important, part of this teaching process involves the values and behavior necessary for the perpetuation of the group. (Inasmuch as this process at times may lead an individual to die for the sake of the group, the function for the group perpetuation appears at least as significant as its function for individual survival.) In the course of acquiring this information, individuals also learn to depend on approval and esteem from their fellows, and to want and approve of the things other members of the group value. This teaching process is called socialization, or enculturation. It proceeds smoothly in some societies and with more difficulty or trauma in others. It is never totally effective, but it is far more so in some societies than in others.

In the following excerpt, take note of what values, behaviors, and beliefs the people try to develop in the child, and what methods they use to achieve their goal. Also note who is responsible for different phases of the socialization, as well as what differences there are in training and expectations for different statuses (such as boy, girl, servant, and so on) in the society.

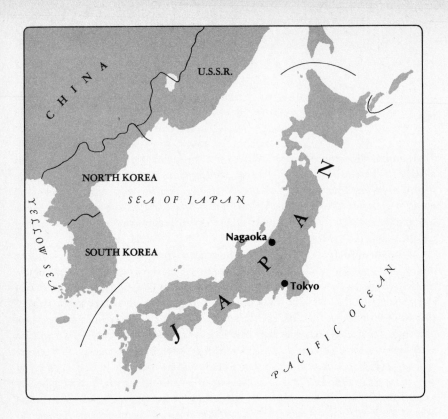

The Education of a Samurai Daughter

We did not have kindergartens when I was a child, but long before the time when I could have been admitted to the new "after-the-sixth-birthday" school, I had acquired a goodly foundation for later study of history and literature.* My grandmother was a great reader, and during the shut-in evenings of the long, snowy winters we children spent much time around her fire-box, listening to stories. In this way I became familiar, when very young, with our mythology, with the lives of Japan's greatest historical personages and with the outline stories of many of our best novels. Also I learned much of the old classic dramas from Grandmother's lips. My sister received the usual education for girls, but mine was planned along different lines for the reason that I was supposed to be destined for a priestess. I had been born with the navel cord looped around the neck like a priest's rosary, and it was a common superstition in those days that this was a direct command from Buddha. Both my grandmother and my mother sincerely believed this, and since in a Japanese home the ruling of the house and children is left to the women, my father silently bowed to the earnest wish of my grandmother to have me educated for a priestess. He, however, selected for my teacher a priest whom he knew—a very scholarly man, who spent little time in teaching me the forms of temple worship, but instructed me most conscientiously in the doctrine of Confucius. This was considered the founda-

*From *A Daughter of the Samurai* by Etsu Inagaki Sugimoto, pp. 17–24. Copyright 1925, 1928 by Doubleday & Company, Inc. Abridged by special arrangement with the publisher.

210

tion of all literary culture, and was believed by my father to be the highest moral teaching of the time.

My teacher always came on the days of threes and sevens—that is, the third, seventh, thirteenth, seventeenth, twenty-third, and twenty-seventh. This was in accordance with our moon-calendar custom of dividing days into groups of tens instead of sevens, as is done by the sun calendar. I enjoyed my lessons very much. The stateliness of my teacher's appearance, the ceremony of his manner, and the rigid obedience required of me appealed to my dramatic instinct. Then the surroundings were most impressive to my childish mind. The room was always made ready with especial care the day of my lessons . . . [it] was wide and light and was separated from the garden porch by a row of sliding paper doors crossed with slender bars of wood. The black-bordered straw mats were cream-coloured with time, but immaculate in their dustlessness. Books and desk were there, and in the sacred alcove hung a roll picture of Confucius. Before this was a little teakwood stand from which rose a curling mist of incense. On one side sat my teacher, his flowing gray robes lying in straight, dignified lines about his folded knees, a band of gold brocade across his shoulder, and a crystal rosary round his left wrist. His face was always pale, and his deep earnest eyes beneath the priestly cap looked like wells of soft velvet. He was the gentlest and the saintliest man I ever saw. Years after, he proved that a holy heart and a progressive mind can climb together, for he was excommunicated from the orthodox temple for advocating a reform doctrine that united the beliefs of Buddhism and Christianity. . . .

My studies were from books intended only for boys, as it was very unusual for a girl to study Chinese classics. . . .

I was only six years old, and of course I got not one idea from this heavy reading. My mind was filled with many words in which were hidden grand thoughts, but they meant nothing to me then. Sometimes I would feel curious about a half-caught idea and ask my teacher the meaning. His reply invariably was:

"Meditation will untangle thoughts from words," or "A hundred times reading reveals the meaning." Once he said to me, "You are too young to comprehend the profoundly deep books of Confucius."

This was undoubtedly true, but I loved my lessons. There was a certain rhythmic cadence in the meaningless words that was like music, and I learned readily page after page, until I knew perfectly all the important passages of the four books and could recite them as a child rattles off the senseless jingle of a counting-out game. Yet those busy hours were not wasted. In the years since, the splendid thoughts of the grand old philosopher have gradually dawned upon me; and sometimes when a well-remembered passage has drifted into my mind, the meaning has come flashing like a sudden ray of sunshine.

My priest-teacher taught these books with the same reverence that he taught his religion—that is, with all thought of worldly comfort put away. During my lesson he was obliged, despite his humble wish, to sit on the thick silk cushion the servant brought him, for cushions were our chairs, and the position of instructor was too greatly revered for him to be allowed to sit on a level with his pupil; but throughout my two-hour lesson he never moved the slightest fraction of an inch except with his hands and his lips. And I sat before him on the matting in an equally correct and unchanging position.

Once I moved. It was in the midst of a lesson. For some reason I was restless and swayed my body slightly, allowing my folded knee to slip a trifle from the proper angle. The faintest shade of surprise crossed my instructor's face; then very quietly he closed his book, saying gently but with a stern air:

"Little Miss, it is evident that your mental attitude to-day is not suited for study. You should retire to your room and meditate."

My little heart was almost killed with shame. There was nothing I could do. I humbly bowed to the picture of Confucius and then to my teacher, and backing respectfully from the room, I slowly went to my father to report, as I always did, at the close of my lesson. Father was surprised, as the time was not yet up, and his unconscious remark, "How quickly you have done your work!" was like a death knell. The memory of that moment hurts like a bruise to this very day.

Since absence of bodily comfort while studying was the custom for priests and teachers, of course all lesser people grew to feel that hardship of body meant inspiration of mind. For this reason my studies were purposely arranged so that the hardest lessons and longest hours came during the thirty days of midwinter, which the calendar calls the coldest of the year. The ninth day is considered the most severe, so we were expected to be especially earnest in our study on that day.

... In those days penmanship was considered one of the most important studies for culture. This was not so much for its art—although it is true that practising Japanese penmanship holds the same intense artistic fascination as does the painting of pictures—but it was believed that the highest training in mental control came from patient practice in the complicated brush strokes of character-writing. A careless or perturbed state of mind always betrays itself in the intricate shading of ideographs, for each one requires absolute steadiness and accuracy of touch. Thus, in careful guidance of the hand were we children taught to hold in leash the mind.

With the first gleam of sunrise on this "ninth day," Ishi came to wake me. It was bitterly cold. She helped me dress, then I gathered together the materials for my work, arranging the big sheets of paper in a pile on my desk and carefully wiping every article in my ink-box with a square of silk. Reverence for learning was so strong in Japan at that time that even the tools we used were considered almost sacred. I was supposed to do everything for myself on this day, but my kind Ishi hovered around me, helping in every way she could without actually doing the work herself. Finally we went to the porch overlooking the garden. The snow was deep everywhere. ... Once or twice a sharp crack and a great soft fluff of spurting snow against the gray sky told that a trunk had snapped

A Japanese winter. For a Samurai education the coldest days were chosen for the hardest tasks. *(Werner Bischof/Magnum)*

under its too heavy burden. Ishi took me on her back and, pushing her feet into her snowboots, slowly waded to where I could reach the low branch of a tree, from which I lifted a handful of perfectly pure, untouched snow, just from the sky. This I melted to mix for my penmanship study. I ought to have waded to get the snow myself, but—Ishi did it.

Since the absence of bodily comfort meant inspiration of mind, of course I wrote in a room without a fire. Our architecture is of tropical origin; so the lack of the little brazier of glowing charcoal brought the temperature down to that of outside. Japanese picture-writing is slow and careful work. I froze my fingers that morning without knowing it until I looked back and saw my good nurse softly crying as she watched my purple hand. The training of children, even of my age, was strict in those days, and neither she nor I moved until I had finished my task. Then Ishi wrapped me in a big padded kimono that had been warmed and hurried me into my grandmother's room. There I found a bowl of warm, sweet rice-gruel made by my grandmother's own hands. Tucking my chilled knees beneath the soft, padded quilt that covered the sunken fire-box, I drank the gruel, while Ishi rubbed my stiff hand with snow.

Of course, the necessity of this rigid discipline was never questioned by any one, but I think that, because I was a delicate child, it sometimes caused my

The Japanese tea ceremony, which follows the precise dictates of etiquette. *(Werner Bischof/Magnum)*

mother uneasiness. Once I came into the room where she and Father were talking.

"Honourable Husband," she was saying, "I am sometimes so bold as to wonder if Etsu-bo's studies are not a little severe for a not-too-strong child."

My father drew me over to his cushion and rested his hand gently on my shoulder.

"We must not forget, Wife," he replied, "the teaching of a samurai home. The lioness pushes her young over the cliff and watches it climb slowly back from the valley without one sign of pity, though her heart aches for the little creature. So only can it gain strength for its life work."

. . . But my lessons were not confined to those for a boy. I also learned all the domestic accomplishments taught my sisters—sewing, weaving, embroidery, cooking, flower arranging, and the complicated etiquette of ceremonial tea.

Nevertheless my life was not all lessons. I spent many happy hours in play. With the conventional order of old Japan, we children had certain games for each season . . . And I believe I enjoyed every game we ever played—from the simple winter-evening pastime of throwing a threaded needle at a pile of rice-cakes, to see how many each of us could gather on her string, to the exciting memory contests with our various games of poem cards.

We had boisterous games, too, in which a group—all girls, of course—would gather in some large garden or on a quiet street where the houses were hemmed in behind hedges of bamboo and evergreen. Then we would race and whirl in "The Fox Woman from the Mountain" or "Hunting for Hidden Treasure"; we would shout and scream as we tottered around on stilts in the forbidden boy-game of "Riding the High-stepping Bamboo Horse" or the hopping game of "The One-legged Cripples."

But no outdoor play of our short summers nor any indoor game of our long winters was so dear to me as were stories. The servants knew numberless priest tales and odd jingles that had come down by word of mouth from past generations, and Ishi, who had the best memory and the readiest tongue of them all, possessed an unending fund of simple old legends. I don't remember ever going to sleep without stories from her untiring lips. The dignified tales of Honourable Grandmother were wonderful, and the happy hours I spent sitting, with primly folded hands, on the mat before her—for I never used a cushion when Grandmother was talking to me—have left lasting and beautiful memories. But with Ishi's stories everything was different. I listened to them, all warm and comfortable, snuggled up crookedly in the soft cushions of my bed, giggling and interrupting and begging for "just one more" until the unwelcome time would arrive when Ishi, laughing but stern, would reach over to my night lantern, push one wick down into the oil, straighten the other, and drop the paper panel. Then, at last, surrounded by the pale, soft light of the shaded room, I had to say good-night and settle myself into the *kinoji*, which was the proper sleeping position for every samurai girl.

Samurai daughters were taught never to lose control of mind or body— even in sleep. Boys might stretch themselves into the character *dai*, carelessly outspread; but girls must curve into the modest, dignified character *kinoji*, which means "spirit of control."

Imagine having to sleep in a particular position! Most people in the United States do not believe it is even possible to teach children to do such things. But different peoples have different assumptions about human nature, and in many societies demands Americans would never even consider imposing are successfully made on children.

People of various societies also value or despise different characteristics and attitudes. Naturally enough, adults in all societies want their children to behave in ways they admire, so in most societies adults try to teach children valued characteristics and to eliminate undesirable traits. The process of teaching the young the beliefs and traditions of the society is called enculturation,° and the process of teaching the young how to get along in the group is called socialization.° This technical distinction is usually ignored, however. Sociologists (and a few anthropologists) tend to use *socialization* to refer to both processes, whereas anthropologists are more prone to use *enculturation* in the same way. Enculturation and socialization are vital for the maintenance of a society, since it is through these processes that people come to want to do what has to be done, that they learn to accept the goals and values of their society and the approved methods of attaining them (as well as the methods not approved). In most societies, the family is responsible for a major part of both processes.

TEACHING VALUES AND NORMS

Few groups require young children to display the degree of self-control that was demanded by the Japanese Samurai class in the past. Not even all groups in premodern Japan expected the same amount of self-control. Ishi, the nursemaid, wept at the sight of Etsu's frozen hand. She told Etsu stories, allowed interruptions, succumbed to pleas for "just one more," and laughed even as she insisted on bedtime. She also did her best to modify the strictness of the discipline without actually disobeying orders. She waded out into the yard with Etsu on her back, so the child could actually take snow off the tree branch herself. This was within the letter but certainly not the spirit of the rule, because as Etsu points out in the excerpt, technically she should also have waded into the snow herself. One gets a sense of Ishi's informality and sympathy even from the short excerpt quoted; it is much more obvious when one reads the whole book.

What were some of the characteristics people in the Samurai class of that time regarded as admirable? What did they expect of their children? How did they go about developing the valued characteristics? The excerpt indicates that

A model of a Japanese country home, somewhat unusual in having a second story, but showing the typical sliding panel walls. *(Courtesy of the American Museum of Natural History)*

both physical and mental control were highly admired and expected; in fact, this is repeatedly emphasized. By the time she was six, Etsu had learned to sit motionless for at least two hours at a time (contrast this with the expected behavior of first-graders in the United States). She felt deeply ashamed when she moved slightly and her teacher dismissed her. She does not complain that her instructor was unjust or unfair, which indicates she had already accepted (internalized°) the values of her society to such an extent that she applied its standards to her own behavior and felt unworthy or inadequate when she failed to measure up.

In some societies, people feel unworthy and deserving of punishment even if no one else knows about their failure to live up to the standards of the society. Such a society is said to be "guilt-oriented." The individual to some extent punishes himself for actual violation or even for anticipated violation of a social norm. In other societies, people feel unworthy only when other members of the group are aware of their failure. Such a society is said to be "shame-oriented." Individuals depend on punishment from some source other than themselves. The anthropologist Melford Spiro says this dissimilarity in societies occurs because of a difference in the number of people involved in socializing a child. When only a few people are involved in the socialization of each child, a guilt-oriented culture is likely to develop, whereas in a society where there are many agents of socialization, or where these agents threaten the child that "others" will do the punishing, a shame-oriented culture is likely to develop (Spiro 1961:120). The two types are theoretical extremes, and in any real society one would expect to find both types of individuals (though perhaps more of one type than the other) and also to find individuals who exhibit a combination of guilt and shame attitudes about different social norms.

Just reading the excerpt, one has difficulty deciding whether the Samurai class in premodern Japan was primarily shame- or guilt-oriented. Other parts of the book, however, indicate that much of Etsu's behavior depended on her perception of what other people thought of her actions. When she knew others did not object or even approved (in a mission school, for example, or after she went to the United States), she was apparently able to adopt new behavior easily. Had she been heavily guilt-oriented, it is unlikely that it would have been so simple for her. (Protestant missionaries, for example, reject wife-lending practices even in societies where such behavior is not only accepted but expected. General missionary resistance to changing their own behavior has even led to martyrdom. Christian missionaries are notoriously guilt-oriented.)

The Samurai class made the basic assumption that physical and mental control were related to the extent that one was either an indication or a cause of the other. In the excerpt Etsu points out that "in careful guidance of the hand were we children taught to hold in leash the mind"—that is, if children learned physical control, they would also attain mental control. Even more explicit is this statement: "It was believed that the highest training in mental control came from patient practice in the complicated brush strokes of character-writing." As evidence that a lack of physical control indicated a lack of mental control, we read, "A careless or perturbed state of mind always betrays itself in the intricate shading of ideographs," and the comment of the teacher when Etsu moved: "Little Miss, it is evident that your mental attitude to-day is not suited for study." Some modern educators have a curiously parallel attitude. Children with reading problems are often placed in special motor-skills classes in the belief that improving their coordination will improve their reading ability. Recent work with mentally retarded children indicates that many may be greatly helped by intensive physical training (Stutz 1974:238–244).

In the Samurai class, physical control might also indicate respect. Etsu mentions the hours she sat "with primly folded hands," listening to her grandmother tell stories. Other statements in the book support the idea that casual movements (particularly of the lower body) in the presence of superiors might be regarded as insulting. (During World War II, prisoners of the Japanese learned this the hard way, but many people mistook the Japanese reaction for just another fiendish way of harassing prisoners.) The Samurai class assumed that physical control could and should be maintained even in sleep. They required girls to sleep in a position that affirmed control. In the United States, people tend to assume that the individual has little or no control over his behavior while he sleeps. At the same time, we also know that sleepers do not normally fall out of bed, urinate, or defecate. As any parent with small children can testify, this is learned, not instinctive, behavior. Holding contradictory assumptions simultaneously is not unusual in cultures; provided both assumptions are part of the traditional belief system, the contradictions are generally ignored by most members of the culture.

Notice that neither Samurai men nor women were supposed to *lack* emotions or feelings; they were simply expected to *control* their manifestation. One could predict that Japanese from the old Samurai class would be dreadfully embarrassed or ashamed to cry openly or to show signs of fear. Anglo-Saxon and early American cultures also place a high value on control of emotion, particularly in public, and assume that such control is evidence of a strong character. Jacqueline Kennedy, for example, was lauded for her "courage" at the funeral of her first husband. In other societies, control over emotions is equated with a *lack* of emotions—Latin Americans often regard North Americans as "cold" and "emotionless" people. Thus, some felt that Mrs. Kennedy's behavior revealed a lack of emotions, rather than courage. Such a difference in basic assumptions and values has led to a great deal of misunderstanding between peoples.

A modern notion, common in the United States, is that all emotions must be expressed in behavior, acted out. Failure to do so is "unnatural," and potentially harmful to the individual. This idea may be the result of some confusion between the psychological concepts of repression—denying the existence of an emotion even to one's self—and behavior control, in which one recognizes the existence of the emotion but refuses to translate it into action. There is evidence that repression may be emotionally harmful, but little evidence that behavior control is. In fact, group life would probably be impossible without some such control. A large number of people almost inevitably have conflicting desires, so attempts to satisfy them all at once would lead to chaos.

CHILD-RAISING TECHNIQUES AND PERSONALITY

It seems reasonable to assume that different demands placed on children in various societies will produce adults who differ. This assumption is correlated with another—that it is possible to instill attitudes and values through certain methods of child-training. The excerpt indicates that the Japanese certainly held the latter assumption. The relationship of child-training practices to both the culture of a society and the personality or character of the adults in that culture has been under study for some time. The standing argument about which is more important, heredity or environment, nature or nurture, has changed focus in recent years. No one is born without a genetic endowment or lacking an environment. A more modern approach regards the adult personality as the result of the interaction of genetic heritage, environment (both physical and social), and idiosyncratic (individually unique) experiences. This can be represented schematically by a triangle or a square (depending on whether the environment is represented by one angle or two). See Chart 7.1.

A more complex representation of the individual notes that the information on which the individual bases action goes through two filters: (1) the physical equipment through which the individual senses the environment, and (2) the mental organization through which sensations are interpreted (Thompson 1975:2–3). These two filters, acting together, provide the basis for individual behavior (see Chart 7.2). Knowledge of the mental organization is essential for accurate prediction of behavior, and much of the content of the mental organization (although by no means all of it) is culturally determined. For example,

Chart 7.1

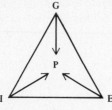

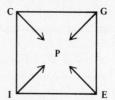

P = personality
G = genetic endowment
E = environment
I = idiosyncratic experiences

P = personality
G = genetic endowment
E = physical environment
C = culture (social environment)
I = idiosyncratic experiences

suppose a yellow blinking light is placed over a deep hole in a path. An individual whose sight is impaired may not see the warning, and may fall into the hole. On the other hand, an individual whose vision is excellent but whose culture does not contain the equation "yellow blinking light = caution, danger" may also fall in.

In studying culture, we are studying the part of an individual's mental organization and interpretation that is learned from and shared with other members of the society. In studying socialization, we are attempting to learn more about how the specific content of the individual's mental organization and interpretations were acquired. We may also want to know what people in the society try to teach others, how successful they have been in doing so, as well as how they did it.

The process of learning, and the interpretation of sensory data, are a major concern of psychologists. Therefore, in this area of study, anthropology is closely related to psychology. The cross-cultural study of the relationship between the individual and the culture is often called psychological anthropology, or culture and personality. Much of the theoretical basis for this subdiscipline comes from the field of psychology, just as many concepts used in studying the distribution of goods and services are related to the study of economics, and many of those used in studying the maintenance of order and organization are related to the study of law and political science.

Chart 7.2. RELATION OF INDIVIDUAL
TO PHYSICAL AND SOCIAL ENVIRONMENTS

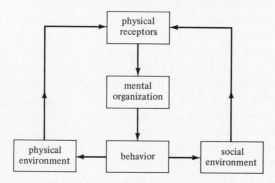

One of the basic assumptions underlying the culture-and-personality field is that people socialized in one culture are likely to have a very different mental organization from people socialized in another. In other words, this assumption rests heavily on the psychological theories that regard childhood experiences and child-training methods as major determinants for adult personality (Barnouw 1973:28–35).

The general physical environment and certain aspects of the social environment are shared by all members of a society. In one of the earlier hypotheses about the relationship between culture and personality, Abram Kardiner (a psychologist) and Ralph Linton and Cora Du Bois (both anthropologists) suggested that people sharing a similar series of experiences as children tend to have similar personalities as adults; that is, they have the basic personality structure° of the culture. Du Bois called the cluster of characteristics that appears most frequently in a society the modal personality° and predicted it would differ from one society to another. This statistically based concept has gained more acceptance than the concept of the basic personality structure (Barnouw 1973:153–154).

As a result of attempts to test these hypotheses, researchers have found that there is much more variation in personality within a society than was predicted. In fact, variations within one society are often as great as variations between societies (Thompson 1975:28, 48–49; Wallace 1952; Kaplan 1954). This indicates that child-training methods—no matter how similar—do not turn out a series of carbon copies of some socially ideal model. Since child-raising methods are only one small part of the social environment affecting the development of personality (see Chart 7.1), it is hard to see why anyone would expect them to have such an extensive impact. In addition, of course, no two people apply the methods in exactly the same way, so although child-training methods in one society may be quite similar in all families, they are never really identically applied to all children, any more than all the children are identical in the first place.

Another general factor is more basic. The most convincing differences between cultures are those that are most easily observed, that is, behavior. There is little question that both in public and in private the French behave differently from Americans, Arabs, or Japanese—all of whom also behave differently from one another in obvious ways. These easily observable differences are largely responsible for the popular belief that there *must* be a "national character," or personality, that is common to at least the "normal" members of one cutlure. This belief depends on the assumption that similar observable behavior reflects similar underlying psychology—or at least, motives. As previous chapters have shown, and as research has borne out, however, people can and often do behave in similar ways from different motives (Devereux 1961:235–239). One does not have to feel altruistic to share food, although one *may*. People may read this book, attend college, chop down trees, or even eat for a variety of different reasons. Any given act may be performed by different people inspired by as many reasons as there are individuals. The same individual may perform the same act for different reasons at different times. Several simultaneous motives may be present for any one action, even though some of the motives are apparently out of the conscious awareness of the actor.

The research techniques used to investigate personality cross-culturally—things like the TAT°, Draw-A-Person test,° and Rorschach°—are designed to reveal underlying, subtle, and even unconscious emotions and attitudes of the individual (Barnouw 1973:301–370). One could therefore anticipate that the results of such research would be more varied than the observable behavior, as they, in fact, are.

Since members of a society are often more concerned with producing proper behavior than proper thoughts, socialization is more apt to be directed to "right doing" than to "right thinking," although some socialization of attitudes is inevitable (Thompson 1975:20, 49). At the same time, however, it is important to note that there are some societies whose members do concern themselves with "right thinking"—especially in regard to the supernatural world. Members of such societies may, therefore, specifically attempt to socialize right thinking as well as right doing. Again, one would expect that socialization directed toward behavior rather than toward one's inner life would produce or permit more variation in motives and attitudes than one would anticipate in societies that stress the socialization of thoughts as well as actions. The regularities that do appear in the research on societies that stress only behavior socialization are consequently more impressive than they would seem at first glance.

The question of how much underlying personality behavior reflects is obviously far from settled for the psychologist or for the anthropologist. This and other questions, such as whether all behavior reflects attitudes equally well (or poorly), whether some behavior is more revealing than other, and how different personalities have to be before they will produce noticeably different behavior, continue to plague researchers in this field. The cross-cultural work of John W. M. Whiting and Irving L. Child indicates some of the cultural effects on at least a few components of personality, but that influence is neither simple nor necessarily direct.

Whiting and Child have been leaders in recent cross-cultural research into the relationship between child-rearing and individual personality. They modified the Kardiner-Linton hypothesis to include more variables, to suggest that while personality is influenced by child-raising practices, these in turn are influenced by the systems the society has developed to provide for the biological needs of its members. The adult personality is then reflected in the belief systems, particularly those centering around medicine (in non-Western societies) and religion. For example, cross-cultural research supports a general hypothesis that harsh parental treatment during infancy is correlated with a belief in a harsh, aggressive spirit world, whereas indulgent treatment is correlated with a belief that the gods can be controlled by proper ritual and do not need to be propitiated (Whiting, 1961:357; Lambert, Triandis, and Wolf 1959:162–169).

One difficulty encountered by researchers in the area of psychological anthropology is the problem of classification. For example, was Etsu's treatment harsh or not? The demands made on her were certainly severe, but there is no indication that she was ever beaten or even struck. Shaming seems to have been a sufficient punishment even at her age. In addition, when she successfully completed her task, she was immediately rewarded with warmth, comfort, food, and approval. Using severity of demands or the strictness of expectation as a criterion, Etsu's treatment might be classified as harsh. Using frequency or type of punishment as a criterion, her treatment might be classified as moderate. Using reward for successful completion of a task as a criterion, her treatment might be classified as indulgent. It is obvious, then, that if results are to be reliable, specific guidelines for classification must be drawn up before research coding and interpretation can proceed. Too many people have done research with vague notions instead of clear, operationally defined concepts, and consequently have ended up with boxloads of data that fail to provide reliable and necessary information on key questions.

Classifying Etsu's attitude toward the spirit world creates almost as much difficulty as classification of her treatment. There is no evidence in the book that Etsu regarded the supernatural world as aggressive, although she did feel "fate" was sometimes hard and unfair. She says Buddhism has a thread of hopelessness in it that she disliked, and she became a fervent Christian as an adult (Sugimoto 1934:137–147). At what point in her life should the classification be made, and on which religion—Buddhism, Shintoism, or Christianity—should it be based? Her autobiography does not clearly confirm or refute any hypothesis, but it does illustrate some of the difficulties of research in the area of culture and personality.

To understand, predict, or direct human behavior, these classification problems have to be solved, or at least clarified. Social learning takes place, according to some researchers, as a result of conditioning, reinforcement, and imitation (Miller and Dollard 1941). Rewards, such as the treatment Etsu received when she successfully completed a hard task, are positive reinforcement toward repeating the behavior that resulted in the treatment. Punishment such as she experienced when she was dismissed by her teacher is called negative reinforcement and tends to discourage repetition of the behavior. Children also may learn by observing what happens to others around them, especially if those other people are ones with whom the child can identify, that is, ones the child wants to be like or already feels like (Bandura and Walters 1963:90–106). The excerpt does not provide examples of this kind of learning but the book mentions numerous instances.

Another cross-cultural study found that sorcery is an important explanation for illness in societies where children are severely punished for sexual or aggressive behavior (Whiting 1961:370). Other studies have shown that aggression is most severely punished in extended households (where a variety of relatives live together) and in polygynous households° (where more than one wife is present). If the suggested relationship between punishment for aggressive behavior and belief in sorcery as a cause of disease is valid, then one should find this belief especially prevalent in societies with extended or polygynous households. Studies so far show that the expected finding does occur in societies with polygynous households, especially when jealousy between wives is great (Whiting 1961:370). The studies therefore support the more general hypothesis that a basic maintenance system° (the polygynous household) leads to certain child-raising practices (punishment of aggressive behavior) which, by producing certain personality characteristics, are reflected in a projective system° (disease is caused by sorcery).

In some societies the child-rearing methods are deliberately chosen to instill certain characteristics. It is clear from the excerpt that at least some of the methods used by the Japanese were of this type. In other societies, however, methods are not consciously chosen. They are used simply because structural factors in the society make them almost inevitable. A woman alone for most of the day with four small children cannot possibly use the same child-rearing methods that a woman living in a large extended-family household has available to her (Minturn and Lambert 1968:551–557). In the studies mentioned above, it is unlikely that polygynous households have any intention of producing a belief in sorcery as the cause of illness when they punish aggression; it is much more likely that aggression is punished simply because living conditions in such complex households would be next to intolerable if everyone were allowed to express aggression whenever he or she wished. The belief in sorcery as a cause of illness is simply an unexpected by-product of the child-rearing methods or of some other factor that produces both the punishment for aggression and the belief in sorcery. Note, however, that these correlations, although subtle, refer to attitudes that are on a more conscious level than those tapped by projective tests such as the TAT or Rorschach. A belief in sorcery is not on the same level of abstraction or subtlety as an Oedipus complex, or latent homosexuality, for example.

In the United States in recent decades, changes in child-raising techniques have been introduced in response to a variety of hypotheses about the effects of certain practices (early weaning, swaddling) on adult behavior. Unfortunately, results do not seem to coincide with predictions, and it is difficult to determine whether the failure is due to faulty assumptions or to other factors in the society that override the effects of child-rearing techniques. (Both positions have supporters and detractors.) One assumption of middle-class Americans—that each child has an innate set of potentials that should be allowed to develop and which can be destroyed by interference—seems to have led to the cross-culturally unique practice of parents deliberately trying to avoid indoctrinating their children (Fischer and Fischer 1966:50). Yet there is no good evidence that the middle-class assumption is correct. In fact, anthropological data would seem to indicate that any innate potentialities are so generalized they could develop in any one of a number of directions. If a child is left without parental guidelines, these potentialities may develop in highly unexpected directions that may not please the parents. A child never develops without *any* guidelines, of course. If parents fail to provide them, the child adopts those of playmates or of individuals at school or elsewhere. The consequences of this haphazard socialization are not easily predictable.

Samurai in Japan certainly had no intention of leaving the socialization of their children to chance or to casual playmates. In addition to the characteristics already mentioned as desirable, they apparently regarded obedience and respect for superiors as quite important. The presence of superiors and inferiors means that Japanese society is not egalitarian,° but of course no human society ever is. Even the simplest society recognizes power differentials at some level (see Chapters 5 and 6). None gives the same power to small children that it gives to adults, for example, and it is difficult to imagine how any could. Comparison of societies on an egalitarian basis usually centers on the ways in which powerful positions are attained and maintained. A society in which such positions are ascribed on the basis of chance factors (race, age, physical appearance, family) is regarded as less egalitarian than a society in which powerful positions are awarded on the basis of individual qualification. If we look at Japanese society as pictured in the excerpt, some of the criteria for superiority and inferiority are apparent. Education, religious training, male gender, and age clearly qualified one as superior. Children, women, and servants were inferior. Some of these qualifications were chance factors (sex, age, family), but others such as education were obtained by individual effort. One might be born a Samurai or a servant, but not educated or a priest.

Respect for superior individuals was expressed in a variety of ways. Avoiding unnecessary movement has already been mentioned. Etsu gives others, such as relative height or comfort. (She never sat on a cushion in her grandmother's presence, and her teacher had to sit on one in spite of his wish, because "the position of instructor was too greatly revered for him to be allowed to sit on a level with his pupil.") Bowing is mentioned several times, as is backing out of the presence of a superior (when Etsu was dismissed by her teacher). All these examples indicate that the Samurai of prewar Japan had a strict and formal code of manners, detailed and precise, with little room for spontaneity or variation. Often in societies of this sort, lower-class individuals are allowed more variation in behavior; in fact, the amount of variation permitted tends to be one of the distinguishing characteristics of social class.

COVERT CULTURE

Since most socialization takes place early, certain behavior tends to become almost automatic and appears "instinctive." It is not, of course. Almost all human behavior is learned, and "proper" behavior varies so much from one group of people to another that it could not possibly be instinctive. But the automatic character of the behavior makes it difficult for someone socialized in one group to move easily into another, for such a person must unlearn accustomed behavior patterns and adopt new ones. Hardly anyone can learn the new responses as well as the people who have been trained in them from childhood. In addition, because these responses are so automatic, it is difficult for members of a class to teach them to others even if they want to. Their reactions have become part of "covert" (hidden) culture.

Covert culture refers to those concepts people take for granted, do not remember learning, and often do not realize they know at all. Behavior motivated by these concepts is assumed to be "natural," the result of "human nature" or "instinct." Yet man seems to have very few instincts. (The term *instinct* is subject to different definitions, unfortunately. Psychologists, biologists, zoologists, and others are still arguing about the "best" definitions of instinct, drives, and reflexes.) Primates—especially humans—have to be taught virtually everything they need to know to survive; ants, bees, and other insects, on the other hand, are genetically programmed to do almost everything necessary for individual or group survival. Man may have some general drives (the argument over this is currently a hot one in anthropology), for companionship, aggression, esteem, or dominance; but if they exist, these drives can be satisfied in a wide variety of ways. Accepting the existence of a drive for dominance, for example, will not help an investigator predict the behavior of a specific individual in a particular situation.

Covert culture often provokes heated debates. Since people assume behavior motivated by covert culture is natural or instinctive, they are apt to be disturbed by behavior that is different, because it is "unnatural" to them. Assumptions about attributes of men and women, sexual behavior, and the human being's innate nature tend to be part of covert culture in most societies. Changes in these are therefore upsetting.

It is patently absurd to think of teaching this instinctive behavior. After all, do bees have to go to school to learn how to make honey? The motives and intelligence of anyone who offers to teach instinctive behavior are obviously open to question. Much of the resistance to sex education in the schools appears to be based on the belief that sexual behavior is instinctive and that early education in it will only cause children to start active practice before the society would like them to. Most of the cross-cultural evidence, however, indicates that sexual behavior is not entirely instinctive. What excites people sexually in one society may "turn them off" in another. Southern European men are excited by the bushy underarms of a woman; Americans are more often repelled by them. Trobrianders (South Pacific Melanesians) are thrilled by biting off each other's eyelashes (Malinowski 1929:334). The "normal" position for sexual intercourse varies from one society to another (Powdermaker 1933:240–241; Malinowski 1929:336; Holmberg 1969:164–165). Even American society provides some evidence that sexual behaviors are learned. Aside from the incidence of sexual problems, known to any psychiatrist, there is one experience common to almost everyone. When young people ask, "How do I know if I am in love?" most adults, relying on instinct, answer, "Don't worry, you'll know all right when it happens," or "If you have to ask, you aren't." Yet even the same adults will usually admit that they themselves were fooled at least once. It is very difficult to fool an instinct. If we want our children to hold to certain values and norms of sexual practice, sex education in the schools is probably advisable. Otherwise, since parents normally give very little instruction in what they regard as proper sexual behavior themselves, and since the behavior is not instinctive, children will get their values and behavior from such random sources as friends, movies, and pornographic literature. These values are unlikely to be ones of which most parents would approve.

Temperament associated with a particular sex is also learned, at least in part. Men are not "naturally" much more aggressive than women (a doubter can watch children playing in any nursery school before cultural conditioning has had time to take full effect). Women are not "naturally" more demonstrative, emotional, affectionate, or kinder than men. It takes twelve to fourteen years of conditioning, using all the weapons at a society's command (such as scorn, ridicule, physical punishment) to teach boys that "men don't cry." If men instinctively did not cry, it would be unnecessary to indoctrinate boys. At some point in history, in Anglo-American cultures, crying came to be thought of as weak or effeminate behavior and consequently inappropriate to the male role. It would be illuminating to trace the development of this concept, since it is fairly recent (biblical personages and even knights of the Round Table wept freely), but there is neither time nor space to discuss it here (Bulfinch n.d.:377, 379, 399, 404). Probably all psychologists can testify to the emotional cost of this particular conditioning to their male patients. In short, while there may be a few differences in innate temperament associated with sex, it is still far from certain precisely what these are, and many of the differences assumed by Americans to be innate are actually learned.

Most nonverbal behavior falls into the category of covert culture. Edward T. Hall and other anthropologists have written at length about the covert aspects of such commonplace things as the use of time and space, walking, sitting, standing, and carrying burdens (Hall 1959, 1965; Birdwhistell 1970:8–9). *Body Language* (Fast, 1970) and *How to Read a Person Like a Book* (Nierenberg, 1972) are two recent publications that have presented, in a popular and easily read form, some of the information available about the nonverbal communication present in body positions and movement. At the moment it is not clear just how much of this "body language" is learned and how much is tied to genetic inheritance. Some is certainly innate. Ethologists° (students of animal behavior) have developed a special descriptive terminology such as *threat-stare, play-face,* (van Hooff 1969:21ff) and so on, to refer to expressions that communicate something to other animals. Many of these physical expressions are species limited; that is, they mean something to members of the same species but not to individuals of other species. Consequently, the labels and descriptions are attached to specific actions only after intensive investigation of behavior, not simply on the basis of what the behavior communicates to the human observer. This is an attempt to avoid anthropomorphizing° (attributing human characteristics and emotions to animals), which can easily cause misunderstandings. When the same ethological techniques of investigation (field observation, mirror-camera recording—i.e., taking pictures with a camera that points in one direction while taking pictures in another, without spoken dialogue—and so on), are employed on human children from non-Western cultures, the results are startling. Eibl-Eibesfeldt, a distinguished European ethologist, photographed Bushmen children in this manner, and the expressions on their faces, as well as the significance of other aspects of body movement, were instantly intelligible to adults from various European cultures as well as from the United States. It was an enlightening experience for anyone who believed that *all* human behavior is learned and consequently unique to each culture. (Actually, if that were true, no communication between different peoples would ever be possible.) From the evidence it is apparent that some aspects of human behavior may be genetically determined, but since it is equally clear that training and learning modify human behavior considerably, the problem lies mainly in determining what is genetic and what is learned. As Bushmen children grow, they learn to control muscles and alter behavior to conform with adult patterns. The threat-stare and play-face of adults, for example, are not so spontaneous or obvious as they are in children. The same is true in all societies, of course. The threat-stare communicates accurately, but most of us learn not to give it under all provocations, since it is only appropriate in certain situations. These situations vary from culture to culture. We also learn not to respond automatically to the threat-stare, and may exercise a number of options, again varying from one culture to another.Thus, although covert culture is not normally "taught" in the formal sense of the word, but to a great degree learned, children tend to imitate, and parents by their behavior and reactions tend to produce, sometimes quite unconsciously, the preferred and expected behavior from their children.

Because some gestures, facial expressions, and postures are learned and vary from one culture to another, all kinds of difficulties—some amusing, some not—can beset individuals who use physical expressions that are commonplace and innocent in their own culture but insulting or threatening in some other culture they happen to enter. For example, the peace sign used today in the United States (the first two fingers on one hand held up, spread apart) meant "V for Victory" during World War II. It would have been dangerous to use it in Nazi Germany, and it is an obscene gesture in some societies. In the United States, men engaged in sports (basketball, baseball, football) continually pat one another on the buttocks to indicate approval after some particularly skillful act or before a crucial play to give encouragement. This gesture is taken for granted by performers and spectators alike, provided it occurs "on the field," but it would be highly inappropriate on a public street or in a restaurant. Yet precise and meaningful as this gesture is, it is part of covert culture; people do it unconsciously, without thinking about it, unless it is called to their attention.

The use of space is also learned. People in some societies tolerate close physical contact; in others, they reject it. In large American cities such as New York, good manners require individuals to give others all the space possible in any given situation. On public transportation, in restaurants where patrons seat themselves, on beaches, "proper" behavior consists in sitting as far as possible from anyone else. If a man sits beside a woman he does not know (or vice versa) when there are alternative places available, it is usually interpreted as a sexual advance. Even if for some reason this is obviously not the case, the behavior is usually regarded as rude and disagreeable. Iroquois Indians are noted for their skill in high steel construction and for their lack of fear of heights. The reasons for this ability are far from clear, but a contributing factor may be walking habits that are part of Iroquois covert culture. Most Iroquois still place one foot directly in front of the other when walking. Unpaved paths on their Onondaga reservation may be as little as six to eight inches wide, whereas similar paths in non-Iroquois areas are rarely less than eighteen inches wide. If one customarily walks in an eight-inch space, one is likely to think of a steel girder as a wide, comfortable walking path.

While covert culture is hidden from us, we all remember learning the concepts of overt culture°—history dates, the proper use of "please" and "thank you," how to play basketball, and the like. We can often specify when we learned certain concepts and from whom. In the United States, hunting technology is part of overt culture. The author of the excerpt in Chapter 5 is aware that he does not know Pygmy hunting technology because he has had little opportunity to learn it. He does not regard the behavior as instinctive (although some authors still write about the "instinctive" tracking abilities of hunting and gathering peoples). Hunting knowledge is covert in some cultures, however. Ways to track and move through cover are learned in such a way and at such an age that people are not conscious of learning them. The behavior simply seems natural. In such cases, people tend to regard outsiders who lack these skills as somewhat retarded, handicapped, and possibly not quite human. The native New Yorker is apt to feel similarly about skills for coping with heavy traffic, either vehicular or pedestrian. Naturally, if an individual lacks an elementary "instinctive" skill, people will not regard him as "normal." The quotation marks are significant, because these skills are *not* instinctive; they simply seem so to people who have acquired them as part of covert culture.

From what has been said, it is obvious that covert culture differs from one society to another. This difference causes misunderstanding between peoples. Note, for example, the reaction of the author to the Pygmy treatment of animals. He admits that when they laughed and imitated the animal's struggles and suffering after they killed the *sindula,* he felt furthest from them. The Pygmies were unconcerned about inflicting pain on animals. They kicked dogs; they singed the feathers off living birds. In modern American-English tradition, the suffering of an animal is as upsetting as human suffering—possibly more so. A person who willfully causes animals to endure unnecessary pain or someone who laughs at such suffering is believed to be emotionally disturbed, cruel, inhuman, and generally untrustworthy or "bad" (and someone brought up in the American-English tradition who does such things may indeed have emotional problems). In their treatment of animals, the BaMbuti behaved in a way that the author's covert culture insisted was characteristic of "bad" people. Consequently, in spite of his intellectual understanding of the Pygmies and his general sympathy with them, he could not help but feel somewhat disturbed and alienated when they exhibited this behavior. Yet in a society where kicking dogs is an expected part of the normal treatment of animals, the behavior does not indicate any character flaws.

Among various peoples, therefore, covert cultural differences may be a source of ill will that increased contact only aggravates, rather than reduces— a fact overlooked by proponents of "togetherness" as the solution to world tensions (Williams 1964:25). The only way dislike brought about by conflicts on the covert culture level can be reduced is for members of both societies to become aware of what is causing the trouble and to develop a tolerance for something emotionally upsetting. It is possible, but far from simple.

Covert culture is extremely difficult to study in one's own culture, of course, precisely *because* it is covert. This is one reason anthropologists go into societies other than their own for extended periods of time (normally a year to a year and a half) as part of their training. Experience with the covert culture of others usually opens one's eyes to one's own, at least partially. The less experience one has with people of different cultures, the greater the proportion of one's own culture that remains covert. (This is one reason why people who are isolated often appear narrow-minded and provincial to those with more experience.)

All culture (including covert) can be studied only through its manifestations (manifestations of culture, remember, are act and artifacts—behavior and the consequences of behavior). Anthropologists study these manifestations and arrive at hypotheses about the concepts motivating them. They check these by asking questions (in the case of covert culture, the answers are never very helpful), or they try to verify the hypotheses by predicting what behavior will occur under various circumstances. If their hypotheses are correct, their predictions will be accurate, or nearly so.

Another aspect of covert culture, and an important one, is language. It is crucial in human socialization. Both animals and humans are socialized through imitation (animals may not need socialization in some areas of life because of instincts), but only the human being is also socialized through language. Language exerts a profound influence on our lives, an influence often greater than most of us realize. According to Edward Sapir, "The fact of the matter is that the 'real' world is to a large extent unconsciously built up on the language habits of the group" (Barnouw 1963:96). Benjamin Whorf suggested that concepts of the nature of space and time are conditioned by language structure. The Sapir-Whorf hypothesis takes the position that individual perception of reality is determined by the structure of the language the individual speaks (Barnouw 1963:97). Holders of this position agree that no true understanding of a culture is possible without complete familiarity with its language, and speakers of different languages cannot possibly perceive reality the same way. (Some philosophers conclude that because no two people ever speak exactly the same language, no individual perceives reality in exactly the same way as any other individual.)

Semanticists and psychologists have explored the effects of language on individual perception and personality. They too conclude that language strongly influences individual perceptions and responses. Differences in meanings and connotations attached to certain words may have disastrous consequences for communication between individuals.

The exact nature and degree of the influence of language on socialization are by no means well understood, however. Critics of the Sapir-Whorf hypothesis point out that some societies with different cultures speak the same language, particularly so far as grammatical structure is concerned. On the other hand, other societies with different languages have cultures that are almost identical (Hoijer 1954b:102–104). The most popular position among anthropologists today would seem to be that language does indeed exert an influence on individual modes of thought, particularly by channeling them along certain lines, but does not actually control perception. In this view the influence of language lies in the fact that it is "the major instrumental means by which people learn to attribute meaning, order, and significance to cultural existence" (Thompson 1975:16). Language systems—shared meanings and rules of classifying, ordering, and combining linguistic elements—are the product of generations of social interactions and experiences of people who share a culture. Newcomers (babies and strangers of all ages) must learn the language system to communicate effectively. Babies usually acquire the rules of the language so early and so informally that they are almost always unaware of most of the mechanical aspects and take them for granted (although later they are forced to relearn many consciously in school). As they learn the rules, growing children also are unconsciously conditioned into concepts "about the way in which the world is structured and operates" (Thompson 1975:15). Adult newcomers, who learn the language slowly and painfully, are generally more aware of the details, and may never fully accept the concepts of the new framework.

Language divides phenomena into distinct categories, based on particular criteria that differ from one language to another, and then labels these categories. As new things in the environment are encountered, children learning the language find as they get more and more competent, that there are convenient classes for filing all the new elements, which are then integrated into the growing conceptual framework—adding to it, making it easier for the children to remember the new information, and also making the new information seem less alien. It is this classification function of language that led Sapir and Whorf to postulate the deterministic effect of language on thought and that has led modern anthropologists interested in cognition° (concept formation and thought) to the assumption that linguistic analysis will reveal significant information about the concepts of the culture.

Most students in the United States are not exposed to even a small part of the full range of the linguistic variations found in the world because the traditional languages taught in schools are all variants of one large language family, Indo-European, and so bear a strong resemblance to each other in the way they categorize phenomena, despite some variation in details. Only a very few colleges and universities offer Asiatic or native-American languages which differ sharply from Indo-European or even Semitic and African language conceptualizations. Yucatec, one of the languages spoken by the Maya in the Yucatan Peninsula (southeastern Mexico), or Navajo (spoken by native Americans in the southwestern United States) would provide the necessary contrast if either were widely taught in North American schools. In counting things, for example, a Yucatec speaker must give first the number (one, two, three, and so on), then the genus classifier (whether the thing is plant, human, or other living creature, or inanimate), then the size or shape classifier (whether the thing is flat-round, long-pointed, and so on) before finally getting to name the thing. Thus, to ask for a tortilla (a round, thin, flat pancake), a person should ask for "one inanimate object, flat-round thing, tortilla" (Thompson 1975:11, 12). Navajo complicates things even further by using quite different verbs with the different-shaped objects, as well as different verbs to describe *how* the object was transferred from one person to another, since they have no general verb equivalent to the English *give*. Such classification differences mean that speakers of these and similar languages rarely give the same answers as English speakers on the sort of tests that ask people to identify the one object in a group that does not match the others, or to group together items that have common characteristics. The story is told of the Aztec scribe who drove his Spanish master to despair because instead of listing the tribute brought according to its value, or categories Spaniards would normally use (such as "gold," "precious gems," and so on) he used Aztec categories and "put all of the durable things together, the round objects all in their proper place, as are the flat things and the cylindrical ones" (Thompson 1975:10). He could not understand the Spaniard's confusion. Similarly, Navajos, unlike English speakers, do not use the same word for a "nice" dress that they use for a "nice" dinner or for a "nice" horse.

This difference in categorizing, conceptualizing, and building the framework for organizing experience has a stronger effect on memory than on perception. Research has shown, for example, that it is easier to remember colors that have names than those that do not, although differences between the colors are perceived (Lenneberg and Roberts 1961:493–502).

The relationship between language and thought is still being explored. The widespread belief that without language there can be no thought has been increasingly challenged by recent work with animals, particularly chimpanzees. Washoe (the chimpanzee who was taught deaf-oral sign language) has answered questions and used signs in other ways that show she is aware of herself as an individual and has a sense of property. She also "talked" to herself with signs when she was alone, indicating a mental life going on in the absence of her trainers or specific cues that were used to get her to respond with signs. Currently, Washoe is living with other chimpanzees, and researchers are watching with great interest to learn whether she will teach her companions to communicate through signs. A variety of experiments with other chimpanzees has indicated that the same ability to communicate through a symbol system is general among them (Gardner and Gardner 1969; Hahn 1971).

Another approach that has made a considerable stir in recent years has been expressed most popularly by Noam Chomsky, who said (among many other things) that the apparent "surface" structure of a language was only a superficial mask for a more significant, underlying "deep" structure that rested on basic cultural, or perhaps even human, characteristics, and that the task of the linguist should be focused more on the problem of revealing the deep structure than on "simple" description (Chomsky 1964:28–29). His theories and criticisms of it are discussed in more detail in the final chapter of the book. If Chomsky's concepts about the relevance of basic human characteristics are accurate, some personality characteristics should also be universal which would account for the ability of humans to communicate at least at some levels across cultures. It might also account for some widespread cultural universals in other than linguistic areas. Children are socialized nonverbally as well as with words. Adults communicate with one another constantly through the way they move, hold their bodies, stand, sit and so on. In this chapter the socialization function of both speech and physical communication is the focus of interest. Parents or other adults communicate verbally and physically with their offspring. Long before a baby has built a vocabulary of words, it has begun to learn from its parents and other people in its environment. The degree of physical contact, and whether it is most often painful or pleasant; the tone of voice, and whether certain tones, intensities, or rates of speech are accompanied by painful or pleasant experiences—all these things teach something, often far more than adults realize or would want them to. The meaning of words comes later, and may never communicate feeling tone as well as some of the other characteristics of both language and physical movement.

We are still learning many things about socialization, the factors that influence the development of adult personalities, and the relationship of these to social institutions. Another subtle relationship between child-rearing and adult institutions has been suggested by David McClelland. His hypothesis is that "the need for achievement is responsible for economic growth and decline" (McClelland 1961:vii). The high-need achievers, McClelland says, are produced by strong independence training and achievement expectations in childhood. The excerpt would tend to support this. Etsu appears to have a strong need to achieve, and she received strong independence training at an early age. Her father seemed to feel the development of self-reliance was crucial for members of a Samurai family. He illustrated the type of training a Samurai child should receive by describing a lioness pushing her cub over the cliff to make it climb up from the valley because "so only can it gain strength for its life work." Japan's economy has been most impressive in its growth and vigor, especially since the end of World War II. If Etsu's training was characteristic of a significant segment of Japanese society, McClelland's hypothesis would seem to have strong support. Of course, it is poor methodology to rely on data such as this excerpt, which can give only an impressionistic idea of possibilities. To test McClelland's hypothesis, one would have to study samples of the Japanese population to determine whether they in fact *are* high-need achievers, whether their childhood training was aimed at fostering independence, whether it succeeded, and whether parents expected high achievement from their children. (The difficulty of relying on the data contained in the excerpt is demonstrated by the ease with which the strong emphasis on obedience and submission plus the reliance on rote memorization in studies could be used as evidence that Japanese child-training was meant to and in fact did produce dependent imitators rather than self-reliant creative individuals.)

In his effort to find out whether children were socialized toward achievement, McClelland, among other things, examined readers given to children in school in various countries. He also took the amount of electricity used per person as an index of economic growth. The results of his research led him to

A class in Niger watching a program on closed circuit educational television. *(UN/ UNESCO/RACCAH Studio)*

state that the socialization of children for achievement caused economic growth; it did not just go along with it. A later study in Nigeria by LeVine partially supported McClelland, but also showed that national complex societies did not socialize all segments of the society the same way (Thompson 1975:53; LeVine 1966). The excerpt makes the same point about Japan. Etsu was certainly socialized differently from Ishi, and Etsu also mentions that other girls were not socialized the way she was. Her father emphasizes the fact that Samurai children were socialized more sternly than children of other classes.

PERSONALITY AND CULTURE: A COMPLEX RELATIONSHIP

The study of human beings is never simple. Most behavioral scientists have long since abandoned the search for a single cause to explain specific behavior, for they recognize that a number of factors, all of which may be important, are involved in any human interaction. In line with this awareness, modern approaches to the relationship between personality or character and culture tend to focus more on the *interaction* among genetic endowment, physical environment, idiosyncratic individual experiences, and sociocultural environment; it is the interplay of cultural demands with other factors that attracts researchers' interest. For example, recent technological advances have revealed unsuspected physical aspects of human behavior. Technology now enables man to travel more rapidly than ever before, and Western culture requires business people to take advantage of the new ease of travel to make their work global in scope. Because of the reported detrimental physical and mental effects of rapid travel combined with the stress of engaging in prolonged and complicated business negotiations, researchers began to study the problem and found that the human has an internal clock which is disrupted by too rapid passage from one time zone to another. "Jet lag" is now one of the factors taken into account in arranging business conferences and athletic schedules. It is probably also one of the factors involved in the periodic attempts by some business people and politicians to put the United States on one time zone, so that when it is 4 PM in Washington it will also be 4 PM in Los Angeles (even though it would just be getting dark in Los Angeles at "midnight"). The assumption has not been fully tested experimentally as yet, but there is some indication that cycles of light and dark are profoundly significant regardless of what the clock indicates. Populations in areas of the far north which have close to twenty-four hours of sunshine a day in the summer and twenty-four hours of darkness a day in winter show considerable changes in activity patterns, sleep habits, and so on, regardless of the fact that the clocks keep the same time, summer and winter.

Studies have been made concerning the relationship of perception to such environmental characteristics as straight lines and right angles (called a "carpentered environment"[o]) or curved lines and no right angles (called a "noncarpentered environment"). People raised in a noncarpentered environment are not as subject to the optical illusions that fool people socialized in a carpentered environment, although they succumb to others (Mussen and Rosenzweig 1973:617–618; Allport and Pettigrew 1957:104–113; Segall, Campbell, et al. 1963:769–771). Other studies have concentrated on the level of certain chemicals produced by the body and present in the blood. Epinephrine, which is produced by the adrenal gland, has, for instance, been correlated with emotional states and sensitivity (or the lack of it) to pain (Schachter and Wheeler 1962:121–128; Science News 1936, 90:425). Further research is necessary to learn how these chemical levels are related to child-raising practices. For example, do high (or low) levels in either parents or children correlate with harsh (or indulgent) child-raising techniques? These studies are revealing a more subtle relationship between the physical individual and his or her culture than had previously been suspected, and are adding to the complexity of the whole area of study. Space does not permit a more detailed discussion, but interested readers can explore the topic further through the references cited.

THE FAMILY: SEX ROLES

Consider the excerpt again. What were some characteristics other than those discussed earlier that the Samurai class wanted to develop in their children? Clearly, patience, endurance, and perseverance were highly regarded. The incident in which Etsu froze her fingers while practicing writing illustrates the value attached to all three. Despite being aware of the damage to her hand, neither the child nor the nurse stopped the session. Such a deliberate disregard for the personal comfort or physical well-being of a child is almost inconceivable in middle-class American culture today. Etsu was expected to finish her task slowly and carefully regardless of discomfort. In fact, the physical discomfort was assumed to contribute to her mental inspiration. It was no accident that her room was cold, since the coldest days had been chosen for the most difficult tasks, and no stove was brought into the room. Etsu's parents went out of their way to make things difficult, not easier, for their daughter.

Even though Etsu was subjected to what in the United States today might be regarded as cruel treatment, once she successfully finished her task, she was wrapped up comfortably, fed warm food her grandmother herself had prepared, surrounded with love, attention, and care. Contrast this with the cold rebuke she received from her teacher when she moved during a lesson. Assuming this difference in reaction to performance was consistent, what child would not prefer the warm, affectionate treatment, even if it meant enduring some temporary physical discomfort? When people a child depends on or feels affection for give either cold or warm reactions according to the child's behavior, it is a rare one indeed who will deliberately choose to prompt the negative reaction. The source of the power of the family to socialize a child should be obvious.(Children who appear to be deliberately provoking are usually just trying to get *some* reaction. Even a negative response is better than being ignored. Parents, teachers, all persons working with very small children who constantly behave "badly" need to look at their own behavior objectively to determine whether they are really rewarding the behavior they *want* or the "wrong" behavior instead.)

The excerpt also indicates that members of the Samurai class made a sharp distinction between training for boys and that for girls. Boys were permitted to sleep in a sprawled-out position, for example; girls were not. Boys studied the Chinese classics; girls normally did not. (Etsu was an exception because she was being trained as a priestess.) There were special games for boys that girls were forbidden to play (although they did do so when no one was watching—perhaps another indication that the society was shame- rather than guilt-oriented). Girls learned the necessary skills for running a household; boys did not.

All societies make some distinction between the training of girls and boys, since no society expects precisely the same behavior from both sexes. Of course, there is a biological component involved—no male is likely to give birth to a child, and no female is likely to sire one. As a result of the child-bearing and nursing functions, most societies have patterns of behavior for women that can be carried out in or close to the home. As mentioned in earlier chapters, no society requires big-game hunting as a normal part of the role of women. Women are hardly ever expected to be deep-sea fishermen or warriors. Women may accompany such expeditions, but it is rarely part of their normal role expectation. With these exceptions, which are based on the functional demands of the situation more than on attitudes, abilities, or inclination, role expectations for women and for men are as varied as any other aspect of culture. Thus, although the role training for men in any specific society is different from the role training for women in that society, it is also likely to be different from the training for men in other societies. The training of male children in one society may include activities restricted to the role of women in another society, and vice versa. For example, in some societies, only the men weave; in others, only the women. Men make pottery in one society, women in another. Margaret Mead has pointed out that in one New Guinea society women are taught to be more aggressive and less interested in dress or adornment than the men, whereas the situation is reversed in the United States (Mead 1950:188–189).

There is a great deal of concern over sex roles in the United States today, due at least partly to a confusion between gender (biological sexual characteristics) and masculinity or femininity (cultural expectations of behavior appropriate to a particular sex). The first is determined genetically, the second, culturally. The first is physical, the second behavioral. For the individual it is

A transvestite, in this case a male impersonating a female as a profession in New York City. (*Jason Lauré/Woodfin Camp & Associates*)

much easier to change behavior than genetic or physical characteristics; but for a group, social expectations are almost as difficult to change as physical characteristics are for the individual, since many people's expectations are involved. Consequently, the individual who wishes, for whatever reason, to behave like a member of the opposite sex faces constant problems from the conflict between social expectations determined by physical appearance and his or her actual behavior. Because so many of the expectations in regard to sex roles are part of covert culture, people who do not behave according to the expectations are often regarded as "abnormal," and their behavior considered "unnatural." A difficulty is, of course, that "unnatural" behavior in one society may be "natural" in another. So when people from two cultures interact, misunderstandings are quite possible. Violation of sex-role expectations tap strong emotions, and consequently attempted changes in this area often produce strong resistance, anger, even violence. The attention of the behavioral scientist in regard to the relationship between culture and personality is often focused on the question, If sex-role behavior is learned, then what happened in the cases of people who either do not know or do not care to practice the appropriate role? How did they get socialized into the behavior they practice and why did socialization into the appropriate role fail to occur?

THE PROBLEM OF FAILURE

All societies have to cope with failures of the socialization process in some areas. A variety of factors may cause such failures. Recent studies indicate, for example, that overcrowding may be as detrimental to human socialization as it has been shown to be for laboratory rats (Ardrey 1970:241–280). Various structural breakdowns in the family can also cause socialization problems. Harry and Margaret Harlow conducted a long series of experiments with monkeys that showed that when monkeys were deprived of all association with other young monkeys or with the mother figures, they did not develop into socially normal monkeys. Even sexual behavior became disturbed. The deprived monkeys did not know how to engage in sexual intercourse and consequently could not reproduce under normal circumstances (so much for instinct!). When the experiments did finally succeed in bringing about reproduction, the deprived monkeys made poor parents. They mistreated their offspring, physically abused them, neglected them, and managed to raise a second generation of disturbed monkeys (Harlow and Harlow 1961:48–55). The implications of these studies for humans appear clear, but researchers are being cautious. Human beings are not monkeys, however closely related the two may be. It is tempting, but perhaps unwise, to generalize from one to the other without modification. One fact does seem inescapable, however: socialization is far more important than has been suspected, even in less complex animals in whom instinctive behavior apparently plays a more powerful role than it does with humans.

There are other reasons for breakdowns in socialization. In a complex society, such as the United States, there are so many different groups involved in socialization (school, peer groups, various subcultures) that young people are almost always subjected to a barrage of conflicting beliefs and values. This may be one of the factors behind the so-called identity crisis faced by many American teenagers. Subjected to strong pressure to identify with groups, and having so many groups to identify with, individuals may find themselves strongly supporting diametrically opposite causes, according to the group they are in at any given time. A thoughtful individual must question such easy adoption of the values of first one and then another group, asking, What am I really like? What do I really believe? Who am I?

In addition, wherever and whenever it occurs, rapid and fundamental change in a society produces special problems of socialization. Premodern societies recently exposed to Western culture and in the process of industrializing perhaps suffer this difficulty even more deeply than does the United States, although the problem of alienation from one's own culture is also highly significant here. But any society caught in the flux of profound change will have difficulty, since many of the things adults were taught, and want to teach their children, no longer apply, yet carry all the emotional force of the past. Young people are often caught between attraction for the "new life" and love or respect for parents who have not, as yet, been able to adjust to the changes. The situation should be familiar to most Americans from the stories of the conflicts between immigrant parents and their American-born children. Now, whole

New and old modes of transportation from two different cultures. Rapid modernization often produces problems of socialization. *(Standard Oil Co. of New Jersey)*

generations with native-born parents are suffering the same conflicts, both in the United States and in other countries. There is no immediate solution in sight, but at least books like *Future Shock* (Toffler 1970) show that people are beginning to grapple with the problem realistically instead of just bemoaning the loss of the "good old days."

Another problem afflicts many modern nations, particularly the United States. Our population is drawn from all over the world and consequently has been socialized in many different cultures. People emigrating to the Western Hemisphere obviously do not shed their values, beliefs, or attitudes at the entry port, although many of their behavior patterns, from necessity, do eventually change (Thompson 1975:27). Actually, the United States as a "melting pot" never really melted much of anything (Glazer and Moynihan 1963:12–17), and remains a multinational, multiethnic society in which there is no true majority. (The so-called WASP majority—white, Anglo-Saxon Protestant, presumably people of English, Welsh, and Scottish descent—actually makes up only 14.4 percent of the population. Add to that group people of German descent—12.5 percent, not all of whom are Protestant—and it still amounts to only about 27 percent of the United States population [*World Almanac* 1975:154].) With people from many different places present in one country, socializing their children at least partly into the cultures they brought with them (or already had here), especially the covert-culture aspects, it should not be surprising that Americans often disagree. The surprising thing is that we agree as often as we do. The "failure" of socialization in the United States may actually be more a problem of successful socialization into many mutually exclusive or at least

Store signs and advertisements in New York, showing contact among several cultures on one street corner. *(Freda Leinwand)*

divergent cultures. For example, a properly socialized traditional Navajo male does not speak to his mother-in-law, and if they are in the same room together, he trys to avoid even looking at her. A properly socialized middle-class WASP male talks to his mother-in-law (preferably politely). If a Navajo male married into a WASP family or a WASP male into a Navajo family, both men would be regarded as badly brought up (examples of socialization failures) by their respective in-laws, but they would be examples of socialization successes in their own families. Studies have shown cultural differences not only between ethnic groups but also between socio-economic classes that would lead to properly socialized people from one group being defined as failures of socialization in the other (Vogt and Albert 1966; Kohn 1966:281–289). (Middle class males are punished for fighting, for example, while lower class males are punished for *not* fighting [Clinard 1974:6–11].)

CRISIS RITES

The study of socialization is, of course, not limited to childhood experiences. Modern researchers are aware that events taking place later in an individual's life may also play a significant part in the development of the adult personality (Thompson 1975:44). Some of these later events may serve the purpose of undoing earlier childhood conditioning; others reinforce it. One experience researchers believe has the function of undoing early conditioning is the puberty rite.° This is one of the *rites de passage*° (passage or crisis rites°) that marks a change in status (van Gennep 1960:2–4). The puberty rite marks the change from child or adolescent to adult. These ceremonies have attracted a great deal of attention from behavioral scientists and there is a voluminous literature on the topic. Puberty rites often involve some sort of ordeal, particularly for males, and a learning experience. The severity of the ordeal and the duration of the instruction period vary widely.

Male circumcision is a frequent feature of puberty rites. The explicit, or manifest, function is to make the initiate a man. Once the operation has healed, a young man is usually free to consider marriage (or sexual intercourse), speak up in the presence of the older men, command respect from the uncircumcised boys (as well as girls and women), and otherwise take on the responsibilities and privileges of adult males. This one act turns a boy into an adult. Contrast this with the ambiguous position of a young man in the United States. Laws vary from one state to another. In some states he can get a learner's permit to drive at fourteen but must stay in school until he is sixteen. He can usually sign a legally binding document when he is eighteen but in some states may not marry without parental consent until he is twenty or twenty-one. He can be drafted at eighteen but in some states cannot drink alcoholic beverages until he is twenty-one. In most places he can be tried in criminal court as an adult when he is over eighteen but the insurance rates for his car remain high until he is over twenty-five. In American society, an individual passes through a transition state for approximately eleven years—from about age fourteen to twenty-five. During this time he is considered an adult for some purposes and a child for others—with the choice rarely left to him. There is no clear-cut ceremony or sign that he is now a full adult member of the society.

A puberty rite often dramatizes and tests certain of the qualities members of the society value and expect of their adults. In some societies, initiates are expected to be brave and show no signs of fear or pain during an extremely painful operation performed without any anesthetic (Gatheru 1965:60). In others, they are not expected to show the same fortitude. Girls usually do not have to undergo such painful ordeals, but in a few societies, they too must endure substantial pain (for example, the Kikuyu practice clitoridectomy°—excision of the clitoris [Gatheru 1965:58]).

Penalties for failure to show the desired characteristics are usually well known. Group contempt, for example, may be expressed by public scorn and humiliation, including spitting on the offending initiate as an immediate reaction, and long-term rejection might even be extended to the initiate's family. The Kikuyu assume that only illegitimate boys show fear during initiation (Gatheru 1965:62).

Rewards for successful endurance are equally clear, and new initiates usually delight in validating their status by demonstrating their superiority over the uninitiated. This serves to reinforce the system; the differences between circumcised and uncircumcised in terms of privileges are so obvious that the uninitiated tend to be strongly motivated to undergo the public ordeal for the sake of its rewards. Refusal to go through a puberty ceremony may mean that an individual will never be taken seriously by the rest of the society. He may be handicapped in any dealings with the people in powerful positions; he may not be able to marry (or even court a wife) and is likely to be left out of the mainstream of adult life.

Whiting and others have studied the correlations between severe puberty rites and other aspects of the society. According to Whiting, the rite serves to break any possible cross-sex identification that might occur because of a male child's close and almost exclusive association with his mother during his early infancy. Under these circumstances, the mother may appear the envied and powerful sex. The severity of the puberty rite emphasizes the boy's identity with his own sex. Whiting feels this explanation is supported by the correlation of severe public puberty rites and either a long postpartum sex tabu or a period of a year or more when the young boy shares his mother's bed (Whiting 1961:361). Frank Young, on the other hand, feels that the rite is an expression of male solidarity and occurs particularly in those societies where male cooperation is important for both economic exploitation of the environment and defense (Young 1962:380–383). Neither of these explanations deals with the problem of female initiation. Fewer societies have female puberty rites, and in those that do, the rites are rarely as painful as circumcision or subincision° (slitting the penis from base to glans, or part way). Most female rites include only such mild ordeals as seclusion, sleeplessness, food tabus, and special, often tiring, activities. A study of female initiation shows that, as with males, severity and genital mutilation tend to be correlated with a possible conflict in sexual identity. Female initiation is also associated with matrilocal° residence and occurs most often in societies where women make a substantial contribution to subsistence (Brown 1963:849–850).

Many puberty rites include a period of training in the norms and beliefs of the society. This period may last from a few days to several years. The so-called bush school may be held for either sex, but it is never coeducational —each school is restricted to one sex. Most often males are the ones who receive the training and go through the public ceremony.

Even when the period of training and isolation is short, there is usually some symbolic representation of norms the society regards as important during the ceremony itself. Kikuyu initiation emphasizes the social value placed on courage and endurance. The women sing what is expected of the initiate, which of course he already knows, having witnessed similar ceremonies himself (Ga-

A puberty ceremony in sub-Saharan Africa. These boys have just been circumcised; when the operation heals, they will be considered men. *(Dr. Kal Muller/Woodfin Camp & Associates)*

theru 1965:59). In some societies an initiate is required to perform actually or symbolically some of the duties that will be expected of him or her as an adult. Among Navajos, for example, female initiates grind corn; in Polynesia they weave mats or make grass skirts; in some African societies men must kill either a valuable food animal or a dangerous one, such as a lion. In the past, many societies required a young man to kill an enemy or successfully complete a difficult or dangerous task (a raid or a vision quest) before he was eligible for the puberty ceremony. All these requirements emphasize the values or behavior that an individual must have mastered to be able to perform his or her adult role successfully.

Since puberty rites generally have a public aspect, the initiate has seen the ceremony many times before participating as a candidate. Thus the rite has a teaching function for the uninitiated spectators. For the candidates and the initiated spectators the rite serves to demonstrate dramatically that the candidates are capable of doing what is expected of them as adults. It makes it easier for the candidates to adopt their new roles and for others to accept them in those roles. This latter aspect may be more important than the literature indicates. One of the difficulties often mentioned by young adults, parents, and observers alike in the United States is getting members of the older generation (especially parents) to accept young people in their late teens and early twenties as competent adults. The United States has no public ceremony that clearly demonstrates to the older generation that the young man or woman in question has mastered the necessary adult skills, information, or values. A puberty rite cannot substitute for a college degree (which shows that its possessor has been exposed to certain aspects of the culture and society), but, equally, no one should demand that college graduation function as a puberty rite and insist on it before admitting a young person to adult status—as seems to happen at some social levels in the United States today.

SUMMARY

A society cannot function unless most members perform approximately as expected. Since it is impossible to force everyone in a society to behave predictably, people have to want to do what they are supposed to do (Thompson 1975:35). In most cases, they learn what that is while they are growing up in the family. As children, they are taught the rules, customs, and traditions of the society, and they are rewarded for approved behavior and punished for incorrect performance. In this way, each child learns to value certain things and to reject or dislike others. The process is called socialization, or enculturation.

Since the individual's personality is affected by the experiences he or she has, particularly during the first few years of life, anthropologists and some psychologists have assumed that cultures making different demands on individuals will tend to have members whose personalities are characteristic of the society and different from those in other societies. The nature of the relationship between personality and culture is complex, however. The demands of a culture do affect the personalities of its members, but they in turn embody the culture and pass it along to their children. Individuals are not simply passive recipients. Each interprets and reworks the culture as he or she lives. The same cultural demands made on different people have different consequences. Culture and personality are dynamically interrelated, with influences going both ways.

The relationship of physical environment, cultural surroundings, and internal human chemistry to personality is also being investigated with a new sophistication, and is turning out to be far more subtle and complex than was originally envisioned.

Research into the interrelationship among various aspects of the culture, child-raising practices, and, ultimately, personality is providing new information. The function of puberty rites in undoing certain childhood conditioning; the relationship of initiation rites to structural features of the culture such as residence patterns, the contribution of women to subsistence, the organization of work groups, and so on; the relationship of basic maintenance systems to child-raising practices; the effect of the adult personality on concepts of disease causation, religious beliefs, or witchcraft; research into all these topics is producing exciting new insights about human behavior. The whole area of socialization, thought processes, education, and personality is an active and vital one in current anthropology.

Some socialization takes place throughout an individual's life, and the society as a whole plays a part in the process, but most of the early and crucial socialization takes place within the family. Chapter 8 deals with the formation and composition of families in different societies.

8 Addition of New Members

Even with the most careful precautions and concern, individual members of the group die. If they are not replaced, the group itself will cease to exist. There are two ways in which any group replenishes its members: it may attract new members from other groups, or it may create new members through reproduction within the society. Attracting people from other groups is less expensive in the short run because an immigrant comes into the society as a productive adult; a child, on the other hand, must be supported for a long time before he can contribute economically to the society. But the difficulty of socializing an adult often offsets this advantage. Reproduction within the group is by far the more common method, for it is efficient and simpler in the long run. (It might be noted in passing that reproduction does nothing directly to contribute to the survival of the individual; *in fact, for female members of the group throughout human history, childbirth has been the major life threat, as it still is in countries lacking modern medical facilities. Reproduction is, however, essential to the survival of the human species. Addition of new members, therefore, meets a group rather than an individual survival need.)*

In this chapter, we focus on the more common method for adding new members. As you read the excerpts in this chapter, observe how people find mates, how they deal with family relationships and inheritance, how they set up households, and what they do if the households break up.

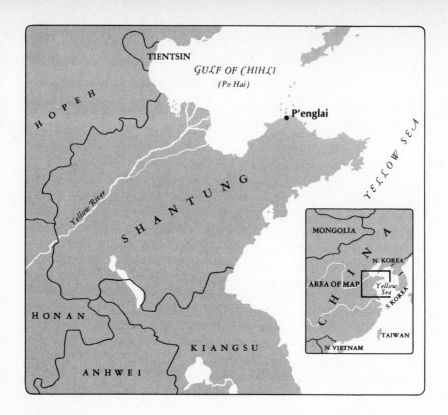

Tradition and the Chinese Bride

My father called me Little Tiger and I was my mother's youngest child.* The name she called me is known to no one now alive. My sister and my brother called me Meimei, Little Sister, and the neighbors called me Hsiao Wutse, Little Five, because I was the fifth child my mother bore. Two died before I was born.

We lived in a courtyard by ourselves when I was born. We lived near the truck garden which had belonged to the family, to my father and my father's uncle. . . .

The garden had once been part of the property of the Temple of the Goddess of Mercy, the Kuan Yin T'ang. Ten generations ago, a Taoist priest came down from the hills . . . and became the abbot of the temple. He was our ancestor. He was a man with a square face and a strong disposition. My grandfather had the same square face and I have it also. That is why my father called me Little Tiger. Also, he said, I had a strong disposition.

Our family had been well to do at one time. We had the land our ancestor left us and my grandfather and his father before him had been among those who worked as overseers on the estates of General Ch'i. When my mother married into the family we owned the garden and the house in the Chou Wang Temple

*Abridged from *A Daughter of Han: The Autobiography of a Chinese Working Woman* by Ida Pruitt, from the story told her by Ning Lao T'ai-T'ai, pp. 11–14, 20, 29–39, 42–43, 46–47, 54–55, 66–67, 70–72. Copyright, 1945 by Yale University Press. Reprinted by permission of Yale University Press.

248

section of the city and some other small houses besides. The family had servants and plenty to eat.

My father was an only son and was spoiled by his father. His parents died when he was seven or eight. He was brought up by his uncle, his father's younger brother, who made his own four sons work in the garden but sent my father to school. The uncle said that in this way he was faithful to his dead brother. My father studied the classics for about eight years, but his studies never amounted to anything. When he was grown, the uncle put him in a shop to learn business.

Money went out, the neighbors said, because my father and his cousins had too good a time, eating and playing. . . . Each year there was less than the year before. When my grandfather died, what was left was divided between my father and his uncle, the younger brother of his father.

My father tried to work in the garden but he had not the strength or the skill and he was ashamed. He sold the garden to one of his mother's aunts, to pay his debts, and went to Chefoo and peddled bread. He knew how to make bread, and carried it around the street in a basket. That was the year I was born. From the time I was conceived, the fortunes of the family went down. The destiny determined for me by Heaven was not a good one.

The neighbors said that my mother was not a good manager, that she could not make the money stretch so as to "get over the years" successfully. At New Year's time great loaves of bread were steamed in the iron cooking basin. If, when the lid of the cooking basin was raised, the loaves shrank, they were thrown into the fire. Sometimes she threw three or four cookings into the fire before the loaves came out round and full. This is what the neighbors said my mother used to do. I never saw it, for we had nothing to throw away when I was growing up.

My mother did not live the life she was brought up to live. A woman in childbed should have at least five hundred eggs to eat. When I was born she had only eight eggs. My mother's father, when he lived, sold oil in the streets, beating a small bronze gong, and supported the family comfortably. My mother had a round face and gentle ways. She was a carefully reared and sheltered person. How could such a person, living behind walls, know how to manage poverty?

. . .

Though each year our living was less than the year before, we had a good life at home. My mother was kind to us. She cooked good things for us to eat and she loved us.

My father was strict but he was good to his family. He taught us manners and what was seemly for a woman to do and what was not seemly.

. . .

When I was three or four years old we moved to the Chou Wang Temple neighborhood, to be near the garden. . . . This was the first time our family had lived in a court with others. The house had a thatched roof. Before we had always lived in houses with tile roofs.

When I was thirteen my parents stopped shaving the hair from around the patch of long hair left on my crown. I was no longer a little girl. My hair was allowed to grow and was gathered into a braid at the back of my head. It was braided in a wide loose plait which spread fanlike above and below the knot that held the hair at the nape of the neck. It was like a great butterfly. Girls do not wear their hair that way now. Part of the hair was separated and braided into a little plait down my back. When the little braid was gathered into the big braid I was a woman, and not allowed out of the gate. . . . And at the age of thirteen I was taught to cook and sew.

My father was a very strict man. We were not allowed, my sister and I, on the street after we were thirteen. People in P'englai were that way in those days. When a family wanted to know more about a girl who had been suggested for a daughter-in-law and asked what kind of a girl she was, the neighbors would answer, "We do not know. We have never seen her." And that was praise.

. . .

My sister was married when she was fifteen, and I was married when I was fifteen. I was eight when my sister was married.

My sister's match was considered a very suitable one. Her husband was only three or four years older than she and he had a trade. He was a barber. And the father-in-law was still young enough to work also. But my sister was a child, with the ways of a child and the heart of a child. She had not become used to housework. She did not know how to mix wheat bread or corn bread. She got the batter too thick or too thin, and so her mother-in-law would scold. She had

Chinese family at dinner. *(Rodale Press, Inc.)*

no experience and could not plan meals. At one meal she would cook too much and at the next not enough. This also made her mother-in-law angry and she would scold. Though my sister had not learned to work she had learned to smoke [opium]. This also made her mother-in-law angry. She would say that my sister was not good for work but only for luxury. So there was bitterness.

Her mother-in-law forbade her to smoke. She took her pipe and broke it into many pieces. My sister made herself a pipe from a reed and smoked when there was no one around. One day her mother-in-law came suddenly into the room. My sister hid the pipe under clothes as she sat on the k'ang. The lighted pipe set the wheat chaff under the bed matting afire, and her mother-in-law beat her. When her husband came home his mother told him the story and he also beat my sister. There was a great quarrel and her mother-in-law reviled her with many words that were too hard to bear.

... My sister went crazy. ... she stayed with us for six months.

And she was not right for all those six months. ... All these six months she talked to herself, and at times she was stiff and still. But she got better and the fits became less frequent.

We asked friends to talk for her to her mother-in-law and husband, and at last it was arranged that they should take her back. A separate house was rented for her and her husband so that they did not live with the old people. She got on with her husband and they liked each other, but still at times she had the spells. ...

Seeing that my sister had so much trouble with a young husband, my father and mother said that I should be married to an older man who would cherish me. When the matchmaker told of such a one and that he had no mother—she was dead—my parents thought that they had done well for me. I was to have an older husband to cherish me, but not too old, and no mother-in-law to scold and abuse me.

Our neighbor, the man who carted away the night soil,° made the match for me. He was a professional matchmaker. He did not care how a marriage turned out. He had used the money. As the old people say, "A matchmaker does not live a lifetime with the people he brings together." The matchmaker hid four years of my husband's age from us, saying that the man was only ten years older than I. But he was fourteen years older. I was twelve when the match was made, and I became engaged—a childhood match. I still had my hair in a plait. I did not know anything. I was fifteen when I was married.

They told me that I was to be a bride. I had seen weddings going down the street. I had seen brides sitting on the k'angs on the wedding days when all went in to see them. To be married was to wear pretty clothes and ornaments in the hair.

I sat on the k'ang, bathed and dressed, in my red underclothes and red stockings. The music sounded and they took me off the k'ang. I sat on the chair and the matrons combed my hair for me into the matron's knot at the nape of my neck. They dressed me in my red embroidered bridal robes and the red embroidered bridal shoes and put the ornaments in my hair. An old man whose parents and wife were still alive carried me out and put me in the wedding chair that was to carry me to my new home. I knew only that I must not touch the sides of the chair as he put me in, and that I was dressed in beautiful clothes. I was a child, only fifteen by our count, and my birthday was small—just before the New Year. We count ourselves a year old when we are born and we all add a year at the New Year. I was counted two years old when I was a month old, for I was born near the end of the old year. I was a child. I had not yet passed my thirteenth birthday. [She continues, but in the third person.]

. . .

The musicians in their green uniforms and red tasseled hats sat by the table in the court. There were those who played on bamboo reed flutes and those who played on wooden horns. At times the cymbals clashed. But during the ceremony of clothing the bride and while the groom, who had come to fetch the bride, drank in another room with the men of the bride's family, it was the flute that sounded. By the different motifs played those who passed by in the street or stopped to watch knew which part of the ceremony was in progress.

. . . It was time for the groom to take the bride home. The musicians stood and played. The wooden horns joined the flutes. The cymbals clashed. The drums boomed. The groom came out of the house door. He was clothed in hired bridal robes, patterned like those of a mandarin's full dress. Once or twice at least in a lifetime every man and woman is equal to the highest in the land. When they are married and when they are buried they are clothed in the garments of nobility.

The father and the brother and the uncle of the bride escorted the groom. They bowed him to his chair. Then the red sedan chair of the bride was brought to the gate . . . All cracks between the chair and the gate were covered with pieces of red felt held by the chairmen to make sure that no evil spirit should enter. A long note of the horn sounded and the bride was carried out kneeling on the arms of an old man. He was a neighbor, a carpenter who was no longer working but was spending the last years of his life in pleasant social pursuits. He was also a doctor . . . who knew what to tell the mothers when their children's bellies ached, and how to keep their faces from scarring when the children broke out with smallpox, and how to break a fever . . . He was also a manager for weddings and funerals, and he was peacemaker for the neighborhood. . . . He was what was known as a whole man. Destiny had been kind to him. His father and mother still ate and slept in his house. . . . His wife, his old partner, was the one with whom he had started forty years ago as a boy of sixteen. He had sons and grandsons. Therefore at wedding ceremonies he was much sought after to bring good luck to the new couples. . . .

Matrons whose husbands were alive patted the bride's garments into place as she folded her arms and legs. They dropped the red curtain before her. . . .

The little procession started off. There were pairs of red lanterns on poles, red banners, and red wooden boards on which were great gold ideographs. The band followed and then came the green chair of the groom. This was followed closely by the red chair of the bride. Her brother walked beside it. He carried a piece of red felt in his hands. It was his duty to hold this between her chair and all the wells and dark corners and temples they passed. He must protect her from the hungry ghosts, the souls of those who have drowned themselves in these wells and are doomed to stay there until they can persuade others to drown themselves and release them. He must protect her from the elementals that lurk in dark corners, the weasel spirits and the fox fairies, and from the little demons in the temples who might follow her home and possess her and make her leave the path of reason and do those things which people do not do. . . . Behind came the cart carrying the perfect couple, the whole couple, a middle-aged man and his wife whose parents and children lived, who were to act for the family in giving her over to her new home.

. . .

Outside of the city the procession veered to the east . . . and went toward the sea and a village lying low and gray on the rocks of a small promontory.

It was a village of fishermen and the groom owned one of the fishing boats. He was also a farmer. . . . It was the family village of the Ning clan. All in the village were of this one clan. . . .

When I got to my new home and the wedding guests had left I found that there was a woman living in the house, a cousin's wife. She had lived there for many years and had borne a son to my husband. We all slept on one k'ang, the four of us. I was such a child that I told her I was glad she was there for I was frightened. Her husband had been gone many years and none knew whether he was alive or dead. . . . She lived with us for more than two years.

My husband's father was also with us. He tilled the family land and in the winter made baskets. . . .

I was but a child. We played games, the village children . . . and I. . . .

. . .

As was the custom, I went home every month to see my mother. But because my husband smoked opium and did not bring home food, I stayed longer with my mother than was the custom. Half of every month I stayed with my husband and half of every month I went home to my mother. . . .

When I left home to go back to my husband's village I would not let my mother see me cry. . . . That was because my older sister always cried and screamed when she had to go back to her mother-in-law. And so my father would scold her.

"What can we do?" he would say. "What is done is done. What good to make such an ado?" So I was always careful not to let them see me weep. My sister's husband was good and brought them money, but her mother-in-law was cruel. I had no mother-in-law but my husband did not bring in money.

. . .

I know now that there is no need to be angry with my parents for my marriage. They did the best they could for me. They thought they were getting a good home for me. Now I know that one's destiny is one's destiny. It was so decided for me.

We slept on the same k'ang, the four of us, until just before Mantze [her first child, a girl] was born. Then the neighbors got rid of the woman for me.

They were all our relatives. They said to her, "Who are you that you should live with them?"

And so she went away. . . .

. . .

Across the west wall from us lived an old uncle and aunt. He was a cousin to my husband's father. They were an old couple with no children and they were very fond of me. . . .

This old uncle was over seventy, a strong old man who loved his wine. He was good to me and hated my husband. The old aunt was a little old woman, over fifty.

I often went to their house and they fed me many meals when my husband brought home nothing for me to eat.

. . .

My husband was twenty-nine when I married him, and he had been an opium eater since he was nineteen. He took everything and sold it for opium. He could not help it. He took everything. I dared not wash a garment and put it out to dry without staying by to watch it. . . . The land had gradually gone. He had sold it.

An opium den in New York City, early in this century. *(Culver Pictures, Inc.)*

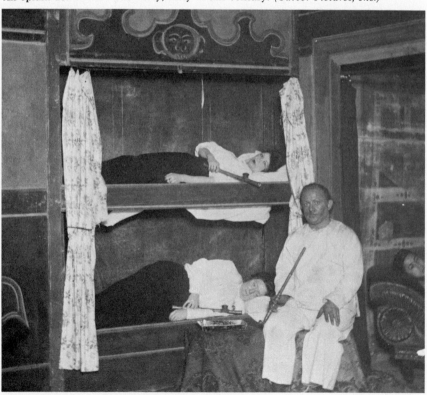

. . .

He was a fisherman. Our village was on the seashore. There are two lives that a man with a family must not lead. One is to be a soldier and the other to be a fisherman. Fishermen go out with the tide. They may sleep all day and go out in the night watches. They learn to be idle and irregular. In the early morning, if the fishing has been successful, they take their catch, great or small, to the city . . . They sell their fish at the market and go to the counting house for their cash. The counting house is in the court of an inn. There they smoke and drink all day. What is there left to bring home? How could they escape the opium habit? And my husband was good natured and friendly. My sister's husband beat her. Mine never lifted his hand to me, but he brought me no food. Half of each month I lived at home with my mother and ate. My brother brought me grain and flour when I lived in the other half in the house of my husband.

When Mantze was born my mother came to my husband's house and took care of me. . . .

When Mantze was two and I was big with another child I left my husband and the village. This was the first time I left him and I went on foot. . . . Respectable women did not walk in the streets of P'englai. We rode on horses and squares of black cloth covered our faces. But I was angry. For three days had we quarreled. He had sold everything I possessed. I had left, of the things my mother had given me at my marriage, only a pair of silver hairpins. I liked those hairpins. He wanted to sell them. I would not let him have them. . . . These three days the four people in our house had only seven small bowls of millet gruel to eat. Then he took the hairpins and sold them for a hundred coppers and smoked his opium. We had nothing to eat. Leading my child, and heavy with the other in me, I started out. I said that we would beg.

. . . I went to my mother's house and they took me in. It was in my anger that I said I would beg, but I knew not how. I went back to my husband and when my child was born it was another girl.

. . .

Our land was gone. The old man, my husband's father, . . . could braid his baskets in town as well as in the country. What he made was barely enough to keep him alone. In town I was near my own people. We sold the house . . . We leased a room in town . . . We had a four-year lease on it. Houses were cheap in those days and easy to get.

I was twenty-one when my mother died and she was only fifty-three.

Day after day I sat at home. Hunger gnawed. What could I do? My mother was dead. My brother had gone away. When my husband brought home food I ate it and my children ate with me. A woman could not go out of the court. . . . I did not know enough even to beg. So I sat at home and starved. I was so hungry one day that I took a brick, pounded it to bits, and ate it. It made me feel better.

How could I know what to do? We women knew nothing but to comb our hair and bind our feet and wait at home for our men. When my mother had been hungry she had sat at home and waited for my father to bring her food,

so when I was hungry I waited at home for my husband to bring me food.
My husband sold everything we had.

. . .

[They began going to a public food kitchen which served gruel.]
One day when my husband handed the baby over to me as usual, saying,
"Nurse her," one of the men in charge of the gruel station saw him do it.
"Is that your man?" said the man from the gruel station. I answered that
he was.
"He is trying to sell the child. He tells people that her mother died . . . "
[The husband did sell the child, but she managed to get it back.]

. . .

The old people tell us that her husband is more important to a woman than
her parents. A woman is with her parents only part of her life, they say, but she
is with her husband forever. He also feels that he is the most important. If a wife
is not good to her husband, there is retribution in heaven.

. . .

. . . People urged me to leave him and follow another man, to become a
thief or a prostitute. But my parents had left me a good name, though they left
me nothing else. I could not spoil that for them.

A peasant home in a village outside Peking. *(Marc Riboud/Magnum)*

In those years it was not as it is now. There was no freedom then for women. I stayed with him.

For another year we lived, begging and eating gruel from the public kitchen.

The father of my children was good for a while, and I thought he had learned his lesson. He promised never to sell the child again and I believed him. Then one day he sold her again and I could not get her back that time.

· · ·

... because he sold her, I left my husband. I took Mantze and went away. I told him that he could live his life and that I would live mine. He lived in the house I had leased but I did not go home. When the lease was up I let it go. I let him live where he would. He lived from one opium den to another. I taught my daughter Mantze to run at the sight of him and to hide. What if he sold her also? I would not live with him.

The story almost has a traditionally happy ending, after some more difficulty. Ning Lao was eventually able to support herself and her remaining child by hiring out as a house servant. Although that was somewhat shameful, it was at least honest, so she preserved the good name of her family. When Mantze was fifteen, Ning Lao arranged her marriage (which also turned out badly). Once Mantze was married, Ning Lao began to live with her husband again. They had another child—a boy—who was his mother's great delight. And with good reason, for girl children were not particularly welcome in traditional China. Marriages had to be arranged for them, at considerable expense. If the marriages were successful, the girls were lost to the family; if the marriages failed, the girls were a continual concern. Boys, on the other hand, were an advantage to the family, and their birth brought high status, and often improved treatment of the mother. If a woman in traditional China (and other societies with a similar concern for male children) was lucky and skillful enough to raise a son to manhood, she could count on having a daughter-in-law to order around. The mother of several sons could look forward to a comfortable and powerful old age—compensation for her problems as a young bride. The mother of daughters, on the other hand, had nothing but a lonely old age to look forward to. It is no wonder that Ning Lao greeted the birth of her son with great pleasure. Then, too, following the birth of his son, Ning Lao's husband cut down on his use of opium (although he never gave it up entirely), and their life together was relatively tranquil until he died. After that, she had her son to console her and to look out for her in her old age.

Most Americans would find it difficult to understand why Ning Lao ever remained married. In the United States today, a woman who would accept the kind of treatment Ning Lao received would probably be regarded as emotionally disturbed. Yet Ning Lao obviously felt she was doing the right thing and did not seriously consider any other course of action (or at least she did not mention any). Why?

MARRIAGE AND THE FAMILY

Part of the answer to this question lies in the meaning of marriage itself. In the American ideal, boy meets girl, they fall in love, get married, and "live happily ever after." Despite the so-called revolution in sexual norms, most people in the United States *do* get married, sooner or later. The same is true in most societies, even those where premarital sex is expected of everyone. One of the reasons is that the family° (as defined below) is a basic social unit in virtually all societies, and a family starts with a marriage.° There are many definitions of the term *marriage,* of course, but the one which seems most useful on a world-wide basis was proposed by Stephens, who said,

Marriage is a socially legitimate sexual union, begun with a public announcement and undertaken with some idea of permanence; it is assumed with a more or less explicit marriage contract, which spells out reciprocal rights and obligations between spouses and between the spouses and their future children [1964:5].

Marriage as defined by Stephens is virtually universal. Even the Nayar and the kibbutz, which may lack the family, have a form of approved sexual union that fits the definition. The Nayar are an Asiatic Indian caste in which, in the past, the wife never saw her husband after the marriage. She continued to live with her mother, sisters, and brothers, and accepeted lovers on an overnight basis. Kibbutzim are communal settlements in Israel in which children are raised together in a community nursery. Notice that there are several societies (including American examples) with forms fitting the definition and approved of by some subculture that are nonetheless illegal according to the formal code of the society (see discussion of marriage forms below). The study and understanding of family systems and societies in general is extraordinarily complex. Political and legal entities frequently do not coincide with cultural and social ones; legal codes do not always (and in complex societies could not possibly) embody all the values current in the society. In complex societies, there are always unwritten laws and informal codes of behavior, and there are always subgroups that hold different (and sometimes conflicting) values and that approve different kinds of behavior.

The term *family* is, if anything, more difficult to define satisfactorily than is *marriage.* When it is used in American society, it is commonly held to mean parents and children—the group called a nuclear family in anthropological literature (Cuber 1968:432–433). Actually, this unit is more often the household than the family. When college students are asked to list the people they regard as members of their family, 95 percent list grandparents, parents' siblings° (brothers and sisters), uncles and aunts by marriage, their own siblings' spouses (brothers- and sisters-in-law) and children (nephews and nieces); 75 percent also included their first cousins (children of their parents' siblings) (Richards, C.: unpublished research).

Family has had almost as many definitions as *instinct.* One of the best-known anthropological statements is George Murdock's:

The family is a social group characterized by common residence, economic cooperation, and reproduction. It includes adults of both sexes, at least two of whom maintain a socially approved sexual relationship, and one or more children, own or adopted, of the sexually cohabiting adults [1949:1].

For years, it was assumed that the family as defined by Murdock was universal, but this assumption was challenged by both M. Spiro and E. K. Gough in separate articles on the basis of their studies among the kibbutzim and Nayar, respectively. Both groups lack common residence of parents and children, and among the Nayar, not even the husband and wife live together (Spiro 1968:68–79); Gough 1968:80–96). As with most other questions about universal human patterns, much depends on definitions. Norman Bell and Ezra Vogel dodge the question by saying that any society recognizing the statuses of father, mother, and offspring has a family system, regardless of how it is constituted (Bell and Vogel, 1968:2). If the term *father* is accepted as referring to the sociological *pater* and not necessarily including *genitor* (Goody 1962:19), then all societies have a family system because all societies recognize these statuses.

Anthropologists have been particularly interested in family structure, because in many simple societies the dynamics of family relationships are the dynamics of the social organization as a whole; that is, almost all the behavior people exhibit toward one another is determined by their family relationships. This may be difficult for a member of a complex society to appreciate. During the first ten years of an American's life, he may very well interact with three or four times as many people (at a conservative estimate) as a member of an isolated small society meets throughout his life. Most of the people an American knows by the time he is out of high school are nonrelatives; a member of a small society may *never* meet a nonrelative.

Societies that are simple technologically may not be at all simple in their family structure. In general, kinship complexity appears to have an almost inverse relationship with societal complexity. That is, complex societies such as those found in the industrial nations of the Western world often have a simpler kinship structure than the technologically unsophisticated, small societies of sub-Saharan Africa, aboriginal Australia, or the interior of Brazil. The number of people recognized and treated as kin, the varieties of specified roles that are tied to certain kinship statuses, and so on, are often richly elaborated in these small, otherwise simple, societies.

Since the family is a basic social unit, the individual in many societies is regarded as a child until the responsibilities of marriage are accepted. Adult status is particularly important for men, because they are most often involved in public decision making. So long as a male is classified as a child, he is excluded (along with the other children and women) from public power. His opinions carry no weight with the "adult" men, regardless of his chronological age. If he wants to have any influence, gain esteem, win prestige, be a man, he must marry. Desire to improve one's status is therefore a major motive that impels males into marriage in many societies, especially in ones where premarital sexual activity is freely practiced and sexual desire per se is thus diminished in significance as a motive in the decision to marry.

A woman may also gain status through marriage, although not so obviously or rapidly. In societies like the traditional Chinese, her main prestige comes only through the birth of children. For a man of China, the tie with the family of orientation° (the one he was born into), the consanguine° tie (a bond of blood relationship) was held to be the most important. For the woman, however, this bond was supposed to be severed at marriage. A woman was expected to separate herself emotionally and physically from her parents and turn her attention to her new family. Children served to cement this new bond. They,

An exchange of vows in a Hindu wedding. For a complex society such as that of the Hindus, the marriage ceremony tends to be elaborate. Here the bride and groom touch hands with the bride's mother (left) and the priest. *(U.P.I.)*

particularly the males, were important to a woman's husband's people and were her main source of status in that family. (Children are so important in some societies that parents change their names at the birth of the first child, and from then on are known as "father of [child's name]" and "mother of [child's name]" rather than by their own names. This practice is called teknonymy° [Holmberg 1969:129].) Frequently, however, a woman has no choice about her marriage, so improvement of status is not a motive for her. Ning Lao was married long before she had any power to effect the decision, any desire to marry, or any knowledge of the consequences of either marriage or nonmarriage. In some societies girls are betrothed at birth, or promised even before birth (Hart and Pilling 1960:15–16). Consequently, status improvement is a motive to marry for males rather than for females.

Why are babies betrothed and girls so quickly married off by relatives (most often by fathers, but sometimes by brothers)? One reason is to ensure wives for themselves by creating obligations on the part of the recipient to return a woman to them—in other words, the betrothal is a form of prestation. Another reason is that giving a female in marriage is a means of creating or cementing an alliance. Americans who have studied history are familiar with this technique as used by royal families in Europe for centuries; but it has been a standard practice in many other parts of the world as well, and in fact is probably one of the most common ways in which human groups extend their ingroup (the group within which cooperative behavior is possible) beyond the limits of blood relationship (Schusky 1974:63).

Both American marriage and the traditional Chinese pattern described in the excerpt comply with Stephens' definition, although they differ from each other. One of the most obvious differences is the way the marriage comes about in the two societies. Generally speaking, societies seem to fall along a continuum on this question. At one extreme, the parents make all the decisions, and the young have no say in the matter, not even veto power. At the other extreme, the young make the decisions of when and whom to marry, and parents may not even meet the prospective spouse until after the wedding. Patterns in most societies fall somewhere in between the two. An American couple arrange their own marriage, sometimes with a little help from friends or parents, after a courtship of anywhere from days to years. During the courtship period, Americans ideally get to know each other well, and reach agreements in potential areas of conflict. Ning Lao, in contrast, had no courtship and had never met her husband before their marriage. Even her parents did not know him. A professional at arranging marriages found the husbands for both Ning Lao and her sister. Most Americans know of professional matchmakers only from stories like *Fiddler on the Roof,* and would probably tend to assume that such situations could never work out very well. Ning Lao's account certainly is not reassuring to supporters of arranged marriages, since all the ones known to her were, even by her standards, disasters. Yet the arranged marriage has been and still is the norm in many parts of the world. Judged by such criteria as the number of children produced, stability, and contribution to the smooth functioning of the society, the record of arranged marriages compares favorably with that of marriages based on romantic love. It is possible that a "love match" provides more personal satisfaction to the participants (although divorce-court evidence does not seem to suggest this). Happiness is a difficult quality to measure, however, and there is little valid information available in any case, so the apparent advantage of the "romantic" marriage in American eyes may be no more than the result of a natural bias in favor of the familiar, best-known, and "right" cultural norm—in other words, ethnocentrism.

In societies where marriage is arranged and managed by the family rather than by the partners themselves, attitudes toward romantic love, if the concept exists at all, are not very favorable. Ning Lao gives no indication of a romantic attachment to her husband. This may not be surprising to Americans, considering his behavior, but it is surprising that she expresses no disappointment about the lack of romance in her marriage, nor even an awareness that it was missing. Her expressions of disappointment are confined to her husband's performance as a provider. It might be possible to get a similar statement from some subgroups within contemporary American culture, but the prevailing stereotype is that marriage is (or should be) based on love. When love is missing, the lack is legitimate grounds for complaint or even divorce. The stereotype of romantic love as a basis for marriage is almost unique to the English-speaking world, although its popularity is growing elsewhere, thanks to Western influence.

When cases of romantic love do occur in parts of the world where marriage is normally arranged, it is often regarded as a misfortune. Such cultures may view romantic love as a dangerous mental aberration that causes people to forget their obligations, fail to perform various duties, neglect important people, and generally behave badly. Legends and folk tales in such countries are full of the disasters caused by romantic love (Goodman 1949:89–132, 480–483). Even English-speaking societies had such stories before the concept of romantic love took firm hold. All the great love stories of the past—Tristan and Isolde, Romeo and Juliet, Hero and Leander, for example—are tragedies. Tristan and Isolde were enchanted by a love potion, and their madness led them to betray their obligations to King Mark, Isolde's husband. Romeo and Juliet both ignored and betrayed obligations to their families, and died. Leander's love for Hero led him to lose his life attempting to see her (Leach 1949:11, 25, 26; Hamilton, E. 1945:135–138).

If husbands and wives do not love each other, why do they stay together? Societies vary widely in the relationship they expect between husband and wife. In some the pair are held together only by their mutual concern for their children or by pressure from their respective families. In many societies the birth of a child is crucial to the perpetuation of the marriage, and childless couples do not stay together long. The birth of a child is consequently an important event, and crisis rites for childbirth occur in as many societies as puberty rites do. Although they may involve only the mother and child, in some societies the father also has an important part to play in the ceremonies. The couvade,° a practice widespread in the Amazon area and among the Island Carib, requires that the father, as well as the mother, be confined at the birth (sometimes for a longer period). In addition, he may complain of labor pains, observe food tabus, and endure various ordeals. The purpose of the couvade is usually said to be to ensure the well-being of the child (Steward and Faron 1959:303, 324, 370).

MARRIAGE RELATIONSHIPS

Why did Ning Lao's parents feel it was necessary to *arrange* her marriage? Why do parents—even in the United States, where love is supposed to be the basis for matrimony—often try to promote a match between their offspring and the child of close friends? Because marriage is not an individual matter, even in the United States. A marriage tends to link two families because of their interest in their respective children, and normally has the potential of creating an even stronger link in the future, because any offspring of the marriage will be a focus of concern for both sets of grandparents. The immediate link between the families is not emphasized in the United States. In fact, it is explicitly denied, as in the saying "I'm marrying *you,* not your family!" used when one potential partner worries aloud about dealing with future in-laws. But even in the United States that statement is only partially correct, and in many societies it is entirely false. In fact, the relationship with affinal relatives (in-laws) has preserved or destroyed marriages in many societies (including our own). Chapter 5 discusses two of the techniques (joking and avoidance) commonly used to prevent or ease tension between affinal and blood relatives. In societies where consanguine (blood) ties to the family of orientation are paramount for both men and women, the conjugal° (marriage) ties may be brittle and relations between the two almost hostile (Schusky 1974:54–55) (see below). However, in most patrilineal° societies (where descent is traced exclusively through males) the relatives have a vested interest in maintaining the match, since it is only through the women brought into the family that the line can be continued. Note the effort Ning Lao's parents made to bring about a reconciliation between Ning Lao's sister and her husband. Note also the accommodation made by the husband's family in providing a separate home for their son and his wife, so that the tension between the mother-in-law and the new bride might be reduced. Maintaining the marriage was also probably the main motivation behind the assistance Ning Lao's in-laws gave to her by feeding her, chasing off her husband's mistress, and so on.

The marriage frequently entails a great deal of initial labor or expense on the part of either or both families. In the United States, most of the expense lies in feeding and entertaining large numbers of people after the wedding ceremony, and it is supposed to be borne by the bride's family. A girl must have the approval and cooperation of her family if she is to have a "big" wedding (unless she has money of her own). In some societies, however, there is a transfer of wealth from one family to the other. When the wealth comes from the bride's family, it is called a dowry.° The dowry may be distributed in different ways: (1) It may be given to the bride herself for the purpose of setting up her new home or for the rearing of her prospective children; (2) it may be given into the control of the husband for similar purposes; or (3) it may be given to the family

of the groom. If the wealth comes from the groom's family, it is called bride°
or progeny price,° or bride wealth° (Hoebel 1966:344–346). This is rarely given
to either the groom or the bride, but usually goes to the bride's family. Generally, the explanation is that the bride or progeny price is given to compensate
the bride's family for the loss of her services or for the loss of the offspring their
daughter will bear. It validates the right of the husband to the services of his
wife, including sexual intercourse, or the right of his family to their children,
or both. Progeny price would not be expected in societies where descent is
matrilineal° (descent traced through women only), of course, since children are
not lost to the family. Bride price may appear even in matrilineal systems,
however, if the family loses the services of an economically important member
in cases of patrilocal° or avunculocal° residence (residence after marriage with
the groom's mother's brother). This matter of where the bride and groom live
after marriage is significant in many ways (see below).

Some societies apparently feel that the reproductive power of a woman is,
in a sense, beyond price, and regardless of the amount of wealth given to the
family in exchange for their daughter, the family that receives the bride is
always in some ways indebted to the family that gives her—unless they can give
a woman in return (Schusky 1974:63). As mentioned earlier, throughout the
world the regular exchange of women between two groups is a common way
of creating or cementing alliances and of developing them beyond the extended family. In some societies, rather than a direct exchange between two
groups, women are exchanged indirectly between several; that is, group A gives
brides to group B, which gives brides to group C, which gives brides to group
A, and so on, making even larger alliances possible than a mutual two-group
exchange. In such a situation, the donor group generally remains somewhat
superior to the recipient group: the groom is usually respectful toward his
in-laws and rarely at ease with them (Schusky 1974:63). Because the marriage
pattern influences, conditions, or determines a variety of relationships among
people, a close study of marriage forms and practices provides a great deal of
information about social organization, particularly in simple societies where ties
of kinship and marriage are almost the only basis for human interactions.

When wealth or labor is involved in a marriage, the families have a vested
interest in the stability of the marriage. They do not want to have to go through
the whole process again for the same people, for one thing. For another, when
wealth is given up, it may be forfeited by the family whose child is at fault in
a divorce. That is, if the offspring of the recipient family is to blame, they may
have to return the wealth. If the offspring of the donor family is at fault, they
may get their child back, but lose their wealth (and then have to spend more
to get their offspring married again!). Such families, therefore, are directly
involved in the success of the marriage. (This may be one reason why they do
not like to leave the choice of partner entirely up to the children.) Even when
a marriage is dissolved by the death of one of the partners and no one is held
to blame, families often try to maintain a tie that has been established with
considerable effort. To this end, they may substitute another person for the
deceased. This pattern is called sororate° if a female substitutes for her sister

and levirate° when a male substitutes for his brother. The Hebrews practiced levirate (Genesis 38:6–26). The most common question an American asks at this point is, "What if the brother (or sister) is already married or there is no brother (or sister)?" Most societies that practice levirate or sororate also permit polygamy° (plural spouses), so taking on an extra spouse is no problem. Such societies are also often unilineal° (tracing descent through only one line), and there are always a number of people called "brother" or "sister" who will serve perfectly well as substitutes for a real brother or sister (see below).

One obvious factor involved in the stability of marriage is the ease or difficulty of obtaining a divorce. If it is difficult or if there is strong social disapproval, there will be fewer divorces. The divorce rate has gone up steadily in the United States as divorce has become easier and more acceptable. In one sense, therefore, a divorce rate represents only the ease with which a divorce can be obtained. It cannot serve as an index of either morality or marital happiness in the society. Another factor in the high American divorce rate is the fact that most people get married. That sounds facetious, but it is not. Many societies have a high rate of consensual unions° (people living together without marriage). The frequency with which people in these societies change mates is never reflected in divorce statistics. Marriage and divorce statistics indicate the official bureaucratic definitions in the society. In many countries these definitions do not reflect closely the realities of the situation.

There have been various studies of the causes of stability in marriage in different societies. Most of them tend to show that divorce rates are closely tied to factors in the social structure of the society. Divorce is generally most frequent in societies where descent is reckoned through the mother and where the social system also tends to emphasize consanguine ties at the expense of conjugal ties, for example (Gluckman 1968:464–468; Ackerman 1968:469–478). Although in no society is divorce fully approved, societies vary in the stringency of the disapproval and in the disruptiveness of divorce. In the United States, divorce and separation are highly detrimental to the children, partly because they are so emotionally dependent on a limited number of people. Since the household is small, a home broken by either divorce or death of a spouse generally lacks an adult representative of one of the sexes. It therefore cannot provide all the necessary models for the proper socialization of the child unless substitutes can be found. In societies with extended-family households, the problem is not so acute. The child is almost always socialized by several adults of both sexes, and the loss of one is not quite so traumatic.

Thus, for a good many reasons, the happiness of the partners, or at least the continuity of their relationship, is a matter of some concern to everyone, even in an arranged marriage. Ning Lao's parents showed this concern when they sought an older man for her after the difficult experience her sister had had with a man her own age. The failure of the marriage was blamed more on the matchmaker (or on destiny) than on a lack of parental concern or arranged marriages in general. As Ning Lao said, "A matchmaker does not live a lifetime with the people he brings together." In her case, he "hid four years" of her husband's age from the parents, which might have made a difference in their plans; and if he knew about it, he also obviously did not reveal the man's careless financial behavior. Naturally, families too try to conceal the faults of their children and find out those of potential spouses. It is obvious that Ning Lao's sister was as disappointing to her in-laws as they were to her, and with good reason; they had not been warned that she could not do the things expected of her. The game of concealing faults or inflating the virtues of potential mates occurs in all societies with arranged marriages, and in fact is incorporated into quite a few folk tales, along with ways of coping with the problem. (The story of Rumplestiltskin begins with a fraud in most versions. The parent of a young girl claims that the daughter can spin gold out of straw—an ability that, if she actually possessed it, would make her a fit wife for a prince. The prince's doubt of the parent's claim leads him to propose the test which leads to the bargain with Rumplestiltskin and the rest of the story.)

American and Chinese marriage patterns are also similar in the elaborate nature of the ceremony that officially finalizes the marriage. The details vary, but in general, friends and relatives are present, and the bride's family is involved in a great deal of expense in both societies. The ceremony constitutes a public announcement of the marriage—one of the aspects that distinguishes a marriage from other types of sexual unions (Stephens 1964:5–6). Since marriage is an approved sexual union in all societies (another characteristic mentioned in the definition), there is no reason to hide it, and there may be several reasons for announcing it. The marriage ceremony is a *rite de passage* that serves a double function of both marking the change of status and publicly announcing the marriage. In small societies, it takes very little to make a new relationship known; the "public announcement" may therefore consist of nothing more than the young couple setting up a house of their own or having a meal together (Powdermaker 1933:151–152). As societies become larger, as the change in status becomes more significant, or as the number of people immediately concerned in the marriage increases, the elaborateness of the public announcement tends to increase too. The ceremony described in the excerpt is fairly elaborate, as befits a complex culture.

MARRIAGE RESPONSIBILITIES AND REWARDS

The reciprocal obligations of American and Chinese marriages also show similarities and differences. A woman of Ning Lao's class, for instance, was expected to know how to manage a household that was generally far more complicated (at least in terms of personnel) than an American one. She was supposed to spend money wisely, to work hard, to bear children, and to defer constantly to her husband. The husband was expected to provide money for the household, to make major decisions, to guide or direct the socialization of the children, and in general to "head" the household. There was no question of sharing authority with the wife; she was subordinate to him and to other members of his family, especially his father, his mother, his older brothers, and his older brothers' wives. Parents were expected to care for and socialize their children properly, and to arrange marriages for them when they were grown; children were expected to be obedient, respectful, and to care for their elderly parents when the time came. The anger and distress of various people involved in Ning Lao's story indicate just how important some of these expectations were. When they were not met, social pressure placed on the guilty individual was severe, so much so that in the case of Ning Lao's sister, it led to a mental breakdown. Yet for all that, the option of dissolving the marriage was not given high priority. Almost any solution seemed preferable—another difference from the modern American situation.

Still another difference results directly from the Chinese system of arranging marriage. Since a girl did not have to date to get a husband, it was possible for "respectable" parents to seclude their young daughters, and the greater the seclusion, the more prestige for the family. Ning Lao said that it was high praise if neighbors could say that they did not know a girl because they had never seen her.

Seclusion of females prior to bethrothal and marriage is usually related to a concern with biological fatherhood and stems from the fact that although there is no doubt about who bears a child, there can be considerable doubt about who has fathered it, unless the female's sexual activity is strictly controlled. American society tends to regard biological relationships as crucial (Schneider 1968:23–25). Because in Western society, generally, determination of biological paternity is vital in inheritance, there is also heavy emphasis on female chastity. The only way biological paternity can be determined with certainty is to ensure that only one male has access to the female. The more emphasis placed on biological paternity (the *genitor* aspect of fatherhood), the more people in the society try to ensure that the female has no sexual access to any male other than her husband: she must be a virgin when married and she must restrict her sexual activity after marriage to her husband. These things are not usually important when (1) descent and inheritance are traced only through women, or (2) the mother's husband is socially regarded as the child's father regardless of biological parentage. In a matrilineal society, the biological father is of little significance. So long as a man's rights to his wife's sexual services are not compromised, he should not be concerned about the men she gets involved with. In much of Melanesia, men generally are not particularly bothered by a wife's affairs, although since individuals vary in all societies, some men are more reluctant to share their wives than others (Powdermaker 1933:247–248; Malinowski 1929:321–324). Even a patrilineal society may regard the sociological father as more important than the biological sire. In some groups, for example, the true father is regarded as the man who fed the mother during her pregnancy and the child during its infancy. The contribution of the man who sired the child (unless he is the same man) is held to be less important in determining fatherhood. After all, the life of the child depended on the man who brought in food. He "grew" the child in a very real sense (Schapera 1941:244–245).

American women were never confined so closely to the home, prior to or after marriage, as Ning Lao, even in the most restrictive periods of our history.

Today, of course, American women are free, at least theoretically, to participate as fully in daily social life as they wish. As indicated earlier, however, American society is far from unique in allowing women to play important roles outside the home. The Pygmy excerpt (Chapter 5) mentioned the active participation of women in the hunt, for example. In societies dependent on horticulture, women do much of the work in the fields (Netting 1968:125). Even societies with plow agriculture sometimes expect women to help in the fields, although such societies are generally more restrictive than those based on other methods of subsistence (Pierce 1964:27–28). (It should be noted here, however, that even if the woman contributes economically, she is almost never expected to be the sole provider for the home in any society, whereas in several societies the man is.)

Respective obligations of spouses vary from one culture to another. It sometimes seems that the male has all the prerogatives and the female all the obligations—as in the present excerpt, for example. But in many cultures, privileges and obligations are more evenly divided—as in the Hopi Indian excerpt on pages 275–283. There are almost no societies, however, that reverse the first example and give men most of the obligations and women most of the privileges. American society is perhaps one of the more extreme in this regard in some areas of family life. In attempts to allow more freedom and independence for women, legislation has sometimes given women special advantages, or the court has consistently interpreted the law to the disadvantage of men in family matters. For example, from a position of virtually no control over her own children in the 1800s, the American woman has moved to an almost

Chinese women at work in a field. *(Rodale Press, Inc.)*

impregnable legal position in which the rights of the natural mother are usually held superior to those of any other individual, including the natural father. In cases of divorce or separation, women almost always receive custody of children (especially if the children are young) unless they voluntarily give up their claim. (Recent agitation for more equal treatment of men and women in the courts has led to some modification of this position—at least in some states.)

One of the basic postulates° in middle-class white American society seems to be that the male parent is relatively unimportant to the emotional well-being of the child, whereas the female is essential (Hoebel 1966:23). Many articles in the popular press paint a gloomy picture of what happens to the home when the wife works. It is assumed that she cannot be a good mother and a working woman at the same time. With the exception of a few novelists, advocates of women's liberation, and some psychologists, no one mentions the effect of a man's job on his family or suggests that *he* cannot be both a good father and a working man. Why not? Ignoring his family role implies that a man is not important to it except as a source of economic support and as a stud to sire children. His career is expected to come first, and if it does, no one seems to think that its precedence might be detrimental to the family. This assumption downgrades the importance of the male partner in the family and is subtly contemptuous of men as fathers.

Regardless of the arrangement, the division of labor in the family serves several functions, some of which were discussed in earlier chapters. One that is significant here is that the division forces members of opposite sexes to depend on each other. If men and women have quite different roles, both of which are important to survival, they cannot exist without each other. This can provide another powerful motivation for marriage and marriage stability (Lévi-Strauss 1960:274–276; Schusky 1974:8).

FORMS OF MARRIAGE

Another similarity between the patterns of American and Chinese marriage as described in the excerpt is that both are monogamous,° that is, have only one spouse for each partner. Actually, the traditional Chinese were polygynous, but in Ning Lao's case, her husband could not even maintain her, and there was no talk of a second wife. In fact, the inability to support another woman is the reason why most marriages are likely to be monogamous even in societies where polygyny is the ideal (Nimkoff 1965:17). In the United States many people practice a pattern referred to as serial polygamy; that is, they have several spouses, but in sequence, not simultaneously.

Because there are only two sexes, forms of heterosexual marriage are limited to a few basic alternatives. It is possible to have one man marry one woman —monogamy, which is statistically the most frequent form in the world, and the only one permitted in all societies. It is not the most popular, however. The favorite form in the majority of societies is polygyny, one man married to several women. If this is the most popular, why is it not the most frequent on a world-wide basis? The answer lies in the birth ratio. Normally, slightly more male than female babies are born. The difference is not great, and because of the slightly higher mortality rate of male babies, the sex ratio in most societies is about even, unless something is done to disturb it—such as killing female babies (female infanticide°) or losing a large number of adult males in hazardous occupations such as warfare. If there are an approximately equal number of males and females in a society, obviously every male cannot have several wives. Usually, only wealthy older men can afford more than one wife. The majority of older men have only one, and young adult men often have none (Hart and Pilling 1964:16–17). Of course, in a society where a few men corner all the wives, *women* will almost all be in polygynous marriages. Thus from a female point of view, polygyny is much more frequent than it is from a male point of view.

In a third possible marriage form, polyandry,° one woman is married to several men. Although polyandry does occur in a few parts of the world, it tends to be rare. Sexual jealousy does not fully explain the rarity, since wife-lending, which should be as rare as polyandry if sexual jealousy were the cause, is fairly common. Polyandry seems to be correlated with female infanticide (and thus a shortage of women) combined with a low economic level (Linton 1936:183; Stephens 1964:45). Another reason for the rarity of polyandry and the frequency of polygyny may be the relation of the marriage form to population

The king of Akure, West Nigeria, and his wives. *(Marc and Evelyne Bernheim/Woodfin Camp & Associates)*

increase. Polygyny is highly productive in terms of numbers; polyandry is not. No matter how many husbands a woman has, she can bear only a limited number of children per year. And a woman who bears a child every year often ages rapidly and dies young. The population therefore cannot increase as quickly in the polyandrous pattern. In polygyny, however, the number of children one man can sire per year is limited only by the number of wives he has and his stamina. Societies that practice polygyny obviously have a survival advantage over polyandrous societies that might be sufficient to account for their greater frequency.

A final possible marriage form is one in which several women are married to several men. This has been called group marriage, communal marriage, or even tribal marriage° (Downing 1970:119–135), and is the rarest form of all. Some anthropologists have suggested that it has never really been viable° (able to survive) or the ideal pattern in any society (Linton 1936:182; Murdock 1949:24), but others have observed group mating in some societies that was accepted, even if not formally recognized as marriage (Holmberg 1969:165, 215). What about current experiments with communal families in the United States in which all spouses are shared? These are not approved sexual unions under American law, of course, but so long as approval is understood to apply only within the group or subculture itself, communal marriage might fit Stephens' definition of marriage. However, there have been too few studies, and most communal marriages have been in existence far too short a time, for

People serving themselves food in a modern commune. *(Dan Budnik/Woodfin Camp & Associates)*

researchers to be certain whether they fit the definition of marriage or are viable. We may know more in a few years.

In trying to determine the frequence of such relatively rare forms of marriage as polyandry and tribal or communal marriage, results depend to a great extent on the definition used. Stephens', like any other, excludes some patterns while it includes others. Ethnographic accounts make it clear that in many societies a woman may be sexually shared by a number of men. Among the Siriono (Bolivian jungle Indians), for example, a man's brothers have unlimited sexual access to his wife, and he to theirs (Holmberg 1969:165). Eskimo men freely share their wives with others, even nonrelatives (Boas 1967:171). (The Siriono are reluctant to go *that* far.) And except for its aspect of immediate reciprocity, wife-swapping in the United States tends to resemble Eskimo and Siriono wife-lending (Bell 1971:74–83). All these forms of wife-lending exist on a temporary basis (although among the Eskimo, when a man lends his wife to travel with another man, the "temporary" period may last weeks, or even months) (Freuchen 1961:58–63). Lack of permanence therefore disqualifies them from consideration as marriage under Stephens' definition.

In addition, in wife-lending and wife-swapping there are virtually no mutual obligations incurred between the man and women. Among the Eskimo, if any obligation is incurred, it is between the borrower and the woman's husband. If the relationship takes place on the woman's initiative, or without the man's asking prior permission, the husband will be righteously indignant, and violence is likely to result. Among the Siriono, too, there are few reciprocal obligations. A woman may sleep with a man for some food, but once the bargain has been made and the deal completed, she is not entitled to any further food from the man—unless she sleeps with him again. Her husband, on the other hand, is obligated to provide her with food even when for some reason or other he is not having intercourse with her (Holmberg 1969:166). A Siriono accepts his wife's having sexual intercourse with his full brothers, and she needs no permission from him, but were she to be discovered extending the same courtesy to more distant relatives or to nonrelatives, there would be trouble (Holmberg 1969:165–166). Similarly, on Lesu (a Melanesian island in the South Pacific) a woman is expected only to get shell currency from her lover to give to her husband. Her lover incurs no other obligations, nor does she (Powdermaker 1933:238). Note how different this is from American customs. On Lesu, a woman who does not collect payment for sexual services is immoral. In the United States this behavior is considered prostitution, and it is generally disapproved. People on Lesu would be equally shocked at a woman who engaged in extramarital sexual intercourse "for love."

In almost all societies, marriage involves a form of civil contract giving the partners property rights (instead of or in addition to moral ones) to certain services, especially (but not exclusively) sexual ones. People outside the partnership who avail themselves of these services without permission are regarded as thieves, and partners who casually give away services the other partner is legally entitled to are generally regarded as equally guilty by members of the society. It is this violation of his property right that infuriates the Eskimo, the Siriono, and the Lesuan alike.

RESIDENCE PATTERNS

Another similarity between marriage as described in the Chinese excerpt and marriage in the United States is that when Ning Lao married, she left home to live with her husband. That is the ideal in American society, although it is not always followed in practice. Ning Lao's marriage is closer to the American ideal than it should be because it does *not* correspond to the Chinese ideal. In the traditional Chinese ideal, the young couple should live with the groom's parents after marriage, as Ning Lao's sister did. This pattern is called patrilocal or virilocal.° The two terms are sometimes used synonymously, although there is a small distinction. *Virilocal* is a more precise term to use for Ning Lao's marriage, since she moved in with her husband who headed his own establishment in his family's village. His father lived with him, but it is clear that the old man was not regarded as the head of the house. If Ning Lao had followed her sister's example and moved into a household dominated by her husband's parents, *patrilocal* would have been the more accurate term to use.

Because there are many more classifications of relatives than there are sexes, residence patterns are much more variable than marriage forms. Patrilocal or virilocal residence patterns are the most frequent forms; matrilocality° is next. Neolocal residence,° in which the young couple establish a residence of their own (the American ideal), is a rarity. Another residence form, unfamiliar to Americans but surprisingly frequent, is the avunculocal, in which the couple moves in with the husband's mother's brother. (There are several practical reasons for this last type of residence form frequency, as will be explained below.)

Residence rules are useful in pointing up probable stress areas in a marriage, such as who has to leave the natal° home and who has helpful relatives nearby (Fischer, J. 1958:508–517). Other things being equal, the individual who has to leave home and who is far from helpful relatives will be subjected to more stress in the marriage. Ning Lao's position was considerably eased by the fact that she was not far from her parents, and they were able to help for a while. If she had gone farther away, she would have been even more at the mercy of her husband and his family, as was her sister.

That the Chinese were aware of the stress on a new bride is indicated in the excerpt by the statement that the bride is supposed to visit her family frequently during the first year of marriage. If the new couple lives too far from the girl's home, however, or if her husband's family is poor, they may be unwilling or unable to afford to send her back on frequent visits. In theory, of course, the husband's relatives are supposed to look after the new bride, make her feel at home, and treat her well, so long as she behaves properly. Ning Lao was rather fortunate. Her husband's people did treat her well and looked out for her as long as they could. Her husband was amiable and did not beat her, even though he was not a good provider. The theory does not always work out that well in practice, however, as the experience of Ning Lao's sister indicates. In almost any society with patrilocal residence, there are anecdotes about treatment of new brides that was so harsh that it drove them to run away or commit suicide (Pierce 1964:83; Fallers and Fallers 1960:81). Of course, it is to the benefit of the groom's family to treat the new bride well. She is, after all, the potential mother of new heirs, essential to the continuity of the line, so it behooves any family to make her a contented wife. There are anecdotes about happy wives, too, but since happiness is rarely as dramatic or exciting as misery, these cases are apt to be overlooked by publishers and authors in favor of more sensational ones (Fernea 1969:39).

What happens in societies where the women do not leave home to live with their husband's people? What if it is the man who has to move away? Is the man subject to as much stress in a matrilocal system (the reverse of patrilocal and virilocal) as the woman is in a patrilocal one? The following excerpt describes a matrilocal system different in this aspect from both the Chinese and the general American patterns.

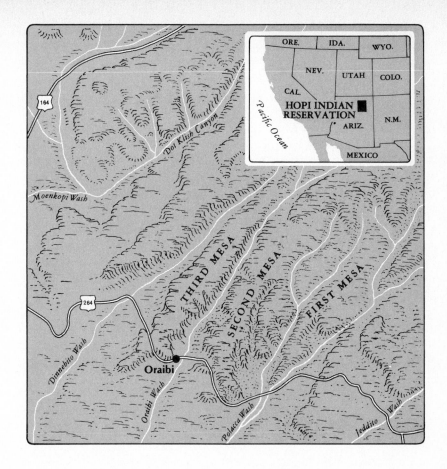

Hopi Indian Life: Courtship and Marriage

In September we returned to the Agency school.* ...

One Friday night at a social with games I was talking to Louise of the Tobacco and Rabbit Clan. She said she was leading a hard life, that neither her father nor her stepfather seemed to care for her. ... I told her softly that if she could like me I would help her. I said, "I love you and I will get food from the kitchen. ... " From then on I began to look after her. ...

. . .

One day Louise told me, to my surprise, that she was the daughter of my clan brother, and therefore my clan daughter. ... This was bad news for me. ... I had not known that Louise was the daughter of my linked-clan brother and therefore my daughter. I knew that our relatives would not like for us to be in

*Abridged from *Sun Chief: The Autobiography of a Hopi Indian,* edited by Leo W. Simmons, pp. 111–114, 116, 131–133, 145, 155, 198, 202–203, 212–223. Copyright, 1942 by Yale University Press. Reprinted by permission of Yale University Press. Talayesva, the Sun Chief, was about sixteen at the time the excerpt starts.

love, and wondered what we could do. . . . we were both worried about it all.

. . .

In November, before Thanksgiving, our superior officer told forty or fifty of us that we were to go to school at Sherman, the nonreservation school in Riverside, California. . . . Louise and I planned to go together.

Before we departed I had another talk with the superintendent. I told him that Louise and I had an agreement to marry, that I was helping to support her, and that it was my right to have intercourse with her. I was not afraid to say this because I knew that for Hopi lovers who are engaged this is the proper thing. . . .

. . .

Louise and I were together on the train part of the time until we reached Riverside. . . . When we had placed our baggage in the Sherman School for Indians, . . . the assistant disciplinarian told us that there would be a football game in the park at three o'clock. . . . We decided to go.

Now Susie, . . . the younger sister of Louise's mother, had gone to Sherman . . . a few weeks before. She came over with a sharp look on her face and took Louise away. I felt uneasy and feared that she might learn about our courtship and complain to our relatives that I was making love to my clan daughter.

. . .

. . . This made me think I had better drop Louise, because her mother's sister might get me into trouble. These thoughts began drawing me away from my first love. . . .

. . .

. . . At the socials I began going with a girl named Mettie from Moenkopi, which caused everybody to call her my girl.

In May, 1909, . . . we . . . packed our things to start for Oraibi.

. . .

. . . As we got off the train in Winslow we found our relatives with their wagons to meet us. . . .

I walked over to the campfire where Mettie was eating with her uncle and some other people. . . . I told her I was going out toward the railroad roundhouse to hunt for game. She whispered back that she would follow. Pretty soon I left with my rifle and hunted around until I saw her coming. We walked together toward the railroad and sat down among some bushes, where we stayed most of the afternoon. It was here that I had Mettie for the first time. I was not afraid to do it, because we were back among our own people. . . .

. . .

. . . When it was time for bed I took my blanket and lay down beside Mettie. Her uncle saw me but said nothing. I had Mettie twice more during the night. We could hear others doing the same thing, for we were sleeping close together. All the fellows were with their girls, for we were now free from the school officials and back with our uncles and fathers.

. . .

. . . I began picking fruit at the Agency in the middle of August and continued until the third week in October, living with my aunt [in Moenkopi] . . . It became public knowledge that Mettie and I were lovers. This pleased her uncles but worried her mother. At first I tried to be careful and safeguard Mettie from pregnancy because she wanted to return to school . . . Later when I found that her mother was so opposed to her marriage, I hoped that Mettie would become pregnant, because that gives a man some advantage over his sweetheart's mother. For when a girl has a baby, the mother usually wants the daughter to marry the child's father.

Other girls came into my life even while I was planning to marry Mettie.
. . .

. . .

. . . Euella came over . . . to get our young clan sister, Meggie, to help her grind corn. . . . I soon went over where the girls were grinding and stood around chatting until I got a chance to ask Euella to slip out to a secret place with me. . . . After a little petting we hurried our pleasures in order to return before her family missed her. This was love-making with my little "aunt" and was the safest kind of all because I could not be expected to marry her, of course. . . .

. . .

[Mettie went back to school. Don was initiated in Oraibi and received his adult name of Talayesva. He returned to Moenkopi and continued his "safe" affair with Euella.]

On Saturday Secaletscheoma put on a dance hoping to please the gods and get help for his sore eyes. I watched the Katcinas all day and slept with Euella that night. The next morning Secaletscheoma asked me to do clown work; but I told him frankly that I was unfit for it. I did not wish to spoil the ceremony by bringing a bad wind, or to have it said that his eyes were no better on my account. My aunt was surprised until I told her the reason. Then she said, "I'm going to beat Euella for cutting me out. . . . " We often joked about love-making, but I never tried it with her. She was much older than I, the niece of my father, and the wife of my ceremonial father's brother . . . Even if she had been younger and unmarried, I would not have touched her because she was of the Sand Clan, like my father. It was all right to make love with a niece of either of my grandfathers—like Euella of the Lizard Clan, for example—but not with my father's close relatives. These aunts had teased me about love-making a great deal; but I had never tried to make a Sand Clan woman, and knew that I never would for that would not be right.

. . .

. . . I was still thinking of Mettie and received a letter from her every week; but some of the girls had written me that she had a Navaho lover, besides two Hopi boys. Mettie's mother had heard of the Navaho and told my relatives that if I waited until Mettie returned, we could marry. She did not want to lose her daughter to a Navaho. I did not want to wait.

. . .

. . . Mark, an uncle of Mettie, . . . also suggested that if I waited until Mettie returned from school I might marry her. "I hear Mettie has a Navaho friend," I replied, "and it is hard to wait. If I can find another lover, I may have to marry her."

. . .

One evening . . . my old pal Louis came from Moenkopi. [Don had gone back to Oraibi.] . . . he was as eager to go out among the girls as ever and . . . said, "I have made love with Iola of the Fire Clan before, but now she does not like me very well." I knew she was staying with her clan sister, Irene, whose parents had gone to the field house at Loloma Spring. Since we could think of no other available lovers, Louis said, "Let's take these girls by force." . . . I knew that Irene was marriageable for me but I did not know whether she wanted me or not. I argued that since Louis had had Iola before, he could get away with it, but it was too risky for me to try forcing Irene. But Louis urged until I finally agreed.

We found the girls grinding corn and decided to sneak into Irene's house and wait in the dark. Finally, as the two entered, Louis grabbed Iola and blew out the light. I caught hold of Irene and quickly assured her that she had nothing to fear. . . . We talked softly for a while and when we heard Louis and Iola at love-making, I begged Irene urgently with words of love and promises of marriage. Finally she said, "It is up to you." Then I led her, with a sheepskin, to another corner of the room where she remained passive but very sweet. After some time, she said, "Now you must ask your parents about our marrying. Let's go and leave this terrible man, Louis." I told her to be a good girl, gave her a nice bracelet, slipped out, went to the roof of my mother's house, and lay down to sleep out under the stars.

. . . When I returned from the surveyors' camp Monday evening, Irene's parents were home. After supper I went to their house. They offered me food, and the father later asked if there was anything he could do for me. Then I asked for the hand of Irene. He replied: "My daughter is not a good-looking girl. If your relatives are willing you may have her." I told him that I had my parents' consent and that they were well pleased. This was a lie, but a necessary one in order to spend the night with Irene. They agreed and arranged for us to have the next room. We had a very good time. . . . All our talk was sweet and I thought there would never be an argument between us. At cockcrow I went home for a nap on the old roof.

At breakfast I raised the subject of marriage. "I spent the night at Huminquima's," I said, "and now I want to marry his daughter, Irene." "What did they say?" asked my mother. I assured her that Irene's parents had already agreed. . . . My father spoke: "Well, I won't object for then you would think I am against you. You are not a good-looking man, and she is not a beautiful woman, so I think you will stay together and treat each other fairly. A good-looking woman neglects her husband, because it is so easy to get another." My spirit was high when I left for work. Riding down the mesa, I waved to Irene, let out a war whoop, beat my horse into a gallop, and thought that I would always be happy.

· · ·

One day the news circulated that Ira was getting married in November, and that my turn would follow four days later, making a double wedding. Both our girls belonged to the ... Fire Clan, and their people make this plan. My brother was worried and complained, "Our father is poor and cannot afford a double wedding. What shall we do?" Then he remembered that our great-uncle ... had approved of our marriages and said, "Perhaps he will buy a buckskin for one of us or give us some sheep for the wedding feast." I replied, "If he doesn't, we will refuse to herd for him." My father took $30 or $40 of my money to help buy the buckskins.

One evening after the crops were harvested, Ira's girl, Blanche, was brought to our house by her mother. She ground corn meal on her knees for three days, remaining in the house most of the time, but Ira was not permitted to sleep with her. I herded, and was told to keep away from Irene because she was grinding white corn meal at her house for our family.

· · ·

[One morning, four days later] Iola ... called to me "Get up and go see what is in your house. I hear you have a pet eagle." I found Irene grinding corn with all her might. She had been brought there by her mother the night before. As I stood in the door and watched her, I felt as though I were dreaming and scratched my head, seeking for words. My mother smiled and said, "Talayesva, don't be foolish." I went out sheepishly, returned to my sleeping place, yanked the cover from Dennis, who was still asleep, and said, "Get up, lazybones, it is your turn next. I am now a man with a wife. . . . "

The aunts of my father's clan, and of my ceremonial and doctor fathers' clans, ganged up and staged a big mud fight with the men of my family. They caught my grandfather, Homikniwa, and plastered him with mud from head to foot. They also poured mud and water all over my father and tried to cut his hair for letting me marry into the Fire Clan. They made all manner of fun of Irene, calling her cross-eyed, lazy, dirty, and a poor cook, and praised me highly, asserting that they would like to have me for a husband. Dear old Masenimka, my godmother, threw mud on my father and uncles and said that she wanted me for her lover. This mud fight was to show that they were very fond of me, and that they thought Irene was making a good choice.

On the third day I began worrying about my coming bath, for I was very ticklish and did not know whether I could stand still under the hands of so many women. A little after sundown my mother told Irene to stop grinding the blue corn and sit by the fire on a soft seat. I had not seen much of her since she came to our house, and when we had spoken it was usually in a whisper. Soon her relatives came to spend the night—the same women who had stripped and bathed Ira. I thought I had never seen so many women, and even those whom I had known all my life seemed a little strange to me. I had little to say all evening, and at bedtime I took my blanket and started out. My father said, "Wait a minute, Talayesva. Where are you sleeping? I want to be able to find you in the morning." When I told him that I was sleeping with Dennis, he replied, "Be sure to leave the door unlocked so that I can wake you early. . . . "

[In the morning] My father struck a match and said, "Get up, son, and come quickly. They are preparing the yucca suds." Then he woke Dennis and asked him to see that I started. . . . When I entered the house, I saw many eyes staring at me. There were Irene's mother and her sisters, Blanche's mother and her relatives, in fact all the women of the Fire Clan, also the women of the Coyote and Water-Coyote clans, and most of my real and ceremonial aunts. They had assembled to give me a bath. My mother was assisting Irene's mother with the yucca suds. I was so timid that I took steps not more than an inch long. My mother said, "Hurry up." I laid back my shirt collar and knelt with Irene before a bowl of yucca suds. My relatives washed Irene's head and her relatives washed mine. Then they poured all the suds into one bowl, put our heads together, mixed our hair and twisted it into one strand to unite us for life. Many women

A Hopi girl, ca. 1892, wearing the coiffure that signifies her unmarried status. *(The Bettmann Archive)*

rinsed our hair by pouring cold water over it. When that was completed, Irene's mother told me to take off my clothes. I felt so uncertain about my loincloth that I made an excuse to go out, ran behind the house, and checked it carefully. When I had returned and undressed, Irene's mother led me outside. My real aunts tried to bathe me first in fun, and scuffled with Irene's relatives. Then Irene's mother bathed me from tip to toe. All the women took their turn bathing me, while I stood shivering in the cold. I had to appear gentle and kindhearted and say to each of them, "I thank you very much." They assured me that they had washed away all remaining traces of youth and had prepared my flesh for married manhood.

I hurried into the house, wrapped myself in a blanket, and stood until Irene's relatives told me to sit down near the fire. Irene's hair was arranged in the married women's style, and her mother advised her to be a good housewife. Irene and I took a pinch of sacred corn meal, went to the east edge of the mesa, held the meal to our lips, prayed silently, and sprinkled it toward the rising sun. We returned to the house in silence and my mother and sister prepared our breakfast. Before Irene's mother left, she built a fire under the piki stone. After breakfast Irene made batter and began baking piki° [paper-thin corn bread].

. . .

My father distributed staple cotton among all our relatives and friends, asking them to pick out the seeds and return it. In a few days we butchered a couple of sheep, and it was announced from the housetop that there would be carding of cotton and spinning in the kiva for my father's new daughters-in-law.

. . .

I herded sheep for my uncle . . . so that he could supervise the spinning for Irene in the Mongwi kiva, while my father had charge of the spinning for Blanche in the Howeove kiva. I returned from the sheep camp in the evening, ate supper with Irene and my family, and went to the kiva to card cotton. I had never learned to spin very well, or to weave at all. Many men were helping us. . . . Finally I was teased and reminded that it was bedtime and that I had better go. We slept together in a separate room in my mother's house. I thought I would never tire of sleeping with Irene, and she agreed that it was a good life.

The brides remained in our house for the rest of November and all the next month, for it was considered bad luck for them to go home in December. . . . The women fetched water and we hauled several wagonloads of wood in preparation for the wedding feast. . . .

In the morning, long before daylight, we arose, built fires under the pots outside, and cooked the mutton stew. Pots were boiling all around our place, and almost all the people in Oraibi were present at the breakfast feast. Then the men assembled in the different kivas to weave. Two of our uncles from Shipaulovi took back cotton string with them to weave the belts. There was work under way in all five kivas in Oraibi. . . .

One day I went to the post office . . . and received five letters . . . The fifth . . . was from my old girl Mettie . . . When I read that, I raised my head for a long breath. The Chief asked, "What is the matter, Don?" "In this letter," I replied, "Mettie says that I will always be hers." I read it to him. He smiled and

said, "I think she means just that. When she comes home, I would go to see her
and cheer her up." I think I would have been more excited over my wedding
if she had been the bride.

. . .

The wedding costumes were completed in January. For each bride there
were two blankets whitened with kaolin, a finely woven belt, and an expensive
pair of white buckskin moccasins. Soft prayer feathers were attached to the
corners of the blankets. Each bride was to wear the large blanket and carry the
small one rolled in a reed case when she returned to her house. The small
blanket was to be carefully preserved and draped about her at death—as wings
to speed her to dear ones in the House of the Dead. The beautiful belt was to
serve as tail to a bird, guiding the bride in her spiritual flight.

There was a feast for our close relatives on the day that the men completed
the wedding outfits. The brides made puddings, and we butchered and cooked
the two sheep that Kalnimptewa had given to us. We gathered at sunset, and
the brides took special pains to be good hostesses and to see that everyone was
happy and well fed. After the meal they cleared the food away, and our great-
uncles . . . made speeches to them: "We Sun Clan people are very thankful that
you brides have come to our household and have taken such good care of us.
You have proven yourselves to be good housewives by feeding us well. The
wedding outfits are completed, and tomorrow you will return to your homes.
We are now the same people, sisters, brothers, uncles, and aunts to each other.
Look on the bright side of each day, treat your husbands right, and enjoy your
lives. Visit us often so that we will be happy." The brides were expected to say:
"Thanks very much for your work on the wedding outfits." . . .

Early in the morning our mother, assisted by her sister, . . . awoke the
brides before daylight, washed their heads, and dressed them in the wedding
outfits. They led them to the door, sprinkled a corn-meal path toward the rising
sun, and placed a prayer feather upon it. The brides stepped out upon this path,
followed it to the end, turned and went to their homes, carrying before them
the small blanket rolled in a reed mat. There they were received by their
mothers and other female relatives, who removed the wedding garments and
tried them on themselves. I remained in bed for another nap and did not see
my bride depart.

The brides and their relatives prepared food to bring to our house in the
evening. About sunset they came with their mothers, bringing a large tub filled
with food. When they returned to their houses, our own relatives were invited
to come and eat. That was the occasion for giving us advice. Our great-uncle
. . . spoke first: "Thank you, my nephews. You are not very good-looking, and
I thought you were never going to marry. I am glad that you have chosen such
fine wives. You know every woman hates a lazy man, so you must work hard
and assist your new fathers in the field and with the herding. When they find
that you are good helpers, they will be pleased and treat you like real sons.
When you kill game, or find spinach or other food plants in the fields, bring
them to your wives. They will receive them gladly. Make believe that your wife
is your real mother. Take good care of her, treat her fairly, and never scold her.

If you love your wife, she will love you, and give you joy, and feed you well. Even when you are worried and unhappy, it will pay you to show a shining face to her. If your married life is a failure, it will be your own fault. Please prove yourselves to be men worthy of your clan."

The next day my parents killed two more sheep, made a stew, and took a large tub of food to our wives' homes. Irene and Blanche invited all their relatives to come and eat, and it was then that their uncles advised them on their family duties.

After the feast in the brides' houses, it was time for them and their relatives to prepare corn-meal gifts in exchange for the wedding costumes. The brides and their relatives ground corn for many days. . . . Many heaping plaques of fine corn meal were taken to our house—perhaps twenty bushels—to be distributed among the relatives who had assisted us. This completed the wedding obligations.

It is customary for the groom to decide when he will move into his wife's house. I remained at my house for about two weeks, visiting Irene every night. Ira stayed three weeks longer. It was necessary for me to go live with Irene early, because her father, Huminquima, was not a very good worker. Before I went, I hauled wood for them like a dutiful son-in-law. I also took part in the Soyal ceremony [one of the major Hopi religious ceremonies], observing the rules of continence. After the Soyal I borrowed Frank's team and wagon and went for an extra large load of wood without telling Irene. I returned late in the afternoon, stopped the wagon at my wife's door, and unhitched. Irene's mother shelled corn for my horses while I unloaded the wood. Irene came to the door and asked me how I liked my eggs. I thought of sneaking home, but, knowing that would never do, I timidly entered the house and ate a little of the scrambled eggs. I soon remarked that I was not very hungry, and hurried out with the shelled corn, feeling that the Fire Clan were very high-tone people. Taking the wagon to my home, I asked my mother for a square meal, which caused her to laugh. About sunset, as I returned from hobbling the horses, Irene came to our house calling, "Come and eat." She invited all my family—according to custom—but they properly declined. I meekly followed my wife to her home and sat down with the family to a dish of hot tamales wrapped in corn-husks and tied with yucca stems. But I ate so slowly that Irene's mother unwrapped tamales and placed them in a row before me. I thought, "This old lady is very kindhearted, perhaps she will do this for me always." But I was mistaken; at breakfast I had to unwrap my own tamales, and was put to work for my wife's people.

This excerpt illustrates marriage based on romantic love and personal choice, but what a difference from courtship and marriage in middle-class America! Some of the differences are obvious, some are subtle, and some of the behavior is simply confusing. Don may have chosen Irene, but at that point similarities between Hopi courtship and marriage and the middle-class United States pattern virtually disappear. In the Hopi excerpt, Don talks of love, but his behavior belies his words from a non-Hopi point of view. If he "loved" Mettie, how could he decide to marry Irene so easily? And why was he unable to wait the short time till Mettie came home, particularly after he knew that her mother no longer opposed the match? Don himself admitted he probably would have been more excited about his marriage if it had been Mettie who was going to be his wife; yet he also said he "loved" Irene. This does not quite fit the prevailing American concept of love.

Look at some of the other differences. In the Hopi situation, uncles, aunts, grandparents, and even more distant relatives are highly involved in the whole process, with the groom's family, not the bride's, apparently bearing the greatest expense. Don's relatives gave each bride in the double wedding two blankets, as well as several other valuable things. Some of the money for the gifts came from Don and Ira, but other sources apparently were a great uncle and the boys' father. In addition, male relatives carded cotton, spun yarn, and helped weave the blankets and belts. The weaving was all done in the kivas—underground rooms where sacred and ceremonial activities were carried on by men only; women were not allowed inside. (The fact that Hopi males, not females, do the spinning and weaving is an example of different sex-role expectations.)

In the Hopi case, the cost of the wedding to the grooms' family was accompanied by the loss of the sons, since Don and Ira moved in with their wives' people. In the Chinese situation, the bride's family bears the expense and the bride and groom usually move in with his parents. Among the Dodoth in Africa the groom's family has the heaviest expense of the marriage, and the bride at first stays with her people, but she later goes to live with her husband and his family (Thomas 1965:83). All this suggests that the expense of the marriage is not necessarily correlated with the residence pattern, but is probably determined by some other factors.

The change in residence meant that Don had some adjustments to make. He was nervous and uncomfortable with his new family. But he could always go home, as he did after his first meal with his in-laws, when he was still so timid he could not eat properly. Notice that the pattern of going back home to ease the transition occurs in the Hopi marriage as well as in the Chinese. These visits do not carry the connotation that "going home to mother" carries in the American system. That is, Don's return (and Ning Lao's) was not the result of a quarrel; it was a normal part of expected behavior. The pattern was built into the system, rather than discouraged by it.

Don's situation differed from Ning Lao's in several ways. He married within his own village and therefore was close to his relatives. Ning Lao moved into another community, one that was occupied entirely by relatives of her husband. Don's marriage was matrilocal, but he lived close by his own relatives. Uxorilocal° residence, which is the reverse of virilocal, is rarely used, partly because females are seldom heads of their own households before they marry. Regardless of the technical label for the residence pattern, it makes a difference when the newly married individual is separated from his or her family of orientation by yards instead of miles. Ning Lao and her sister would have had an easier time if they had lived next door to their parents.

Another factor that made Don's marital adjustment easier was that he was free to move about; he was not confined to the house and courtyard of his in-laws. He could get off by himself, could get his own food if necessary, and could easily leave for good, if he cared to. Ning Lao had fewer options. In her culture it was not proper for women to be seen on the street alone. She was not free to go out to work, was not trained to do anything outside the home (she said she did not even know how to beg), and was not free to travel when and where she pleased. Don was; consequently, he was under far less pressure.

This difference in mobility is another of the factors that tends to make

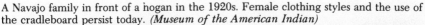

A Navajo family in front of a hogan in the 1920s. Female clothing styles and the use of the cradleboard persist today. *(Museum of the American Indian)*

marriage in matrilocal systems less stable than patrilocal marriage. Marital stability is not necessarily an indication of marital satisfaction and may often be the result of the difficulty involved in changing or leaving the situation. Since it is relatively easy for a male to leave a matrilocal marriage (compared to the problems a woman has in leaving a patrilocal one), societies with matrilocal residence might be expected to have a higher divorce rate, and they do. Dozier reports that the Tewa rate of 20 percent is low in relation to other Pueblo peoples (most of whom are matrilocal) (Schusky 1974:42). Mobility is not the only factor contributing to the high divorce rate, of course. Other factors will be discussed later.

Don's residence pattern corresponded to the Hopi ideal, whereas Ning Lao's varied from the Chinese. The ideal residence pattern in American society is different from either of the ideals presented in the excerpts. Here, the young couple is supposed to set up their own home in a clearly independent household. This neolocal pattern is actually not very common. Although a young couple may have a separate household in many societies, the new household is often dominated by one set of parents or the other, and this is contrary to the American ideal (Richards, A. I. 1964:210; Richards, C. 1963:25–33). In the United States, young people want to be "on their own," although in practice, during the first few years of marriage they may not be able to be for economic or other reasons. There are an amazing number of residence patterns, and the variety of terms for them would easily fill half a page. Almost every possible combination has been tried somewhere. Sometimes there are a series of stages in a marriage, each one correlated° (varying or associated) with a different residence pattern. For example, Navajos during the first years of marriage tend to live several months first with one set of parents (often the wife's) and then with the other. After several years, they usually settle down on a homestead of their own (Richards, C. 1963:27; Rapoport 1954:57; Kluckhohn and Leighton 1946:57).

INHERITANCE PATTERNS

In most societies, residence rules are related to the inheritance pattern; they support it, or else they help solve problems posed by conflicts between the inheritance of family affiliation and inheritance of land or power. Patrilineal inheritance, tracing descent through the male line, is usually associated with patrilocal or virilocal residence, as in the excerpt on China. Matrilineal inheritance, tracing the line through the mother, often occurs with matrilocal residence, as illustrated by the Hopi excerpt. In both cases, the residence and inheritance patterns reinforce each other. It must not be thought, however, that patrilineal or matrilineal inheritance is the only way people trace descent.

Some Americans may think of their society as patrilineal because of the inheritance of family name, and because historically many of the countries from which American ancestors came are or were patrilineal. However, since the child is biologically the result of a combination of an equal number of genes from both parents, American society (which is aware of and concerned about this) leans heavily to bilateral inheritance° (inheritance from both sides), except in the matter of family name, which is inherited patrilineally. Bilateral inheritance creates an overwhelming number of relatives (in ten generations there are 1,024 ancestors and a lot more "cousins") if all relationships are equally emphasized and remembered. In addition, no one but full brothers and sisters have quite the same set of relatives (as any chart of three generations will show). What happens, as a rule, is that people emphasize the ties they are interested in and ignore the rest (just as members of the Daughters of the American Revolution emphasize ties to ancestors who fought on the American side and ignore any ties to British soldiers). The resulting group has been called a kindred, a ramage,° an ambilineal descent group°, a nonunilineal descent group°, and more recently, a cognatic descent group° (Schusky 1974:35, 37). A bilateral society may also emphasize the nuclear family and ignore all relatives more distant than first cousins (Schusky 1974:27–34).

Patrilineal and matrilineal systems are both examples of unilineal descent, that is, descent which is traced through only one sex, or "line." In a patrilineal system, because descent is traced or passed through males only, females belong to the group but cannot pass the family membership to their children. Their children belong to the family of the father. Matrilineal systems are in some ways mirror images of patrilineal ones; that is, descent is traced through the females. Men belong to a family but cannot pass membership to their children. A man's children belong to their mother's family. (As will be seen, however, matrilineal systems are not entirely mirror images of patrilineal ones.)

A common error Americans make trying to understand a unilineal system is that they exclude one sex entirely. They exclude females from a patrilineal system and males from a matrilineal one. Yet males and females are full members of both matrilineal and patrilineal families. Girls are members of the patrilineal family at least until they marry, and in some societies for as long as they live, married or not. In other societies they are adopted into the family of their husband when they marry. In a matrilineal system, men are usually permanent members of their natal family (the one they are born into) and this is one of the factors that keeps a matrilineal system from being a mirror of a patrilineal one. The fact that men universally exercise public power also complicates the situation in a matrilineal system. The larger and more complex a system is, the more formal public power there is to exercise and distribute, and in a matrilineal system, the greater the number of adjustments that need to be made, until, possibly, the system is not viable. It may be significant that none of the major large civilizations has been matrilineal.

In the excerpt just read, Don's children would belong to Irene's family, and Ira's to Blanche's. But Blanche and Irene were clan sisters. What would that mean to the children? Unilineal systems have several kinds of groups that are not normally found in a bilateral system. First, a group of brothers in a patrilineal system (or sisters in a matrilineal one) establish families that can obviously trace their relationship to one another. This is a lineage.° As generations pass, the specific connecting links may be forgotten, but the members still

assume that they are related and that they are all descended ultimately from
a common ancestor, even if they cannot prove it. This group is called a clan,°
sib,° or gens° (Murdock 1949:67). (*Sib* is more popular in the United States, *clan*
in England.) The main difference between a clan (or sib) and a lineage is
that in a lineage the connection between families can be demonstrated through
genealogies, whereas in a clan it cannot. This definition creates problems in the
field, because in the course of their research anthropologists sometimes learn
how families are connected when the people themselves do not know. Is the
group to be called a lineage then, or is it still a clan? Different anthropologists
answer the question in different ways. Since Irene and Blanche were members
of the same matrilineal clan, their children would be too. Members of the same
clan frequently regard each other as members of the same family, and call each
other brother and sister. They are usually forbidden to marry, and have the
same general obligations to each other as children of the same mother and
father would, although in large societies where members of a clan may be
spread over a large geographic area and consequently cannot interact with any
frequency, distant clan members will probably be treated more formally and
with less warmth. Actually, the same thing happens in the United States when
full brothers and sisters live miles apart and may treat close friends at least as
warmly as they treat each other. The frequency of interaction has a lot to do
with how fully theoretical obligations are met in practice.

A larger group, called a phratry,° may be created when several clans regard
themselves as somehow related or linked. In the Hopi excerpt, Don mentioned
that Louise, his first love, was the daughter of a linked clan brother and therefore technically his daughter too. This shows that the Hopi had phratries. Phratries often have the same functions as clans, and marriage within the phratry
therefore may be forbidden.

Unilineal lineages, clans, phratries, and so on usually form corporate
groups. That is, for many purposes they act as a legal person (Schusky 1974:39).
Land or other forms of wealth may be owned by the clan, which usually redistributes it regularly to members, as individuals and nuclear family needs
change. The clan often acts as a unit in disputes with other clans. Individuals
within a clan are then regarded by outsiders as functionally equivalent; in cases
of feud, for example, *any* member of an enemy clan is legitimate prey, or in
cases of wrongdoing, members of the clan are collectively responsible for the
offense of one, as in the case of the Hurons in Chapter 3.

A still larger grouping occurs when the entire society is divided into two
parts, each of which is called a moiety.° Membership in a moiety may be based
on kinship or on some other factor such as religion, politics, geographic location,
or common interest. Membership is usually ascribed, but occasionally it may be
a matter of individual choice. When it is based on kinship, the moiety may
consist of many independent nuclear familes, or it may be subdivided into
phratries, clans, or lineages. Complexity of kinship organization increases
steadily from nuclear family to extended family to lineage to clan to phratry to
moiety. Additional complexity may be created by the introduction of some
intermediate steps, such as a lineage segment (Sahlins 1964:181–200) or a half-

clan (I Chronicles 6:61). Both Don and Ning Lao were members of clans. Although the Chinese excerpt does not describe any clan function specifically, inasmuch as Ning Lao went to her husband's village, where everyone resident was a member of her husband's clan, it would appear that land ownership might have been a function, at least at one time. Other parts of the excerpt, however, make it clear that, economically, individual families were more or less on their own. Ning Lao's life would have been much easier if she had been able to depend on clan financial support when her husband turned out to be such a poor provider. The Hopi excerpt mentions a very important clan function—the regulation of sex and marriage. Don also mentioned another: financial help from relatives, particularly at the time of his marriage.

Unilineal descent carries with it other complications for American students. For one thing, it often discriminates among kinds of cousins. In the American system no distinction is made between cousins. There is not even a special term to distinguish males from females; all are lumped together as "cousins." The children of siblings are technically first cousins to each other, the children of first cousins are second cousins to each other, and so on, but this distinction is made by adding modifiers (*first, second*), not by using completely different terms. Many contemporary Americans are not even sure just what relationship a third cousin is, anyway. In a unilineal system, however, certain people we would call cousins are members of the family and others are not. In a patrilineal system, children of the males are in the patrilineal family whereas children of their sisters are not. Similarly, in a matrilineal system, children of the females are in the matrilineal family, but children of their brothers are not. For Don this meant that children of his sister were in his own clan but that his and his brother Ira's children would not be. Don's children and his sister's children (first cousins in our terms) would therefore be in different clans. In any unilineal system, the children of one sex will be in different clans from the children of siblings of the opposite sex. Technically, these first cousins are called cross-cousins,° meaning that the father of one is the brother of the mother of the other. The children are related through parents who are opposite-sex siblings (see Charts 8.1 and 8.2).

If Don's system had been patrilineal instead of matrilineal, the situation would remain the same so far as his children and his sister's children being in different clans is concerned, but in this case, his children would have been in his clan and his sister's children in some other. Don's and Ira's children would have been in the same clan, as the children of Blanche and Irene (clan sisters) were in the matrilineal Hopi. These first cousins (the children of brothers, or the children of sisters) are called parallel cousins.° In matrilineal systems, parallel cousins who are children of sisters are always in the same clan. Children of brothers may not be (although since both Ira and Don married Fire Clan girls, the children were in the same clan in that case). If Don and Ira had been in a patrilineal system, then their children (parallel cousins who are children of brothers in a patrilineal system) would have been in the same clan. (In a patrilineal society, children of sisters are also technically parallel cousins, but since they belong to their fathers', not their mothers', families, they will not be in the

Chart 8.1. PATRILINEAL
Bifurcate merging

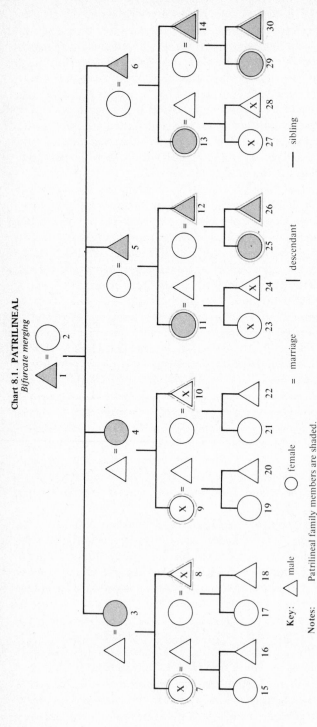

Key: △ male   ○ female   = marriage   — sibling

= marriage | descendant   — sibling

Notes: Patrilineal family members are shaded.

Individuals marked **X** are cross-cousins to shaded individuals *in the same generation.*

Individuals in the same generation outlined in gray call each other "brother" and "sister." 11 and 12, 13 and 14, 25 and 26, 29 and 30 are brother and sister in American terminology, but 11 and 12 are parallel cousins to 13 and 14, and 29 and 30 are parallel cousins to 25 and 26. They would *not* call each other "brother" or "sister" in the United States. If they used any kinship term at all, it would be "cousin."

Individuals outlined in dotted lines are technically parallel cousins (7 and 8 parallel to 9 and 10), but usually do not call each other "brother" or "sister" in a patrilineal system because they are parallel matrilineally—through the female line.

11, 12, 13, and 14 would call both 5 and 6 "father"; 25 and 26, 29 and 30 would call both 12 and 14 "father" (since 12 and 14 call each other "brother"), and would call both 11 and 13 "father's sister" (since 12 and 14 call 11 and 13 "sister").

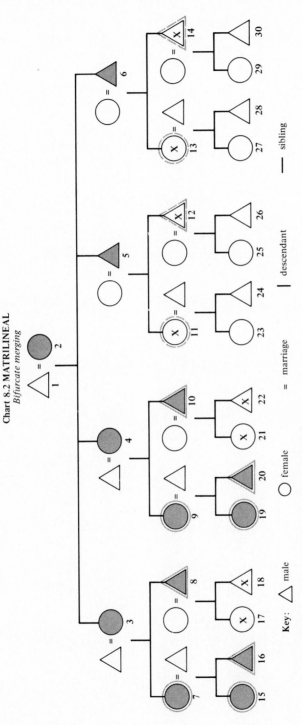

Chart 8.2 MATRILINEAL
Bifurcate merging

Key: △ male ○ female = marriage | descendant — sibling

Notes:

Matrilineal family members are shaded.

Individuals marked **X** are cross-cousins to shaded individuals *in the same generation.*

Individuals in the same generation outlined in gray call each other "brother" and "sister." 7 and 8, 9 and 10, 15 and 16, 19 and 20 are brother and sister in American terminology, but 9 and 10 are parallel cousins to 7 and 8, and 19 and 20 are parallel cousins to 15 and 16. They would *not* call each other "brother" or "sister" in the United States. If they used any kinship term at all, it would be "cousin."

Individuals outlined in dotted lines are technically parallel cousins (11 and 12 parallel to 13 and 14), but often do not call each other "brother" or "sister" in a matrilineal system because they are parallel patrilineally—through the male line.

7, 8, 9, and 10 would call both 3 and 4 "mother"; 15 and 16, 19 and 20 would call both 7 and 9 "mother" (since 7 and 9 call each other "sister"), and would call both 8 and 10 "mother's brother" (since 8 and 10 call 7 and 9 "sister").

291

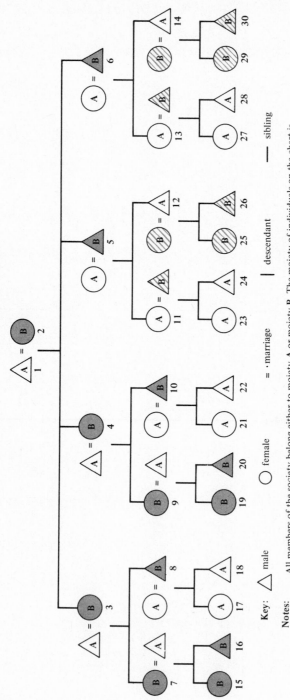

Chart 8.3. EXOGAMOUS MATRILINEAL MOIETY

Key: △ male   ◯ female   = · marriage | descendant   — sibling

Notes:

All members of the society belong either to moiety **A** or moiety **B**. The moiety of individuals on the chart is indicated by the letter **A** or **B** in every case.

Members of the matrilineal *family* are shaded gray.

Members of moiety **B** (the moiety of the matrilineal *family* charted) who are *not* also members of the matrilineal family have cross hatching instead of gray shading.

In this type of moiety system, *all* parallel cousins (traced through either matrilineal or patrilineal lines) are in the same moiety, while all cross-cousins are in the opposite moiety.

same family unless their fathers are also brothers or the society has exogamous°
moieties; the same is true in reverse in a matrilineal system, where the children
of brothers are also technically parallel cousins. See Chart 8.3.)

The separation of cross-cousins into different clans is a process called bifurcation,° since it splits the matrilineal and patrilineal lines of descent. It excludes
descendants of the females from the family in a patrilineal system and descendants of the males in a matrilineal system. When parallel cousins call each other
"brother" or "sister" (as they do in many societies), the pattern is called bifurcate merging,° because although the matrilineal and patrilineal descent lines

Table 8.1. Kinship Terms

Descent Type	Same Term for	Distinct Term for
Parental generation[*]		
Bilateral–generational	mo, mo si, fa si	no one
	fa, fa bro, mo bro	no one
Bilateral–lineal	mo si, fa si	mo
	mo bro, fa bro	fa
Unilateral–bifurcate merging	mo, mo si	fa si
	fa, fa bro	mo bro
Unilateral–bifurcate collateral	no one	mo, mo si, fa si
	no one	fa, fa bro, mo bro
Ego's own generation[†]		
Bilateral—Hawaiian	sibling, cross-cousin, parallel cousin	no one
Bilateral—Eskimo	cross-cousin, parallel cousin	sibling
Unilineal—Crow, Omaha, Iroquois	sibling, parallel cousin	cross-cousin
Unilineal—Sudanese	no one	sibling, cross-cousin, parallel cousin

[*] In the bilateral-generational type, all related females in the parental generation are
called by the same term, and all related males in that generation are called by the same term.
At the opposite extreme is the unilateral–bifurcate collateral, where "mother", "father"
"mother's siblings", and "father's siblings" are each distinguished by a separate term.

[†] In the Hawaiian system, all relatives of the same generation call each other by the same
term, equivalent to "brother" or "sister" in American terminology. At the opposite extreme, in the Sudanese system, siblings, cross-cousins, and parallel cousins are all distinguished
by separate terms. Therefore, Sudanese follow the same principle of terminology for one's
own generation that bifurcate collateral does in the terminology for the parental generation.

split, the parallel lines are continually merged with siblings (Hoebel 1966:335–336) (see Charts 8.1 and 8.2).

KINSHIP PATTERNS

Kinship terms have been of interest to anthropologists for some time because of the way that they are thought to reflect attitudes and behavior. At the very least they provide clues to how members of the society classify relationships. The terminology of kinship systems can be ranged along a continuum according to the number of distinctions made between kinds of relationships (see Table 8.1). At one end are bilateral-generational systems which tend to lump all or most relatives together and distinguish people only by sex and/or generations. For example, people using such a system would have one term to apply to all male relatives in the generation above theirs. Usually translated as "father," the term would be better translated as "male, related to me, a generation older," since it includes not only the biological father but his brothers, full and classificatory° (classified as such in a given society but not in the American kinship system), and also the maternal uncles (the mother's brothers, full and classificatory). Similarly, the term translated "mother" would be better translated "female, related to me, a generation older," since it includes the biological mother, her sisters, full and classificatory, and the father's sisters, full and classificatory. This system, by the way, was very confusing to missionaries who assumed the poor savages did not know their own fathers or mothers. In ego's own generation the terms usually translated as "brother" or "sister" include not only full brothers and sisters but maternal and paternal parallel cousins and cross-cousins—thus giving plenty of "brothers" and "sisters" for the next generation to call "father" and "mother." The prototype (the society in which it was first reported in detail) for the bilateral-generational system is Hawaiian. (The term "ego" is used to give readers a starting point in a chart. It means "I"— so a reader can pick a symbol as "that's me," and read the chart from the viewpoint of that symbol. "Ego's own generation" would refer to the people represented by the symbols in the same generation as the one chosen to represent one's self, and so on.)

At the other end of the continuum are societies that distinguish each kind of relationship by a separate term (see Table 8.1). They have a term for "father," another term for "father's brother," and still another term for "mother's brother." Similarly, "mother," "mother's sister," and "father's sister" are all distinguished by separate terms. In ego's own generation, siblings are distinguished from parallel cousins, which are also distinguished from cross-cousins by a separate term. These systems are called unilateral–bifurcate collateral, and the prototype is Sudanese.

In between the extremes are societies like our own, in which parents are distinguished by a separate term but parents' siblings are lumped together as "uncles" or "aunts." In the United States this classification includes even affinal relatives (in-laws), since the mother's or father's brothers' wife is called "aunt," and the mother's or father's sister's husband is called "uncle." In ego's own generation, full or half siblings are distinguished, but all cousins, cross or parallel, male or female, are lumped together as "cousin." This term is also often extended to include in-laws. The prototype of this type of system, which is called bilateral-lineal, is not American but Eskimo.

The remaining major category of kinship systems is the unilineal–bifurcate merging, and the prototypes are Crow, Omaha, and Iroquois—depending on minor variations within the basic theme. In these systems "father" and "father's brothers" are classed together, but "mother's brother" has a separate term. "Mother" and "mother's sisters" are classed together, while "father's sister" has a separate term. (This kind of distinction makes good sense. Even in the United States, if ego's father died, ego's mother could possibly marry the paternal uncle —the father's brother—if he were single and wanted to marry her, but she could never marry the maternal uncle, because he is her own brother [Schusky 1974:1]. Of course, she is *unlikely* to marry her dead husband's brother for many reasons, which probably explains why the distinction between uncles is not made in English. Nevertheless, the utility of such a distinction in certain societies is clear.) The terms translated as "brother" or "sister" really mean "male (or female) of my clan in my generation."

Kinship terms are almost always reciprocal; that is, someone I call "brother" is almost certain to call me "sister." Someone ego calls "mother" will most likely call ego "son" or "daughter." Kinship systems are also internally consistent. That is, it is unlikely that one mother's brother would be called "uncle" and another called "cross-cousin," or any term other than "uncle." These two characteristics are a great help in investigating kinship systems.

A few characteristics, not common to many systems but occuring now and then, pose traps for the unwary researcher. In some societies, for example, there are separate sets of terms used by men and by women. That is, the same relative, a cross-cousin, for example, would be called "x" by a man and "y" by a woman, even though the relative is related to them both in the same way. There may also be completely different sets of terms to use when talking *about* someone and when talking *to* someone (respectively called terms of reference° and terms of address°). This is not common in the United States, although it may occur. We would use "uncle" to refer to our father's brother, and in talking *to* him, if we used any kinship term at all, we would still call him "uncle." But in some societies "uncle" might be used to refer to him and a totally different term used to talk to him. We do the same occasionally, as when we talk *about* "father" but call that person "dad." It would be just as correct to call him "father" or refer to him as "dad," however, whereas in the societies that have two separate sets of terms, one is never used when the other is appropriate.

Another problem some systems pose for the investigator is the use of alternate ways of reckoning relationship. In many small societies people are often related to each other in a number of ways. Since certain relationships carry certain obligations, people generally use the term that activates the particular obligation they want the other person to assume, and another term when they want to avoid an obligation they might have to assume in turn. For exam-

Chart 8.4. MATRILINEAL
Consequences of cross-cousin marriage

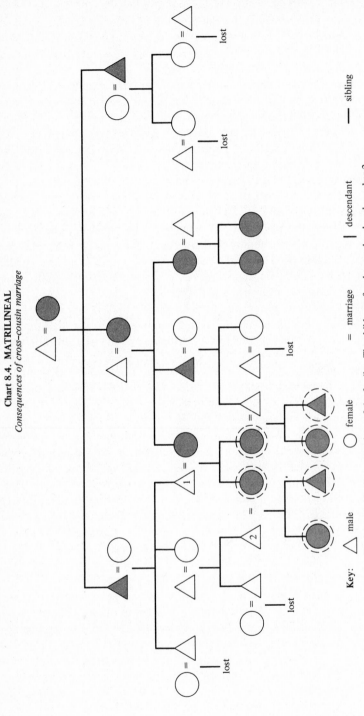

Key: △ male ○ female = marriage | descendant — sibling

Notes: Shaded individuals are members of the family. The children of males number 1 and number 2 (circled individuals) would have been lost to the family if the males had not married a cross-cousin (a father's sister's daughter). In a patrilineal system, a man would have to marry his mother's brother's daughter to have the same effect.

ple, a man wanting to borrow something, or get help, might address a relative as "uncle," tracing the relationship through certain individuals. Not wishing to be obligated, the kinsman, instead of responding "nephew," which would indicate his acceptance of the responsibility of an uncle, might respond "cousin" instead, tracing the relationship through other individuals, and thus rejecting the request. It is particularly easy to do this kind of optional kinship reckoning with cognate descent groups, who figure kinship bilaterally and therefore emphasize the ties they prefer while ignoring those they are not interested in (Schusky 1974:37).

Anthropologists often use kinship terminology for the information it gives about marriage patterns and incest. For example, some terms applied to cross-cousins mean "potential wife" or "potential husband." That is because in quite a few societies cross-cousins are preferred as marriage partners. There is little agreement on the reason for this popularity of cross-cousin marriage, but in a unilineal system it does have the effect of reuniting the parts of the family that have been split off by bifurcation (see Chart 8.4). This does not seem sufficient to account for all the cases, and the search for additional motives continues.

Cross-cousin marriage is regarded as incestuous (between true first cousins) by most Americans, although not by people in societies where it is practiced. Marriage between people regarded as close kin (i.e., incest) is rejected in all societies, although the relatives classified as "close" vary, and, as the excerpt shows, sexual relations are not always prohibited even when marriage is forbidden. (Since the traditional American system forbids sexual relations outside of marriage, we do not normally make that distinction.) The so-called incest tabu exists in all societies in the sense that certain relatives are regarded as too closely related for sexual relations to be acceptable between them. In some societies the prohibition is fairly explicit; in such cases the incest tabu is obvious. In others, sexual relations between certain relatives are literally unthinkable, and apparently do not occur. Under these circumstances, it is difficult to speak of an actual tabu, since it is unnecessary to prohibit anything really unthinkable. In any case, attempts to explain and understand this phenomenon have occupied researchers for decades. Part of the difficulty lies in the fact that societies vary in the specific relationships they prohibit. Only the mother-son incest prohibition approaches universality. Father-daugher sexual relations are usually forbidden, and brother-sister relations are also generally barred, but exceptions are found. In some societies, for example, brother-sister marriage has been required. The ancient Egyptian, Hawaiian, and Inca cultures are the best known examples, but even in those, brother-sister marriage was expected only of royalty and was barred to commoners.

Unilineal societies may carry the incest prohibition much further than bilateral cultures in certain relationships (such as parallel cousins), yet allow marriage between other categories of kin that would be forbidden in a bilateral society like that of the United States (e.g., cross-cousins). When a society follows a unilineal–bifurcate merging pattern for generations, people may call each other "brother and sister" and be restricted by incest regulations although they have only the most tenuous biological relationships. On the other hand, the same society that regards as incestuous a relationship Americans would accept with no qualms might very well encourage the marriage of first cross-cousins, which many Americans *would* regard as incestuous, or the marriage of a man and his sister's daugher, which is definitely an incestuous match in the United States (Evans-Pritchard 1965:215).

Why do incest regulations exist? Are they necessary? One assumption has been that inbreeding would have harmful genetic effects. Yet how could this have been a conscious reason in societies with no understanding of genetics? Moreover, biologically a cross-cousin is as close as a parallel cousin, yet many societies require marriage with a cross-cousin but regard parallel-cousin marriage as incest. One of the earliest explanations was that people brought up together are not sexually attractive to each other. This explanation was more or less discredited by Freud, who held that, on the contrary, people brought up together would naturally be attractive to one another, and to avoid the disruptive effect of sexual competition within the family, stringent prohibitions had to be set up. The clinching argument seemed to be that one does not have to prohibit something if it is literally unthinkable. Some recent cross-cultural evidence seems to indicate that the first explanation is sounder than the Freudian argument would make it seem. Among the Chinese, a child bride is sometimes brought into the groom's house to be raised with her future husband. Although there is no cultural brother-sister tabu in this situation, of course—in fact, the pair are constantly encouraged to act as husband and wife—the pair almost always find each other sexually unattractive when it is time to consummate the match. This form of marriage produces fewer children and has a higher divorce rate than does the usual marriage pattern (Wolf 1966:883–898; Westermarck 1921; Freud 1920:294).

Claude Lévi-Strauss, a modern theorist, relies heavily on a structuralist° explanation. He regards incest prohibitions as essentially arbitrary and cultural (since they are so variable), rather than anything demanded by biological imperatives. He says that incest regulations force families to depend on one another, just as the division of labor forces individuals to depend on one another. This creates a larger number of interdependent people and gives the group a survival advantage. Groups with incest regulations therefore prospered, whereas those who were inbred died out not so much for biological reasons as for social ones (Lévi-Strauss 1960:261–285).

Group affiliation is not the only thing that can be inherited, of course. Wealth, personal belongings, power, and a variety of intangible things also pass from one generation to the next. These may not move in the same manner as group affiliation. When a child inherits one type of thing from one parent and a different sort of thing from the other parent, the pattern is called double descent.° The Huron (Chapter 3) may have had this system, since Lahontan said they inherited their body from their mother but their soul from their father (Lahontan 1931:122). Inheritance from the father in the realm of the supernatural is supported by Jean de Brebeuf, who claimed the Huron received their supernatural charms from their fathers (Talbot 1956:71). Double descent also occurs in Africa (Ottenberg 1968:3–5). When girls always inherit only from their

mothers and boys only from their fathers, the pattern is called parallel inheritance.° It is occasionally found in various parts of the world (Bock 1969:133). A
society may have several patterns, one for group affiliation, another for certain
types of things, and still another for different categories of things. Thus American society is bilateral for wealth and patrilineal for family name.

We have seen that residence rules in a patrilineal system are usually patrilocal or virilocal—as in the excerpt about Ning Lao in traditional China—and
similarly, as in the Hopi excerpt, that matrilineal inheritance occurs with matrilocal residence.

In certain circumstances, however, the residence pattern does not coincide
with the inheritance of group affiliation. If marriage must take place with an
outsider, the orderly succession of inherited power may cause complications in
a matrilineal society, for example, since public power is almost always in the
hands of the men. If land cannot pass out of the possession of the corporate
matrilineal group and yet men inherit land, this may also create problems. As
long as marriage takes place within the same village (endogamy,° marriage
within the social unit), the transfer of power or land poses no real problem. In
a matrilineal system, a man's heirs are his sister's children, not his own. The
matrilineal line of succession runs from a man to his nephews instead of from
father to son, the patrilineal pattern familiar in the Western world. When
marriage is endogamous in the village, a man's heirs are available for training,
supervision, and work on the land that will ultimately be theirs. They can take
over a well-known system with a minimum of disruption, since they play accustomed roles with familiar people.

There are times, however, when marriage is not endogamous but exoga-
mous (requiring people to marry outside a particular group), sometimes because marriage within the group would require incestuous relations, sometimes
for economic or political reasons (Schusky 1974:67, 68). Village exogamy, combined with matrilineal inheritance, gives rise to particular strains in the matrilineal system that the patrilineal system does not have to face. To begin with,
a man and his sister would never be living in the same village under either
matrilocal or patrilocal residence patterns. A man and his matrilineal heirs
would thus be in different villages, which would cause all kinds of problems. For
example, if residence is matrilocal, as it normally would be in a matrilineal
system, a man would leave his village but his sister would stay in it. If he
inherited land in his home village, he would not be around to work it. If he
inherited power through his mother, he would not be around to claim it.
Patrilocal residence does not solve the problem either, because then the sister
leaves the home village but the brother stays in it, so his heirs are not around
to claim power or work land. Some societies have solved the problem with
avunculocal residence (residence with the groom's mother's brother). In this
way, if a man has power or land to pass on to his sister's sons, they are living
with him. His young nephews tend to move in as adolescents and bring wives
back to his house or village when they marry. Residence in this case may appear virilocal or even patrilocal, since the couple appears to move into the
groom's village or his family's home, but actually it is the village and home of

the groom's maternal uncle, not the village in which the groom was born. When the groom's children grow up, they will move away into the village of his wife's brother (to whom they are heirs), and he will receive his nephews (his sister's children), who are *his* heirs. It is a complex system from an American point of view, but apparently fairly simple in practice. It results in different areas of tension, of course. Under this system, the fact that the maternal uncle is far more of an authority figure than the father has various ramifications for father-son relationships. For example, Malinowski, who worked in such a society, found little trace of an ambivalent attitude toward the father. Father-son relations were relaxed and warm. Rather, the tension appeared between uncle and nephew. If Malinowski's observations were accurate, the genesis of the Oedipus complex described by Freud probably lies in rivalry over power, not sex (Malinowski 1953). (Psychologists have still not made sufficient use of the natural experimental situations that exist in different cultures, although some steps have been made in this direction, as mentioned in Chapter 7.)

The division of loyalties that matrilineal systems place on a man are probably more responsible than any other single factor for the fact that matrilineal systems are less frequent than patrilineal ones. Since males exercise the power of the corporate group, and since husbands do not belong by birth to the corporate group, that group (clan, lineage, or whatever) continues to make demands on the birth-related male for his time, energy, and interests even after he marries. Unlike the woman in the patrilineal system, he is not expected to cut his ties with his family of orientation—in fact, he is often forbidden to. Consequently, his conjugal family (his wife and children) must always compete for his attention with his consanguine family (his mother, his sisters, and their children, who are his heirs). The ties to the consanguine family make the conjugal, or marriage, bond brittle and place greater strain on the marriage (Schusky 1974:42).

SUMMARY

All societies regulate the sexual behavior of their members. At a minimum the society classifies individuals into permissible and nonpermissible sexual partners through incest rules. The specific relationships prohibited or permitted vary widely from one society to another. In order to have any incest prohibitions at all, of course, it is necessary to recognize kinship affiliations. Membership in or exclusion from a kinship-based group is determined in various limited ways. A child can be affiliated through his mother, his father, or both parents. Societies organized around affiliation through one parent rather than through both have a variety of characteristics in common, such as the occurrence of lineages and clans, discrimination of cross-cousins and parallel cousins, frequently including preferred cross-cousin marriage, and levirate and sororate. The latter is made easier by another practice frequent in unilineal societies —classificatory kinship, in which relationship terms are extended to include relatives who would be excluded in American kinship terminology.

Marriage exists in all societies, although the family (as defined by Murdock) does not. Marriage may be arranged entirely by the parents and be a matter for general extended family concern, or it may result from the independent choice of the young couple and be regarded as entirely their own business. Wealth frequently changes hands at a marriage. Sometimes it is the bride's family that must distribute wealth, sometimes it is the groom's, and sometimes both families exchange items. In any of these cases, the young couple usually must depend on assistance from their families to marry.

Stability in marriage obviously depends neither on romantic attachment nor on happiness. Ning Lao's marriage was stable, in the sense that she married only once and was never divorced, but it certainly was neither romantic nor happy. Don's marriage, based on romantic love of a sort and his own choice, was also stable in the same sense as Ning Lao's, but it too falls short of the American ideal of a happy marriage. (The American divorce rate, however, shows quite clearly that a substantial number of marriages based on this ideal founder.) Stability in marriage does not seem to have much to do with Judaeo-Christian morality, either. Ning Lao's husband was hardly a shining example of "goodness." He had one premarital and extramarital affair; he had one illegitimate child we know about (he may have had more). He smoked opium, did not provide for his family, and sold one of his children. Yet he never sought a divorce and lived with Ning Lao again as soon as she let him. He fathered another child by her. His marriage was certainly stable in the sense of enduring. Don also fails to provide a model for Judaeo-Christian morality, at least so far as his sexual behavior is concerned. He engaged in a variety of premarital and extramarital affairs, but this behavior did not affect the stability of his marriage.

Residence after marriage varies widely from one society to another, and is occasionally variable even within the same society. A change in residence places some stress on the individual who has to leave home, particularly if he or she is cut off from supportive relatives. Residence rules may reinforce the group affiliation pattern or serve to correct problems when group affiliation and some important element in the society are not passed along in the same way from one generation to the next.

The family is a major source of socialization for the young. It is frequently the group within which they first learn the values and traditions of their culture and internalize the beliefs and rules that make it possible to function in society and enjoy doing it. Socialization is not the only answer to the question of why individuals support their society, however. Without a feeling of esprit de corps and morale, human beings—apparently alone of all the animals—do not have the motivation to continue living. Where do people find answers to the questions of why they live and why they should want to go on? In the next chapter, we discuss the problem of maintaining morale and motivation, another prerequisite for the survival of society.

9 Maintaining Morale and Motivation

Human beings have always asked, Why am I here? What is it all for? Why do we do what we do? They are often anxious about the future, death, and many other things beyond their control. The human seems to be the only animal who broods about the future. For a society to survive, for the individual members to survive, they need not only material things such as food, clothing, and shelter but also a reason for living and for behaving responsibly. People must have a feeling of loyalty to the group, a feeling of satisfaction and a sense of rightness in what they do and what is expected from them. Otherwise they give up as individuals or as members of society, and either they or the society fails to survive. For a society to function well, its members must have reasonably high morale and a motivation to live, to live according to its norms. What is the source of this morale, this motivation? Much of it comes from an individual's socialization, but this is not the only source. Art, folklore, literature, music, drama, and religion also provide man with answers, with motivation, and with morale.

In this chapter we focus mainly on religion, which seems to have some priority over the fine arts. Archeological evidence suggests that the arts have long had as a major purpose the service of religion. Once established in general culture, however, many of the arts began to serve independently to bolster morale and motivation.

In the following excerpt, note what seem to be the major worries of people in the society, the questions they ask, and the source or the type of answers they receive. What kind of specialists do they have? How is life made exciting, interesting, and more secure for them?

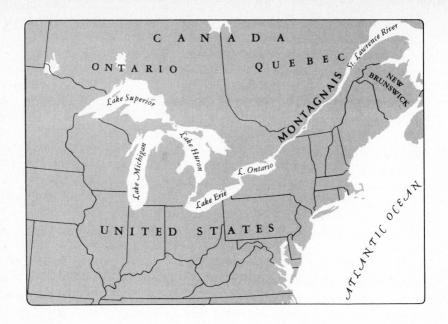

Sorcery and the Montagnais

Towards nightfall, two or three young men erected a tent in the middle of our
Cabin; they stuck six poles deep into the ground in the form of a circle, and to
hold them in place they fastened to the tops of these poles a large ring, which
completely encircled them; this done, they enclosed this Edifice with Cas-
telognes [woolen blankets], leaving the top of the tent open; it is all that a tall
man can do to reach to the top of this round tower, capable of holding 5 or 6
men standing upright.* This house made, the fires of the cabin are entirely
extinguished, and the brands thrown outside, lest the flame frighten away the
Genii or *Khichikouai,* who are to enter this tent; a young juggler slipped in
from below, turning back, for this purpose, the covering which enveloped it,
then replaced it when he had entered, for they must be very careful that there
be no opening in this fine palace except from above. The juggler, having entered, began to moan softly, as if complaining; he shook the tent at first without
violence; then becoming animated little by little, he commenced to whistle, in

---

*Abridged from "Le Jeune's Relations, 1634," in Ruben G. Thwaites (ed.), *The Jesuit Relations
& Allied Documents* (Cleveland: Burrows Bros., 1897), Vol. 6, pp. 163–171, 193–201. Odd-numbered
pages are in English; even-numbered, in French. The report by the French Jesuit Paul Le Jeune was
made after he had spent a winter with the Montagnais Indians in eastern Canada. The complete report
is published in Vols. 6 and 7.

a hollow tone, and as if it came from afar; then to talk as if in a bottle; to cry like the owls of these countries, which it seems to me have stronger voices than those of France; then to howl and sing, constantly varying the tones; . . . disguising his voice so that it seemed to me I heard those puppets which showmen exhibit in France. Sometimes he spoke Montagnais, sometimes Algonquain, retaining always the Algonquain intonation, which, like the Provençal, is vivacious. At first, as I have said, he shook this edifice gently; but, as he continued to become more animated, he fell into so violent an ecstasy, that I thought he would break everything to pieces, shaking his house with so much force and violence, that I was astonished at a man having so much strength; for, after he had once begun to shake it, he did not stop until the consultation was over, which lasted about three hours. Whenever he would change his voice, the Savages would at first cry out, . . . "listen, listen"; then, as an invitation to these Genii, they said to them, . . . "enter, enter." At other times, as if they were replying to the howls of the juggler, they drew this aspiration from the depths of their chests, *ho, ho.* I was seated like the others, looking on at this wonderful mystery, forbidden to speak; but as I had not vowed obedience to them, I did not fail to intrude a little word into the proceedings. Sometimes I begged them to have pity on this poor juggler, who was killing himself in this tent; at other times I told them they should cry louder, for the Genii had gone to sleep.

Some of these Barbarians imagined that this juggler was not inside, that he had been carried away, without knowing where or how. Others said that his body was lying on the ground, and that his soul was up above the tent, where it spoke at first, calling these Genii, and throwing from time to time sparks of fire. Now to return to our consultation. The Savages having heard a certain voice that the juggler counterfeited, uttered a cry of joy, saying that one of these Genii had entered; then addressing themselves to him, they cried out, . . . "call, call"; that is, "call thy companions." Thereupon the juggler, pretending to be one of the Genii and changing his tone and his voice, called them. In the meantime our sorcerer, who was present, took his drum, and began to sing with the juggler who was in the tent, and the others answered. Some of the young men were made to dance, among others the Apostate [Pierre Antoine Pastede-chouan, the Montagnais interpreter who had been baptized and then had turned back to his native religion], who did not wish to hear of it, but the sorcerer made him obey.

At last, after a thousand cries and howls, after a thousand songs, after having danced and thoroughly shaken this fine edifice, the Savages believing that the Genii . . . had entered, the sorcerer consulted them. He asked them about his health (for he is sick), and about that of his wife, who was also sick. These Genii, or rather the juggler who counterfeited them, answered that, as to his wife, she was already dead, that it was all over with her. I could have said as much myself, for one needed not to be a prophet or a sorcerer to guess that, inasmuch as the poor creature was already struck with death; in regard to the sorcerer, they said that he would see the Spring. Now, knowing his disease,—which was a pain in the loins, or rather an infirmity resulting from his licentiousness and excesses, for he is vile to the last degree,—I said to him, seeing that he was otherwise healthy, and that he drank and ate very heartily, that he would not only see the Spring but also the Summer, if some other accident did not overtake him, and I was not mistaken.

After these interrogations, these fine oracles were asked if there would soon be snow, if there would be much of it, if there would be Elks or Moose, and where they could be found. They answered, or rather the juggler, always disguising his voice, that they saw a little snow and some moose far away, without indicating the place, having the prudence not to commit themselves.

So this is what took place in this consultation, after which I wished to get hold of the juggler; but, as it was night, he made his exit from the tent and from our little cabin so swiftly, that he was outside almost before I was aware of it. He and all the other Savages, who had come from the other Cabins to these beautiful mysteries, having departed, I asked the Apostate if he was so simple as to believe that the Genii entered and spoke in this tent. He began to swear his belief, which he had lost and denied, that it was not the juggler who spoke, but these *Khichikouai* or Genii of the air, and my host said to me, "Enter thou thyself into the tent, and thou wilt see that thy body will remain below, and thy soul will mount on high." I did want to go in; but, as I was the only one of my party, I foresaw that they might commit some outrage upon me, and, as there were no witnesses there, they would boast that I had recognized and admired the truth of their mysteries.

. . .

I must set down here what I saw them do on the twelfth of February. As I was reciting my hours [prayers] toward evening, the sorcerer began to talk about me: *aiamtheou,* "He is making his prayers"; then, pronouncing some words which I did not understand, he added: *Niganipahau,* "I will kill him at once." . . . Just as I was thinking that he wanted to take my life, my host said to me, "Hast thou not some powder that kills men?" "Why?" I asked. "I want to kill some one," he answered me. I leave you to imagine whether I finished my prayers without any distraction; for I knew very well that they were disinclined to kill any of their own people, and that the sorcerer had threatened me with death some days before,—although only in jest, as he told me afterward; but I did not have much confidence in him. . . . I wished to learn if they had me in mind, and so I asked them where the man was that they wished to kill; they answered me that he was in the neighborhood of Gaspé, more than a hundred leagues away from us. I began to laugh, for in truth I had never dreamed that they would undertake to kill a man a hundred leagues away. I inquired why they wished to take his life. They answered that this man was a Canadian sorcerer, who, having had some trouble with ours, had threatened him with death and had given him the disease from which he had suffered so long, and which was going to consume him in two days, if he did not prevent the stroke by his art. I told them that God had forbidden murder, and that we never killed people; that did not prevent them from pursuing their purpose.

My host, foreseeing the great commotion which was about to take place, said to me, "Thou wilt have the headache; go off into one of the other cabins near by." "No," said the sorcerer, "there will be no harm in his seeing what we do." They had all the children and women go out, except one who sat near the sorcerer; I remained as a spectator of their mysteries, with all the Savages of the other cabins, who were summoned. All being seated, a young man comes bearing two pickets, or very sharply-pointed sticks; my host prepares the charm, composed of little pieces of wood shaped at both ends like a serpent's tongue, iron arrow-points, pieces of broken knives, bits of iron bent like a big fishhook, and other similar things; all these are wrapped in a piece of leather. When this is done, the sorcerer takes his drum, all begin to chant and howl, and to make the uproar of which I spoke above; after a few songs, the woman who had remained arises, and goes all around the inside of the cabin, passing behind the backs of the people who are there. When she is reseated, the magician takes these two stakes; then, pointing out a certain place, begins by saying, "Here is his head" (I believe he meant the head of the man whom he wished to kill); then with all his might he drives these stakes into the ground, inclining them toward the place where he believed this Canadian was. Thereupon my host comes to assist his brother; he makes a tolerably deep ditch in the ground with these stakes; meanwhile the songs and other noises continue incessantly. The ditch made and the stakes planted, the servant of the sorcerer, I mean the Apostate, goes in search of a sword, and the sorcerer strikes with it one of these pickets; then he descends into the ditch, assuming the posture of an excited man who is striking heavy blows with the sword and poniard; for he has both, in this act of a furious and enraged man. The sorcerer takes the charm wrapped in skin, puts it in the ditch, and redoubles his sword-cuts at the same time that they increase the uproar.

Finally, this mystery ends, and he draws out the sword and the poniard all covered with blood, and throws them down before the other Savages; the ditch is hurriedly covered up, and the magician boastfully asserts that his man is struck, that he will soon die, and asks if they have not heard his cries; they all say "no," except two young men, relatives of his, who say they have heard some very dull sounds, and as if far away. Oh, how glad they make him! Turning toward me, he begins to laugh, saying, "See this black robe, who comes here to tell us that we must not kill any one." As I am looking attentively at the sword and the poniard, he has them presented to me. "Look," he says, "what is that?" "It is blood," I answer, "of what? Of some Moose or other animal." They laugh at me, saying that it is the blood of that Sorcerer of Gaspé. "How?" I answer them, "he is more than a hundred leagues away from here." "It is true," they reply, "but it is the Manitou; that is, the Devil, who carries his blood under the earth." Now if this man is really a Magician, I leave you to decide; for my part, I consider that he is neither Sorcerer nor Magician, but that he would like very much to be one. All that he does, according to my opinion is nothing but nonsense to amuse the Savages. He would like to have communication with the Devil or Manitou, but I do not think that he has. Yet I am persuaded that there has been some Sorcerer or Magician here, if what they tell me is true about diseases and cures which they describe to me; it is a strange thing, in my opinion, that the Devil, who is visible to the South Americans, and who so beats and torments them that they would like to get rid of such a guest, does not communicate himself visibly and sensibly to our Savages. . . .

Unfortunately, Le Jeune never revealed whether the Gaspé sorcerer died. Apparently he was so sure of his evaluation of the situation that he never bothered to check after he returned to Jesuit headquarters in Quebec. Our curiosity must remain unsatisfied.

Le Jeune lived with the Montagnais to learn their language and to convert as many of them as possible. He was terribly sincere, and he firmly believed in the existence of a supernatural that intervened in the lives of men. In this he and the Montagnais agreed. Le Jeune, however, was convinced that *manitou* (the Montagnais name for the supernatural) was the Christian devil. In 1634, the suggestion that a supernatural being worshiped by other peoples might be equated with the Christian God would have been regarded as scandalous or blasphemous.

A magician undergoes convulsions in order to prophesy the outcome of his tribe's forth-coming war expedition. From an eighteenth-century engraving. *(The Bettmann Archive)*

BELIEF SYSTEMS

Le Jeune did not realize how many beliefs he and the Montagnais held in common. Their differences in behavior were so apparent and Le Jeune's bias was so strong that he was unable to examine the Montagnais belief system with any objectivity. A careful study of his full report, however, reveals many of the Montagnais religious beliefs, and incidentally sheds light on Le Jeune's concepts too. A list of concepts and practices is given in Tables 9.1 and 9.2.

It is easy to see from Table 9.1 that Le Jeune and the Montagnais shared more beliefs than either of them realized. First, both believed in supernatural beings with will and consciousness. In addition, both believed that men and the supernatural can interact; that one individual can harm another by means of the supernatural; and that there is a variety of supernatural beings capable of a variety of actions. Both Le Jeune and the Montagnais believed that man has a soul that can separate from the body; that supernatural beings know what the future holds and what is happening in other parts of the world; that the supernatural can be used as protection against supernatural attack.

There is no major area of the globe entirely free from such beliefs, even today, although they may appear in different combinations in specific individuals or groups. The belief in supernatural beings with will and consciousness is called animism° and is one of the most widespread concepts about the supernatural. The belief was first defined by E. B. Tylor (Tylor 1965:10–21), who noted its almost universal occurrence and suggested that it had developed from speculation about dreams, which are consciously experienced by almost everyone. Tylor also described a special kind of belief in supernatural beings—the worship of animals and of natural features of the environment—that he called "nature worship" (Tylor 1965:10). R. R. Marett, another student of religion in the same period, coined the term animatism° for a belief in the life force of usually inanimate natural objects (LaBarre 1964:26–29). This term is so close in sound to the word *animism* that it has plagued generations of students. Moreover, the distinction between animism and animatism is not always easy to determine in actual religious systems; it is sometimes impossible to learn whether an individual worships a spirit housed in a rock (animism), or believes that the rock itself has an awareness, consciousness, and supernatural powers (animatism). The people of a society themselves may not be sure, or they may disagree on the correct interpretation. Tylor's term is the more useful here and the one we shall use, since people who venerate a rock can be classified as nature worshipers in any case.

Another widespread belief is that the supernatural is a mindless force, analogous to electricity, with *no* will, awareness, or consciousness. This concept is called mana° and is similar to the Western idea of luck. It is not so pervasive as the concept of animism, although it appears in many parts of the world. Mana can be used for either good or evil purposes, since the force itself has no awareness and is no more intrinsically good or evil than electricity. Objects, locations, people, and animals can have mana. If a person knows how to deal with the mana in something, he can use it to bring himself good fortune, but

Table 9.1

Montagnais Concepts (based on excerpt)	Le Jeune's Concepts (based on excerpt and other sources)
1. There are a variety of supernatural beings (*Khichikouai*—spirits of the air).	1. Same: demons; evil spirits; a specific evil force called the Devil; a good supernatural being called God (and other names); angels and other beings allied with God.
2. Flame (or light) frightens them.	2. Same, applied to evil spirits only. God, angels, and so on are not frightened by anything.
3. The spirits manifest their presence physically (speak aloud, answer questions, shake walls, and so on).	3. Same, although God and the good supernatural beings rarely do so, and are never undignified about it.
4. The spirits can predict the future and know what is happening in other parts of the world.	4. Same. God not only knows everything, past, present, and future, but personally causes or allows it to happen.
5. Humans have souls that can separate from their bodies.	5. Same.
6. Supernatural beings can interact with each other and with humans or human souls.	6. Same.
7. Singing and dancing are appropriate in religious ceremonies.	7. Singing is appropriate but dancing is not.
8. Humans can cause disease and kill through supernatural means. They can protect themselves the same way.	8. People may use evil spirits this way, but God cannot be used. God can protect people or cause them to die, but at God's volition, not theirs. God forbids murder. (Le Jeune said "real" magicians among the Montagnais might have cured or caused disease at one time, so he clearly believed it was possible.)
9. Weak or unauthorized individuals might be harmed by witnessing a ceremony. (Le Jeune was warned that he might get a headache; women and children were sent out.)	9. Witnessing a church service could be only beneficial. A ceremony involving evil spirits might harm weak, evil people, but could not hurt truly good ones, weak or strong.
10. Irrelevant conversation threatens to spoil ceremonies. (Presumably, the spirits would be scared off.)	10. Irrelevant conversation is improper or offensive at any time, but would never frighten good spirits or spoil a ceremony, except by annoying participants.

if he is untrained or supernaturally weak (a child, for example), contact with the mana may bring him disaster, just as contact with a high-tension wire may harm an unprotected person. The attitude toward mana is therefore ambivalent. Everyone wants to increase his own store of mana, and thereby his good fortune, but everyone also wants to avoid contact with more mana than he is equipped to control. Individuals with a great deal of mana (which is usually indicated by their fine health, wealth, and general good fortune) are dangerous to others and are therefore feared, respected, envied, and admired. Objects that belong to them or things they handle may become infested with an unusual amount of mana, making them dangerous to people who have a lesser amount. Contact with such people and their belongings is often hedged about with tabus.° The terms *mana* and *tabu* come from the South Pacific, where these concepts have been elaborately developed. The important difference between the concepts of mana and animism is that animistic beings have awareness and will, whereas mana does not. One cannot plead or bargain with mana, but it can be thoroughly controlled by anyone with the proper knowledge. Supernatural beings are less predictable or controllable, but they can be reasoned with, propitiated, and even outwitted. There is no clear evidence in the excerpt that the Montagnais had a manalike concept of the supernatural, but data in Le Jeune's full report indicate that they might have had.

Le Jeune and the Montagnais both believed that men can harm each other by supernatural means, and both believed the cause and the cure of most diseases are supernatural. Le Jeune attributed some diseases to "natural" causes, but believed all could be cured by God, and that some—particularly epidemic diseases—might be sent by God to punish individuals or whole societies: diseases caused by men using the supernatural are manifestations of the devil's power and are not the work of good supernatural beings. The Montagnais did not make such fine distinctions: they apparently felt that all diseases, at least all serious ones, are supernaturally caused, either by the supernatural acting independently or at the command of some sorcerer. Because the belief that the supernatural is the ultimate cause of all disease is widespread, in most societies religion is intimately involved in the treatment of illness. In the United States large segments of the population believe that prayer is an important supplement to medicine, and some groups depend almost entirely on supernatural treatment (Eddy n.d.:1–17).

From the list of beliefs given above, it is more difficult to determine the differences between Le Jeune and the Montagnais than it is to discover similarities. Some apparent differences are actually only modifications of shared concepts. For example, both shared the general belief that men and the supernatural interact. The Montagnais, however, believed that the spirits speak aloud to men and answer their questions. Le Jeune did not agree. As a Christian, he held that such communication can occur only under special circumstances with special individuals (Joan of Arc, for example). As the report indicates, he obviously did not accept the idea that the spirits engage in casual chitchat about the weather with a cabinful of Indians. Both Le Jeune and the Montagnais believed man has a soul that can separate from his body, but Le Jeune held that this normally occurs only after death. As in the case of visions, there might be exceptions, but he thought they were rare, and certainly not the almost routine occurrences that the Montagnais thought them to be.

Other beliefs held by the Montagnais were unacceptable to Le Jeune even in modified form; some he felt applied only to evil spirits. He did not believe that good supernatural beings are frightened by flame (although Christian folk belief would accept the idea that light, especially daylight, is frightening to evil spirits). The Montagnais thought that the spirits whistle, hoot like owls, and shake tent walls. Le Jeune did not believe that good spirits engage in such antics, and although he might have agreed that evil spirits can behave that way, it is clear from the report that he tended to blame all the noise and activity on the Montagnais sorcerer himself.

In Le Jeune's religious system, human beings have no certain control over the forces of good. They can supplicate or by performance win the good will or pity of the supernatural, but the suggestion that they can in any way control God is abhorrent. The concepts of the Montagnais were very different. To them, the supernatural is subject to human control; one only had to know the proper method. This difference between control and persuasion is often accepted as one of the distinctions between magic and religion, magic being defined as a system for control over the supernatural (Hoebel 1966:467). In general, anthropologists have accepted this definition, and regard magic and religion as two different approaches to the supernatural distinguished by the presence or absence of the power to control. Not all agree, however. A. van

A religious specialist treating a patient in South Africa. *(SATOUR)*

Gennep, an early theorist, regarded religion as a body of theory and concepts about the supernatural, and magic as the techniques for dealing with the supernatural based on those beliefs. He placed religion and scientific theory on the same analytical level as two different conceptual approaches to understanding the universe. Magic, the practice based on religion, was therefore on the same analytical level as what we call technology (and van Gennep called "science") —the practice based on scientific theory (van Gennep 1960:13). Van Gennep's definition is easier to apply than the other, because all religious systems attempt to influence the supernatural in some way. Using his definition, all techniques for doing so are designated magic, regardless of whether they are thought to coerce the supernatural, and all beliefs about the supernatural are classified as religious concepts, whether they depict the supernatural as subject to human control or as an omnipotent being whose good will depends upon man's submission. Van Gennep's definition helps one avoid the ethnocentric trap of regarding practices of familiar systems as "religious" and those of unfamiliar systems as "magical."

The question of the universality of magic and religion is often raised. The answer is largely a matter of definition. To Le Jeune and other Jesuits, whose definition of religion included specific beliefs (in one God, in the divinity of Jesus, in the virgin birth, and in a host of other dogmas), the Montagnais either had no religion or worshiped the devil. Definitions used by anthropologists today vary, but can be roughly summed up: Religion consists of attitudes and beliefs about the supernatural. Based on this definition, most anthropologists state that all societies have some form of religion. But some anthropologists regard this definition as unsatisfactory. For one thing, it leaves the word *supernatural* undefined; for another, many students of religion have pointed out that the distinction between the "natural" and the "supernatural" is by no means universal, nor is it consistent even in societies that make such a distinction. Most of the Western world would classify as supernatural all phenomena beyond human power to cause, sense, control, or comprehend. Instances of such phenomena will vary according to the technology of each society, so that a precise definition of the word that will hold across cultural boundaries has not yet been made. What can be said so far is that all socieites appear to have concepts and beliefs dealing with what the Western world would classify as the supernatural. Perhaps an anthropological definition should read as follows: Religion consists of attitudes and beliefs about what Western civilization classifies as supernatural. Although this definition is ethnocentric, it makes it possible to categorize practices and beliefs for analysis, and perhaps even more important, makes explicit something that has long been implicit in the definition.

The anthropologist Murray Wax has suggested that the whole concept "religion" is a "folk category of the Western Judaeo-Christian tradition," and that the category may not exist in other parts of the world (Wax 1968:228). He prefers a classification based on "magical" and "rational" thinking. Magical thinkers, according to Wax, regard the universe as "a 'society,' not a 'mechanism'; that is, it is composed of 'beings' rather than 'objects' " (Wax 1968:235). He regards this classification as less ethnocentric than the other.

Whichever definition of magic or of religion is accepted, there are certain similarities in practices that can be identified. Much of the behavior for manipulating the supernatural uses materials that have been in contact with the person or thing to be affected, mimics the desired result, or both. James Frazer classified such behavior under the general term *sympathetic magic*, based on what he called the Law of Sympathy, which assumes that things act on each other even at a distance because of a "secret sympathy" between them (Frazer 1955:52). Frazer also divided this general principle into two subordinate laws: the Law of Similarity or Imitation, and the Law of Contagion or Contact. The first states that things that resemble each other influence each other, like produces like, and effect resembles its cause; the second states that things once in contact continue to affect each other after contact is broken (Frazer 1955:52ff.). Le Jeune's report describes one Montagnais ritual based at least partly on imitative magic. The charm used in the assassination sorcery contained things that could cut and wound. The sorcerer made dagger thrusts and sword slashes

A meeting of a group interested in the occult. *(Thomas Höpker/Woodfin Camp & Associates)*

in the air to harm his opponent. The presence of blood on the weapons was confirmation that the thrusts had actually penetrated the body of his enemy. Had the Montagnais sorcerer also used something formerly in contact with his opponent's body (such as clothing, fingernail or hair clippings, or excrement), he would have been using the Law of Contagion.

Sorcery and witchcraft are practiced in many parts of the world today, with a recent resurgence of so-called satanic cults in Europe, England, and the United States. Many practices reminiscent of the Middle Ages have been adopted by elements of modern society once thought immune to such beliefs (Holzer 1971:4–6, 71–85). Sorcery is the term usually reserved for magic practiced with evil intent, but magic for socially acceptable goals also uses the same principles. Thus the Nootka put a model of a swimming fish into the river when salmon runs are delayed, and peoples in many parts of the world engage in ritual sexual intercourse to encourage fertility in the plant and animal worlds (Leach 1949:867).

Read Le Jeune's excerpt again and you will find evidence of a profound and yet subtle difference between European and American Indian religious concepts that Le Jeune probably never realized existed. Le Jeune's God prohibited murder, yet Le Jeune accepted the idea that evil supernatural beings might assist humans to kill other humans. He divided the supernatural world (and the natural world as well) into categories of good and evil beings. His God, the saints, angels, and other assorted supernatural beings were "good" and would never under any circumstances do anything that Le Jeune would regard as "evil." Misfortunes that befell men were held to be the work of the devil or were merited punishment for man's sins and therefore "good" for him. The Montagnais had no such dichotomy of good and evil beings. Some supernaturals were more powerful than others, or had special competence in certain areas, but none was regarded as invariably good or bad. The Montagnais beliefs were characteristic of those of American Indians in general; the Old World good-evil dichotomy hardly seemed to exist in the New World. The Indian approach was incomprehensible and reprehensible to European clerics (as it is to many people today), although it was certainly attractive to less pious Frenchmen.

All of what Robert Redfield has called the Great Traditions° have attached moral values to the supernatural, whereas most of the Little Traditions (like that of the Montagnais) have not (Redfield 1960:40–59). From parts of Le Jeune's report it is clear that to the Montagnais, violation of a supernatural regulation, such as the requirement that certain animal bones be burned instead of given to dogs, was a dangerous and even a stupid thing to do, since it might result in hunting failure, but it was not "wrong" in the European sense. A man could do it if he could get away with it, but he was taking a risk. Behavior that harmed another person was "bad," but there was little concern over supernatural punishment; instead, the wronged individual was likely to retaliate immediately (and violently) with the full support of public opinion. Sins—offenses against the supernatural—were of consequence only if the supernatural reacted, and then were of general concern only if the reaction appeared to threaten the society as a whole. At that point, the individual's actions were judged "crimes"—

offenses against society—and social pressure was directed against him (see Chapters 5 and 6).

This classification led to the evaluation of actions in context. Stealing from another Montagnais was a crime, but since Europeans were not Montagnais, stealing from them was not. It was also proper to take another person's belongings in retaliation for certain offenses. Stealing, therefore, was not intrinsically bad; it was classified as wrong according to who took from whom and under what circumstances. Apparently, if a Montagnais got away with something normally regarded as a "crime" or a "sin," he felt no guilt about it and was unconcerned unless he became ill. In that case his act might be used by a religious specialist as an explanation for his sickness, which was attributed to retaliation by a sorcerer or a supernatural. The Montagnais (like many other peoples) had a concept of an afterlife, but one's fate was not determined so much by one's conduct during life as by the circumstances of death and the subsequent treatment of the body. (Compare Norse beliefs that men who died in battle went to Valhalla, whereas those who died naturally did not—saint or sinner in life, it made no difference.)

Still another contrast between Le Jeune and the Montagnais lies in the degree of exclusiveness of the belief system. Christianity is classified as an "exclusive" religion. It rejects inclusion of gods from other systems (although a surprising number turn up as "saints" with new names but old ceremonies). Since the Christian God is believed to be omnipotent and in control of the entire universe, belief in other gods is assumed to be either mistaken or the

A view of the Jerusalem skyline at sunset. The Christian, Jewish, and Islamic faiths are examples of exclusive religions. *(Marvin Newman/Woodfin Camp & Associates)*

worship of evil supernatural beings. The Christian, Islamic, and Judaic religions will not permit believers to hold other religious beliefs simultaneously. An inclusive religion, on the other hand, permits believers to accept a variety of different beliefs simultaneously. A member of an inclusive religion sees no difficulty in participating in his own religion and in Christian services as well.

Exclusive religions are apt to proselytize more often than are inclusive ones. Le Jeune himself was a missionary. In his system, it was possible for people born into one religion to become members of another—the Christian faith— simply by accepting certain beliefs and undergoing certain rituals. The rituals are examples of the class of ceremony called *rites de passage* by van Gennep (van Gennep 1960:3), other examples of which have been mentioned in Chapters 7 and 8. Such ceremonies mark the transition of an individual from one status to another, and all societies have them in some form. The ceremonies may involve the supernatural and so be religious in nature, or they may be secular. Because they so often deal with dramatic events in the life cycle, they are sometimes called crisis rites.

All the Great Tradition religions accept converts (although Judaism still does so reluctantly). Tribal religions, on the other hand, are limited to members born or adopted into the group (Dobyns 1960:114–117, 444–458). Christianity began as a tribal religion; it took explicit doctrinal change to open the belief to non-Jews (Walker 1959:23). The change was vital to the spread of Christianity, which otherwise would have remained a Jewish sect. Two tribal religions cannot compete for recruits, since neither has a mechanism for accepting any. Members of tribal religions often resist conversion to one of the Great Tradition religions because they do not believe such a thing is possible. Le Jeune was often frustrated in his attempts to convert the Montagnais to Christianity by this lack of comprehension. When he pointed out that the French regularly violated Montagnais tabus without any of the expected unpleasant consequences, the Montagnais were unshaken in their faith because they did not think the two situations were comparable. The French were not Montagnais, so what they did in regard to tabus was irrelevant. When Le Jeune tried to insist that the Montagnais abide by certain restrictions, they could not understand why they should have to abide by French rules. They persisted in thinking in terms of a French heaven for the French and a Montagnais afterworld for themselves. Relatives of converts had themselves baptized so they could all be in the same afterworld, or refused baptism because they did not want to be separated from nonconverts after death. Some individuals who claimed to have visited heaven and returned insisted that the Montagnais were badly treated there by the French. The idea of a single heaven and hell was a difficult concept to communicate.

PRACTICES

If we compare the two lists of practices taken from the excerpt and other sources (Table 9.2), we see that the Montagnais and Le Jeune differed more in

Table 9.2

Montagnais Practices (based on the excerpt and other sources)	Le Jeune's Practices (based on the excerpt and other sources)
1. A separate temporary structure for religious purposes was set up inside their dwellings when needed.	1. Not usual. Permanent buildings or parts of buildings especially for religious purposes were more common.
2. All lights and fires were extinguished for ceremonies.	2. Reverse. Candles were often *lit* for religious purposes.
3. The main religious specialist was hidden out of sight; a second, not hidden, questioned the spirits who were presumably speaking through the first.	3. Different. In public ceremonies, religious specialists were not hidden from view. Supernatural beings were not interrogated, and did not speak through human lips.
4. All the spectators were expected to participate by singing, dancing, calling out to spirits, and generally following directions—apparently spontaneous ones—from the specialist.	4. Similar but not identical. Spectators were expected to participate by singing, reciting special prayers, and giving formalized, memorized responses, or by silent meditation. No part was spontaneous except meditation.
5. Women and children were normally excluded from the ceremony, except for an occasional specialist (female) who might assist.	5. Different. Women and children were expected to attend, but only as participating spectators (although male children might assist occasionally).
6. The specialist mimicked events he wanted to cause, actively involved himself with supernatural beings, asked questions, and so on. He was possessed.	6. Different. The specialist prayed and led responses, but never questioned supernatural beings or mimicked events. He was not normally possessed during ceremonies.
7. Specialists attempted to control and direct the supernatural beings, and tried to kill someone.	7. Different. Specialists did not try to control the supernatural; they only asked for favors.
8. Specialists had few fixed routines in ceremonies, but some had personal prohibitions or obligations connected with the supernatural.	8. Different. There were general obligations (prayers, etc.) on all specialists that were required despite difficulties in carrying them out. The routine of ceremonies was fixed.
9. Every individual sought some supernatural power, through dreams and visions. Specialists got more power through visions of especially powerful supernaturals, or by having a series of visions instead of the customary single one.	9. Different. The average individual did what he was told to do by the specialists. The specialist became one through long study in special schools but he sought knowledge, not supernatural power.

their practices than they did in their beliefs. Among other things, Christians usually have permanent religious buildings separate from their homes and do not normally erect a special structure inside the house for each ceremony. Most of the major Christian groups do not expect their religious leaders to go into a trance or to be hidden from sight during ceremonies. Christians tend to be suspicious of trances and of hidden activities.

The role of women in Christian ceremonies is almost unique among the world's religions. On the one hand, women are supposed to be devout specta-

A worshiper in Guatemala. *(Jacques Jangoux)*

tors, present at almost all ceremonies. On the other hand, until recently women were not supposed to participate in the ceremonies *except* as spectators or in very minor roles. In many of the other religions of the world, women are either excluded entirely from participation or even observation of many ceremonies or else are permitted to become religious specialists themselves. Le Jeune reports that women (except for one with a special role to play) were excluded from the Montagnais ceremonies. This complete exclusion of women must have seemed strange to the Jesuit, and the active participation of the only female exception, even stranger. Moreover, in Le Jeune's religion, nonspecialists were not allowed the sort of active role the Montagnais seemed to expect from their average male citizen (and the exceptional female).

The Montagnais differed from Le Jeune's society in the kinds of specialists they had. All except the simplest of societies have specialists who deal with the supernatural. (In the simplest societies, each individual acts as his own "specialist," but even there, some may be recognized as better at it than others.) The Montagnais, with a relatively simple society based on hunting, had at least two types of part-time religious specialists. Neither of these behaved the way Le Jeune expected such persons to behave in *his* system. In other words, the French and Montagnais roles of the religious specialist had quite different contents. Le Jeune distinguished the two Montagnais types by using the term *juggler* for one and either *sorcerer* or *magician* for the other. From Le Jeune's point of view, the term *juggler* was more derogatory; it meant a trickster, a ventriloquist, a sleight-of-hand artist. He compared the juggler at one point to the puppeteers of France. A magician or sorcerer, on the other hand, was one who could interact with evil supernatural beings. Although Le Jeune called one of the Montagnais a magician or a sorcerer, he wrote that he would leave it to the reader to decide "if this man is really a Magician." Le Jeune obviously thought he was not. A more subtle indication of Le Jeune's skepticism is that when he wrote about a "real" magician or sorcerer in this excerpt, he used a capital "M" or "S," but when he wrote about the Montagnais specialist, he always used a lower-case *m* or *s*.

Several characteristics of the religious specialists that anthropologists call shamans° are mentioned by Le Jeune in the excerpt. A shaman is supposed to have personal supernatural power, whereas a priest does not. Le Jeune indicates that the Montagnais believed the juggler could separate his soul from his body and could continue to control it. His detached soul could shake the tent and could attract supernatural beings to the tent. The disembodied spirit could also make a variety of noises. In other reports of similar ceremonies, the religious specialist might be bound before being placed in the tent (Leach 1949:56–57). The activity that then takes place is regarded as proof that the spirit, and not the physical body of the specialist, is making its presence felt and heard. On some occasions, the bound specialist disappears from the tent and appears outside after the ceremony. (Perhaps this is what Le Jeune observed when he mentioned that the juggler "made his exit from the tent and from our little cabin so swiftly, that he was outside almost before I was aware of it.")

A shaman often intervenes with the supernatural world for the benefit of someone. A priest generally explains the will of the supernatural, but his intervention, if any, is usually limited to suggesting a course of action to petitioners and occasionally performing a ritual or prayer for them. Le Jeune describes the effort made by one specialist to attract the spirits and by another to interrogate them. In the second ceremony, he reports the attempt of one sorcerer to use the supernatural against another. In some societies, a shaman may invade the supernatural world and even do battle with supernatural beings to compel them to grant human wishes (Howells 1962:127).

Another characteristic of shamans is that they are highly individualistic and neither learn nor teach a highly organized body of doctrine. A shaman may learn a few specialized techniques from other shamans, but such knowledge is individually held and individually passed from one to another. Most of the shaman's power and knowledge comes from direct personal revelation obtained through visions and dreams. A priest° is a member of an organized group of religious specialists and learns an organized body of doctrine, often in a special school. The Montagnais had no such school or organized doctrine. Other parts of Le Jeune's report indicate that the Montagnais specialists were highly individualistic. Their specialists are accordingly classified as closer to shamans than to priests. The distinction between a shaman and a priest is useful for purposes of analysis, but as is true of so many human patterns, the behavioral reality is often closer to a continuum than to a dichotomy. Many religious specialists seem to behave in ways that are intermediate between the analytical extremes. In dealing with specific societies, anthropologists have therefore tended to use a term in the local dialect, or to translate it, if possible, into such terms as "star gazer" or "fortune teller."

Le Jeune mentions several other characteristics of religious behavior. One was that absolute darkness was required for the ceremony, the spirits being reluctant to approach in the light. This fondness for darkness and dislike of light as characteristic of spirits is a belief held the world over. Many religions believe that night is a time for heightened supernatural activity. Folk Christianity, particularly in the past, generally assumed that nocturnal spirits were evil. A form of light is involved in almost all Christian ceremonies, and expressions such as "ye are the light of the world" form a part of Christian religious writings. Other Middle Eastern religions (for example, Zoroastrianism) also correlate darkness with evil and light with good, but such a correlation is by no means universal.

Participants in the Montagnais ceremonies were expected to sing and dance. In native-American rituals, dance is often a form of prayer as important to the proper conduct of a ceremony as verbal prayers and songs. The removal of dancing from religious ceremonies is almost unique to Christianity and may have been a reaction to its importance in other religions that were regarded as devil worship.

When the spirit or soul was separated from the shaman's body, it manifested its presence by sparks and noises. Thus, the hooting of owls and the strange voices mentioned in the excerpt are still regarded by some native Americans as evidence of supernatural activity. The owl particularly is frequently associated with the supernatural, perhaps because of its nocturnal activities. Le Jeune reported that the Montagnais disagreed about exactly what happened inside the tent during the ceremony. Some felt that the shaman had actually disappeared; others thought only his soul moved. Le Jeune regarded this disagreement as evidence that the Montagnais beliefs were false, since *his* system had no tolerance for disagreement. The Montagnais, without a formally organized doctrine, were less concerned with individually variant beliefs.

Spirit possession of religious specialists is another characteristic found the world over. It is known in Christianity, although it has usually been regarded as characteristic of fringe sects, or as possession by the devil. Saints or individuals capable of performing miracles have not usually been regarded so much as possessed by supernaturals as being able to influence or attract their favor in some way.

THE ORIGINS OF RELIGION: SOME HYPOTHESES

What is the origin of religion? Why do humans engage in this kind of behavior at all? A believer would answer by pointing out the need to take some account of the supernatural world, but that answer does not satisfy everyone. Is it possible to find another basis for the origin of religion? As far as we know, human beings are the only animals who wonder where they came from, or what their purpose in life may be. Wolves, sparrows, ants—all go through life untroubled by the search for identity or meaning that bedevils the human being. Modern theology and much of modern philosophical thinking are still devoted to the search for understanding, for purpose, for some higher or more certain reality than what appears immediately obvious. The human also is apparently the only animal who can lose motivation and, as a result, die. Other animals may give up the struggle because of exhaustion or privation, but apparently only humans can worry or brood themselves into suicide. A detailed discussion of all the hypotheses that have been advanced to account for this behavior or for the origin of religious beliefs is too complex and extensive for us to take up here. We can, however, make a beginning.

How old is religion? How long have humans engaged in religious behavior? What is the earliest evidence of such activity? These are questions we can answer. The earliest documents recovered so far are from the cradle of civilization in Mesopotamia, and they reveal an already well-established system. Religion began long before writing. Evidence from earlier periods is necessarily indirect, but inferences have been made from the available data, and analogies from modern or historical religious systems have been used to support those inferences.

Art, dating from the Upper Paleolithic period (in Europe some 25,000 to 15,000 years ago), is helpful. Cave paintings of creatures that are part human, part animal, can hardly be representations of reality; they are more likely symbolic of supernatural or imaginary beings. Small figurines with exaggerated female sexual characteristics and no facial features, hands, or feet are also more likely representations of a fertility principle than portraits. Some of the famous cave paintings of the type found at Altamira in Spain or Lascaux in France show wounded animals. One suggestion is that these paintings were made to ensure success in the hunt by imitating the desired result (Howell 1965:148). If this suggestion is correct, the paintings would indicate that one of the major principles of magic (the Law of Imitation) had already been developed. Some of the paintings were done in virtually inaccessible parts of the caves. Their location is difficult to explain on the basis of an esthetic motivation for art. In other cases, several paintings were superimposed, although other parts of the cave walls were left empty. Again, this is difficult to explain if the paintings were being done for esthetic reasons. If, however, one speculates that a particular spot was believed to be supernaturally powerful, then the choice is a logical one. The cave paintings therefore suggest that some of the major concepts of religion had developed by this time. (Cave art is discussed at greater length on page 329.)

The cave paintings are not the first evidence we have of religious beliefs, however. Neanderthal, who lived 70,000 to 150,000 years ago during the last glacial period, and whose skeletal remains are associated with the cultural assemblage known as Mousterian,° buried his dead, sometimes with grave offerings, and often sprinkled or painted them with red ocher° (a natural iron-oxide pigment) (Chard 1969:222). We do not know anything else about the religious beliefs of this early kind of human, but we assume from the burial evidence that he believed in some sort of afterlife.

For an earlier time, we cannot rely heavily on present evidence. It has been suggested that Peking man, a type of *Homo erectus*° who lived from 250,000 to 500,000 years ago, may have extracted brains from the skulls of his dead for religious purposes (Roper 1969:427ff.). So many alternative explanations have

A prehistoric cave painting of a deer hunt in Spain. *(Courtesy of the American Museum of Natural History)*

been advanced for the available evidence, however, that we cannot make even that tentative suggestion with any certainty. As more and more information is accumulated on the early human forms, it is possible that we will be able to answer questions about the antiquity of religion with more confidence. At present, it appears that Neanderthal may have been the first to have had some form of religion, but future discoveries may reveal that religion is even older.

THE FUNCTIONS OF RELIGION

What accounts for the wide distribution and persistence of religion? Why do people react with so much emotion to a threatened change in religion? (Witness the furor over the American Supreme Court decision to keep prayers and Bible reading out of the school; the protests over changes in the Roman Catholic Mass; the turmoil over the Pope's encyclical *Humanae Vitae*.) One approach to these questions has been to concentrate on the functions religion seems to serve in society. The various hypotheses by anthropologists and sociologists seem to fall into three major categories:

1. Religion relieves anxieties in areas of life over which man has little or no control.
2. Religion integrates and binds together members of the society.
3. Religion justifies and explains customs and traditions.

In Le Jeune's report of the first ceremony, questions were asked by the sorcerer about weather conditions, the location of game, and the outcome of specific cases of disease. An examination of ceremonies in other parts of the world frequently reveals a similar preoccupation with weather, food sources, and individual well-being. These are all matters that bear on individual and consequently on societal survival. They are all areas in which humans, particularly non-Western peoples, have little or no control. Humans everywhere are concerned with health (particularly when it is bad) and with food (particularly when the supply is not adequate or reliable). The relationship of the weather to food is obvious for agricultural peoples, but weather is also significant to hunters, although not in quite the same way. The Montagnais depended on snow in winter to track game more easily. With snowshoes, they could travel over deep snow that exhausted or confined heavier mammals such as moose, elk, and deer. The spirits' pronouncement that they saw "a little" snow must have been disheartening to the Montagnais, but at least they would not sit in camp waiting for snow. The moose were far away, which was also bad news, but at least a man could hunt other game and would not waste his time trying to find moose.

Le Jeune scorned the spirit response in regard to the health of the sorcerer and his wife because the prophecies seemed obvious to him, but were they so obvious to the sorcerer? The sorcerer's own disease may have been uncomfortable enough to make him uneasy about the possible outcome. In the case of his wife, he might have hoped that the spirits could suggest a course of action to save her. In any event, even though the prediction about his wife was bad, he was no longer anxious, because he *knew* what would happen: in situations such as his, an unpleasant certainty is often less difficult to bear than uncertainty. The second ceremony Le Jeune described indicates how an individual may alleviate fear by positive action. It would therefore seem that the Montagnais evidence supports the hypothesis that religion serves to relieve anxiety. On the other hand, religion may also create anxiety. The Christian sinner, the Navajo who touches a corpse, the Polynesian who breaks a tabu—all suffer varying degrees of anxiety directly caused by religion. However, the religion itself usually provides a way to cope with such anxieties.

Another function suggested for religion is that it serves to integrate the community. There are many activities that bind people together, of course, and not all of them can be classed as religious. Suggesting that one function of religion is to integrate a community is *not* the same as saying that *only* religious rites integrate a community or that integration of a community is the *only* function of religion. The adult males of the community described by Le Jeune were called in to cooperate in the ceremonies. In the ritual aimed at killing an enemy sorcerer, the situation clearly defined group members as defending one of their own against external hostility. Both ceremonies emphasized the bonds

A meeting of Black Muslims in the United States. Greater numbers of followers seem to be attracted to religious movements in a society under stress. *(Roger Malloch/Magnum)*

between group members and reinforced their sense of community. But women and children were excluded from these ceremonies. Would this not work against the integration of the society? The very fact of exclusion could add to the solidarity of the men and could even increase a sense of solidarity among the women, since they were all in the category of excluded people. Historical documentation reveals integrative elements other than religious ones that bound women and children into the larger society. The Montagnais example as presented in the excerpt supports the hypothesis that religion may serve an integrative function for at least some segments of society.

The description of other rituals also tends to support the hypothesis. Any of the crisis rites, religious or otherwise, serves to integrate a society by uniting people in a cooperative endeavor, by clearly making public a change in the status of members, and by reaffirming group concepts. (Reciting values or behaviors appropriate to the new status is often a part of crisis rites.) When crisis rites involve the supernatural, religion is again playing an integrative role in the society. A related binding force is the special relationship individuals or groups within a society may feel themselves to have with an animal or object in their environment. Ceremonies involving these totems° serve to integrate the society. The strength of the bond that some peoples feel toward totems has intrigued researchers for years, yet the similarity of totemism to modern Western practices of selecting a group mascot or symbol went unnoticed for some time (Linton 1936:424–426). The use of a group symbol is clearly integrative regardless of whether the supernatural is involved. When it is involved, then once again religion is helping to integrate the society.

Another type of religious behavior, called revitalization,° nativistic revival,° or messianic movement,° is also of interest. Under certain circumstances, a society may experience a religious upheaval. A charismatic leader appears, a "new" doctrine is promulgated (which actually may be only a modification of an old doctrine), followers are attracted, converts with strong, even fanatical, convictions increase, and the whole society may be swept up in a mass movement that often radically and permanently changes the nature of the system. Studies of such cases seem to indicate that they occur when a society is suffering severe stress or has just passed through a period of disaster and demoralization (Mooney 1965:2ff.). The new religious formulation appears to strengthen and reunify the society. Not enough is known about these movements yet to be able to explain precisely why they have this effect. One suggestion is that the new doctrine relieves anxieties caused by the stress and provides an acceptable rationale for changes (or persistences) in behavior. By doing this, the movement reestablishes the morale and motivation of individuals in the society. Since this is a prerequisite for survival, a revitalization movement once again makes a system viable.

The integrative hypothesis has been criticized on the basis that religion has caused considerable friction and conflict both within and between societies. Violent confrontations based on religion still occur today (the current Protestant-Catholic trouble in Northern Ireland is an example, and the Middle Eastern situation is aggravated by the religious differences of the participants).

However, cases where religion divides rather than integrates all appear to be instances of competition between two or more belief systems. Apparently, so long as there is only one religious system within a society, it serves to integrate the members of that society. Competition between two or more systems, however, creates intense factionalism and may completely rupture the society. The most severe competition between religious systems occurs if both are exclusive and missionary religions. Exclusive tribal religions cannot compete for members because of the belief that one must be born into the religion and cannot convert. If the tribal religions are inclusive, they will tend to amalgamate and believers will simply add to the number of supernatural entities they worship.

Religion is also said to support the values of the society by providing an explanation and justification for customs and traditions. The short excerpt by Le Jeune does not illustrate this characteristic, but his longer report does. For example, bones of certain game animals were burned rather than being thrown to the dogs, because the Montagnais believed the generalized spirit of these animals would be offended if the bones were eaten by dogs and that the spirit would then not permit any more of the animals to be caught. Le Jeune and other Europeans were continually being frustrated in their attempts to change Indian behavior (as distinct from their beliefs) because the Indians protested that the new behavior was offensive to the supernatural or that continuation of the old behavior was essential to maintain good relationships with the supernatural.

Conflict between members of rival religions in Northern Ireland. *(Leif Skoogfore/ Woodfin Camp & Associates)*

These functions (which are not necessarily the only possible functions a religion may perform in a specific society) help to explain the emotion an attack on religion arouses. To believers, an attack on their religion cannot be regarded simply as a matter of criticism of some abstract philosophical hypothesis. It is a threat to their personal survival, to the society in which they live, and to the values in which they believe. It should not surprise anyone that missionaries very often become martyrs.

OTHER MORALE BUILDERS

Religion is not the only aspect of culture that contributes to maintaining morale and motivation, of course. Art is another, and has been mentioned briefly in connection with religion. Its history, so far as we can tell, is almost as old as religion itself, and if the refinement of stone tools beyond functional necessity can be classed as "art," then it may be much older. Tools begin very early to show an elaboration that seems to be esthetic rather than functional. But beyond this elaboration, we do not know what art—if any—may have been practiced by early hominids (such as *Homo erectus* or the australopithecines). Did they, for example, make baskets, or use animal skins or internal organs to transport liquids and other things? If so, did they decorate them? We do not know, for if any art forms did exist, they were confined to perishable materials and left no traces. All we can say for certain is that the history of art may be much older than any evidence we have.

With the appearance of unmistakable *Homo sapiens,* however, a great deal of artistic evidence appears on the archeological scene, relatively suddenly—painting, carving, and a variety of decorative elements in tools and clothing. We do not know the reason for this apparently sudden florescence of art. It may have had something to do with the biological evolution of the human brain, or it may be more related to preservation of evidence. Or there may have been other factors involved. Additional research may shed some light on the situation (Chard 1975:175–176).

There are traditionally three classifications of the art of this prehistoric period: chattel (or *art moblier,* sometimes also called portable art), cave art, and rock art (Chard 1975:180). Humans of this time appear to have been much like ourselves in mental and physical characteristics (Marshack 1972:11, 24–25; Chard 1975:175), although their knowledge of the world, and world view, may well have been quite different. Nevertheless, they do seem to have been like us even in subtle ways, because their art still arouses emotions in us across the millennia—though, again, whether these are the same emotions they felt, we cannot be sure.

Portable, or chattel, art was of several different sorts. There were small figurines with exaggerated sexual characteristics, for example. Some, polished from much handling, were apparently carried around for quite a while, held, and rubbed, or hung around the neck. It has been suggested that these were worn or used as charms or amulets, although it has also been suggested that they were kept simply because they were esthetically pleasing to their owners (Chard 1975:184). Other statuettes that show no evidence of use or wear were apparently discarded almost as soon as they were made. These may have been used to illustrate a myth or legend or to reassure someone in a crisis situation such as childbirth (Marshack 1972:286–287).

In addition to the figurines, there were beads, necklaces, pendants, and other objects of personal decoration. Attractive shells and pieces of amber were among the first objects (together with flint and obsidian) to move along the earliest long-distance trade routes known.

Cave art is familiar to the modern educated person. The famous painting in the caves of southwestern Europe (France and Spain) have been the subject of numerous books, films, and television specials. Carvings in the same areas and by the same peoples are less well known but are also impressive. The motives that inspired the paintings probably inspired the carvings as well. A new approach to the carvings and paintings of prehistoric man by Alexander Marshack suggests motivations other than religious ones. Much of the art work can be related to seasonal or lunar motifs and may have had either calendrical or explanatory uses. According to Marshack, some of the nonrepresentative markings were apparently made to keep track of the phases of the moon or certain other time-sequenced events. Representational carvings or paintings, he suggests, illustrated stories, possibly explanatory, about those events (1972).

Although some of the paintings and carvings are in almost inaccessible places, and therefore were not, apparently, meant for exhibition, others are in large caverns; on the basis of their location and other evidence, it would seem that the latter were meant to be viewed, at least at the time of special ceremonies such as initiation rites (Chard 1975:185; Marshack 1972:15). There may also have been paintings or carvings closer to living areas, but since these areas were not sealed off from erosion as were the others, the intervening 20,000 to 30,000 years could have destroyed all traces.

Rock art involves painting and carving either on sheltered rock faces or on independent and free-standing rocks. The age of these art forms is very difficult to determine, unless the rock either has been buried by or is itself covering, something of fixed date. In addition, since the rock art is far more exposed to the effects of weather than even the cave art, it is poorly preserved (especially the paintings), and most of it is probably not very old.

From ethnographic accounts we know that some rock art is done today to illustrate important myths and legends (Gould 1969:147–148), and some to alleviate boredom (Navajo children herding sheep have been responsible for some rock drawings, for example), but rarely if ever is any done for esthetic motives alone. There is no good reason to think prehistoric rock art was motivated differently.

Huge rock statues, heads, or other forms of monolithic carvings have been found in many parts of the world. It is sometimes hard for members of highly mechanized societies geared to the digital read-out clock to believe that prehistoric peoples with simple tools could have made these enormous artifacts. But with enough time and effort, people using simple tools can accomplish a great

deal. It is now known that the technological abilities of early humans were quite impressive. By the time of *Homo sapiens,* people were as intelligent as we; they simply were not as knowledgeable. But given the information and tools they had to work with, prehistoric peoples were as efficient and ingenious at solving problems as we are (Marshack 1972:24–25; Wauchope 1962:23–27).

All these artistic endeavors apparently satisfied psychological needs of prehistoric peoples as they do the needs of modern individuals—whether these needs were precisely the same or different in some way. From the fact that we appreciate a great many of the things made by prehistoric peoples, one could assume that the needs were similar, if not identical. Color, variety, and something perceived as "beauty" have been valued in most societies of which we have any record. Prehistoric textiles, feathered cloaks, decorated tools and utensils are still impressive or lovely to look at; temples and other monumental structures were painted and otherwise attractively decorated; shells, feathers, colored stones, and various decorative minerals were used in ways that even today are regarded as beautiful. Yet art also provides an example of one of the central problems in understanding humanity. While art may communicate across both centuries and cultural boundaries with some people, tastes differ and in some cases there may be no communication even within one culture. What constitutes beauty continues to be a source of argument, and concepts of beauty—like other concepts—appear to be mostly learned.

Storytelling is another way of maintaining morale and motivation. It is probably as old as true language, but there are no unequivocal traces of it until the development of written language. Most paintings and sculptures of prehistoric peoples consist of single scenes, or single and multiple group pictures— not of sequences like a comic strip. If, as Marshack suggests, they were used in some cases to illustrate stories, we have no way of knowing today what the stories were or what the connecting links were, if any, between scenes (1972:40). Yet Marshack's approach is convincing in many ways. The painting on cave walls *could,* in many instances, illustrate some of the earliest stories recorded: accounts of the gods and goddesses or culture heroes (individuals who are said to have taught the ancestors of a particular society how to do things and the proper way to live); explanations for seasonal events, geographic features, human customs, animal characteristics; tales of animals and of people interacting and having a common language; and so on (Marshack 1972:169–340). Whatever the antiquity of storytelling, virtually all human groups, present or known past, have practiced it and still do, most commonly to account for the origin of things, to instruct the young, and to entertain all ages. The ability to tell a story in a way that will amuse, excite, or impress an audience that has heard the same one hundreds of times before is greatly prized. Expert storytellers are in demand and highly respected as a rule. A story does not have to be new to be

One of the Colossi of Memnon, a monument to one of the god-kings of Egypt. *(Elliot Erwitt/Magnum)*

popular, and people of some societies seem to prefer old favorites, although people in other societies reward the innovative as well as the polished narrator.

Conversation and storytelling were, for centuries, the main sources of information, instruction, and entertainment, and in many parts of the world where literacy is not widespread, they still are. The feats of memory performed in such societies are impressive. For years, it was assumed that oral history could not be trusted, and there are still cautions that must be observed in its use, but today it is recognized that at least some peoples have preserved certain aspects of their history with reasonable accuracy for centuries (Saggs 1960:772).

The study of folklore attracted a great deal of attention during the nineteenth century when some researchers noticed that particular themes were widely found in the oral literature of the world. Certain story ideas, found in areas far apart with no history of contact between their peoples, were assumed by some folklorists to have spread from one center, and much effort was put into trying to trace them to their point of origin. Like the people who thought all civilization spread from Egypt, these folklorists believed that every legendary hero was a manifestation of the sun god and therefore had been inspired by Egyptian or some Middle Eastern mythology. Other people were searching in the folklore of the world for confirmation of biblical stories, such as the creation of Adam and Eve, or the Flood. Every story of an inundation was taken as verification of the story of Noah and therefore as proof of the reliability of the Bible. Naturally a number of controversies swirled around the important figures in the field. Max Müller was one of the most famous scholars and he aroused the ire of many researchers because he insisted that none of the important figures in folklore and legends had ever existed. All, from Asian to African to North and South American heroes, were manifestations of the Sun God myth. Müller developed an elaborate methodology for analyzing legends to support his theory. One of the more effective counterattacks against him was by Henri Gaidoz, who believed that many legends recorded (if in exaggerated form) exploits of real people. Using Müller's own techniques, he "demonstrated" that Müller did not really exist but was himself a manifestation of the Sun God myth (Gaidoz 1884:73–88). One of the most convincing arguments against the extreme diffusionist° approach came from Sigmund Freud, whose postulation of universal human psychological processes attempted to explain the frequent appearance of certain themes without resorting to any theory of a spread from a single center. The modern approach is somewhere between the two extremes. Folklore today is collected to be appreciated for its own sake, to be analyzed for what it may reveal about a society's world view, and to be compared with other examples for themes that might reveal either the psychological unity of man *or* past contacts with other peoples. Some stories can easily be shown to have traveled amazing distances (apparently all the world loves a good story), but others seem to have developed independently. In general, the more elaborate or fantastic the details and the more arbitrary the connection between elements of identical or closely similar tales that show up in two widely separated parts of the world, the more likely it is that a single story has traveled. However, stories dealing with common human experiences or emotions, such as rivalry between siblings, between males over a woman (or women over a male); desertion or abandonment of children, spouses, or parents; being orphaned; quarreling with relatives for almost any reason; jealousy; greed; and so on, are quite likely to be independent inventions.

Storytelling, in any case, has contributed greatly to the maintenance of morale and motivation in the past, and still does, although the stories are now told (in complex societies) through the medium of books, magazines, newspapers, movies, and television instead of being recited around campfires, at feasts, or during special ceremonies.

Music is another source of entertainment that helps maintain morale and motivation. Again, the origin and antiquity are uncertain. Chimpanzees rhythmically beat on their chests and call in a particular way before starting some displays (van Lawick-Goodall 1971:45, 66–67), a characteristic which may have been a forerunner of music. Whistles and drums are found in almost all cultures, suggesting a possible early evolution of these instruments. Music based only on drums and the human voice is often simple both in rhythm and tone, though not necessarily. The best examples of complex music using few and simple instruments come from Africa where, in some societies, vocal and drum music has as many as a dozen separate rhythms combined in intricate patterns to give

Musical drums and players in South Africa. *(SATOUR)*

a sum that is greater than its parts in a way analagous to the symphony in Western music (Bohannan 1971:81–82). Music, as it is known in the complex cultures, however, appears to be a relatively late development. There is no space in an introductory text for a full discussion of the complexity of music in different cultures. It is an aspect of life that has been seriously neglected by anthropologists in general, partly because few have had the necessary training to study it adequately in the field. Like linguistics, it requires considerable skill to note music by hand. Modern recording equipment, however, should make investigation and "note-taking" in the field much easier in the future. Ethnomusicology is a recognized subfield of anthropology that is seriously understaffed, but it may be that with the modern equipment interest will grow as better material is brought back from the field by relatively untrained researchers for study at home by specialists.

Another area that has been rather neglected is the dance. Its antiquity is suggested by some of the cave paintings and rock art which appear to represent dancing figures. Nearly all societies of the world have some form of dance, the most common probably being dances that imitate animal behavior or that tell a story. Modern photographic equipment makes recording dances for later analysis a simpler procedure than it used to be, but even in the earlier years of American anthropology, some excellent films were taken (for example, Mead's *Trance and Dance in Bali,* available through New York University). Gertrude Kurath is an anthropologist who has probably made the most extensive studies of dance patterns. She devised ways to record dance patterns but, unfortunately, few anthropologists have learned these well enough to use them in the field (*cf.* Kurath 1950, 1954). Again, improved equipment may make it possible for relatively untrained people to bring back material for expert study.

Storytelling, music, and dance have been combined in a few cultures to make a form of drama, but the history of the theater, true drama itself, is virtually limited to complex cultures and the relatively recent past. This area, too, has not been well studied. The neglect is somewhat surprising, since several of the early anthropologists were artists in their own right. (Ruth Benedict was a poet who wrote under the name of Anne Singleton, and Edward Sapir was a concert pianist, for example.) In complex cultures, various forms of drama and theater have significantly served the functions of maintaining morale and motivation, but a full exposition of the history of the theater in complex societies would require at least another book (*cf.* Brockett 1974).

Another neglected area that plays a significant part in maintaining morale and motivation is games and play in general. Play is not unique to humans, of course; in fact, all mammals play as young animals. Adult animal play is rare, however, except among some of the higher mammals. Jane van Lawick-Goodall has recorded a number of instances of adult chimpanzees, both male and female, joining the young in games of tickling, chasing, and play fighting (1971:107–109, 153–158). Humans, on the other hand, regularly engage in play both as young and as adults. In fact, most societies have special games designed particularly for adults. The most widespread adult games are the making of string figures and a variety of gambling games; competitions of skill for males, such as racing or spear-throwing, are also quite common. Games have been divided into categories of games of skill, chance, and strategy, with the aim of correlating specific child-training, cultural, and personality characteristics with the relative emphasis members of a particular society place on different types of games (Roberts, Arth, and Bush 1959:604; Roberts, Hoffman, and Sutton-Smith 1965:26–29). Another researcher has compared the emphasis on violent games with the occurrence of violence in a society, to test the hypothesis that violent games act as a catharsis and consequently reduce the ingroup violence (Sipe 1975). The results (which contradict the hypothesis) are somewhat ambiguous and controversial, yet the research suggests some interesting correlations that would seem to justify additional study.

Native Americans played several kinds of games, including lacrosse, which has become a modern popular sport. Another game is known only through prehistoric paintings and the large ball courts that were used for playing it. These are found throughout Mesoamerica° and in the American Southwest. Details of how the game was played have not yet been entirely discovered, although some general ideas have been deduced. Many of the native-American games involved gambling, and European missionaries disapproved strongly of the extent to which various groups were addicted to betting. In many parts of the world, including native America, games were and still are played in connection with religious ceremonies, or at least have a supernatural component. This was true, for example, in Europe and the early historic Middle East where Greek and earlier civilizations engaged in a variety of sports and contests that had supernatural aspects. Minoan bull-vaulting, known from paintings and carvings, is only one example (Hawkes 1968: plate 9; Hutchinson 1968: plate 16).

All these activities provide entertainment as well as fulfilling some of the functions also met by religion. In addition, all of them, music, storytelling, painting, sculpture, games, and the rest, have been involved with religions in many societies. During recorded history, at least, all the arts have served to entertain, instruct, and inspire men. There is no reason to assume that their function when they first appeared was substantially different. They almost surely enhanced the effectiveness of religion and have shown throughout history a strong capacity to assist in the maintenance of morale and motivation in their own right, even when they were not directly tied into the service of religion.

SUMMARY

One of the prerequisites for the survival of a society is the maintenance of morale and motivation among its members. Human beings seem prone to questions about the value of life and what they are doing as members of society. They must have justification for and receive satisfaction from doing what needs to be done in the society. Religion and the arts have served to provide answers to those difficult human questions mentioned in the introduction to this chapter, or at least to distract people from thinking about the questions, and to make life a joyous, interesting experience worth living. Today, due at least partly to the secularization of society, to the compartmentalization of life, and to the specialization of roles, many people in industrial societies are not firm believers in a religion, and also are not willing or able to practice the various arts; they are, at most, spectators. Since "art" in all its forms has been relegated to a secondary place in society, regarded as "impractical," called a "luxury frill" in educational systems, and removed almost entirely from vocational and technical schools (except those directly connected *with* the arts), and since religion is usually regarded as even less "practical" than art, the average citizen is apt to have comparatively little contact with either. The current crisis experienced by many people over the question of the meaningfulness of life may be partly due to this isolation from what have been throughout human history the main sources of morale and motivation.

In modern society, particularly recently, individuals have been torn by doubts about the worth of many of the basic assumptions, values, and practices of the system. It is extremely difficult, perhaps impossible, to arrive at an objective conclusion that one way of life is better than some other. In most societies of the past and in a few of the present, such questions have been settled by an appeal to tradition (this is the way our fathers did it, so it is good enough for us), to ethnic group pride (I am a Hopi and this is the Hopi way), or to the supernatural (this way is best because it is the way God commanded). All these reasons provided most members of a given society with a reason for "right" behavior and with a deep satisfaction and security when they performed properly in the expected manner. The rewards for meeting expectations, however demanding, were consequently greater than the difficulties and frustrations encountered in trying to meet them. Perhaps a perception of this satisfaction is the source of the idyllic picture of "savage life" so often presented by the uneasy and critical members of an industrialized society.

Today, none of these ancient supports seems acceptable to members of mass industrial societies. There have been attempts to shore up customs by appeals to logic, to utility, to humanitarianism, or to some other rational foundation, but so far nothing has gained the general emotional commitment of earlier methods. Until something is found that can permit or create the kind of satisfaction and security people previously obtained from the proper performance of their societal roles, modern societies will continue to be disrupted by the dissatisfied, the alienated, and the discontented.

10 Concepts and Trends in Anthropology

Human beings have been interested in their fellow creatures and their history for centuries. C. Leonard Woolley reports that there was a kind of museum in Ur, one of the earliest sites of civilization (Woolley 1965:204). Herodotus is famous for his descriptions of "foreign" cultures. Since the beginning of writing (and possibly long before), there has been speculation about foreign or "different" cultures and about the possible reasons for the variations. Anthropology —the study of the human being—is only the most recent label attached to this interest.

A SHORT DESCRIPTION OF THE FIELD

Modern anthropology, as practiced in the United States, is divided into two major areas. One, physical anthropology,° deals with man as a biological organism (this is the only part of the discipline most Europeans call anthropology). It includes the study of physical variation in man, human diseases, human physical development, geographic distribution of biological characteristics, processes of evolutionary change, and any other physical or biological matters involving man. Because of the interest in evolution, some physical anthropologists have also engaged in extensive study of primates other than man and in paleontology° (the study of fossils). Very little information from physical anthropology was used in this book, and that mostly in the first chapter. The other major division of anthropology deals with the human individual as a social and cultural being. Here human concepts are studied through the behavior stemming from them. This division has three distinct branches: linguistics,° archeology,° and cultural anthropology.

Linguistics is the study of language. People interested in this field have occasionally pursued their studies without paying any but incidental attention to the speakers or the meaning of the sounds made. They have concentrated on sound patterns and the organized structure of the speech itself. (Many, of course, have studied other culturally motivated human behavior besides speech or have concentrated on ascertaining the meaning of words. Still, linguists often differ from other anthropologists in being less involved with the people they study.) Linguistics is among the most "scientific" of the divisions of cultural anthropology. (Its closest rival in this area is the study of kinship, which also has a vigorous methodology and perhaps the most sophisticated body of theory in the social sciences [Schusky 1974:65].) It has elegant and sophisticated theories as well as rigorous methodology. The earliest linguistic studies were concerned with structure, grammar, and sounds. Many linguists today concern themselves primarily with describing the sound patterns and grammar of a language. They look for patterns and regularities in the ways sounds in a particular language are combined to make meaningful utterances, and the ways these are combined to make longer and more complex meaningful utterances. The terms *words* and *sentences* are so bound to our own language that linguists have developed an entire vocabulary of their own. Phonetics,° which deals with the transmission, production, and reception of sounds, is not usually a primary concern of the linguist, although for practical purposes, all must learn some method of phonetic transcription of a language in order to study it properly. Linguists are generally more concerned with phonemes° (single speech sounds) or a group of similar ones that function the same way in a particular language (Sturtevant 1947:16). Each of the various sounds that go to make up a phoneme is called a allophone. Naturally, these vary from one language to another, and it is from the last part of the word *phonemic* that anthropologists took the term *emic* to refer to the approach that studies a culture from the point of view of someone in it. The term *phonetics* provided the word *etic* to refer to a classification based on some outside, set standard. Linguists refer to the smallest unit of meaning, made up of one or more phonemes, as a *morpheme,*° and distinguish two types, free and bound. The free morphemes we would call words, but the bound ones are only (from our point of view) parts of words—the *s* of *dogs* that turns one dog into more than one, or the *er* that turns the verb *count* into the noun *counter,* the person or thing that counts (Bloomfield 1933:177–178).

Linguists today have gone far beyond these beginnings, and no longer confine themselves to questions of structure. Morris Swadesh, for example, through studies of the regularities of change in sounds and vocabulary developed a method he said could date the separation of peoples who spoke related tongues. This approach, called glottochronology, is based on the hypothesis (tested on languages of people with a written history) that (1) certain terms, such as words for parts of the body, fire, water, and so on, do not change rapidly, or easily drop out of a language; (2) that sounds change in a regular way; and (3) that both types of changes occur at a more or less constant rate. Consequently, by studying the amount and kinds of changes that have taken place in the key vocabulary list of two distinct but related languages, it is possible to tell how long the speakers of those languages have been separated. Although each of the assumptions in the hypothesis has been challenged, glottochronology has provided some helpful suggestions about prehistoric relationships and migrations of people speaking distinct but related tongues (Swadesh *et al.* 1954:361–377). Another significant figure in modern linguistics is Noam Chomsky. His attack on traditional and structuralist approaches to linguistic studies started a ferocious controversy that as yet shows few signs of disappearing.

The traditional approach to the analysis of language is to categorize parts of an utterance into previously defined categories (such as subject, object, noun, verb, and so on) in order to make the whole utterance meaningful for study (Harrison 1970:4). Structuralists who regard others as mentalists consider themselves empiricists. They attempt to analyze a sentence by dividing it into its natural parts and not assuming or attributing to it any hidden meaning. Parts of speech such as nouns are defined by what they do (the grammatical environment they regularly appear in), not what they mean (Harrison 1970:5–8).

Transformational grammar makes a major departure from this approach. First, it emphasizes something both structuralists and traditionalists ignore, that many utterances are ambiguous, that is, that they can be interpreted in more than one way. Chomsky says that for an adequate linguistic description the

X-ray of an Egyptian mummy in its case.

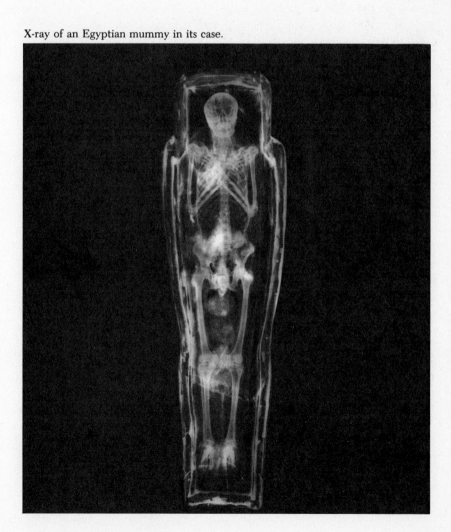

analyst must account for what the speaker must know to understand the utterance as well as what is said. The surface structure is what is said, the deep structure is what must be known to either produce or understand an utterance (Harrison 1970:9–11). Transformationalists also hypothesize that there are universal principles of grammar and that every child is born with an understanding of them (Harrison 1970:22; Grinder and Elgin 1973:209–210). Although the basic premises may be accepted, some of the implications and interpretations suggested by Chomsky have been strongly criticized or rejected. The most serious criticisms charge that Chomsky has said nothing that other linguists have not said before (and said more simply), that he has misrepresented other linguistic approaches in order to attack them, and that his approach, by mixing levels of analysis, confuses more than it clarifies. The arguments are so complex and technical that a beginner cannot be expected to follow them, but it is

A general view of an archeological dig in the Marquesas Islands in the South Pacific. *(Courtesy of the American Museum of Natural History)*

important to realize that not all linguists regard Chomsky as the savior of the field, although others apparently do. (For an example of the two sides, read reviews of Chomsky's works by Burling [1955:160–162], Lamb [1967:411–415], and Steiner [1969].) Some of the objections to Chomsky's hypotheses about universal and innate human mental characteristics are repeated in the criticisms directed toward Lévi-Strauss, another proponent of a mentalist approach (see pages 298).

Traditional linguistic study in anthropology is closer to the natural sciences in many ways than other approaches to the study of human behavior. The biological mechanisms for speech, the fine distinctions and variable combinations of sounds that make up words, the orderly patterning of sound combinations, the sound changes that occur, apparently without conscious interference by the speakers, are all subject to a mechanical and mathematical treatment that has not so far been possible with most other forms of human behavior. Perhaps the person who has most nearly attained the scientific elegance of the linguist is Birdwhistell in his studies of physical movement (1952). As in some linguistic approaches, it is possible in the study of human motion to separate the physical characteristics from the communication function meaning of the behavior.

Archeology at times can be as divorced from human behavior as linguistics. Some archeologists have concentrated on the physical characteristics of artifacts such as pottery, metal objects, or stone tools to such an extent that these implements have completely overshadowed their makers. Other archeologists have paid more attention to the human behavior that resulted in or made use of the artifacts found. Classical archeologists traditionally were interested in reconstructing the past. In their almost exclusive concentration on the art objects and inscriptions of early civilizations in the Mediterranean area, however, they discovered much about kings, rulers, and the upper classes, but very little about the daily life of ordinary people, and they ignored the rest of the world almost entirely. Traditionally, archeologists working in this area have been allied with classics departments rather than with anthropology. In recent decades, anthropologists using a wide variety of new techniques for analysis and recovery have been concentrating on a fuller reconstruction of past cultures not only in the Mediterranean area but all over the world. The trend in this direction has led to articles calling archeology the new social science. Archeological data are used in this book especially for material included in the first and second chapters.

Throughout this text, however, we have been primarily concerned with the third branch, cultural anthropology. In the United States the term *cultural anthropology* is more or less restricted to this branch, although both archeology and linguistics deal with culture at least occasionally, and their data (artifacts or verbal behavior) are all culturally motivated. In most of the rest of the world, what Americans call cultural anthropology is referred to as *ethnology*° and is regarded as distinct from anthropology. The British compromise and refer to *social anthropology*. Unless all these terms are kept in mind, books on "anthropology" written by Europeans can be confusing to Americans.

Only a brief introduction to the field of cultural anthropology (or ethnology or social anthropology) is contained in this volume. For example, each of the separate topics discussed in Chapters 1 through 9 could serve as the basis for one or more college courses. The data of anthropology are incredibly rich, and any introductory text can present only a bare minimum or run the risk of overwhelming the student. Two major interesting areas of anthropology have not even been mentioned as such, since they are broad enough to encompass all the topics we have discussed. Applied anthropology (also called culture change) and theory were left for this chapter, although some theoretical concepts have been integrated into previous chapters when appropriate.

It should be clear by now that anthropology is a field that offers something for almost everyone. If a student's interest lies in chemistry or biology, he or she could easily specialize in some phase of physical anthropology; if in law, the subdiscipline of primitive law and government beckons; if in the area of economics, the subfield of economic anthropology is open; if in the humanities, particularly art, folklore, music, or dance, these fields, too, are recognized subdisciplines in anthropology. The field of culture and personality is closely allied with psychology, while that of social organization is closer to sociology. There is virtually no field of interest that does not relate to anthropology in some way. Even nuclear physics has become involved in the development of more accurate ways to date archeological and paleontological material.

DIRECTED SOCIAL CHANGE

Applied anthropology is one of the most exciting and controversial areas of anthropology today, because it is immediately involved in problems of directed social change. This involvement raises a host of ethical questions. Who has the right to judge other people? Who says that one way of life is better than another? What justification has anyone for changing the lives of other people? None of these questions is easy to answer, although some people seem to think they are. Many individuals would immediately insist that no one has any right to judge other societies, that one way of life is just as good as another, and that no one has the right to direct other people's lives. However, it becomes difficult to maintain this aloof perspective when, for example, people plead for help to stop an epidemic that is wiping out their children. It is difficult to tell them that since one system is just as good as another, their own medical concepts and techniques should be able to cope with the epidemic. If their system were effective, they would not be asking for help. The fact that their system cannot cope with the epidemic in the sense of saving lives, whereas Western medical technology *can*, suggests that it may be possible to show that one system really *is* better than another, at least for some purposes. At that point the ideal of cultural relativity° is threatened and must be either abandoned or radically modified.

Perhaps Western medicine is more effective for treating certain kinds of sickness, but medicine is only one aspect of culture. Even if we can evaluate medical concepts comparatively, can we judge others? And if we can, should we? Can we not just help people with their medical problem and leave the rest of their culture alone? This is the position many people, including doctors who actually deliver medical help, have taken. They are there to heal the sick, and they have no intention of meddling with the rest of the culture. Unfortunately, that is impossible. Culture is an organized whole, not a random collection of bits and pieces. It is not possible to change one part without having any effect on the rest. If we put ourselves in the position of simply delivering treatment, is that not a new imperialism? The have-not countries must depend on outsiders to save their very lives. What people would not resent this, and resent the society that kept a monopoly on its vital medical knowledge? Most human beings want some control, particularly in the matter of life and death. They not only want treatment, they want to understand the process and be able to practice it themselves. Are we being fair if we deny the information to them? Most people would answer no on humanitarian grounds alone, regardless of the political implications denial would have. So we find ourselves committed to helping countries that ask for aid, not only by giving them treatment, but also by training their own people in modern medical technology and concepts.

Western medicine does not consist simply of injections, pills, and surgery. It is based on a coherent body of theory that must be imported along with techniques if the whole system is to work. We must at least teach the germ theory of disease, since it is the cornerstone of our medical technology. The germ theory, however, is almost certain to be in disagreement with medical concepts in premodern societies, and these concepts are apt to be imbedded in religion. Remember that weather and disease control are the two main topics with which religion is involved around the world. The germ theory may run counter to the recipient society's religious concepts; if people accept the basic concepts of Western medicine, their belief in their own religious system may weaken. If one area of religious faith is undermined, other areas of religion are usually weakened too. Since only medical concepts are being introduced, nothing is available to replace lost religious faith. This can be disastrous for the culture if no one has anticipated the problem.

Besides endangering the religion of the society and thereby running the risk of undermining the morale and motivation that keeps it vital, other areas of life will be affected by the introduction of modern medicine even if the germ theory is never accepted by the majority of the people. Western medicine teaches that health depends on certain sanitary practices. Regular baths and the careful disposal of excrement are not whimsical notions. They have the practical functions of reducing vermin, skin problems such as impetigo,° and dangerous disease organisms.

In trying to introduce modern Western medicine to societies that have asked for it, changes have to be promoted with regard to where people urinate and defecate; what they eat and how they prepare it; how often they wash themselves and their clothing, and so on. In addition, by reducing the death rate in these countries without also slowing the birth rate, modern medicine is making a major contribution to the population explosion that is rapidly making the earth too small for us all. If urination, defecation, diet, and cleanliness are thought to be sensitive topics, wait till birth control is attempted! Changing the sexual habits of a people is usually incredibly difficult, yet can the attempt be avoided? Moreover, there the change agent is doing just what we said should not be done at the start of this section, and it does not seem to matter whether the change agent is a member (or employee) of the governing group in the country being changed or an imported specialist. If local elites attempt to bring about the changes described, they are almost sure to be accused of being puppets of Yankee imperialists, communist dupes, Uncle Toms (or an equivalent term), or the sad products of brainwashing. Change agents, native or foreign, will inevitably have been trained outside their own country and, tragically, usually find themselves as alienated from their own people as any outsider would be. The *change* itself is the problem, more than the agent.

Faced with this thicket of complications, it might seem the more judicious part of humanitarianism to refuse medical assistance or information to those requesting it. But imagine the screams from the rest of the world. Besides, have we any right to play God and doom people to die when we could save them? Especially if they ask for our help? This moral dilemma is one most of the younger generation (and many of the older) have so far either not realized or have refused to face. It is much easier just to parrot the simple answers of cultural relativism mentioned at the beginning of this section.

A Nigerian emir (religious leader) at the procession celebrating the end of Ramadan— the Moslem month of fasting. *(Marc and Evelyne Bernheim/Woodfin Camp & Associates)*

How can the unhappy consequences of change be avoided? While it may not be possible to escape them entirely, their effects can certainly be reduced. If people working in other cultures—in any capacity whatsoever—accept the facts that (1) culture is an organized whole and (2) changing one part is bound to cause changes in other parts, they will realize that to do their job well they must understand the specific culture of the society they are working in and some of the dynamics involved in culture function and change (see below).

THEORY: A BRIEF SURVEY

In this context, the importance and relevance of theory should be obvious. Theory attempts to explain interrelationships and systems so that they can be better understood, predicted, and directed. Trying to work in a cross-cultural situation without some theoretical understanding is like looking for a gas leak

A village couple at a family planning center in India. *(United Nations/Farkas)*

with a lighted candle: if the task is accomplished, it will probably be at the expense of everything around.

Unfortunately, theory is still weak in cultural anthropology. Data continue to pour in, and all the information has not yet been integrated into a single coherent body, although attempts have been made by people like Leslie White (1949) and, more recently, Marvin Harris (1964, 1968). We do know a great deal on a concrete factual level about the dynamics of human interaction and social processes. Yet in spite of being several decades old, this information is not general public knowledge but is restricted to the relatively few people in the social science disciplines of psychology, sociology, labor relations, and so on, as well as occasional individuals in other disciplines who have encountered it (and understood it) in some course in college or learned it through firsthand experience. It is rarely taught at any level lower than college, and there it is only systematically taught in a few courses. Yet more information is constantly being added to that already available, and new theories are constantly being formulated or tested without more than the barest hint (and that frequently garbled) escaping to the general public. The average individual probably knows more about how to make an atom bomb than how to reduce conflict in an organization or how to harness competition for socially useful rather than disruptive ends.

Generally, in anthropology, a rash of data production has been followed by a spell of attempting to digest the mass of facts. Theories and generalizations spawned during such a phase have prompted more field research to test them. Because most of the theories have not survived without major modification, the process is still one of cycles, each of which adds a bit of real understanding.

Even though the task is far from complete, considerable progress has been made in understanding and organization of data over the years. As recently as 1940 there were still some people (such as Alfred Kroeber) who were masters of the entire field of anthropology, including the physical, archeological, linguistic, and ethnological branches. This is not possible today. Although all well-trained anthropologists have some familiarity with every branch, no one can now claim expertise in all. The data explosion has hit the social sciences too.

One of the earliest "schools" in anthropology was the so-called evolutionist approach, which held that all societies had passed through various stages of development from primitive to civilized. (This view did not, as most people think, stem from Darwin's theories of biological evolution; on the contrary, cultural evolution was a well-established concept by the time of Darwin. Indeed, Darwin's theory of natural selection and evolution was embraced by many as providing confirming evidence and a mechanism for cultural evolution [Harris 1968:25–27; de Waal Malefijt 1974:121–123].) The most famous exponents of this approach were Edward Tylor and Lewis H. Morgan. Tylor and Morgan did not have quite the same formulation, however. Tylor was more flexible in that he did not try to place every society into a specific category of "savagery," "barbarism," or "civilization," which he recognized as an ideal scheme, not a rigid pattern that every society followed in lock step (de Waal Malefijt 1974:141). Morgan's theories were both more rigid and more comprehensive. He subdivided each of the stages of savagery, barbarism, and civilization into lower, middle, and upper divisions, with diagnostic criteria for each. Then he attempted to classify each known society into its appropriate box. He tried to identify an evolutionary sequence not only in the totality of human culture but also in separate areas such as subsistance and technology (which provided most of his criteria), family structure, marriage, sociopolitical organization, economic concepts, and so on. Morgan also attempted to relate the various stages of these different segments of social life to each other, and thereby developed "a diachronic and synchronic system of unprecedented structural and chronological scope" (Harris 1968:183). Both Morgan and Tylor used the comparative method to study society, and both relied heavily on data from the field—but provided by others. (Neither spent much time in the field himself, although Morgan did have more firsthand contact with other cultures than Tylor because of the convenient nearness of native Americans.)

These "founders" of anthropology provided a framework on which later anthropologists have been able to build. Naturally enough, there were many errors made by all of the early theorists. Later researchers have criticized Morgan, Tylor, Bachofen, McLennan, and in fact every one of their contemporaries for a variety of faults, many of which were unavoidable given the knowledge available and the general intellectual climate of the time. Harris notes, however, that for all their faults, many of the hypotheses and theories these early students of human behavior developed are still valid and useful. His major criticism of Morgan, for example, is that he failed "to discover a systematic relationship between technoeconomic and social structural parameters" (1968:184), but he levels that same criticism against almost all past and present theorists.

The rigidity and apparent unilineality of Morgan's approach has been the major source of the criticisms of later researchers (de Waal Malefijt 1974:51–52), inasmuch as the pattern of unilinear evolutionary development did not stand up under the impact of additional data. It has been almost entirely abandoned in American anthropology, although it *still* crops up occasionally in newspapers and in popular articles. Since World War II, however, a modified version has been revived. Leslie White is the major proponent of this so-called neoevolutionist school. He claims that an index and a cause of the evolution of culture is control over energy. As more energy per capita is controlled, social organization and other aspects of culture necessarily change (Harris 1968:636; Woods 1975:6–7; de Waal Malefijt 1974:317). The way it is usually interpreted, this is theory on the level of abstraction that deals with human culture as a whole. Julian Steward, also a "neoevolutionist," argued that theories on that level of abstraction are not particularly useful in explaining particular developments in specific societies, or in making specific predictions and plans for direction. Steward, therefore, sought to establish the concept of what he called multilinear evolution, with research focused on cross-cultural comparisons of parallels on an empirical, easily verifiable level (Harris 1968:642–643; Woods 1975:7; de Waal Malefijt 1974:318). Harris denies that White is limited to the general and ignores the particular, however (1968:642–4), and the whole question has become bogged down (as many issues in the sciences have a tendency to do) in an argument over who said what first and what this or that person *really* meant. (Controversies of this nature have a way of becoming particularly lively after the theorists in question are dead and can no longer explain.) Such arguments are often entertaining but rarely productive. The problem seems partly due to the fact that there are many different levels of abstraction possible in studying the human being (or anything else). There are also many different levels of units of analysis, from sub-subatomic particles to the universe as a whole or from barely visible individual physical movements (called actones by Harris (de Waal Malefijt 1974:321) to the behavior of humans as a species. People who are most interested in one level have a tendency to misunderstand or undervalue work done on another level (of either abstraction or unit of analysis). Even less useful than the controversies resulting from this tendency, however, are those arising from pronouncements by people who confuse or mix levels entirely. Arguments of this sort are semantic and logical nightmares that rarely lead to any new insights or developments.

The controversy over whether White, Steward, Morgan, or someone else is "right" is as futile as the argument over "the" cause of human behavior. All of the significant theorists provided some useful insights and drew some valid conclusions. In the scientific community today, unilinear evolution as applied to the overall culture of any specific society is a dead issue. But most anthropologists would accept certain evolutionary generalizations *applied to human culture as a whole:*

1. It is possible to demonstrate a continuum from simple to complex in several areas of human behavior such as law, government, technology, and economy. It is not necessary, however, to postulate that every society experiences each level, or even that change has always occurred in the direction of simple to complex. (We know of societies that have abandoned agriculture to take up hunting and gathering, for example, although the latter is usually regarded as a simpler subsistence form.)

2. In certain aspects of culture such as economy, law, and technology, complex developments are *dependent* on preexisting simpler forms, although these need not have been developed in the society with the complex form. (Thus the development of the equipment for riding a horse—saddle, bridle, bit, stirrup—could not have occurred until after animal domestication; yet the society that first rode horses was apparently *not* the society that first domesticated animals.)

Mischa Titiev (a well-known anthropologist currently associated with the University of Michigan) presented four generalizations (he called them "laws") that apply to the development of humankind as a whole:

1. The law of increasing reliance on culture
2. The law of expanding use of natural resources
3. The law of the declining percentage of individual knowledge, with its corollaries (*a*) increasing specialization and (*b*) necessary cooperation
4. The laws of the conservation of time and human muscular energy (Titiev 1963:369–382).

Modification of some of these generalizations has been necessary. For example, the rules of the conservation of time and human muscular energy do not hold completely in certain aspects of life, such as religion, recreation, and art. Games are not usually promoted on the basis that one is quicker or easier to play than another. A new religious belief is not adopted because it is faster and less physically demanding to practice. Innovations are not accepted in art solely because they are easier and quicker. The law of increasing utilization of natural resources also needs some modification, since there is good evidence that industrialization has actually decreased utilization of the food resources exploited by hunters and gatherers. There may have been an overall increase in the variety and quantity of exploited resources *in general,* and certain resources—such as minerals—may be exploited much more intensively, but this increase has not occurred in *all* resources. Despite these minor modifications, Titiev's laws of tendencies are useful to know and can easily be applied to situations of culture change. The importance of the law of the declining percentage of individual knowledge and its corollaries has already been stressed several times. Innovations that run counter to trends are less likely to be adopted than those which promote them.

No single society can be shown to have passed through all the stages of simple to complex in all aspects of life where such a progression has been found. Societies change, appear, disappear, combine, and separate. There is not one that has an unbroken continuity back to the beginning of human history, yet all are equally old in the sense that the members of any one have as long an evolutionary history as the members of any other.

Diffusionist Theory

Another approach that attempted to explain the specific characteristics of individual social systems was the diffusionist, which focused on the distribution of specific characteristics called traits.° A few exponents went to the extreme and tried to trace *all* cultures to a single origin. This approach is still popular in the nonscientific literature. People who attribute all civilization to Atlantis, Lemuria, or visitors from outer space; or, less fancifully, Polynesian culture to the South American Andes, or New World civilizations entirely to China are intellectual descendants of the extreme diffusionist school.° One of the most exaggerated positions was promoted by G. Elliot Smith, who attributed all civilization to Egyptian missionaries fanning out over the world to spread Egyptian culture and the worship of the sun god. Smith's exaggerated position has spawned numerous controversies (Wauchope 1962:21–25).

Not all difussionists were as extreme as Smith, of course. Most, however, relied less on field research than did Tylor, Morgan, or others of the evolutionist school. One of the most useful sources for the diffusionists (and for other theorists) which was based on at least some sort of field data was a collection of religious beliefs and practices from all over the world, organized into several volumes by Sir James Frazer as *The Golden Bough* (1955). It remains a classic. Frazer's ideas and data inspired a great many people, including the anthropologist Malinowski, who studied with Frazer and then began to develop his own theories about cultural processes (see below). A major criticism of Frazier's work (and of many diffusionists) is that customs (often used to "prove" contact) are described out of context and consequently are often not nearly as much alike as they seem at first glance.

A more complex diffusionist formulation than Smith's postulated several centers of culture that spread a variety of patterns. The complex interaction of all these was held to be responsible for the astonishing variations in culture found in different parts of the globe. Wilhelm Schmidt and Fritz Graebner, who were primarily responsible for this hypothesis, formed what was known as the culture-historical° school (Herskovits ·1951:510–514), better known by its German name *Kulturkreiselehre* (usually translated "culture circle school"). The basic theories of the school, inspired by Friedrich Ratzel—founder of anthropogeography° in the nineteenth century—stated that nonfunctional similarities between two cultural items indicate diffusion regardless of how far apart the cultures are geographically (the Criterion of Quality or Form), and that the more individual items there are in the two cultures that show similarity, the higher the probability they are related (Criterion of Quantity) (Harris 1968:384). Using these two basic criteria, Graebner and Father Schmidt identified three or four (depending on whether Schmidt's or Graebner's construct is accepted) major grades of culture circles, each grade containing several *Kreise* ("circles"; singular, *Kreis*)—elements that seemed to be associated and to migrate together. (Harris regards the grades as simply the old savagery-barbarism-civilization stages in new guise [Harris 1968:385].) The migration of peoples who had different *Kreise* led to contact between *Kreise,* and consequent dropping, blending, or adding of traits—thus forming all known cultures. The process of tracing the various threads through all the changes grew overwhelmingly complex. As de Waal Malefijt puts it, "In other words, the system did not work, and in fact all it proved was that the cultural spread and development did *not* take place in the ways posited by the *Kulturkreis* scholars" (1974:170). The German researchers collected a tremendous amount of detailed information in the process of trying to test their hypotheses, however, and this mass of material is still significantly valuable today, even though the theory inspiring its collection has virtually gone the way of the concept of unilinear evolution. (It is a tribute to the *Kulturkreis* scholars' careful and thorough work that the material they gathered can be used for other purposes.) The modern descendants of the *Kulturkreiselehre* no longer look for single centers from which *Kreise* diffuse, but they still trace historical connections between cultures on the basis of the distribution of culture elements° (Fischer, J. 1971:personal communication).

The extreme diffusionists and even the culture-historical school were eventually discredited by the continuing influx of new data. Critics pointed out that many of the traits diffusionists labeled as identical bore only a superficial resemblance to one another and were actually no more alike than the words *nein* in German and *nine* in English. Alexander Goldenweiser (1933) pointed out that for some things there is a "limitation of possibilities." That is, there are a finite number of ways to make an effective canoe paddle or a container to hold water.

A round piece of cloth (or even wood) will not work well for either purpose. As mentioned in Chapter 8, there are only four basic forms of heterosexual marriage. Consequently, if similarly shaped water jars or similar marriage forms appear in different parts of the world, there is no need to postulate diffusion to explain the similarity; the limitation of possibilities and independent invention will do.

On the other hand, the possible decorations for water jars are almost infinite. Therefore, if two water jars found in widely separated parts of the world are not only of identical shape but also have the same coloring and decoration (particularly if the decoration depicts some fabulous creature that never really existed), the jar becomes good evidence of diffusion between the two places; it indicates that there was some type of contact, either direct or indirect. The more complex the items being compared and the more arbitrary the associations between the component parts, the more likely they are to be related if they closely resemble each other. Conversely, the more simple the two items and the more closely they copy something found in nature, or the more functional the associations between component parts, the more likely they are to have been independently invented, unless there is good evidence to prove otherwise.

Even though the extreme diffusionist position has been largely abandoned, the significance of diffusion to cultural development is widely recognized today. Human beings are not highly original but they are quite imitative. Throughout human history, a good idea has spread with amazing rapidity, even when transportation was unmechanized. The spread of ideas without any accompanying physical objects is called stimulus diffusion° and is much more difficult to trace, of course, than the diffusion of material objects. Enough cases of stimulus diffusion have been documented, however, for us to know that it occurs, probably more often than we think. Linton illustrates this fact in his classic description of a "100 percent American," pointing out that almost everything an American believes and does has its origins outside the United States (Linton 1937:427–429). The importance of understanding the process of diffusion should be obvious.

There is a well-known truism that it is difficult to make people change, but this particular truism is false unless it is modified. It is ironic that some of the same people who talk about the difficulty and slowness of change may complain about the rapid spread of Coca-Cola. Change agents who cannot induce people to cut down their herds to help erosion control or cannot persuade them to kill animals to stop the spread of hoof-and-mouth disease find themselves equally unable to stop the spread of marijuana smoking, the manufacture of illegal liquor, or some other "undesirable" practice: people are not necessarily resistant to change, per se; they just will not always change in the direction the change agent wants them to. Many times this resistance to a particular change shows the intelligence of the resistors. Well-meaning but ignorant change agents have caused tremendous social and individual human damage in certain cases. (As an example, the introduction of steel axes to one group of Australian natives by missionaries destroyed the aboriginal power structure and mechanism for social control leading to disastrous social disorganization [Sharp 1952:69–90].) Most of the cases reported in the anthropological literature involve change originating outside a particular society but the processes of change (and the potential for damage) are the same wherever the change originates. Understanding these processes can prevent or alleviate much of the disruption.

Diffusion is one of the basic mechanisms by which change occurs; that is, before people can change, they must be aware of alternatives. Ideas, practices, and physical objects all diffuse from one society or from one person to another.

We know several things about the process of diffusion:

It is a selective process, proceeds at varying rates, is reciprocal, . . . It is affected by the duration and intensity of contact, similarity of the two groups and relative cultural integration. New items are commonly subjected to reinterpretation in form, function, or meaning by the receiving group and some areas of culture are more resistant to change than others . . . a technological change can set off a series of linked changes [Woods 1975:25–26].

Knowledge even of these simple principles can, if wisely used, minimize damage, and assist in promoting a smoother, easier transition process.

Studies of trait distribution, so widely used by diffusionists, have led to other theoretical concepts. The concept of "culture area,"° for example, is still in limited use today (Wissler 1922). This idea was originally developed by Clark Wissler to assist museum curators in organizing their material for display purposes (Herskovits 1951:183). Put simply, it states that people in one geographic area resemble each other culturally more than they resemble people elsewhere; the boundaries of a culture area are drawn both geographically and culturally. The concept saves a great deal of work. For example, all the tribes in the American Plains culture area resemble the Piegan in basic outline. Everyone who has read this book and can remember details from the first excerpt already knows something about other native Americans of the Plains, such as the Cheyenne, Arapaho, Sioux, Comanche, Pawnee, and so on. They all depended on the buffalo, which they hunted much the same way as the Piegans in the first excerpt did. They all lived in movable skin-covered lodges (the tepee), usually made in more or less the same manner. They all had roughly the same division of labor and depended on the horse for transport. They all essentially lacked pottery, agriculture, and canoe travel. Their social and political organizations were similar in broad outline and even their religious beliefs were similar. Details of each culture varied to the extent that tribes could be distinguished by the arrows they left in their victims or by the tracks their moccasins made, but the basic resemblances were striking.

Knowing in detail about one group in a culture area makes it possible to concentrate on the specific ways in which a new culture differs from the one already known. This can be an obvious help to a doctor, anthropologist, or some other change agent going to work in a large geographic area such as the upper Amazon drainage. He does not have to learn a completely new set of data for each of the tiny tribes he may encounter. Once he understands the basic patterns of the culture area, he can concentrate on details, and feel, correctly, that he already knows something about each new group he meets.

George P. Murdock has made the most significant contribution to organizing the massive amount of data accumulated during the first half of the twentieth century by establishing the Human Relations Area Files (HRAF). He set up a classification system that could be used to arrange ethnographic data (Murdock 1950). Into the HRAF were then coded vast bodies of material, both published and unpublished, on different peoples in the various culture areas of the world. This classification has been quite useful for certain kinds of research, although some people may have tried to get more out of the material than is there. There has been criticism that data are not always reliable and that cross-cultural comparisons have sometimes compared things that were not actually comparable. Still, for many researchers, HRAF makes easily available material that would take a lifetime of work to accumulate on one's own. (Students can also make good use of the files to write papers on carefully defined problems within one society. Hardly any library in the world would have available *all* the sources classified in the files.) If all this material is ever properly computerized, it will make an even more useful research tool.

As anthropologists became familiar with more and more cultures, they noticed that each one seemed to have a distinct "style." The personality or character of the members of each culture seemed distinguishable. The French, for example, were obviously different in behavior and temperament from the English, Russians, Japanese, or Americans. The relationship between culture and personality became a major focus of interest. Ralph Linton and Cora Du Bois, working with the psychoanalyst Abram Kardiner, developed the concept of the modal personality—a cluster of personality traits that appear most frequently in a culture (Barnouw 1963:110) (see Chapter 7). Ruth Benedict, one of the early pioneers in American anthropology, thought that each culture was organized around a central pattern she called a configuration.° This pattern encouraged certain personality developments and inhibited others. She also said that the main configuration could be correlated with psychological types, such as Dionysian and Apollonian (Benedict 1934:79). Her hypothesis had no sooner been expressed than other anthropologists began to modify it on the basis of additional data. Morris Opler pointed out that most cultures were not organized around one focus but had several, which he called themes° (Opler 1945:198–206). Hoebel followed much the same track, only he used the term *basic postulates°* to refer to the major concepts that gave a culture its unique character (Hoebel 1964:13).

Other anthropologists became interested in what people of different cultures regard as "good" or "bad." (Of the several anthropologists who became absorbed in the study of values, Clyde Kluckhohn is probably one of the best known.) This whole line of development, with its primary concentration on beliefs, feelings, values, and so on, places an emphasis on the mental, or ideational, component of human endeavor, and thus comes into major conflict with the "materialistic" approach which is relatively (or entirely) unconcerned with the meaning, the subjective experience, of culture. The "emic-etic" conflict mentioned earlier is a part of the same controversy.

This entire argument seems to be aggravated by the dichotomous° approach that perpetually afflicts students of human behavior. Trying to categorize people's actions into neat little boxes for analysis is tempting but dangerous. As has been mentioned frequently, most of the time a continuum is a better concept for analyzing human behavior than are limited, mutually exclusive categories. Analog computation fits human actions better than digital; the scale is better than either-or classification. So with the question of *either* materialistic *or* ideational-mentalistic anthropology. The human being is an animal, but an animal whose thought processes are more complex than any other's. There is a dynamic interrelationship between the individual and the group, the environment and the culture, the technology and the value system, that cannot be understood by studying one aspect, no matter how carefully, alone.

As an example, think back to the discussion on the development of agriculture in Chapter 2. An increase in population combined with a lack of new territory in which to follow the usual pattern of fission and migration posed not one survival threat but two. First, how to get food enough to feed the increased population, and second, how to keep peace within the growing group so that they did not destroy themselves through internal conflict. (The same two problems, incidentally, are confronting the world today, on a much larger scale.) Potential solutions to these problems lay in two different ranges, one centering in the technological realm—agriculture, horticulture, intensive fishing, or nomadic herding were some of the options developed there—and the other in the sociopolitical realm. Exactly what all the options in the sociopolitical area were, we are not yet sure, but they certainly had something to do with changed forms of leadership. These changed patterns were both a response to the specific problems and a step that made additional technological options available. The transition from a 25-to-50-person hunting band to a larger, more permanently based population made possible the beginning of complex technology, but it also necessitated forms of government different from those of the hunting band. As suggested earlier, the hunting-gathering pattern of informal leadership, total adult participation in decision making, explicit denial of *anyone's* right to give orders that must be obeyed (as shown in the BaMbuti example of Chapter 5), would not and does not work in a farming village of 500 to 1,000 members. But a change in leadership pattern, in turn, is not possible without some change in the ideas about how people should relate to others, the nature of authority, the respective "rights" of leaders and followers, the appropriate matters for leaders to decide, the degree of participation in the decision of other members of the group, and so on. There is no evidence to indicate that such changes in ideas are likely to occur in the absence of a crucial reason for them, that is, some threat to the group's survival that makes a change essential. But—and this is a significant "but"—there is no guarantee that they will occur in the presence of the threat either. Many groups undoubtedly tried options that did not work and so did not survive. This same sort of interdependence of multicausal factors has recently been suggested as being responsible for the first appearance of the state form of social organization (Wright and Johnson 1975:284–285).

Given that some change in structure was essential to cope with the problems mentioned above, was there ever a situation or a time when there was only one viable option open? Theoretically, it is possible that some threats to group survival could be solved only one way, but the diversity of cultures that have existed and even to some extent continue to exist bears witness that several solutions to common problems are viable. At the same time, the very real similarity that does exist among all hunting and gathering societies, or all horticultural ones, also suggests that the number of viable solutions is not infinite. Whether this limitation is imposed by the biological characteristics of human beings, by the logistic demands of the situation, or (as is more likely) by varying amounts of both has not yet been determined. This problem of accounting for specific diversity within general similarity is at the core of anthropological thinking—or *should* be, according to one recent writer (Jarvie 1975:256–257).

In any case, we are left with the question of why particular options were chosen by specific societies. Harris, the materialist's major proponent, would have these first choices determined by the technoenvironmental circumstances —the things members of the society can do given their cultural equipment and the environmental possibilities. Values would then develop to support the choices dictated by necessity until these values were felt to be "right." In the first and second chapters the explanation of value change (from an emphasis on

Bushman hunters in South Africa. *(Courtesy of the American Museum of Natural History)*

generosity and mobility in hunting-gathering societies to an emphasis on accumulation and residential stability in agricultural societies) was fundamentally a
materialist explanation. Ideationalists tend to reverse things and regard the
nature of human thinking processes as the cause of particular options. Lévi-
Strauss, a major proponent of this position, therefore regards values as explanations for behavior rather than the reverse. In Chapter 7, the explanation of the
incest tabu (as a way humans brought about alliances outside the immediate
family) is essentially an ideational one. The whole argument is reminiscent of
the chicken-egg controversy. With humans, both values and situational demands must be taken into account. From available evidence it would seem that
some initial choices are particularly significant on whatever basis they were
made because of the way they affect subsequent options. That is, once a commitment to the sanctity or value of human life has been made by members of
a society, certain later options in scientific research, medicine, law, education,
and so on, will be more (or less) attractive than others. Some options will be
rejected, or accepted only after considerable struggle. It is because of this
conditioning and modifying influence that the ideational component of culture
cannot be safely ignored. But the materialist component cannot be safely ignored either since some options will simply not fit the demands of the physical
situation as well as others. (Regardless of how much you approve of canoeing,
it won't work as transportation in a desert.)

CURRENT VITAL ISSUES

Values, themes, configurations, or basic postulates are crucial concepts in
applied anthropology. New elements introduced into a culture may be accepted or rejected by its members on the basis of how well these elements fit
with the fundamental concepts of the culture. Elements that are accepted are
often reworked to conform more closely to the underlying organization of the
culture. (Some American Indian groups, taught to screen doors and windows,
but never really understanding why, reworked the innovation by leaving doors
propped open and failing to repair holes in the screen.) A change agent who
tries to introduce something that is incompatible with this basic structure is
bound to have difficulty. To succeed, he has to change either the basic structure
of the culture (which is almost impossible to do) or his innovation. If the basic
themes and values are known, the innovation can be preadapted to fit better,
and the inevitable reworking may be anticipated. It may even be possible to
guide the reworking to ensure that it does not invalidate the entire change.

Margaret Mead, the anthropologist who is best known to the American
public, pointed out that it might be easier to introduce almost an entire new
culture at once rather than to try to change an old one bit by bit (Mead
1956:411). Partial changes always create so many problems of adjustment and
the new clusters of traits are so unpredictable at the present state of knowledge
that a massive rapid change is sometimes both simpler and safer. In the process
of attempting to unravel the tangled skein of cause and effect between the

problems posed by biology and physical reality and the human being's ideational response to them, the concept of the psychic unity of the human continues to play an important role. Usually attributed to Theodor Waitz in a work
published in 1859 and strongly supported by Adolf Bastian in 1895, its modern
champions are Lévi-Strauss and Noam Chomsky. The position as set forth by
Bastian is that there are a restricted number of basic ideas common to all
humankind which serve to organize human experience (de Waal Malefijt
1974:134–135). If correct, this would set some limits to the options, not that are
possible, but that man would think of. Some mental commonality seems essential, or communication between individuals and especially between people of
different cultures would not be possible. Just how much unity there is, or how
specific the similarity might be, is the focus of controversy. But some unity
would account for the frequent reoccurrence of certain patterns without resort
to diffusion. It would place the same sort of limitation on innovation of concepts
that functional demands place on material innovation. Of course, the same
material functional demands may also be responsible for more abstract cultural
limitations. As pointed out in Chapter 8, because there are only two sexes, there
are limits on the possible number of forms of heterosexual marriage. Such
limitations do not demand underlying psychic unity. This is basically the position of the materialists (Harris 1968).

The interest in psychic unity is related to the whole question of the relationship between culture and the individual personality (called either psychological anthropology or culture and personality) and is a vital one today. The
focus of attention has changed somewhat from national-character and modal-
personality studies to searches for specific cross-cultural uniformities and generalizations (such as the studies by Whiting mentioned in Chapter 7). In addition
to these cultural generalizations, there has been an upsurge in cognitive anthropology, that is, in the study of the "mental principles and processes that
give structure, organization, and meaning to human experience and behavior"
(Thompson 1975:2–3). This involves not only the activity called thinking but
also the process by which information and thought are channelled or patterned.
Cognitive anthropology, which has developed strongly since about 1950, is
chiefly concerned with the relation of cognition to culture as expressed through
language, and thus is sometimes termed ethnosemantics. Using the rigorous
methodology of linguistics, attempts are made to map out the boundaries of the
meanings of words used in a particular culture (Berlin 1970:3–18). The assumption is that significant aspects of the way people in the society categorize and
express reality will be embodied in their language (Thompson 1975:7–8). This
interest is an *indirect* outgrowth of the hypotheses of Benjamin Whorf and
Edward Sapir, who were pioneers in studying the relationship between language and culture, and who suggested that language has a more pervasive and
subtle effect on thought and perception than anyone had previously suspected.
The rejection of the extreme Sapir-Whorf position, however, meant that cognitive anthropology in general took a different road, and owes more to the perspectives of Goodenough and Wallace than to Sapir and Whorf. Cognitive
anthropologists are in the ideational-mentalist camp, and thus usually are op-

posed to the materialist approach currently staunchly represented by Harris (Thompson 1975:10). An example of the cognitive approach has been the work of Berlin and Kay on cross-cultural color classifications. They discovered that there are only eleven areas on a standard color chart that serve as foci for the basic color terms of any language, and that 70 percent of the spectrum is never selected as a focus. All languages have terms for black and white. Beyond that, if the number of terms is known, one can predict what colors will be distinguished. For example, if a language has only three terms, they will be black, white, and red; if it has five, they will be black, white, red, green, and yellow (Berlin 1970:6–8).

At about the same time that the interest in values and personality and culture was beginning to occupy the attention of some American anthropologists, others were trying to understand specific patterns in a society by looking at how they functioned. Bronislaw Malinowski and Alfred Radcliffe-Brown were the principal leaders in this approach (Keesing 1964:150–155), yet they themselves differed to the point that Radcliffe-Brown held himself to be an "antifunctionalist," at least in regard to Malinowski's functionalism° (Radcliffe-Brown 1949:320–331, as quoted in Harris 1968:546). Radcliffe-Brown and followers—known as structural functionalists—conceived of a social structure° (an "ordered arrangement of social elements or processes") (de Waal Malefijt 1974:195) whose parts were functionally integrated. The function of a particular institution° was the part it played in this integration; the function of culture as a whole was to integrate individual people into the social system (Radcliffe-Brown 1958:62). Malinowski, on the other hand, looked to function more in terms of the part an institution played in meeting individual biological needs, which he classified on two levels: primary, basic biological needs for survival, and derived needs which arose from the culture itself—learned needs, in a sense. To Malinowski, institutions were sets of behavior patterns organized around an integrating principle such as reproduction, occupation, status, and so on (de Waal Malefijt 1974:202–203).

The sociologists Talcott Parsons and Robert Merton have used structural functionalism and functionalism as much as American anthropologists have (de Waal Malefijt 1974:209–211; see the discussion of manifest and latent function, which is Merton's concept, in Chapter 5). There have been severe criticisms directed against all functionalist approaches (Harris 1968:529–542), but functionalism is by no means dead in modern anthropology; it is of practical importance to programs of directed culture change, for example, since it is essential to know precisely how something functions in a society before it is safe (or in some cases even possible) to change it.

One of the most popular theoretical approaches in cultural anthropology today is structuralism, whose chief exponent is the French anthropologist Claude Lévi-Strauss. (Some of his hypotheses have already been mentioned in Chapter 8.) Structuralism accounts for the presence of certain behavior by the demands of the mind itself—the formal underlying structure—and not by the values (conscious or unconscious) held by members of the culture. Values would be a consequence of the formal structure, rather than a causal factor. Thus

Lévi-Strauss attributes incest prohibitions to the fact that there is an innate, fundamental dichotomy drawn in the mind between the "self" and the "other." Reciprocity alleviates the psychological insecurity resulting from this (Harris 1968:491). The incest tabu compels the reciprocal exchange of women and is therefore due to innate mental structure rather than to frustrated human desires or the fear of biological damage through inbreeding. Similarly, the division of labor has little to do with innate male-female differences; it exists instead because it forces people to depend on each other, again serving the basic structure of the mind (Lévi-Strauss 1960:261–285). This resort to an innate, panhuman mental structure, with a limited number of concepts common to all humans, is what places Lévi-Strauss currently at the head of the ranks of the "rationalists" or "mentalists" among anthropologists. These people regard culture as the result of the working out of the innate tendencies of all normal minds, tendencies such as conceptualizing the world in two opposing categories. These common logical principles are used by the mind to organize the raw materials of experience, and because they are common to all humans, comparisons and cross-cultural understanding are possible (de Waal Malefijt 1974:328).

In addition to the ethnosemanticists, who generally agree with Lévi-Strauss, the linguist Noam Chomsky came to much the same conclusions about inborn logical principles, shared by all normal people, and applied this to language. His concept of deep structure is closely analogous to Lévi-Strauss's concept of the innate logical principles of the human mind (de Waal Malefijt 1974:333–334).

The critics of Lévi-Strauss point out that since he insists that the inborn underlying principles may be totally outside the awareness of the individual (in fact, usually are), there is no way of verifying their existence. The "reality" Lévi-Strauss refers to as more real than the concrete world (de Waal Malefijt 1974:330) may be "real" only in the head of Lévi-Strauss. Harris in particular takes issue with him because he, as Harris puts it, is simply substituting "a universal mental duality of self and other" for "a universal instinctual dread of sleeping with one's mother" (1968:492). Criticisms against Chomsky are made on similar ground (Lamb 1967; de Waal Malefijt 1974:334).

The view of the human as a "rational" being, as held by Chomsky, Lévi-Strauss, and their followers, is certainly more attractive than the mechanistic one held by behaviorists such as B. F. Skinner—who is accused of regarding all human behavior, including language, as conditioned responses (de Waal Malefijt 1974:334)—or the hardly less rigid materialist position of Harris (1965). Still, a main concern of critics of both Chomsky and Lévi-Strauss is that if language and culture are based on inborn principles or concepts, then language and culture themselves must both be, to some extent, inborn and predetermined (de Waal Malefijt 1974:335); but if this is the case, how can such universals—be they called instinct, innate logical principles, or "human nature"—result in the diversity of human culture, language, and behavior? According to Jarvie, this paradox of human similarity in diversity is the main philosophical problem with which anthropology must deal, because both the similarity and the differences are real (1975:256–257).

The argument partly revolves around a difference in point of view. If the focus of interest is on human similarities, then the discovery of universals is desirable and perhaps necessary to explain these similarities; but if the focus of interest is on human variability, then of necessity the search must be for factors that could account for the differences. Both approaches are valid. All human beings are in certain ways alike (they would never be mistaken for birds or horses, for example), but on the base of their general similarity is built both the uniqueness of individual personality and the diversity of human cultures. To understand human beings it is important to know both the elements common to all *and* the factors that contribute to specific differences. Just as the individual personality is a composite of internal and external factors, of biological givens interacting with environmental constants and ideosyncratic historical events, so each society and each culture is a composite of the same environmental constants interacting with the specific unique individuals in the society at a particular time, who are in interaction with each other, using the patterns of beliefs, norms, and values that they, their fellow members, and their ancestors developed over time *through* their interaction.

Structuralism is not an entirely new approach. Alfred Kroeber suggested it in his work on culture as superorganic (1917:163–213). According to the Redfield definition given at the beginning of this book, culture is an underlying formal structure of learned and shared concepts that motivates observable behavior. Émile Durkheim regarded underlying social structure as responsible for much of human behavior (1951). The main difference among these views lies in the locus of the "superorganic" structure: the society (Durkheim), the culture (Kroeber and Redfield), or the individual mind (Lévi-Strauss). Lévi-Strauss has given new impetus to the concept that culture is a shared mental phenomenon that changes according to its own rules and is at least partly unlearned, or innate.

OTHER AREAS OF INTEREST

Several major areas of current interest have been discussed so far—applied anthropology, psychological anthropology, ethnosemantics and theoretical conflicts. Other areas in which interest and research attention have been increasing in the last decade are urban anthropology, industrial anthropology, medical anthropology, educational anthropology, and the use of computers in model- or system-building as well as in analysis.

Industrial anthropology is still mainly the province of physical anthropologists, who have been involved in it for some time in matters of design and industrial safety. Cultural anthropologists have started moving into the field, however, and may continue to do so as management employs more minority-group members and begins to run into the inevitable cross-cultural misunderstandings.

Urban anthropology is an obvious development. As anthropologists began studying more complex societies such as that of India, it was inevitable that they would become involved in studying cities. The subcultural differences between rural and urban populations in a single society or between different classes within one city are often of the same magnitude as cultural differences between separate societies. To a middle class WASP (White Anglo-Saxon Protestant), Chinatown in New York, Spanish Harlem, or the black ghetto is as culturally alien as a foreign country, and the reverse may be equally true. Anthropology has much to contribute to the understanding of urban problems, since so many of these problems are generated by cross-cultural contacts. At present, most urban studies are made by sociologists, but anthropological interest in the area is increasing rapidly.

Medical anthropology includes both the study of non-Western medical concepts and the problems of introducing Western medicine to various parts of the world (including parts of the United States). The cultures of medical practitioners and medical institutions are also subjects for study. More and more medical schools and hospitals are employing anthropologists to find answers to persistent and perplexing problems or are including anthropology as part of their training programs.

The interest in educational anthropology (the cross-cultural study of educational methods, goals, and content) is fairly recent, but it is growing rapidly. Several publications dealing with educational systems and educational technology in various parts of the world have recently appeared. An offshoot of this has been a growing interest in the teaching of anthropology itself in this country at levels earlier than college. Under the sponsorship of the American Anthropological Association, a package for high-school programs has been developed that is being widely used (cf. American Anthropological Association 1966, 1968, 1971). It is too early yet to assess these attempts, but increasing familiarity with the basic concepts and data from anthropology could help to alleviate some of the problems mentioned earlier. In this subfield as well as in the others mentioned, interest will probably increase in the future.

The use of computers is a fairly new development for anthropologists, who have traditionally shied away from mathematical approaches. For years, one of the main differences between anthropologists and sociologists was that sociologists used the survey for collecting data which were then analyzed by statistical methods, whereas anthropologists used participation-observation and made a qualitative analysis of their data. Recently, however, archeologists have turned to computers to analyze the thousands of pottery shards found in rich sites, and cultural anthropologists have begun to use surveys and computer analysis. Even more recently, cultural anthropologists have begun to experiment with computers for building model cultural systems. It is still too early to tell how productive this trend will be, but it is likely to draw increasing attention. Still another trend that seems to have a significant potential for the future is indicated by SOPA—Society of Professional Anthropologists. This society is specifically for professionals with anthropological training who are working in a variety of occupations, using anthropological skills, but not labeled anthropologists. Possibilities of that sort are open to people with degrees lower than the doctorate.

THE FUTURE

What is the most likely future direction for anthropology? At the present time many anthropologists are concerned about several apparent major threats to the discipline. First, there has been a recent loss of recruits, or at least the growth of the field has ceased. Second, there appears to be an intellectual disorganization and stagnation, accompanied by a loss of purpose and enthusiasm (Jarvie 1975:254–255). Third, the reputation of anthropology has suffered publicly recently because a number of undercover agents from various countries and organizations have claimed to be anthropologists as a cover for their secret activities. Revelation of these cases seems to have cast public suspicion on the whole field, but actually, very few anthropologists have ever knowingly acted as spies. In addition, a number of people claiming to be anthropologists but having virtually no anthropological training have gone into various parts of the world in search of some sort of personal fulfillment. Their behavior has often alienated the people they were involved with to the detriment of later genuine attempts to work there. Then, as in every field, there have been incompetent, insensitive practitioners. Archeologists in particular have aroused the wrath of people by "stealing" things they dug up, including human bones, which native Americans could, in many cases, justly claim as the remains of ancestors. Like every profession, anthropology has had its share of people who have been more successful at antagonizing people than at understanding them. Unfortunately, because the discipline still has relatively few people in it and is practiced in societies where not many people have heard of it and even fewer know precisely what it entails, an anthropologist who follows such an incompetent into the field sometimes may not be given the opportunity to convince the people he or she wants to work with that not all anthropologists are alike. Indeed, it seems that people who have traditionally been studied by anthropologists have become more and more reluctant to accept researchers.

Despite the fact that complaints against anthropologists are, in some cases, justified, in others they are highly exaggerated and are motivated more by political concerns than from genuine wrongs suffered. Vine Deloria, for example, a native American, never hesitates to criticize anthropologists and ask what they have ever done for native Americans (cf. 1969, 1970), conveniently forgetting that anthropologists championed the native-American cause long before it became popular (and long before native Americans were able to do much themselves) and that almost all of the successful claims cases, which returned millions of dollars to cheated tribes, were won with the indispensible aid of anthropologists (Nickerson 1975:404).

There are other reasons for the loss of people who once welcomed—or at least accepted—study. Emerging African nations, developing Latin-American countries, and similar people of the so-called Third (and Fourth) World have begun to view anthropologists with hostility and suspicion, sometimes only because they come from rich, industrialized, or former colonial powers. At other times the resentment results from anthropologists' honest and accurate reports which are interpreted as hostile because they do not paint a glowing or impressive picture of the country.

Another problem in the discipline arises from the fact that professional caution, or particular political positions, have made some highly competent anthropologists reluctant to participate in government-sponsored activities. As a result, jobs that anthropologists would seem best qualified to do have been going by default to members of other disciplines. Those members, lacking anthropological skills, have often made unnecessary errors, adding to the extensive literature of failures in change or assistance programs. It will take some positive action to reverse these trends.

In general, the most serious threat faced by anthropology seems to be a loss of confidence. In a recent article Jarvie points out that anthropologists seem to have lost touch with their own beginnings, and seem to have forgotten the goals and aims of the discipline. A sense of confusion and even hopelessness has struck some of the newer members of the profession as old theories have been abandoned while new ones are not yet accepted, and cries of doom have been sounding on all sides (1975:255). Jarvie is cautiously optimistic, however, for some sound reasons. He says:

I regard theoretical breakdown as a fundamentally healthy event. If what we want is intellectual progress, better explanation, then the breakdown of existing theories is a prerequisite; we cannot supercede a theory until we know where it goes wrong [1975:255].

He regards the continuing debate as crucial to the advancement of the field, and suggests that in the "anthropology of anthropology" we may move in the right direction (1975:264). In any case, some move is necessary to recapture the sense of excitement and high adventure that permeated the field in the 1940s and 1950s. The big argument between phenomenology and empiricism, common to all the sciences, and the controversy between the materialists and the mentalists in anthropology (essentially the same argument), will continue to generate heat (and perhaps some light) in the next decades. Phenomenology is far too complex a topic to discuss here but briefly. Phenomenologists take the position that to understand anything one must know how the observer perceives it. This subjective interpretation is the only one that is significant and so-called objective reality is really impossible to achieve because it is observed and reported by people whose perceptions and interpretations control the process. Most empiricists, on the other hand, believe that subjective phenomena cannot be scientifically studied and therefore must be excluded from scientific endeavor as much as possible. They work continually on methodology to reduce or eliminate the personal element of the researchers, something the phenomenologist insists cannot be done. An interesting recent development is the move by some empiricists to begin scientific study of subjective phenomena (Tart 1972:1203–1205). If the phenomenologists, who are basically antiscience, succeed in dominating the field of anthropology entirely, it will mean the end of the scientific study of humanity (which, of course, is what proponents of that position regard as necessary or desirable) (Jarvie 1975:261–263). Given the strength of the empiricists, it seems likelier that, at the most, the discipline will split more formally than it has to date, and *both* positions will continue to attract followers.

One serious problem must be confronted in the coming decade, since it is currently causing a bitter controversy in anthropological circles, and that is the problem of the most appropriate apportionment of involvement and objectivity —the question of where, when, and how the personal values of the anthropologist should be engaged. Although the issue is not precisely either theoretical or methodological, it affects both areas. There is no simple answer to the question, but many people are trying to provide one. There are extremists on both sides: those who feel objectivity cannot be attained and should not be sought and those who feel that values have no place in any field that claims to be a science.

Most anthropologists probably prefer some position between the two extremes, but a hot controversy is raging about just where along the continuum the field and its practitioners should be. Anthropologists are human beings, citizens of particular political entities, and bearers of particular cultures. In studying other peoples, they have traditionally made use of their personal characteristics by reporting their own reactions as fully as possible when they have participated in the study culture. In other words, they tried to use their own cultural biases to increase understanding rather than to obscure it. Since Malinowski's time, anthropologists have always undergone a considerable amount of field training to make them alert to their own biases and to teach methods of research that would help them avoid the biases that remain covert. Although they participated as much as possible in the daily life of the peoples they studied, anthropologists traditionally were supposed to remain analytical, aloof from any long-range real consequences of the research. The first anthropologists to engage in applied research were looked upon somewhat skeptically, for in the eyes of many, this was no longer "pure" research. But now anthropologists, in common with other scientists, have become increasingly concerned about the use to which their research is being put. They have begun to criticize one another because some do work for financial sponsors of which others disapprove, because some fail to protect informants adequately from detrimental consequences of the research, or because some allow their research results to be censored and withheld from the profession. In addition, some anthropologists have felt that their professional associations should take a strong stand on political questions, whereas others think they should not.

Both involvement and objectivity are probably essential at different points in anthropology. Part of the controversy seems to come from confusion over when objectivity is (or is not) appropriate, and who should be allowed to make significant decisions. Involvement of values is probably inevitable in decisions over what research should be done and who should pay for it. Anthropologists are human, and each will probably do a better job if studying a topic he or she prefers. Money for research comes from public and private sources. The values of the anthropologist and those of the people who control the funds enter into decisions over what research will be supported and actually done. Harris has made the point that with the limited financial and manpower resources available, anthropologists should be very careful to allocate these in ways most likely to advance knowledge, and not to fritter them away on enjoyable, fancy, but unproductive research (1968:3).

Research that is evaluated by those who control the money as urgent, significant, or most promising for some purpose or other will probably get funds. Of course, it is difficult to determine in advance what research will be productive. It is probably impossible to make an objective decision, so the real question is whose values should determine the choice—those of the scientists, the elected officials, the people providing the money, or the chosen money managers. Naturally, researchers want to be able to decide what to study; they may even feel that they know best what *should* be studied. Similarly, the people footing the bill want some say in the matter. In addition, if those controlling the funds are using public money, they are normally accountable in some way and therefore must be able to justify their decisions either to other elected officials (Congress, for example) or to the public at large. If the funds are provided by private individuals, it may be possible to ignore public values, but then the individuals who provide the funds must be satisfied. Because their values may be quite different from the general public ones, they provide some source of diversity in what research eventually is supported. Those managing public funds are not noted for their support of unusual projects.

Adding fuel to an already heated controversy, some anthropologists have taken it upon themselves to act as the conscience for the whole profession. Other anthropologists, who feel perfectly capable of making moral decisions themselves, resent this. Just as medical doctors may be prepared to accept a code of ethics regarding their treatment of patients, but not any regulation of what branch of medicine they should specialize in, anthropologists may be ready to accept an ethical code dealing with their relationships to the people they study, but not any dictates as to what they should study or for whom they should work.

Another thorny issue is what happens to the results of the research. There is a strong objection to anthropologists' being subjected to censorship, but there is an equally strong objection to disseminating information that might be used in some way against the study group. It is, however, difficult to both conceal and reveal the same information. It is also difficult to determine just what information might be used "against" a people at some future date. Furthermore, the decision as to what is harmful is in itself a value judgment. What would be interpreted as damaging by one group in the controversy might be regarded as beneficial by another.

Values also enter the picture legitimately and inevitably in the choice of method used. Ethical values do not permit the use of methods that will cause embarrassment or harm to the people being studied. Cost and time available are also values that affect the ultimate decision about the method to use.

The fact that values concerning choice of problem, choice of sponsor, dissemination of results, methods used, and so on, must enter into the research process at various points, does not mean that values must or should be involved everywhere. The philosophical concern over the basic concepts that the anthropologist takes into the field, the knowledge that the presence of the observer alters the situation to some degree, the awareness that preconceived categories may not fit the field data, the recognition that the observer frequently has emotional reactions and becomes involved with the people studied, all have led some anthropologists to feel that values cannot be eliminated from any stage of the process, and probably should not be. A rejoinder to this position is that

Science argues about the world, a world that was there before there was science, and which will be there after science has gone, hence a world in some if not all respects existing independently of science. There is a world and a science of that world, phenomena and observers of those phenomena, facts independent of theories, knowledge independent of social status, kinship connection, cultural or linguistic membership, political power, or ritual condition. The objects of this world are not arbitrary; they are what has been found problematic and hence what wants explanation. Anthropology is cross-cultural, implicitly where not explicitly, and hence inevitably and correctly uses concepts and categories that are not indigenous but as it were external to the *lebenswelt* of the culture described (Gellner 1973:199). . . . a social group is there before an anthropologist visits it, and I see no logical or moral objection to the anthropologist wishing to get an approximate picture of what that social group is like and how it works when he is not there. Of course he can do that only by going there and hence altering the situation, but again, he can make a harmless analytical abstraction [Jarvie 1975:262–63].

It is, of course, difficult to be objective about behavior that violates one's own covert culture, but it can be attempted. People in other professions have been trained to be objective. Good medical doctors will not overlook a potentially fatal disease just because they dislike the patient, nor will they refuse to recognize an embarrassing problem because they like the patient. Surely anthropologists can be equally objective studying other cultures. Doctors recognize their own lack of objectivity regarding medical problems in their own families and customarily send intimate friends and family members to other doctors for diagnosis and treatment. Similarly, anthropologists recognize that there are special problems involved in studying their own culture and usually are not permitted to do so for their first field experience. A peculiar exception to this is that both American and English institutions, when training foreign-born anthropologists such as Asiatic Indians, Pakistanis, or Africans, often encourage them to study their own cultures. They thereby lose a fine opportunity to have an anthropologically trained outsider make a study of American or English culture. In addition, it forces the foreign anthropologist to miss a valuable part of his training. Why allow foreign anthropologists to do something most American or English anthropologists are forbidden to do? The answer seems to be that anthropologists normally study "foreign" cultures, and an African or Indian culture is "foreign" (to the American or Englishman of course), so it is therefore acceptable—ethnocentrism in its worst form!

Deliberately falsifying or distorting data in any way contravenes the whole purpose of science; it is incompatible with any serious study of human behavior. Behavioral scientists who do more than slightly disguise their study populations to protect them from curiosity seekers are doing incalculable harm to the understanding of people. Honest mistakes cause trouble enough without deliberate distortions. Understanding of genetics was hampered for almost twenty years by one researcher's insistence that he had proof of the inheritance of acquired characteristics. When independent observers finally could examine the evidence, they found it was fraudulent. Scientists had been hoaxed and theories based on the "proof" were useless. The concept was dropped from genetics until a Soviet scientist named Lysenko resurrected it. Because of political intervention by Stalin, scientists who opposed Lysenko were silenced. Politics could not control growing plants, however, and experiments based on the inheritance of acquired characteristics which were designed to improve Soviet agriculture uniformly failed (*Encyclopaedia Britannica* 1970, 13:614–617). The inability of plants and animals to respond genetically in a dialectically proper Marxist manner eventually led to the reduction of restraints in this area, allowing geneticists once again to follow where the data led them.

Because most people writing about human behavior have a particular position to support, their statements are often self-seeking and therefore suspect. Where can the city planner, or anybody who wants to improve the human condition, turn for the accurate information needed? If even the behavioral sciences are distorting their data to serve their own interests, however sincere those interests may be, who can be relied on? No one can make any sensible plans in the absence of reliable data. If a population is increasing by 4 percent per year and food production is increasing only 2 percent in the same period, it will not help anyone to be told the opposite. People will starve, because they need real food, not false statistics.

In summary then, values in anthropology are probably inevitable in choices over what is to be investigated, whose support will be accepted, and what is to be done with the results of the research. Arguments can and will continue over who should decide these questions—the anthropologists themselves, the financial supporters, public officials, a professional association, or some combination of all of these. Values must not be allowed to distort the data themselves, however. Regardless of what choices are made in other aspects of research, the data must be gathered and reported as accurately and objectively as possible, or there is no hope for any increased prediction or understanding of human behavior.

Anthropology, as a field, is faced with serious choices in this area which may determine its future usefulness as a science of the human being. If it is to continue as a science, there are a variety of areas that will probably receive increased attention: education, medicine, industry, urban centers, cognition, psychology, the use of computers for model-building, and the application of anthropology. Other areas not apparent at present may prove to be exciting and fruitful. The field is one that offers promise for future generations who are particularly interested in the proper study of humans—people (Pope 1958:107).

Bibliography

ACKERMAN, CHARLES
1968 "Conjunctive Affiliation and Divorce," in Norman W. Bell and Ezra F. Vogel (eds.), *A Modern Introduction to the Family.* New York: Free Press, pp. 469–477.

ALLPORT, G. W., AND T. F. PETTIGREW
1957 "Cultural Influence on the Perception of Movement: The Trapezoidal Illusion among Zulus," *Journal of Abnormal and Social Psychology* 55:104–113.

AMBROSE, STEPHEN F.
1975 *Crazy Horse and Custer.* Garden City, N.Y.: Doubleday.

AMERICAN ANTHROPOLOGICAL ASSOCIATION
1966, 1968, 1971 *Studying Societies, Patterns in Human History.* New York: Macmillan.

ARDREY, ROBERT
1963 *African Genesis.* New York: Dell.
1970 *The Social Contract.* New York: Atheneum.

ARMILLAS, PEDRO
1964 "Northern Mesoamerica," in Jesse Jennings and Edward Norbeck (eds.), *Prehistoric Man in the New World.* Chicago: University of Chicago Press, pp. 291–329.

ASCH, SOLOMON E.
1955 "Opinions and Social Pressure," in H. Laurence Ross (ed.), *Perspectives on the Social Order.* McGraw-Hill, pp. 204–207.

BANDURA, A., AND R. H. WALTERS
1963 *Social Learning and Personality Development.* New York: Holt, Rinehart and Winston.

BARNOUW, VICTOR
1963 *Culture and Personality.* Homewood, Ill.: Dorsey.
1971 *An Introduction to Anthropology.* Homewood, Ill.: Dorsey.
1973 *Culture and Personality,* rev. ed. Homewood, Ill.: Dorsey.

BASTIAN, ADOLF
1895 *Ethnische Elementargedanken in des Lehre vom Menschen.* Berlin: Weidmann'sche Buchhandlung.

BAUER, PETER, AND BASIL S. YARNEY
1957 *The Economics of Underdeveloped Countries.* Chicago: University of Chicago Press.

BEALS, ALAN R.
1964 *Gopalpur.* New York: Holt, Rinehart and Winston.

BELL, NORMAN W. AND EZRA F. VOGEL
1968 *A Modern Introduction to the Family.* New York: Free Press.

BELL, ROBERT R.
1971 *Social Deviance.* Homewood, Ill.: Dorsey.

BELSHAW, CYRIL S.
    1965 Traditional Exchange and Modern Markets. Englewood Cliffs, N.J.: Prentice-Hall.

BENEDICT, RUTH
    1934 Patterns of Culture. New York: New American Library.

BENNETT, JOHN W., AND MELVIN M. TUMIN
    1964 "Some Cultural Imperatives," in Peter B. Hammond (ed.), *Cultural and Social Anthropology.* New York: Macmillan, pp. 9–21.

BERLIN, BRENT
    1970 "A Universalist-Evolutionary Approach in Ethnographic Semantics," in Ann Fischer (ed.), *Current Directions in Anthropology.* 3(3, pt. 2):3–18. Washington, D.C.: American Anthropological Association.

BIGELOW, ROBERT
    1969 The Dawn Warrior. Boston: Little, Brown.

BIRDWHISTELL, RAY
    1970 "Ways We Speak Body Language," *New York Times Magazine,* May 31, pp. 8–9.
    1952 Introduction to Kinesics. Louisville, Ky.: University of Louisville Press.

BLOOMFIELD, LEONARD
    1933 Language. New York: Henry Hart.

BOAS, FRANZ
    1967 The Central Eskimo. Lincoln, Neb.: University of Nebraska Press.

BOCK, PHILIP K.
    1969 Modern Cultural Anthropology. New York: Knopf.

BOHANNAN, PAUL (ED.)
    1960 African Homicide and Suicide. Princeton, N.J.: Princeton University Press.
    1967 Law and Warfare. Garden City, N.Y.: Natural History Press.
    1971 Africa and Africans, rev. ed. Garden City, N.Y.: Natural History Press.

BRACE, C. LORING
    1964 "A Consideration of Hominid Catastrophism," *Current Anthropology* 5(1): 3–19, 32–38.

BREBEUF, JEAN DE, S.J.
    1897 "Huron Relation of 1636," in R. G. Thwaites (ed.), *Jesuit Relations & Allied Documents,* Vol. 10. Cleveland: Burrows Bros.

BROCKETT, OSCAR G.
    1974 History of the Theater, 2nd ed. Boston: Allyn and Bacon.

BROWN, JUDITH K.
    1963 "A Cross-Cultural Study of Female Initiation Rites," *American Anthropologist* 65(4):837–853.

BUETTNER-JANUSCH, JOHN
    1966 Origins of Man. New York: Wiley.

BULFINCH, THOMAS
    n.d. Bulfinch's Mythology. New York: Modern Library.

BURLING, ROBBINS
    1959 "Review of Noam Chomsky's Syntactic Structures," *American Anthropologist* 61:160–162.

BUSHNELL, G. H. S.
   1968 The First Americans. New York: McGraw-Hill.

CAMPBELL, BERNARD G.
   1966 Human Evolution. Chicago: Aldine.

CARNEIRO, ROBERT L.
   1968 "Slash and Burn Cultivation Among the Kuikuru and Its Implications for Cultural Development in the Amazon Basin," in Yehudi A. Cohen (ed.), *Man in Adaptation: The Cultural Present.* Chicago: Aldine, pp. 131–145.

CHAGNON, NAPOLEON A.
   1968 Yanamamo: The Fierce People. New York: Holt, Rinehart and Winston.

CHARD, CHESTER A.
   1969 Man in Prehistory. New York: McGraw-Hill.
   1975 Man in Prehistory, 2nd ed. New York: McGraw-Hill.

CHILDS, EBENEZER
   1906 "Recollections of Wisconsin since 1820," in Lyman C. Draper (ed.), *Collections of the State Historical Society of Wisconsin,* Vol. 4. Madison, Wisc.: The State Historical Society of Wisconsin.

CHOMSKY, NOAM
   1964 Current Issues in Linguistic Theory. The Hague: Mouton and Co.

CLARK, ELMER T.
   1937 Small Sects in America. Nashville, Tenn.: Cokesbury Press.

CLIFTON, JAMES (ED.)
   1968 Introduction to Cultural Anthropology. Boston: Houghton Mifflin.

CLINARD, MARSHALL B.
   1974 Sociology of Deviant Behavior, 4th ed. New York: Holt, Rinehart and Winston.

CLINTON, DEWITT
   1817 A Memoir of the Antiquities of the Western Parts of the State of New York Addressed to the Honorable Samuel L. Mitchill a Vice-President of the Literary and Philosophical Society of New York. Read before the society, 13 November 1817.

COHEN, YEHUDI A.
   1968 Man in Adaptation: The Cultural Present. Chicago: Aldine.

COOK, EARL
   1971 "The Flow of Energy in an Industrial Society," *Scientific American,* 224(3): 134–144.

COOK, SCOTT
   1966 "The Obsolete 'Anti-Market' Mentality: A Critique of the Substantive Approach to Economic Anthropology," *American Anthropology* 68(2):323–345.

CUBER, JOHN F.
   1968 Sociology: A Synopsis of Principles. New York: Appleton-Century-Crofts.

DELORIA, VINE, JR.
   1969 Custer Died for Your Sins. New York: Macmillan.
   1971 We Talk, You Listen. New York: Macmillan.

DEVEREUX, GEORGE
   1961 "Two Types of Modal Personality Models," in Bert Kaplan (ed.), *Studying Personality Cross-Culturally.* Evanston, Ill.: Row, Peterson.

DE WAAL MALEFIJT, ANNEMARIE
　　1974 Images of Man. New York: Knopf.

DOBYNS, HENRY F.
　　1960 "The Religious Festival." Ph.D. thesis, Cornell University, Ithaca, N.Y.
　　1966 "Estimating Aboriginal American Population," *Current Anthropology* 7(4):
　　395–416, 440–444.

DOBYNS, HENRY F. AND ROBERT C. EULER
　　1970 Wauba Yuma's People. Prescott, Ariz.: Prescott College.

DOWNING, JOSEPH
　　1970 "The Tribal Family and the Society of Awakening," in Herbert A. Otto (ed.),
　　The Family in Search of a Future. New York: Appleton-Century-Crofts, pp. 119–
　　135.

DRUCKER, PHILIP
　　1963 Indians of the Northwest Coast. Garden City, N.Y.: Natural History Press.

DURKHEIM, EMILE
　　1951 Suicide. New York: Free Press.

EDDY, MARY BAKER
　　n.d. Science and Health. Boston: published by trustees under the will of Mary Baker
　　G. Eddy.

EDEY, MAITLAND A.
　　1972 The Missing Link. New York: Time-Life Books.

EKHOLM, GORDON F.
　　1964 "Transpacific Contacts," in Jesse Jennings and Edward Norbeck (eds.), *Prehis-
　　toric Man in the New World.* Chicago: University of Chicago Press, pp. 489–510.

EKVALL, ROBERT B.
　　1968 Fields on the Hoof. New York: Holt, Rinehart and Winston.

ENCYCLOPAEDIA BRITANNICA
　　1966, 1970 Warren E. Preece (ed.) 24 vols. Chicago: William Benton.

EVANS-PRITCHARD, E. E.
　　*1965 The Position of Women in Primitive Societies and Other Essays in Social An-
　　thropology.* London: Faber and Faber.

FALLERS, L. A. AND M. C. FALLERS
　　1960 "Homicide and Suicide in Busoga," in Paul Bohannan (ed.), *African Homicide
　　and Suicide.* Princeton, N.J.: Princeton University Press, pp. 65–93.

FARBER, BERNARD
　　1966 Kinship and Family Organization. New York: Wiley.

FAST, JULIUS
　　1970 Body Language. New York: M. Evans.

FEDERAL BUREAU OF INVESTIGATION
　　1973 Uniform Crime Reports for the U.S. Washington, D.C.: F.B.I.

FERNEA, ELIZABETH WARNOCK
　　1969 Guests of the Sheik. Garden City, N.Y.: Doubleday.

FISCHER, ANN (ED.)
　　1970 Current Directions in Anthropology 3(3, pt. 2). Washington, D.C.: American
　　Anthropological Association.

FISCHER, JOHN L.
   1958 "The Classification of Residence in Censuses," *American Anthropologist* 60(33):508–517.

FISCHER, JOHN L. AND ANN FISCHER
   1966 *The New Englanders of Orchard Town, U.S.A.* New York: Wiley.

FORDE, DARYLL
   1968 "The Kazak: Horse and Sheep Herders of Central Asia," in Yehudi A. Cohen (ed.), *Man in Adaptation: The Cultural Present.* Chicago: Aldine, pp. 299–309.

FORTES, MEYER
   1962 Marriage in Tribal Societies. Cambridge, England: Cambridge University Press.

FOSTER, GEORGE M.
   1965 "Peasant Society and the Image of Limited Good," *American Anthropologist* 67:293–315.

FRANKFORT, HENRI
   1964 "The Cities of Mesopotamia," in Peter B. Hammond (ed.), *Physical Anthropology and Archeology.* New York: Macmillan, pp. 344–361.

FRASER, L. M.
   1937 Economic Thought and Language. London: Adam and Charles Black.

FRAZER, SIR JAMES GEORGE
   1955 The Golden Bough. London: Macmillan.

FREUCHEN, PETER
   1961 Book of the Eskimos. Greenwich, Conn.: Fawcett Premierbook.

FREUD, SIGMUND
   1920 A General Introduction to Psychoanalysis. Translated by Joan Riviere. New York: Liveright.

GAIDOZ, HENRI
   1884 Comme quoi M. Max Muller n'a jamais existé. Etude de mythologie comparée. *Melusine* 2:73–88.

GARDNER, R. A., AND B. T.
   1969 Teaching Sign Language to a Chimpanzee. Science 165:664–672.

GATHERU, R. MUGO
   1965 Child of Two Worlds. Garden City, N.Y.: Doubleday.

GELLNER, ERNEST
   1973 Cause and Meaning in the Social Sciences. London: Routledge and Kegan Paul.

GILBERT, GEORGE B.
   1939 Forty Years a Country Preacher. New York: Harper & Row.

GLAZER, NATHAN, AND DANIEL PATRICK MOYNIHAN
   1963 Beyond the Melting Pot. Cambridge, Mass.: MIT Press.

GLUCKMAN, MAX
   1968 "Estrangement in the African Family," in Norman W. Bell and Ezra F. Vogel (eds.), *A Modern Introduction to the Family.* New York: Free Press, pp. 464–468.

GOLDENWEISER, ALEXANDER
   1933 History, Psychology and Culture. New York: Knopf.

GOODE, WILLIAM J. (ED.)
1964 Readings on the Family and Society. Englewood Cliffs, N.J.: Prentice-Hall.

GOODMAN, HENRY (ED.)
1949 Selected Writings of Lafcadio Hearn. New York: Citadel Press.

GOODY, ESTHER N.
1962 "Conjugal Separation and Divorce among the Gonja of Northern Ghana," in Meyer Fortes (ed.), *Marriage in Tribal Societies.* Cambridge, England: Cambridge University Press, pp. 14–54.

GOUGH, KATHLEEN
1968 "Is the Family Universal—the Nayer Case," in Norman Bell and Ezra F. Vogel (eds.), *A Modern Introduction to the Family.* New York: Free Press, pp. 80–96.

GOULD, JULIUS, AND WILLIAM L. KOLB (EDS.)
1969 A Dictionary of the Social Sciences. New York: Free Press.

GOULD, RICHARD A.
1969 Yiwara: Foragers of the Australian Desert. New York: Scribner.

GREER, SCOTT A.
1965 Social Organization. New York: Random House.

GRINDER, JOHN T., AND SUZETTE H. ELGIN
1973 Guide to Transformational Grammar. New York: Holt, Rinehart and Winston.

HAHN, EMILY
1971 "Chimpanzees and Language," *New Yorker,* Dec. 11, 1971, p. 54.

HALL, EDWARD T.
1959 The Silent Language. Greenwich, Conn.: Fawcett.
1965 "Territorial Needs and Limits," *Natural History Magazine* 74:12–19.

HAMBLIN, DORA JANE
1973 The First Cities. New York: Time-Life Books.

HAMILTON, EDITH
1945 Mythology. Boston: Little, Brown.

HAMILTON, MILTON D. (ED.)
1951 "Regulations for the Indian Trade at Fort Stanwix, February, 1762," *Papers of Sir William Johnson,* Vol. 10. Albany, N.Y.: State University of New York Press, pp. 389–391.

HAMMOND, PETER B.
1964 Cultural and Social Anthropology. New York: Macmillan.
1964 Physical Anthropology and Archeology. New York: Macmillan.

HARLOW, HARRY F., AND MARGARET K. HARLOW
1961 "A Study of Animal Affection," *Natural History Magazine* 70(10):48–55.

HARRIS, MARVIN
1964 The Nature of Cultural Things. New York: Random House.
1968 The Rise of Anthropological Theory. New York: Crowell.
1972 "You Are What They Ate," *Natural History* 81(7):24–25.
1972 "Riddle of the Pig," *Natural History* 81(8):32–36.
1974 Cows, Pigs, Wars and Witches. New York: Vintage.

HARRISON, JOHN F.
1970 Linguistics and Two Revolutions. Lexington, Ky.: Transylvania University, unpublished paper.

HART, C. W. M., AND ARNOLD R. PILLING
1964 The Tiwi of Northern Australia. New York: Holt, Rinehart and Winston.

HAWKES, JACQUETTA
   1968 Dawn of the Gods. New York: Random House.

HERSKOVITS, MELVILLE J.
   1951 Man and His Works. New York: Knopf.

HIGGINS, BENJAMIN
   1959 Economic Development: Principles, Problems, and Policies. New York: Norton.

HOEBEL, E. ADAMSON
   1960 The Cheyennes. New York: Holt, Rinehart and Winston.
   1964 The Law of Primitive Man. Cambridge, Mass.: Harvard University Press.
   1966 Anthropology: The Study of Man, 3rd ed. New York: McGraw-Hill.

HOGBIN, IAN
   1971 "Polynesian Ceremonial Gift Exchanges," in Alan Howard (ed.), *Polynesia.* Scranton, Pa.: Chandler, pp. 27–45.

HOIJER, HARRY (ED.)
   1954a Language in Culture. American Anthropological Association Memoir No. 79, Vol. 56, No. 6, Part 2. Washington, D. C.: American Anthropological Association.
   1954b "The Sapir-Whorf Hypothesis," in Harry Hoijer (ed.), *Language in Culture.* American Anthropological Association Memoir No. 79, Vol. 56, No. 6, Part 2. Washington, D.C.: American Anthropological Association, pp. 92–105.

HOLLOWAY, RALPH L., JR.
   1967 "Tools and Teeth: Some Speculations Regarding Canine Reductions," *American Anthropologist* 69(1):63–67.

HOLMBERG, ALLAN R.
   1969 Nomads of the Long Bow. Garden City, N.Y.: Natural History Press.

HOLZER, HANS
   1971 The Truth About Witchcraft. New York: Pocket Books.

HOMANS, GEORGE C.
   1950 The Human Group. New York: Harcourt, Brace and World.

HOSTETLER, JOHN A., AND GERTRUDE ENDERS HUNTINGTON
   1967 The Hutterites in North America. New York: Holt, Rinehart and Winston.

HOWARD, ALAN (ED.)
   1971 Polynesia. Scranton, Pa.: Chandler.

HOWELL, F. CLARK
   1965 Early Man. New York: Time-Life Books.

HOWELLS, WILLIAM
   1962 The Heathens. Garden City, N.Y.: Doubleday.

HSU, FRANCES L. K.
   1961 Psychological Anthropology. Homewood, Ill.: Dorsey Press.

HULSE, FREDERICK S.
   1971 The Human Species, 2nd ed. New York: Random House.

HUTCHINSON, R. W.
   1968 Prehistoric Crete. Middlesex, England: Penguin Books.

ISAAC, BARRY L.
   1971 "Business Failure in a Developing Town: Pendumbu, Sierra Leone," *Human Organization* 30(3):288–294.

JAMESON, JOHN FRANKLIN
   1909 Narratives of New Netherlands 1609–1664. New York: Scribner.

JARVIE, I. C.
  1975 "Epistle to the Anthropologists," *American Anthropologist* 77: 253–266.

JENNESS, DIAMOND
  1959 *The People of the Twilight*. Chicago: University of Chicago Press.

JENNINGS, JESSE, AND EDWARD NORBECK (EDS.)
  1964 *Prehistoric Man in the New World*. Chicago: University of Chicago Press.

JONAS, GERALD
  1974 "Reporter at Large: Into the Brain; Fifth International Interdisciplinary Conference," *New Yorker* July 1, 1974, pp. 52–69.

KAPLAN, BERT
  1954 "A Study of the Rorschach Responses in Four Cultures," *Papers, Peabody Museum of American Archeology and Ethnology*, 42(2).

KAPLAN, BERT (ED.)
  1961 *Studying Personality Cross-Culturally*. Evanston, Ill.: Row, Peterson.

KEESING, FELIX N.
  1964 *Cultural Anthropology*. New York: Holt, Rinehart and Winston.

KEARNEY, MICHAEL
  1969 An Exception to the "Image of Limited Good," *American Anthropologist*, 71(5):888–890.

KEMP, WILLIAM B.
  1971 "The Flow of Energy in a Hunting Society," *Scientific American* 224(3):104–115.

KIPLING, RUDYARD
  1936 *All the Mowgli Stories*. New York: Doubleday, Doran.

KLUCKHOHN, CLYDE, AND DORTHEA LEIGHTON
  1946 *The Navaho*. Cambridge, Mass.: Harvard University Press.

KORFMANN, MANFRED
  1973 "Sling as a Weapon," *Scientific American* 229(4):34–42.

KOHN, MELVIN K.
  1966 "Social Class and Parent-Child Relationships," in Bernard Farber (ed.), *Kinship and Family Organization*. New York: Wiley, pp. 281–289.

KROEBER, A. L.
  1917 "The Superorganic," *American Anthropologist* 19:163–213.

KRONENBERGER, LOUIS (ED.)
  1951 *Alexander Pope, Selected Works*. New York: Modern Library.

KURATH, GERTRUDE P.
  1950 "A New Method of Choreographic Notation," *American Anthropologist* 52:120.
  1954 "A Basic Vocabulary for Ethnic Dance Descriptions," *American Anthropologist* 56:1102–1103.

LABARRE, WESTON
  1964 "Animism" in Julius Gould and William L. Kolb (eds.), *A Dictionary of the Social Sciences*. New York: Free Press, pp. 26–29.

LACY, DAN
  1972 *The White Use of Blacks in America*. New York: McGraw-Hill.

LAHONTON, BARON DE
  1931 *Dialogues curieux et mémories de l'Amérique septentrionale*. Baltimore: Johns Hopkins Press.

LAMB, SYDNEY
   1967 "Review of Chomsky's 'Current Issues in Linguistic Theory and Aspects of the
   Theory of Snytax,'" *American Anthropologist* 69:411–415.

LAMBERT, WILLIAM W., LEIGH MINTURN TRANDIS, AND MARGERY WOLF
   1959 "Some Correlates of Beliefs in the Malevolence and Benevolence of Supernatural Beings: A Cross-Cultural Study," *Journal of Abnormal and Social Psychology* 58:162–169.

LANGNESS, L. L., AND J. C. WESCHLER
   1971 Melanesnia. Scranton, Pa.: Chandler.

LANTIS, MARGARET
   1952 "Eskimo Herdsman: Introduction of Reindeer Herding to the Natives of
   Alaska," in Edward Spicer (ed.), *Human Problems in Technological Change.* New
   York: Russell Sage Foundation, pp. 127–148.

LASWELL, FRED
   n.d. Barney Google and Snuffy Smith. King Features.

LEACH, MARIA (ED.)
   1949 Dictionary of Folklore, Mythology and Legend. 2 vols. New York: Funk &
   Wagnalls.

LEAKEY, RICHARD E. F.
   1973 "Australopitheunes and Hominines: A Summary on the Evidence from the
   Early Pleistocene of Eastern Africa," in Sir Solly Zuckerman (ed.), *Symposium of
   the Zoological Society of London* 33:53–69.

LEE, RICHARD B., AND IRVEN DEVORE (EDS.)
   1968 Man the Hunter. Chicago: Aldine.

LEE, RICHARD B., AND IRVEN DEVORE (EDS.)
   1968 "What Hunters Do for a Living, or, How to Make Out on Scarce Resources,"
   in Richard B. Lee and Irven DeVore (eds.), *Man the Hunter.* Chicago: Aldine, pp.
   30–48.

LE GROS CLARK, SIR WILFRED E.
   1967 Man-Apes or Ape-Men? New York: Holt, Rinehart and Winston.

LE JEUNE, PAUL
   1897 "The Relation of 1634," in R. G. Thwaites (ed.), *Jesuit Relations and Allied
   Documents,* Vols. 6 and 7. Cleveland: Burrows Bros.

LENNEBERG, ERIC H., AND JOHN M. ROBERTS
   1961 "The Language of Experience: A Study in Methodology," in Sol Saporta (ed.),
   Psycholinguistics: A Book of Readings. New York: Holt, Rinehart and Winston, pp.
   493–502.

LEONARD, JONATHON N.
   1973 The First Farmers. New York: Time-Life Books.

LESSA, WILLIAM A., AND EVON Z. VOGT (EDS.)
   1965 Reader in Comparative Religion, 2nd ed. New York: Harper & Row.

LEVINE, ROBERT A.
   1966 Dreams and Deeds: Achievement and Motivation in Nigeria. Chicago: University of Chicago Press.

LEVINE, ROBERT A., AND BARBARA B. LEVINE
   1966 Nyansongo: A Gusii Community in Kenya. New York: Wiley.

Lévi-Strauss, Claude
    1960 "The Family," in Harry Shapiro (ed.), *Man, Culture and Society.* New York: Oxford University Press, pp. 261–285.

Levy, Marion J.
    1964 "Contrasting Factors in the Modernization of China and Japan," in William J Goode (ed.), *Readings on the Family and Society.* Englewood Cliffs, N.J.: Prentice-Hall, pp. 225–230.

Linton, Ralph
    1936 The Study of Man. New York: Appleton-Century-Crofts.
    1937 "One Hundred Percent American," *American Mercury* 40:427–429.

Linton, Ralph (ed.)
    1949 Most of the World. New York: Columbia University Press.

Livermore, Mary A.
    1890 My Story of the War. Hartford, Conn.: A. D. Worthington.

Llewellyn, K. N., and E. A. Hoebel
    1941 The Cheyenne Way: Conflict and Case Law in Primitive Jurisprudence. Norman, Okla.: University of Oklahoma Press.

Lorenz, Konrad
    1963 On Aggression. New York: Bantam.

Madsen, William
    1964 The Mexican-Americans of South Texas. New York: Holt, Rinehart and Winston.

Malinowski, Bronislaw
    1929 The Sexual Lives of Savages. New York: Liveright.
    1953 Sex and Repression in Savage Society. London: Routledge and Kegan Paul.
    1966 Crime and Custom in Savage Society. Totowa, N.J.: Littlefield, Adams.

Marshack, Alexander
    1972 The Roots of Civilization. New York: McGraw-Hill.

Martin, Paul S., George Quimby, and Donald Collier
    1947 Indians Before Columbus. Chicago: University of Chicago Press.

Matthiessen, Peter
    1969 Under the Mountain Wall. New York: Ballantine.

McClelland, David C.
    1961 The Achieving Society. New York: Van Nostrand.

Mead, Margaret
    1950 Sex and Temperament in Three Primitive Societies. New York: New American Library.
    1956 New Lives for Old. New York: Dell.

Miller, N. E., and J. Dollard
    1941 Social Learning and Imitation. New Haven: Yale University Press.

Minturn, Leigh, and William Lambert
    1968 "Motherhood and Child Rearing," in Norman W. Bell and Ezra F. Vogel (eds.), *A Modern Introduction to the Family.* New York: Free Press, pp. 551–557.

Mooney, James
    1965 The Ghost Dance Religion. Chicago: University of Chicago Press.

MORRIS, DESMOND (ED.)
1969 *Primate Ethology.* Garden City, N.Y.: Anchor Books.

MUNSELL, JOEL
1850 *The Annals of Albany.* Albany N.Y.: published by the author.

MURDOCK, GEORGE PETER
1949 *Social Structure.* New York: Macmillan
1950 *Outline of Cultural Materials,* 3rd ed. New Haven, Conn.: Human Relations Area Files.
1968 "The Current Status of the World's Hunting and Gathering Peoples," in Richard B. Lee and Irven DeVore (eds.), *Man the Hunter.* Chicago: Aldine, pp. 13–20.

MUSSEN, PAUL, AND MARK R. ROSENZWEIG
1973 *Psychology: An Introduction.* New York: D. C. Heath.

NETTING, ROBERT McC.
1968 *Hill Farmers of Nigeria.* Seattle: University of Washington Press.

NETTLESHIP, MARTIN, R. DALE GIVENS, AND ANDERSON NETTLESHIP (EDS.)
1975 *War: Its Causes and Correlates.* Paris: Mouton.

NEW YORK STOCK EXCHANGE
1969 *Fact Book.* New York: New York Stock Exchange.

NICKERSON, GIFFORD S.
1975 "Review of Jeannette Henry (ed.), The American Indian Reader, Book One: Anthropology and Book Two: Education," *American Anthropologist* 77:403–405.

NIERENBERG, GERARD I.
1972 *How To Read A Person Like a Book.* New York: Cornerstone Library, Inc.

NIMKOFF, M. F. (ED.)
1965 *Comparative Family Systems.* Boston: Houghton Mifflin.

OLIVER, DOUGLAS L.
1971 "Horticulture and Husbandry in Solomon Island Society," in L. L. Langness and J. C. Weschler (eds.), *Melanesia.* Scranton, Pa.: Chandler, pp. 52–67.

OPLER, MORRIS E.
1945 "Themes as Dynamic Forces in Culture," *American Journal of Sociology* 51:198–206.

ORCHARD, WILLIAM C.
1929 *Bead and Beadwork of the American Indian.* New York: Heye Foundation.

OSWALT, WENDELL H.
1966 *This Land Was Theirs.* New York: Wiley.

OTTENBERG, SIMON
1968 *Double Descent in an African Society.* Seattle: University of Washington Press.

OTTO, HERBERT A.
1970 *The Family in Search of a Future.* New York: Appleton-Century-Crofts.

PACKARD, VANCE
1972 *A Nation of Strangers.* New York: David McKay.

PADDOCK, WILLIAM, AND PAUL PADDOCK
1967 *Famine.* Boston: Little, Brown.

PFEIFFER, JOHN E.
  1972 The Emergence of Man, 2nd ed. New York: Harper & Row.

PIERCE, JOE E.
  1964 Life in a Turkish Village. New York: Holt, Rinehart and Winston.

PILBEAM, DAVID
  1972 The Ascent of Man. New York: Macmillan.

POPE, ALEXANDER
  1951 "Essay on Man," in Louis Kronenberger (ed.), *Alexander Pope: Selected Works.* New York: Modern Library.

POSPISIL, LEOPOLD
  1964 The Kapauku Papuans. New York: Holt, Rinehart and Winston.
  1967 "The Attributes of Law," in Paul Bohannan (ed.), *Law and Warfare.* Garden City, N.Y.: Natural History Press, pp. 25–41.

POWDERMAKER, HORTENSE
  1933 Life in Lesu. New York: Norton.

PREMACK, ANN J., AND DAVID PREMACK
  1972 Teaching Language to an Ape. Scientific American 227:92–99.

PRICE-WILLIAMS, DOUGLASS R.
  1968 "Ethnopsychology I: Comparative Psychological Processes," in James Clifton (ed.), *Introduction to Cultural Anthropology.* Boston: Houghton Mifflin, pp. 304–315.

PRUITT, IDA
  1945 A Daughter of Han: The Autobiography of a Chinese Working Woman. New Haven, Conn.: Yale University Press.

QUINN, DAVID BEERS
  1955 The Roanoke Voyages 1584–1590. 2 vols. London: Hayluyt Society.

RADCLIFFE-BROWN, A. R.
  1949 "Functionalism: A Protest," *American Anthropologist* 51:320–323.
  1958 Method in Social Anthropology. M.N. Srinibas (ed.), Chicago: University of Chicago Press.

RADCLIFFE-BROWN, A. R., AND DARYLL FORDE
  1964 African Systems of Kinship and Marriage. New York: Oxford University Press.

RAGUENEAU, PAUL
  1898 "Relation of What Occurred in the Country of the Hurons . . . in the Years 1647 & 1648," in R. G. Thwaites (ed.), *The Jesuit Relations and Allied Documents.* Vol. 33. Cleveland: Burrows Bros.

RAPOPORT, ROBERT
  1954 "Changing Navajo Religious Values," *Papers of the Peabody Museum.* Vol. 41. Cambridge, Mass.: Harvard University Press.

RAPPAPORT, ROY A.
  1971 "The Flow of Energy in an Agricultural Society," *Scientific American* 224(3): 116–133.

REDFIELD, ROBERT
  1941 The Folk Culture of the Yucatan. Chicago: University of Chicago Press.
  1960 The Little Community and Peasant Society and Culture. Chicago: University of Chicago Press.

RICHARDS, A. I.
>   *1964* "Some Types of Family Structure Amongst the Central Bantu," in A. R. Radcliffe-Brown and Daryll Forde (eds.), *African Systems of Kinship and Marriage.* New York: Oxford University Press, pp. 207–251.

RICHARDS, CARA E.
>   *1957* "The Role of the Iroquois Women," Ph.D. thesis, Cornell University, Ithaca, New York.
>   *1958* "Of Vikings and Long Houses: A Reply to Att. Mallery," *American Anthropologist* 60(4):1199–1203.
>   *1963* "Modern Residence Patterns Among the Navajos," *El Palacio,* Spring–Summer, pp. 25–33.
>   *1969* "Presumed Behavior: Modification of the Ideal-Real Dichotomy," *American Anthropologist* 71(6):1115–1116.
>   *1975* "The Concept and Forms of Competition," in Martin A. Nettleship (ed.), *War, Its Causes and Correlates.* Paris: Mouton, pp. 93–108.

RICHARDSON, F. L. W., JR., WITH JAMES BATAL
>   *1949* "The Near East," in Ralph Linton (ed.), *Most of the World.* New York: Columbia University Press, pp. 461–547.

ROBERTS, JOHN M., MALCOLM J. ARTHUR, AND ROBERT R. BUSH
>   *1959* "Games in Culture," *American Anthropologist* 61:597–604.

ROBERTS, JOHN M., HANS HOFFMAN, AND BRIAN SUTTON-SMITH
>   *1965* "Pattern and Competence: A Consideration of Tick-tack-toe," *El Palacio:* Autumn, pp. 17–30.

ROPER, MARILYN KEYES
>   *1969* "A Survey of the Evidence for Intra-Human Killing in the Pleistocine," *Current Anthropology* 10(4, pt. 2):427–450, 456–459.

ROSS, H. LAURENCE (ED.)
>   *1955 Perspectives on the Social Order.* New York: McGraw-Hill.

SAHLINS, MARSHALL D.
>   *1964* "The Segmentary Lineage: An Organization of Predatory Expansion," in Peter B. Hammond (ed.), *Cultural and Social Anthropology.* New York: Macmillan, pp. 181–200.

SAPORTA, SOL (ED.)
>   *1961 Psycholinguistics: A Book of Readings.* New York: Holt, Rinehart and Winston.

SCHACHTER, STANLEY, AND L. WHEELER
>   *1962* "Epinephrine, Chloropromazine, and Amusement," *Journal of Abnormal and Social Psychology* 65:121–128.

SCHAPERA, I.
>   *1941 Married Life in an African Tribe.* New York: Sheridan House.

SCHNEIDER, DAVID M.
>   *1968 American Kinship: A Cultural Account.* Englewood Cliffs, N.J.: Prentice-Hall.

SCHULTZ, JAMES WILLARD
>   *1964 My Life as an Indian.* Greenwich, Conn.: Fawcett.

SCHUR, EDWIN M.
>   *1965 Crimes Without Victims.* Englewood Cliffs, N.J.: Prentice-Hall.

SCHUSKY, ERNEST L.
>   *1974 Variation in Kinship.* New York: Holt, Rinehart and Winston.

SCIENCE NEWS
1966 "Study Shows Biochemical Link: Tolerance for Pain and Sensory Deprivation," November 19, 1966, p. 425.

SEGALL, M. H., AND D. J. CAMPBELL
1963 "Cultural Differences of Perception of Geometric Illusions," *Science* 139:769–771.

SELEKMAN, BENJAMIN M.
1947 *Labor Relations and Human Relations.* New York: McGraw-Hill.

SERVAN-SCHREIBER, J. J.
1968 *The American Challenge.* New York Atheneum.

SERVICE, ELMAN R.
1966 *The Hunters.* Englewood Cliffs, N.J.: Prentice-Hall.
1971 *Profiles in Ethnology,* rev. ed. New York: Harper & Row.

SHAPIRO, HARRY L.
1960 *Man, Culture and Society.* New York: Oxford University Press.

SHARP, LAURISTON
1952 "Steel Axes for Stone Age Australians," in Edward H. Spicer (ed.), *Human Problems in Technological Change.* New York: Russell Sage Foundation, pp. 69–90.

SIMMONS, LEO W.
1966 *Sun Chief: The Autobiography of a Hopi Indian.* New Haven, Conn.: Yale University Press.

SIMPSON, RICHARD L., AND IDA H. SIMPSON
1964 *Social Organization and Behavior.* New York: Wiley.

SIPES, RICHARD G.
1975 "War, Combative Sports and Aggression: A Preliminary Causal Model of Cultural Patterning," in Martin Nettleship, R. Dale Givens, and Anderson Nettleship (eds.), *War: Its Causes and Correlates.* Chicago: Aldine, pp. 749–761.

SLOAN, ALFRED P.
1941 *Adventures of a White-Collar Man.* In collaboration with Boyden Sparkes. New York: Doubleday, Doran.

SPENCER, ROBERT F., AND JESSE D. JENNINGS
1965 *The Native Americans.* New York: Harper & Row.

SPICER, EDWARD H.
1952 *Human Problems in Technological Change.* New York: Russell Sage Foundation.

SPIRO, MELFORD E.
1961 "Social Systems, Personality and Functional Analysis," in Bert Kaplan (ed.), *Studying Personality Cross-Culturally.* Evanston, Ill.: Row, Peterson, pp. 93–127.
1968 "Is the Family Universal—The Israeli Case," in Norman W. Bell and Ezra F. Vogel (eds.), *A Modern Introduction to the Family.* New York: Free Press, pp. 68–79.

SRINIVAS, M. N.
1955 "The Social System of a Mysore Village," in McKim Marriott and M. N. Srinivas (eds.), *Village India. American Anthropological Association Memoires* No. 83, Vol. 57 (3pt. 2):1–35.

STEINER, GEORGE
   1969 "Chomskian Revolution in Linguistics," *New Yorker,* November 15, pp. 217–218.

STEPHENS, WILLIAM N.
   1964 The Family in Cross-Cultural Perspective. New York: Holt, Rinehart and Winston.

STEWARD, JULIAN H.
   1968 "Causal Factors and Processes in the Evolution of the Pre-Farming Societies," in Richard B. Lee and Irven DeVore (eds.), *Man the Hunter.* Chicago: Aldine, pp. 321–334.

STEWARD, JULIAN H., AND LOUIS C. FARON
   1959 Native Peoples of South America. New York: McGraw-Hill.

STURTEVANT, EDGAR H.
   1947 An Introduction to Linguistic Science. New Haven: Yale University Press.

STUTZ, SARA D.
   1974 "New Hope for Retarded Children," *Readers' Digest* December, pp. 238–239.

SUGGS, ROBERT C.
   1960 "Historical Traditions and Archeology in Polynesia," *American Anthropologist* 62:764–773.

SUGIMOTO, ETSU INAGAKI
   1934 A Daughter of the Samurai. Garden City, N.Y.: Doubleday, Doran.

SUMNER, WILLIAM GRAHAM
   1911 Folkways. Boston: Ginn.

SWADESH, MORRIS, ET AL.
   1954 "Time Depth of American Linguistic Groupings," *American Anthropologist* 56:361–377.

SWARTZ, MARC J., VICTOR J. TURNER, ET AL.
   1966 Political Anthropology. Chicago: Aldine.

TALBOT, FRANCIS X., S. J.
   1956 Saint Among the Hurons: The Life of Jean de Brébeuf. Garden City, N.Y.: Doubleday.

TART, CHARLES T.
   1972 "States of Consciousness and State-Specific Sciences," *Science* 176:1203–1209.

TAYLOR, GEORGE ROGERS
   1962 "The Transportation Revolution," *Economic History of the U.S. Vol. 4.* New York: Holt, Rinehart and Winston.

TERKEL, STUDS
   1970 Hard Times. New York: Pantheon.

THOMAS, ELIZABETH MARSHALL
   1959 The Harmless People. New York: Vintage.
   1965 Warrior Herdsmen. New York: Vintage.

THOMPSON, RICHARD A.
   1975 Psychology and Culture. Dubuque, Iowa: Wm. C. Brown Co.

THWAITES, RUBEN G. (ED.)
1896–1901 *The Jesuit Relations and Allied Documents.* 73 vols. Cleveland: Burrows Bros.

TITIEV, MISCHA
1963 *The Science of Man,* rev. ed. New York: Holt, Rinehart and Winston.

TOFFLER, ALVIN
1970 *Future Shock.* New York: Random House.

TURNBULL, COLIN M.
1962 *The Forest People.* New York: Doubleday.

TYLOR, EDWARD B.
1965 "Animism," in William A. Lessa and Evon Z. Vogt (eds.), *Reader in Comparative Religion,* 2nd ed. New York: Harper & Row, pp. 10–21.

VAN GENNEP, ARNOLD
1960 *The Rites of Passage.* Chicago: University of Chicago Press.

VAN HOOFF, J. A. R. A. M.
1969 "The Facial Displays of Catarrhine Monkeys and Apes," in Desmond Morris (ed.), *Primate Ethology.* Garden City, N.Y.: Doubleday Anchor Books, pp. 9–88.

VAN LAWICK-GOODALL, JANE
1971 *In the Shadow of Man.* Boston: Houghton Mifflin.

VOGT, EVON Z., AND ETHEL M. ALBERT (EDS.)
1966 *People of Rimrock: A Study of Values in Five Cultures.* Cambridge, Mass.: Harvard University Press.

WAITZ, THEODOR
1858–72 *Anthropologie der Naturvolker.* 6 vols. Leipzig: F. Fleischer.

WALKER, WINTON
1959 *A History of the Christian Church.* New York: Scribner.

WALLACE, ANTHONY F. C.
1952 "The Modal Personality Structure of the Turcaraca Indians, as Revealed by the Rorschach Test," *Bureau of American Ethnology Bulletin,* no. 150.

WAUCHOPE, ROBERT
1962 *Lost Tribes and Sunken Continents.* Chicago: University of Chicago Press.

WAX, MURRAY
1968 "Religion and Magic," in James Clifton (ed.), *Introduction to Cultural Anthropology.* Boston: Houghton Mifflin, pp. 224–242.

WEIDENREICH, FRANZ
1939 "Six Lectures in Sinanthropus Pekinensis," *Bulletin of the Geological Society of China,* no. 19.

WESTERMARCK, EDWARD
1921 *The History of Human Marriage.* London: Macmillan.

WHITE, EDMUND, AND DALE BROWN
1973 *The First Men.* New York: Time-Life Books.

WHITE, LESLIE A.
1949 *The Science of Culture.* New York: Grove Press.

WHITING, JOHN W. M.
1961 "Socialization Process and Personality," in Francis L. K. Hsu (ed.), *Psychological Anthropology.* Homewood, Ill.: Dorsey Press, pp. 355–380.

WILKINSON, THOMAS O.
1964 "Family Structure and Industrialization in Japan," in Richard L. Simpson and Ida H. Simpson (eds.), *Social Organization and Behavior.* New York: Wiley, pp. 123–127.

WILLIAMS, ROBIN M., JR.
1964 *Strangers Next Door.* Englewood Cliffs, N.J.: Prentice-Hall.

WILSON, GODFREY, AND MONICA WILSON
1965 *The Analysis of Social Change.* Cambridge, England: Cambridge University Press.

WISSLER, CLARK
1922 *The American Indian.* New York: Oxford Press.

WOLF, ARTHUR P.
1966 "Childhood Association, Sexual Attraction and the Incest Taboo: A Chinese Case," *American Anthropologist* 68:(4):883–898.

WOODS, CLYDE M.
1975 *Cultural Change.* Dubuque, Iowa: Wm. C. Brown Co.

WOOLLEY, C. LEONARD
1965 *Ur of the Chaldees.* New York: Norton.

WORLD ALMANAC
1975 New York: Newspaper Enterprise Association, Inc.

WRIGHT, HENRY T., AND GREGORY A. JOHNSON
1975 "Population, Exchange and Early State Formation in Southwestern Iran," *American Anthropologist* 77:267–289.

YANG, MARTIN C.
1945 *A Chinese Village.* New York: Columbia University Press.

YOUNG, FRANK W.
1962 "The Function of Male Initiation Ceremonies: A Cross-Cultural Test of an Alternative Hypothesis," *American Journal of Sociology* 67:379–396.

ZINSSER, HANS
1935 *Rats, Lice and History.* Boston: Little, Brown.

ZUCKERMAN, SIR SOLLY (ED.)
1973 *Symposium of the Zoological Society of London,* no. 33.

Glossary

achieved status a status attained through one's own efforts.

affinal relatives in-laws.

altruistic motivated by an unselfish concern for the welfare of others.

ambilineal descent *see* kindreds.

animatism the belief that inanimate or nonsentient things, such as rocks, trees, and wind, have a will and a consciousness of their own.

animism the belief in a supernatural being or beings with consciousness and will.

anthropogeography study of the geographical distribution of humans along with their relationship to the physical environment.

anthropomorphising attributing human characteristics to animals, things, or abstract concepts.

archeology the study and reconstruction of past cultures through their artifacts and the physical traces of their activities.

ascribed status a status assigned to a person by virtue of certain possessed characteristics.

atlatl a spear thrower, usually wood. It may also be made of bone, ivory, or a similar solid material.

Australopithecus an early hominid, first found at Taung, South Africa, described and named by Raymond Dart in 1924. There is a controversy over whether it is ancestral to humans.

avunculocal residence the residence of a married couple with the groom's mother's brother.

barter an exchange wherein goods or services are given directly for other goods or services. No medium of exchange such as money is used.

basic maintenance system a system that satisfies the biological survival needs of a group, such as a means of subsistence.

basic personality structure the personality structure common to people in a society as a result of common childhood experiences.

basic postulates assumptions that may either be true or false about the nature of things.

bifurcate merging a system of kinship terminology that excludes one line of descent from the family (bifurcation) but combines cousins of the other line with siblings (merging).

bifurcation the excluding of descendants of one line from the family, for example, descendants of males in a matrilineal system and descendants of females in a patrilineal system.

bilateral inheritance equal inheritance from both parents.

bolas a weapon composed of two or more stone balls tied together on long strings, thrown to entangle birds or game animals.

bride price wealth transferred from the groom's family to the bride's family as part of the marriage process.

bride wealth *see* bride price.

buckskin tanned deer hide.

bung the plug that stops the hole in a barrel.

capital wealth in any form that is used or could be used to produce more wealth.

capstan an upright windlass. A large cylinder with a cable or hawser (thick tow rope) wound around it. It usually has several spokes at the top so more than one person can help turn it and a ratchet to keep it from slipping back as force is released.

carpentered environment an environment characterized by straight lines and right angles.

caste an endogamous social group whose members are ascribed to it at birth for life.

chilblains painful swellings or sores caused by exposure to the cold.

chinook the warm wind on the west central and north central plains of the United States in winter.

civilization a technical term referring to a society that possesses a set of attributes such as monumental public works, writing, and science. It is not to be confused with "civilized" in the sense of "urbane" or "sophisticated."

clan a unilineal descent group whose members assume they have a common ancestor but cannot trace their precise relationship to each other.

class a special group whose members have approximately the same socioeconomic status. Membership in a class, unlike that of a caste, may be changed.

classifactory kinship a variety of relationships combined under one term. For example, "uncle" is a classifactory term since it applies to mother's brother, father's brother, mother's sister's husband, and father's sister's husband.

clitoridectomy excision of the clitoris.

cognatic descent *see* kindreds.

cognition the process of knowing or perceiving.

Cold Maker the Piegan personification for the cold winter weather.

competitive cooperation group cooperation to accomplish a group goal, combined with individual competition to see who can do the most to help attain that goal.

configuration the overall orientation or characteristic around which a culture is organized; it provides a focus or a style that permeates the entire culture.

conjugal pertaining to marriage.

conjugal family family formed by marriage, usually restricted to husband, wife, and their offspring; may include other people related by marriage.

consanguine related by blood.

consanguine family family whose members are all related by blood-descent ties, not by marriage.

consensual union the relationship of a couple willingly living together without being married.

copyright property rights to a particular organization of words or sounds (as in music).

correlated related to or varying with something.

correlation the degree of mutual correspondence between two variables (e.g., two sets of data, two kinds of social phenomena).

coulée a deep gulch or ravine, usually dry much of the year.

counterculture group a group whose culture is opposed to the culture of mainstream society.

couvade the custom in which the father ritualistically imitates the pregnancy and delivery of the mother.

covert culture those concepts which people take for granted, do not remember learning, and often are not aware they know.

crime an offense against people or society.

crisis rite a ceremony marking a major change of status. It is also called *rite de passage*, or passage rite.

cross-cousins children of opposite-sexed siblings, for example, the relationship of a child of a father's sister or a mother's brother to one's self.

cultural relativity the idea that one culture is just as valid as any other, and that the characteristics of a culture can be evaluated only in the context of that culture.

culture those organized concepts, manifest in act and artifact, learned and shared by man as a member of society.

culture area a geographic area within which separate societies have cultures that share more characteristics with each other than they do with cultures outside the area.

culture-bound accustomed to thinking solely in terms of the values and beliefs of one's own society and culture.

culture elements separate characteristics that go to make up a whole culture; sometimes called culture traits.

culture historical Herskovits' term for German "Kulturkreiselehre" or culture circle (sphere) school. A school of thought with heavy emphasis on tracing the distribution and origin of culture traits.

DAP Draw-a-person test developed by Karen Machoner in which the subject is asked to draw a person of either sex. After the picture is drawn, the subject is given more paper and asked to draw a person of the sex opposite to the one already drawn.

dichotomy dividing something into two usually opposing parts.

diffusion the process by which cultural concepts move from one society to another.

diffusionist school the school of thought that attempts to explain all culture as the product of diffusion from a single center or, at most, from a few sources.

dimorphism having two forms, as when one sex is routinely twice as large as the other.

divination the attempt to foretell the future or reveal the unknown by the use of techniques usually involving communication with the supernatural.

dominance control or influence over others. Any social group, human or animal, has a dominance structure. A dominant individual has preferential access to space, sex, food, or other "good things."

double descent descent in which one sort of thing (such as land or physical appearance) is traced through one parental line and another sort of thing (such as money or intellectual qualities) are traced through the other line. A child inherits from both parents, but inherits different kinds of things from each.

dowry wealth transferred from the bride's family to the groom's family, the groom, or the bride as part of the marriage process.

dumb barter *see* silent barter.

egalitarian pertaining to equality.

emic classification of characteristics of a society according to the way in which members of that society classify them.

eminent domain the right of a government to take private property for public use, giving just compensation to the owner.

emulative competition competition in which one attempts to outdo one's rival by better performance (*cf.* predatory competition).

enculturation the teaching of beliefs and traditions of a society to the young or the uninitiated.

endogamy marriage within the social unit.

ethnocentric judging all other groups by reference to the standards, values, and characteristics of one's own group.

ethnology the study of different cultural systems.

ethologists people who study animal behavior by means of prolonged observation of the whole behavior repertoire of the animal in the wild.

etic classification of characteristics of a society according to some external system of analysis.

exogamy marriage outside the social unit.

extended family a group that includes relatives other than the parents and offspring.

extended households those in which a variety of relatives other than the members of the nuclear family live.

family a social unit normally begun with marriage, consisting of adults of both sexes and the offspring, real or adopted, of one or more of them. It is regulated by custom and law and defined in terms of the relationships between the members.

family of orientation the family one is born into or grows up in.

family of procreation the family that one begins after marriage.

female infanticide the killing of female babies.

fish weirs traps to catch fish, built in shallow water, usually stretching across a stream, river, or estuary.

flintlock the firing mechanism of a gun in which gunpowder is exploded by a spark produced by sticking a piece of flint in the hammer against a piece of metal. It is obsolete.

folkways customs and traditions observed by people in a society; positive beliefs about how to act.

foragers individuals who harvest the wild produce (animal or vegetable) of their environment but consume it on the spot instead of collecting it to share with others.

formal sanction a punishment or reward that is explicit, known in advance, and impersonally applied to all. As punishment it frequently involves force and is usually applied by specialists.

functionalism the concept that a specific pattern in a culture can be explained by the purpose it currently serves rather than by its history.

functional status a status based on what one does in a society, such as that of a carpenter or plumber.

generic referring to the genus.

genitor the biological sire.

gens a patrilineal group whose members assume they have a common ancestor but cannot trace their precise relationship to each other; a synonym for "clan."

government a network of statuses whose primary roles are political.

grave goods artifacts placed in a grave with the body.

Great tradition term coined by Robert Redfield to apply to major religious systems that contain a moral or ethical value orientation.

harrow *see* spring-tooth harrow.

hominid in the human line of descent.

Homo erectus a form of early man, also called pithecanthropines; Peking Man and Java Man are classified in this group.

Homo sapiens man, human being; the scientific name for the only living species on the genus *homo*.

Homo sapiens neandertalensis a form of man with distinctive physical characteristics, dating from about 125,000–50,000 years ago, first found in the Neander Valley in Germany in 1856.

horticulture a form of food production depending on hand tools, with mixed crops rather than single crop fields; also called gardening.

hospice an inn, or a refuge for the sick or poor.

impetigo a contagious skin disease caused by staphlococci. The skin appears to blister, the blisters break, and a heavy scablike crust forms. Removing the scab and washing the area with green soap (a disinfectant soap) is the usual treatment.

incest tabu the prohibition of sexual intercourse, marriage, or both with relatives regarded as especially close.

informal sanction a punishment or reward that is spontaneous; it varies according to the circumstances and the individuals involved. As punishment it usually involves shame or ridicule and is most often applied by nonspecialists in law enforcement.

institution a set of norms or rules focusing around a particular aspect or problem in society. Examples of institutions are the religious and economic systems.

internalize to incorporate in oneself the values, concepts, and so on of another person or of a group.

inundate to overflow or to cover with, as with a flood.

Java Man type of primitive man known from fossil remains found in Java in 1891; also called Pithecanthropus erectus.

kindreds groups of people who regard themselves as related in some way by blood or marriage.

kumamolimo the central meeting place of the BaMbuti Pygmy religious ceremony called the molimo.

latent function a real but unintended function (sometimes unrecognized by the society).

law a rule or command in a society backed up by severe sanctions applied with the approval of society; also called a legal norm.

levirate marriage of a man to his brother's widow or of a woman to her deceased husband's brother.

lineage a unilineal descent group whose members can trace their relationship to each other.

linguistics the study of the structure of language.

lodge a type of native American dwelling; may refer to skin, brush, or log structure, either earth-covered or not.

mana a supernatural force with no will, awareness, or consciousness.

manifest function a function explicitly intended by members of the society.

market an exchange involving a number of buyers and sellers with the price varying according to what is asked and paid by the people involved.

matrilineal inheritance descent traced through the female line.

matrilocal residence after marriage in which the bride and groom live with or near the bride's parents; sometimes used synonymously with "uxorilocal."

Mesoamerica the part of the New World lying between the southern boundary of the United States and the northern boundary of Colombia, especially the parts in which high civilizations developed.

messianic movement a religious revival usually occurring when a society is under severe stress. It is generally headed by a charismatic leader who serves as a prophet, messiah, or martyr.

Miocene a geological term referring to the third epoch of the Tertiary Period in the Cenozoic Era.

modal personality the cluster of personality traits that appears most frequently in a culture.

moiety one of two parts of a society.

molimo a ceremony of the BaMbuti Pygmies and the instrument used in it.

money a medium of exchange that is durable, portable, standardized, divisible, and relatively stable in value.

monogamy the practice of having only one spouse at a time.

mores folkways particularly involved with social welfare; they usually consist of stringent tabus or prohibitions rather than prescriptions of positive action.

morpheme smallest meaningful unit in a language.

Mousterian a particular assemblage of artifacts, dating from 40,000 to 150,000 b.p. (before present) and most often associated with Neanderthal man.

mulcted fined.

natal family the family into which one is born.

nativistic revival a mass movement, frequently religious, usually occurring when a society is under severe stress and attempting to reestablish a lengendary or remembered glorious past.

Neanderthal an early form of man with wide distribution dating from between 40,000 and 150,000 years ago. There is some controversy among experts as to whether this form is ancestral to modern man or is a side branch that became extinct.

Neanderthaloids similar to but not necessarily the same as Neanderthals.

neolocal residence after marriage in which the bride and groom move to a new home where they are relatively independent of both sets of parents.

night soil human excrement.

nonlineal descent *see* kindreds.

nuclear family parents and offspring.

obligatio rights and duties.

ocher a natural iron-oxide pigment, usually red or yellow.

overt culture those concepts of which people are aware and consciously teach or learn.

Paleolithic old stone age.

paleontology the study of fossils; a branch of geology.

parallel cousins children of same-sexed siblings.

parallel inheritance girls inherit only from their mothers and boys only from their fathers.

parfleche a rawhide container, usually shaped like a box or a suitcase, used for storage or transport, especially of food.

particularistic exchange an exchange in which the emphasis is on the social relationship between participants rather than on the economic aspect.

pater the sociological male parent.

patrilineal inheritance descent traced through the male line.

patrilocal pertaining to a marriage arrangement in which the bride and groom live with or near the groom's parents; sometimes used synonymously with "virilocal."

Peking Man a type of primitive man of about 475,000 B.C., whose fossil remains were first found near Peking, China, in 1929.

pemmican meat pounded together with fat and berries and dried; a nourishing food, easy to store.

percussion cap a small metal cap containing gunpowder that explodes when struck.

personalistic exchange economic decisions made on the basis of social or personal factors.

phonemes in linguistics, a class of closely related speech sounds (phones) regarded as a single sound and represented in phonetic transcription by the same symbol.

phonetics the production or recording of sounds of speech.

phratry a group of lineal clans.

physical anthropology the branch of anthropology that deals with man as a biological organism.

piki paper-thin cornbread.

polyandry the practice of having more than one husband at a time.

polygamy the practice of having several spouses at one time.

polygyny the practice of having more than one wife at a time.

porcelain ceramic artifacts. In the *Jesuit Relations* it usually refers to trade beads which quickly replaced shell. (It was, however, sometimes also used to refer to strung shell.)

power the ability to make binding key decisions.

predatory competition when individuals attempt to defeat their rivals by destroying or exploiting them rather than by outperforming them (*cf.* emulative competition).

prestation the giving of a gift to create a social obligation.

priest a member of an organized group of religious specialists who learns an organized body of doctrine, often in a special school.

private law the injured party has the right to revenge himself on the offender if he can.

progeny price wealth transferred from groom's family to bride's family; a synonym for "bride price." It gives the groom's family rights over the offspring (real or potential) of the match.

projective system a belief system of a society which deals with an aspect not easily subject to scientific experimental proof (religion, mythology, explanations of disease causation in premodern non-Western societies, and so on).

property a concept referring to a valuable thing and the collection of rights and obligations regarding it.

property right a right to control, exploit, use, enjoy, or dispose of a valuable thing.

puberty rite a ceremony to mark passage from adolescence or childhood to adulthood.

public law a system wherein society takes the part of the injured person and specialized members apprehend, judge, and punish the offending individual.

quirt a short-handled whip, usually with a braided rawhide lash.

ramage *see* kindreds.

Ramapithecus one of the dryopithecines, classed by most authorities as the first in the hominid line.

reciprocity services or goods provided in return for the same or equivalent things.

redistribution the turning over of goods to a central location or organization which then distributes them to other members of the society.

reference *see* terms of reference.

rennet the membrane lining of the stomach of a calf, or an extract of this, used to curdle milk.

reparations payments in the nature of fines from offenders to victims.

replicable able to be duplicated.

revitalization a renewal or revival that breathes new life into a culture under stress that has been growing disorganized.

rite de passage a ceremony that marks a major change in status; also called "rite of passage," "passage rite," or "crisis rite."

role the behavior expected of an individual in a particular status.

role conflict when two or more of an individual's roles (with conflicting expectations) are activated simultaneously.

Rorschach otherwise known as the inkblot test, devised by Hermann Rorschach, in which a series of bilaterally symmetrical inkblots (some in color, some black and white) are shown in a specific order to subjects who are asked to tell what they see in them.

sagittal crest a ridge of bone running from back to front in the middle of the skull.

sanction reward or punishment.

scalar status a status determined by rank or access to wealth and power.

shaman a religious leader who is highly individualistic, does not have an organized doctrine, and usually intercedes with the supernatural on the side of man. His knowledge usually comes from direct revelation.

sib a unilineal descent group whose members assume they have a common ancestor but cannot trace their precise relationship to each other; a synonym for "clan."

siblings brothers and sisters.

silent barter an exchange that takes place without face-to-face contact. Goods are left at a mutually agreed upon site, and people return at a later time to complete the exchange.

sin an offense against the supernatural

sindula the water chevrotain, an animal hunted by the BaMbuti Pygmies in Africa.

smooth-bore musket a gun without rifling (grooves) in the barrel; it is not very accurate except at very close range.

socialization teaching people how to get along in a group.

social norm something that members of a society agree should or should not be done.

social structure the network of statuses, roles, organizations, and institutions forming the framework within and by which members of the society engage in social interaction.

sondu an antelope, hunted by the BaMbuti Pygmies in Africa.

sororate marriage of a woman to the widower of her sister, or of a man to his deceased wife's sister.

spring-tooth harrow a farm implement with teeth that spring back and forth, used to break up clods of earth left after plowing.

status a position in a society.

stimulus diffusion the spread of ideas rather than physical artifacts.

structuralist one who explains culture and human behavior in terms of social structure.

subincision slitting the penis all or part way from the base to the glans.

sutler a person who follows an army to sell supplies—especially food and liquor—to soldiers.

tabu (taboo) a prohibition or caution usually but not always involving the supernatural.

TAT Thematic Apperception Test designed by C. D. Morgan and H. A. Murray, in which the subject is shown a series of pictures and asked to tell stories about them.

team competition competition in which a number of people cooperate with each other against another group of people.

teknonymy naming parents after their children (e.g., mother of Ann, father of David).

terms of address kinship terms that apply to a person used when talking to that person.

terms of reference kinship terms that apply to a person used when talking about that person to someone else.

themes major basic concepts of a culture that underlie most of its observable behavior and articulated beliefs.

toque a round, close-fitting cap.

totem something in nature that is believed to have a special and significant relationship with a particular group.

train a wooden sled with runners, usually drawn by one horse; used on the frontier.

traits discrete observable characteristics of a culture; the smallest meaningful and observable parts of a culture.

transhumance seasonal shifting of people from one area to another.

transvestite a person who dresses like a member of the opposite sex.

travois two long poles, two ends on one side which were crossed over the back of a horse, with the other ends dragging on the ground. Goods and people were transported on nets of rawhide or rope strung between the poles.

tribal marriage two or more males married to two or more females; also called group marriage or communal marriage.

unilineal tracing descent through one side of the family, either the father's or the mother's (*cf.* matrilineal and patrilineal).

universalistic exchange exchange with emphasis on economic rather than social factors.

universalistic system one in which economic decisions are made on the basis of technical factors such as cost, quality, or efficiency, rather than on the basis of social factors.

usufruct the right to make use of something.

uxorilocal the reverse of virilocal; residence after marriage in which the bride and groom live in the bride's parents' home. It is sometimes used synonymously with "matrilocal."

vermillion bright red mercuric sulfide (or any other similar red earth) used as a pigment; also refers to a bright yellowish-red color.

viable able to survive.

virilocal residence after marriage in which the bride and groom live in the groom's home. It is sometimes used synonymously with "patrilocal."

Name Index

Subject Index

abstraction, 47, 206, 224, 347, 348

accumulation, 53, 54, 73, 74, 133, 134, 356

activity patterns, 6, 12, 15, 27, 29, 80, 92, 205, 235, 242

affiliation, 286, 298, 299, 300, 301

affinal, 121, 263, 294; *see also* in-laws

afterlife, 90, 316, 317, 323

age, 95, 172, 177, 179, 204, 208, 225

aggression, 14, 18, 19, 20, 47, 222, 223, 224, 226, 227, 237

agriculture, 13, 29, 36, 51–54, 69, 70–76, 78–80, 82, 85, 86, 89, 90, 92, 103, 106, 107, 114, 133, 136, 139, 145, 147, 148, 324, 348, 352, 354, 356, 367

alcohol, 7, 75, 103, 135, 242, 254, 255

alienation, 92, 229, 239, 336, 344, 362

Amish, 87, 205

ancestors, 66, 67, 248, 286–288, 331, 360, 362

animals, 5–10, 15, 19, 22, 31–34, 45, 50, 51, 55, 65, 71, 72–73, 79, 81–85, 107, 121, 136, 137, 156–163, 173, 174, 227, 230, 234, 238, 309, 315, 322, 326, 331, 334, 348, 351, 354; domestic, 33, 34, 37, 58, 62, 64, 65, 68, 71, 72, 81–83, 85, 91, 107, 136; game, 6, 21, 23, 27, 31, 32, 33, 34, 36, 37, 42, 43, 45, 46, 50, 68, 109, 150, 156, 157, 158, 159, 276, 282, 306, 324, 327

animism, 309, 311

anthropologist, xv, 13, 28, 32, 54, 120, 163, 167, 173, 176, 216, 217, 221, 222, 227, 230, 231, 233, 271, 288, 294, 312, 313, 324, 334, 346, 352, 353, 356, 358, 361, 363, 364, 365, 366, 367

anthropology, xv, 220, 226, 244, 245, 258, 334, 337, 341, 342, 346, 347, 352, 354, 355, 359, 361, 362, 363, 367; applied, 342, 356, 360; cultural, xv, 337, 338, 341, 342, 346, 358, 361

anxiety, 50, 73, 90, 168, 172, 195, 207, 208, 303, 324, 325, 326

archeological evidence, 37, 43, 53, 54, 69, 70, 72, 75, 80, 81, 83, 85, 303, 328

archeologists, 16, 45, 75, 361, 362

archeology, 328, 337, 346

architecture, 75, 77, 214

art, xv, 50, 96, 206, 212, 303, 322, 328, 331, 334, 335, 336, 341, 342, 349; *see also* paintings; sculpture

artifact, xv, 31, 47, 84, 137, 230, 331, 341

assumptions, 200, 216, 218, 219, 221, 224, 226, 231, 269, 338

atlatl, 24, 43; *see also* spear

attitudes, 25, 47, 63, 85, 86, 87, 135, 199, 202, 205, 216, 219, 222, 224, 236, 239, 294, 311, 313; toward accumulation, 74; toward animals, 157, 158, 161, 229; toward death, 10, 25, 29, 48; toward land, 73, 79; toward life, 29, 30; toward nature, 59, 64, 87; toward police, 194; toward time, 88; toward violence, 19, 25, 148; toward women, 59, 85, 101

australopithecines, 17, 28, 328

authority, 76, 163, 166–167, 175–177, 180–185, 187, 188, 197, 198, 200, 207, 266, 354

avunculocal, 264, 273, 299

BaMbuti, 46, 154–164, 167–169, 171, 174, 176, 188, 189, 194, 195–197, 199, 200, 204, 206, 229, 268, 354

band, 12, 16, 27, 31, 40, 42, 52, 69, 74–76, 91, 92, 105, 107, 160–162, 164, 165, 170, 175, 176, 188, 199, 200, 204, 206, 354

barbarians, 80, 84, 85, 346, 350

barter, 119, 121, 136

basketry, 37, 154, 155, 157, 158, 160, 161, 163, 195, 249, 253, 255, 328

beads, 7, 26, 39, 100, 102, 135, 329

bedding, 35, 64, 76, 100, 215, 242, 276

behavior, 47, 48, 82, 143, 153, 165–166, 171, 172, 177, 194, 206–208, 219, 221–223, 226, 227, 228, 230, 234, 236, 237–239, 244, 258, 259, 294, 314, 327, 334, 356, 360, 366; human, 47, 54, 120, 223, 225, 228, 234, 245, 337, 341, 347, 354, 359

beliefs, xv, 23, 47, 202, 205, 208, 215, 218, 222, 232, 239, 243, 309, 312, 313,

About the Author

Cara Richards is chairman of the department of psychology and soc[...] at Transylvania University in Lexington, Kentucky. Born in Bayonn[...] she received her B.A. from Queens College in 1952. She was awarde[...] Ph.D. from Cornell University in 1957 after completing research for he[...] s on the Onondaga Iroquois in New York State. She served as resident [...] ologist for the Navajo-Cornell Field Health Research Clinic for a year and then for two years was associated with the Cornell-Peru project in Lima, Peru. Her publications include a number of articles and a book, *The Oneida People*.